STUDIES IN
CONTEMPORARY
JEWRY

The publication of
Studies in Contemporary Jewry
has been made possible through the generous assistance
of the Samuel and Althea Stroum Philanthropic Fund,
Seattle, Washington

THE AVRAHAM HARMAN INSTITUTE
OF CONTEMPORARY JEWRY
THE HEBREW UNIVERSITY
OF JERUSALEM

ETHNICITY AND BEYOND: THEORIES AND DILEMMAS OF JEWISH GROUP DEMARCATION

STUDIES IN
CONTEMPORARY
JEWRY
AN ANNUAL
XXV

2011

Edited by Eli Lederhendler

Published for the Institute by
OXFORD
UNIVERSITY PRESS

OXFORD
UNIVERSITY PRESS

Oxford University Press, Inc., publishes works that further
Oxford University's objective of excellence
in research, scholarship, and education.

Oxford   New York
Auckland   Cape Town   Dar es Salaam   Hong Kong   Karachi
Kuala Lumpur   Madrid   Melbourne   Mexico City   Nairobi
New Delhi   Shanghai   Taipei   Toronto

With offices in
Argentina   Austria   Brazil   Chile   Czech Republic   France   Greece
Guatemala   Hungary   Italy   Japan   Poland   Portugal   Singapore
South Korea   Switzerland   Thailand   Turkey   Ukraine   Vietnam

Copyright © 2011 by Oxford University Press, Inc.

Published by Oxford University Press, Inc.
198 Madison Avenue, New York, New York 10016

www.oup.com

Oxford is a registered trademark of Oxford University Press.

All rights reserved. No part of this publication may be reproduced,
stored in a retrieval system, or transmitted, in any form or by any means,
electronic, mechanical, photocopying, recording, or otherwise,
without the prior permission of Oxford University Press.

Library of Congress Cataloging-in-Publication Data
Ethnicity and beyond : theories and dilemmas of Jewish group demarcation / edited by Eli Lederhendler.
p. cm. — (Studies in contemporary Jewry, ISSN 0740-8625; 25)
"The Avraham Harman Institute of Contemporary Jewry, the Hebrew University of Jerusalem."
Includes bibliographical references and index.
ISBN 978-0-19-979349-5 (alk. paper)
1. Jews—Identity. 2. Jews—United States—Identity. 3. Jews—Europe—Identity. 4. Jewish diaspora.
I. Lederhendler, Eli. II. Makhon le-Yahadut zemanenu 'a. sh. Avraham Harman.
DS143.E84 2011
305.892'4—dc22
2010037524

1 3 5 7 9 8 6 4 2

Printed in the United States of America
on acid-free paper

STUDIES IN CONTEMPORARY JEWRY

Founding Editors

Jonathan Frankel (1935–2008)
Peter Y. Medding
Ezra Mendelsohn

Editors

Richard I. Cohen
Anat Helman
Eli Lederhendler
Uzi Rebhun

Institute Editorial Board

Michel Abitbol, Mordechai Altshuler, Haim Avni, Yehuda Bauer, Daniel Blatman, Jonathan Dekel-Chen, Sergio DellaPergola, Sidra DeKoven Ezrahi, Amos Goldberg, Yisrael Gutman, Hagit Lavsky, Pnina Morag-Talmon, Dalia Ofer, Gideon Shimoni, Dimitry Shumsky, Yfaat Weiss

Managing Editors

Laurie E. Fialkoff
Hannah Levinsky-Koevary

International Advisory and Review Board

Abraham Ascher (City University of New York); Arnold Band (University of California, Los Angeles); Doris Bensimon (Université de la Sorbonne); Bernard Blumenkrantz (Centre National de la Recherche Scientifique); Henry Feingold (City University of New York); Martin Gilbert (Honorary Fellow, Merton College, Oxford University); Zvi Gitelman (University of Michigan); S. Julius Gould (University of Nottingham); Paula Hyman (Yale University); David Landes (Harvard University); Heinz-Dietrich Löwe (University of Heidelberg); Michael A. Meyer (Hebrew Union College-Jewish Institute of Religion, Cincinnati); Alan Mintz (Jewish Theological Seminary of America); Gerard Nahon (Centre Universitaire d'Études Juives); F. Raphaël (Université des Sciences Humaines de Strasbourg); Jehuda Reinharz (Brandeis University); Monika Richarz (Germania Judaica, Kölner Bibliothek zur Geschichte des Deutschen Judentums); Ismar Schorsch (Jewish Theological Seminary of America); Michael Walzer (Institute for Advanced Study); Bernard Wasserstein (University of Chicago); Ruth Wisse (Harvard University)

Preface

Quite some years ago—in 1987, to be specific—Ezra Mendelsohn devoted the symposium in the third volume of *Studies in Contemporary Jewry* to the topic of "Jews and Other Ethnic Groups in a Multi-ethnic World." The intervening years have witnessed important transitions in both the terms and the questions that scholars bring to bear on the subject of "ethnicity" in general, Jews in particular, and the nature of the interactivity between Jews and others. In the realm of American academic life, especially, forays into the question of Jewish ethnicity in the past two decades have faced a significantly altered terrain.

Perhaps more than anything else, the influential turn to multicultural (often in place of multiethnic) paradigms signaled a significant challenge to those involved in contemporary Jewish studies, because—as the distinguished American cultural historian David Hollinger has pointed out—the foundational notions of multiculturalist ideology rested on a prior classification of nearly all "culturally diverse" groups along non-essentialist but still quasi-fixed axes determined by "color" (the "racial pentagon"). Under that particular aegis, there was little to be said concerning the "minor" specificities that were once the bread and butter issues of ethnic and cross-ethnic studies, such as those distinguishing between Americans of Irish, Italian, German, Jewish, and Polish origin. "The key point about multiculturalism," Hollinger recently reiterated, "is that there has been almost no place in it for Jews."[1]

Hollinger's suggested alternative, as he pointed out in an address to American Jewish historians, is a bid to move beyond the ethno-communal paradigm to adopt a post-identity-politics, post-ethnic, "post-Jewish" historiography. That is: to break out of the mold of constructed boundaries that has predefined the labels of recognized "diversity" (and its limited number of beneficiaries) and embrace instead "the insight that the creative influence of religious and ethnic communities often lasts well beyond the time when individuals and families have been deeply embedded in [their own particular] communities."[2] To fix what may be "wrong" with the multicultural agenda, Hollinger prescribes, we have to reinvent a definition of ethnicity that, in itself, is "post-ethnic" in its sensibilities and priorities. His notion of "post-ethnic" and "post-Jewish" (also "post-Black" and "post-Catholic") points toward a sensitivity to demographics, politics, and ideas as filters of "ethnic" influences in the wider public sphere.

Having had occasion in some of my recent work to note the paradoxical spin-offs of recent research on the ethnic aspects of Jewish social identity, I, too, have voiced some concern over the utility of the older terminologies.[3] And in his own reconsideration of the larger themes and conflicts raised in the contemporary study of Jews and

Judaism, one of my close colleagues in Israeli academia, Moshe Rosman, also chose to tackle the new disposition of older definitional problems. "How Jewish is Jewish history" as he put it, when Jewish society is "a 'hybrid' component of the 'hegemonic' society and culture . . . within which Jewish identity, culture, and society are 'constructed'"?[4]

Taking the discussion to a further level would seem to be a worthwhile venture. That was my agenda when undertaking to invite a group of leading and innovative scholars to participate in a wide-ranging discussion of the terms "ethnic," "ethnicity," and "identity" as these apply to Jews, past and present, individually and collectively. Beyond bold, general statements that delineate the relevant concerns in the widest sense but leave us wondering about their implementation, I felt that it might be possible in a series of smaller, sharply defined studies to generate further insight into the actual permutations and uses of these categories, in the light of recent theory.

Although originally we had hoped to be more global in our reach, the vicissitudes of academic publishing produced a more America-centered discussion than we had planned for. That is not necessarily a bad thing, given the fuller and multifocal treatment thus accorded to the American and American Jewish case. Nor does the current group of essays constitute in anyone's mind anything more than a partial foray into an ongoing discussion.

Nevertheless, it pleases me that the first essay in the present series, authored by Ewa Morawska (herself a transnational scholar in every sense) devotes much attention to several non-American case histories before embarking on the discussion of an America-based study—ex-Soviet Jews in Philadelphia, whose post-migration experience is compared with that of a similar population in Tel Aviv.

Equally general in its geographical applicability is Uzi Rebhun's analysis of the plural dimensional aspects of ethnic research, which in some crucial ways forms a counterpart to Morawska's basic arguments.

Tony Michels is one of a number of scholars who have been engaged in close dialogue with Hollinger's notions regarding post-ethnicity.[5] In the symposium in this volume, Michels' essay most clearly represents the historical discipline, bringing us a case history from the period between the two world wars. In line with the social-scientific approaches delineated in most of the other essays, Michels' contribution suggests a way in which ethnic Jewishness and "ethnic identity" generally might be utilized in novel, sometimes counterintuitive ways.

With Joel Perlmann's discussion of interethnic marriage and its relationship to the demographics of ethnic group stability, we enter into two crucial spheres of discourse: first, the definitional basis for "ethnicity" in the American context, and second, the contextual intergenerational framework that is necessary for any serious understanding of ethnic phenomena. Perlmann's defense of the contextualized and specific utility of "ethnicity," even in a discursive realm that acknowledges the murky origins of the term "ethnic" as distinct from "racial," is a critical move that offers to defuse the fraught politics of the theoretical debate in this regard.

In Perlmann's essay as well as in the unconventional fieldwork underlying the sociolinguistic survey reported on by Sarah Bunin Benor and Stephen M. Cohen, ethnic markers are distinctly behavioral. That is, particular behaviors (marriage and child rearing, institution-building, religion, and language) are the foreground of what is meant by "ethnic" identity—as opposed to inchoate concepts such as "symbolic ethnicity" that pertain rather to subjective and intangible aspects of self-identification with group labels. In their essay, "Talking Jewish," Benor and Cohen provide examples that seem to affirm what Hollinger suggested: to reiterate, that "religious and ethnic communities [exert an influence that] often lasts well beyond the time when individuals and families have been deeply embedded in [their own particular] communities." Thus, as reflected in this study, while not only Jews may be expected to "talk Jewish," "talking Jewish" is still bound to crop up in particular ways in in-group conversations. However, their study also seems to suggest other ramifications: namely, what can occur when some people become re-embedded in communities at the sub-ethnic level. Thus, "talking Jewish" gives some indication that Jews distinguish themselves from other Jews, as the authors argue, by infusing their vernacular English with Jewish-based particularity.

In undertaking a reevaluation of "identity" as a standard, if much-debated, component of the "ethnicity" field, Bethamie Horowitz distinguishes between the individual-level and the group-level dimensions, and indicates how the terminology in the field has shifted, as mediated by changes in American culture and social relations.

In preparing this symposium, we have departed from previous practice by inviting comment on their colleagues' presentations by several other scholarly experts. Both Riv-Ellen Prell and Jonathan D. Sarna are particularly well qualified to serve as commentators on the American Jewish experience, and their remarks help us, as readers, to take stock of the entire group of outstanding essays in this diverse discussion.[6]

Finally, it should be noted that the fine essay by Hagit Lavsky on German Jewish migration history in the interwar decades of the 20th century, published separately as a freestanding article, could also have been included in our wide-ranging discussion of ethnic phenomena. Migrant populations, after all, are the historical agents directly responsible for the addition of new ethnic categories in their receiver societies. Lavsky carefully denotes the subtle calibration of German Jewishness, not just according to global group labels but also with regard to distinct class, age, occupational, and institutional variables, as these were articulated in the encounter between immigrants and the receiver societies. Moreover, she sheds light on the way in which those differences came to be negotiated quite differently in three separate countries: the United States, England, and pre-state Israel (the Palestine *yishuv*), leading to a post-migration constellation of three different ex-German Jewish identities. This painstaking statistical and historical study, therefore, should certainly be read in tandem with the symposium on ethnicity and the Jews, even if its primary focus is not on the reevaluation of ethnicity theory per se, but rather the redefinition of key issues in German Jewish migration history.

This 25th volume of *Studies in Contemporary Jewry* appears at an important juncture in our own institutional history. The trio of extraordinary scholars who were responsible for founding the journal and guiding all of its previous volumes into print—Ezra Mendelsohn, Peter Medding, and the late Jonathan Frankel—are a hard act to follow. My own thanks to them joins the heartfelt gratitude of all of my colleagues on the staff and editorial group that now continues the work of publishing a quality annual survey of contemporary Jewish scholarship. Joining the editors' group as of this year are my colleagues at the Hebrew University and members of the

Department of Jewish History and Contemporary Jewry: Richard I. Cohen, Anat Helman, and Uzi Rebhun. I wish also to thank the Samuel and Althea Stroum Fund and the Lucius N. Littauer Foundation for providing us with the resources for publishing this volume.

Last but certainly not least, Laurie Fialkoff and Hannah Levinsky-Koevary are, as always, the lifeblood of this enterprise. The continuity in service and expertise that they have provided over the years has been doubly felt in this transition year, for which all of us are truly appreciative.

E.L.

Notes

1. David A. Hollinger, "Communalist and Dispersionist Approaches to American Jewish History in an Increasingly Post-Jewish Era," *American Jewish History*, vol. 95, no. 1 (Sept. 2009), 17. See also Hollinger, *Postethnic America: Beyond Multiculturalism* (New York: 1995); idem, "Jewish Identity, Assimilation, and Multiculturalism," in *Creating American Jews*, ed. Karen Mittelman (Philadelphia: 1998), 52–59; cf. Richard D. Alba, *Ethnic Identity: The Transformation of White America* (New Haven: 1990).

2. Hollinger, "Communalist and Dispersionist Approaches," 21.

3. Eli Lederhendler, *Jewish Immigrants and American Capitalism, 1880-1920: From Caste to Class* (New York: 2009), ix–xviii.

4. Moshe Rosman, *How Jewish is Jewish History?* (Oxford: 2007), 53 (see also the review by Nils Roemer in this volume, 170–172).

5. See Hollinger's comments on Michels' work ("Communalist and Dispersionist Approaches," 12, 16) and Michels' rejoinder in the same publication: "Communalist History and Beyond: The Potential of American Jewish History," *American Jewish History*, vol. 95, no. 1 (Sept. 2009), 61–71.

6. Uzi Rebhun's contribution to this volume, originally framed as a third commentary, appeared to us as a self-sustaining argument in its own right, and is therefore presented as such. This late editorial decision explains why his essay was not commented upon by our two discussants.

Contents

Symposium
Ethnicity and Beyond: Theories and Dilemmas of Jewish
Group Demarcation

Ewa Morawska, *Ethnicity as a Primordial-Situational-Constructed Experience: Different Times, Different Places, Different Constellations*   3

Tony Michels, *Communism and the Problem of Ethnicity in the 1920s: The Case of Moissaye Olgin*   26

Joel Perlmann, *Ethnic Group Strength, Intermarriage, and Group Blending*   49

Sarah Bunin Benor and Steven M. Cohen, *Talking Jewish: The "Ethnic English" of American Jews*   62

Bethamie Horowitz, *Old Casks in New Times: The Reshaping of American Jewish Identity in the 21st Century*   79

Uzi Rebhun, *Jews and the Ethnic Scene: A Multidimensional Theory*   91

Riv-Ellen Prell, *The Utility of the Concept of "Ethnicity" for the Study of Jews*   102

Jonathan D. Sarna, *Ethnicity and Beyond*   108

Essay

Hagit Lavsky, *German Jewish Interwar Migration in a Comparative Perspective: Mandatory Palestine, the United States, and Great Britain*   115

Book Reviews
(arranged by subject)
Antisemitism, Holocaust, and Genocide

Susannah Heschel, *The Aryan Jesus: Christian Theologians and the Bible in Nazi Germany*, CHRISTOPHER R. BROWNING   147

Steven T. Katz, Shlomo Biderman, and Gershon Greenberg (eds.),
    *Wrestling with God: Jewish Theological Responses during and after
the Holocaust*, BARBARA U. MEYER   149

History and the Social Sciences

Gur Alroey, *Hamahpekhah hasheketah: hahagirah hayehudit mihaemperiyah
    harusit 1875–1924* (The quiet revolution: Jewish emigration from
the Russian empire 1875–1924), LLOYD P. GARTNER   153

Edith Bruder, *The Black Jews of Africa: History, Religion, Identity*,
    SHALVA WEIL   155

Beth B. Cohen, *Case Closed: Holocaust Survivors in Postwar America*,
    SHARON KANGISSER COHEN   156

Henry L. Feingold, *Jewish Power in America: Myth and Reality*, MICHAEL
    SCOTT ALEXANDER   158

Jonathan Frankel, *Crisis, Revolution, and Russian Jews*, FRANÇOIS GUESNET   160

Lloyd P. Gartner, *American and British Jews in the Age of the
    Great Migration*, JONATHAN D. SARNA   162

Zvi Gitelman and Yaacov Ro'i (eds.), *Revolution, Repression,
    and Revival: The Soviet Jewish Experience*, VLADIMIR LEVIN   164

Nadia Malinovich, *French and Jewish: Culture and the Politics of
    Identity in Early Twentieth-Century France*, ARI JOSKOWICZ   168

Moshe Rosman, *How Jewish Is Jewish History?* NILS ROEMER   170

Charlotte Schoell-Glass, *Aby Warburg and Anti-Semitism: Political
    Perspectives on Images and Culture*, trans. Samuel Pakucs Willcocks,
WALTER CAHN   173

Aviva Weingarten, *Jewish Organizations' Response to Communism and to
    Senator McCarthy* (trans. Ora Cummings), DEBORAH DASH MOORE   175

Arkadii Zeltser, *Evrei sovetskoi provintsii: Vitebsk i mestechki
    1917–1941* (Jews of the Soviet provinces: Vitebsk and
shtetlekh 1917–1941), ANNA SHTERNSHIS   177

Religion, Literary, and Cultural Studies

Glenda Abramson, *Hebrew Writing of the First World War*,
    MICHAL BEN-HORIN   179

Justin Cammy, Dara Horn, Alyssa Quint, and Rachel Rubinstein (eds.),
    *Arguing the Modern Jewish Canon: Essays on Literature and
Culture in Honor of Ruth R. Wisse*, JORDAN FINKIN   182

Ben-Zion Gold, *The Life of Jews in Poland before the Holocaust: A Memoir*, EZRA MENDELSOHN — 186

Benjamin Harshav, *The Polyphony of Jewish Culture*, ALAN MINTZ — 189

Mitchell Bryan Hart, *The Healthy Jew: The Symbiosis of Judaism and Modern Medicine*, AMOS MORRIS-REICH — 192

Tova Hartman, *Feminism Encounters Traditional Judaism: Resistance and Accommodation*, EINAT RAMON — 193

Meri-Jane Rochelson, *A Jew in the Public Arena: The Career of Israel Zangwill*, MATTHEW SILVER — 195

Anna Shternshis, *Soviet and Kosher: Jewish Popular Culture in the Soviet Union, 1923-1939*, JAMES LOEFFLER — 198

Barry Trachtenberg, *The Revolutionary Roots of Modern Yiddish, 1903–1917*, DAVID G. ROSKIES — 201

Zionism, Israel, and the Middle East

Avraham Burg, *The Holocaust is Over; We Must Rise from Its Ashes*, ALLAN ARKUSH — 204

Laurence J. Silberstein (ed.), *Postzionism: A Reader*, ALLAN ARKUSH — 204

Motti Golani, *The British Mandate for Palestine, 1948: War and Evacuation*, MOSHE NAOR — 206

Anat Helman, *Or veyam hikifuha: tarbut tel avivit bitkufat hamandat* (Urban culture in 1920s and 1930s Tel Aviv), ORIT ROZIN — 208

Arie Morgenstern, *Hastening Redemption: Messianism and the Resettlement of the Land of Israel* (trans. Joel A. Linsider), JODY MYERS — 213

Avinoam J. Patt, *Finding Home and Homeland: Jewish Youth and Zionism in the Aftermath of the Holocaust*, ADA SCHEIN — 217

Arieh Bruce Saposnik, *Becoming Hebrew: The Creation of a Jewish National Culture in Ottoman Palestine*, HANNAN HEVER — 220

Matthew Silver, *First Contact: Origins of the American-Israeli Connection; Halutzim from America during the Palestine Mandate*, DEBORAH DASH MOORE — 226

Contents for Volume XXVI — 229

Note on Editorial Policy — 231

Symposium
Ethnicity and Beyond: Theories and Dilemmas of Jewish Group Demarcation

Ethnicity as a Primordial-Situational-Constructed Experience: Different Times, Different Places, Different Constellations

Ewa Morawska
(UNIVERSITY OF ESSEX)

This essay argues for a flexible, context- and actor-dependent understanding of ethnicity, and illustrates this proposition by means of three sets of historical cases of Jewish communities compared and contrasted over time and across space. The first set examines the same group compared over time: commercial middle-class Jews in Venice during the period of residential dispersion (14th and 15th centuries) and in the ghetto era (early 16th through 17th centuries). The second comparison reconstructs the changed compositions of ethnicity over time among the same people, German Jewish intelligentsia in the socialist movement in Berlin at the turn of the 20th century and in the interwar period. Finally, the third set compares the same group across space: Soviet/post-Soviet Jews in Tel Aviv and in Philadelphia from the late 1980s until the present.

The concept of ethnicity in the social sciences has usually referred to common descent and culture that provide the basis of group social boundaries and members' identity.[1] While social scientists generally agree on the general referents of the concept of ethnicity, they have vigorously debated the nature of this shared bond. Three distinct understandings have been proposed. The earliest one views ethnicity as a primordial attachment to one's group and its values and traditions. Primordial attachments are those that stem from the "givens," or more precisely (as culture is inevitably involved in such matters), the assumed givens of social existence. The congruities of blood, speech, custom, and so on are seen to have an ineffable and at times overpowering coerciveness in and of themselves. One is bound, ipso facto, to one's kin, one's neighbor, one's fellow believer—not merely because of personal affection, practical necessity, common interest, or incurred obligation, but also, in great part, by virtue of some unaccountable absolute import attributed to the very tie itself.[2]

The second understanding of the nature of ethnic ties and identities, formulated in opposition to the primordial thesis, represents them as contingent on circumstances and thus, by definition, impermanent. The circumstantial representation of ethnicity has two subtypes: situational and instrumental. Situational ethnicity refers to memberships and identities that are deployed or made relevant by in- or out-group actors in response to specific societal situations and are likely to change accordingly. The instrumental understanding of ethnicity views it as activated by group members to serve specific material or political purposes and reshaped according to these ends.[3]

The third understanding views ethnicity as a social construction by actors of loyalties and identities in the process of engaging their environment. This approach shares with circumstantial representation a notion of ethnicity as emerging from the interaction between social situations and in-/out-group actors, but it is less circumstantial in that it allows for ethnic formations to endure beyond the demands of the moment.[4] Belonging as well to the representations of ethnicity as a constructed phenomenon is the notion of symbolic ethnicity, which refers to an optional association with "things ethnic": social ties, cultural rituals, and/or self-identification by choice rather than by social prescription or a current set of circumstances.[5] An important distinction between this view and the social construction understanding is that symbolic ethnicity can be an individual orientation or practice that is not anchored in its carrier's social surroundings.

While the advocates of the different representations of ethnicity sketched here continue to debate their positions, a novel and interesting proposition has recently appeared to resolve the differences among them, by allowing for context-dependent and, thus, changing constellations of primordial, circumstantial, and constructed components to make up ethnic practices and identities. I find particularly promising Steve Fenton's proposition to treat primordial, situational, instrumental, and constructed ethnicities as *ideal types* to be tested and revised against the specific historical conditions in which concrete ethnic practices and identities of particular group members evolve and transform.[6] Changing economic, political, and social-cultural circumstances, this approach posits, induce social actors—here, ethnic group members—to give their ethnic practices and identities specific meaning, relevance, and functions; or, in terms of the understanding proposed here, to form particular constellations of primordial, circumstantial, and constructed elements of their ethnicity in their interaction with the host environment.

The concept of ethnicity has generally been used in relation to established native national minorities and to populations of foreign origin settled in a host country. In this essay, we will be concerned with both of these cases. The syncretic conceptualization of ethnicity that I am proposing here allows for different combinations of both in-group and out-group elements. These include the use of language, cultural orientations, customs, religious beliefs and practices, social networks, and identities. Moreover, the specific constellations of these features and the scope and intensity of their primordial and situational components depend on the historical circumstances of ethnic group members' experience in relation to the majority or receiver society.

A similar idea of the interactive and, thus, flexible notion of ethnicity in its application to the Jewish experience was once offered by Raphael Patai in his historical overview of Jewish communities "the world over" across time, who noted that:

a certain degree of acculturation to the non-Jewish environment has taken place in every Jewish Diaspora.... Each of these Jewish ethnic groups exhibits its own combination of Jewish and non-Jewish traits. The Jewish traits themselves are of two kinds: old ones, going back to earlier ages and countries of Jewish sojourn, including some... that date back to Biblical Hebrew origins; and new ones, which themselves may be several generations old, but which have developed locally and therefore are likely to represent a certain divergence from corresponding traits that are the result of other local developments.[7]

The syncretic approach proposed here calls for identification of the specific characteristics of the surrounding society and the ethnic group itself that make up the context in which the particular meaning of ethnicity is being defined in each examined historical case. In line with David Myers' formulation in his reflections upon Jewish identities across various geopolitical contexts, Jewish ethnicity is viewed here as "a hybrid creation composed of different strands of influence" that are exerted by changing circumstances of Jewish lives.[8]

Here it should be noted that existing, especially comparative, studies of ethnic groups' identities and social-cultural practices point to some general factors that contribute to the specific constellations of ethnicity across time and space. These include, on the side of the receiver society, attitudes and practices of exclusion and inclusion of "others" by the dominant or majority group(s) in the realms of economy, civic-political life, social relations, and cultural participation. Ethnic group characteristics that usually have an impact on the form and "contents" of ethnic identities and practices include the number as well as the residential and occupational concentration of group members; their economic position vis-à-vis the dominant/majority group(s); the similarity or difference of the typical cultural capital of group members in relation to that of the dominant or majority group(s) in the receiver society; the relative inwardness (exclusivity) or openness of group self-representations, religion, and shared social-cultural practices; and the proportion and social-political role of the post-migration, native-born members (second-generation-plus) of the group.

Comparative studies are particularly useful in highlighting the importance of the circumstances in which ethnicity is being defined.[9] Social-historical studies of Jewish communities with a systematic comparative objective traditionally have been rare, in part because of the isolation of Jewish historiography within its own field, and in part (not unrelatedly) because of the notion underlying these studies of the transtemporal uniqueness of Jewish history.[10] The comparative examination here of time- and place-specific contingencies of Jewish ethnicity shares its purpose with a collection of essays titled *Comparing Jewish Societies* (1997), probably the most explicitly methodologically informed work in this field published in recent years. Like Todd Endelman, the editor of that volume, I would like my analysis to "make a case for viewing Jewish history in a comparative perspective."[11] The "external" comparisons (Jewish groups compared with non-Jewish groups) in the Endelman volume aim to counter Jewish historians' traditional representations of Jewish experience in terms of its taken-for-granted uniqueness. The primary intention of my "internal" comparisons, which examine sets of Jewish populations or groups across time and space, is to demonstrate the integral embeddedness of Jewish experience in its historical surroundings and, thus, its context-dependent and changing character.

The examination of the five comparative cases presented here—Venetian middle-class Jews in the period of residential dispersion in the 14th and 15th centuries and the ghetto in the 16th and 17th centuries; Jewish socialists in Berlin at the turn of the 20th century and in the interwar period; and present-day Soviet/post-Soviet Jews in Tel Aviv—is based on my analysis of secondary sources, about 60 studies in total, followed up where possible by my interrogation of their authors.[12] Information about the sixth case, Soviet/post-Soviet Jews in Philadelphia as the compare-and-contrast match of Tel Aviv Jews, comes from my own ethnographic study of the Jewish community in the former city.[13]

An important caveat is in order before we proceed with the analysis. Against this author's conscience but due to the lack of relevant information in the sources that served as the basis of this project, the comparative examination presented here is sadly genderless. A critical consideration of the gendered nature of Jewish identities and group membership is particularly lacking in studies of middle-class Italian Jews and German Jewish socialists in the periods of interest here (in both cases, in lieu of systematic gender analysis, sporadic references are made to individual women of outstanding status in the public forum or, more often, to "Jewish women and family life").

In each set of comparative cases I first summarize the larger-society economic and political context in which each examined group lived and, within it, the group's social and demographic characteristics. I then identify the major features of ethnic identity and participation of the examined Jewish groups as reconstructed from available studies (or, more precisely, following the interpretations I found most persuasive). Next, I point out the main characteristics of the surrounding environment and the Jewish groups themselves that have contributed to those particular ethnic configurations.

Commercial Middle-class Jews in Venice: Residential Dispersion (14th–15th Centuries) versus Life in the Ghetto (16th–17th Centuries)

It was only in the later part of the 14th century that an estimated 700–800 Jews residing in the area of Venice (many of whom were occupied in being pawnbrokers to the city's poor or else were secondhand merchandise traders) were authorized to live in the city itself, provided that they would settle only on *terraferma*, the Venetian mainland, and would spend only short periods of time in the capital city.[14] By the turn of the 16th century, a growing number of Jews—expellees from Spain and southern parts of Italy, refugees from the wars conducted by the Venetian republic with its competitors, and international traders from the Ottoman empire—began to settle in Venice. This growing "spread" of Jews "all over the city" bothered many Venetians and especially the Catholic clergy. Consequently, in 1516, the Venetian government issued a decree requiring all the Jews to reside together. Accordingly, they were "segregated on the island already then known as the *Ghetto Nuovo*[15] [and], when the space available on that island proved to be insufficient, the Jews were assigned two additional adjacent areas, the *Ghetto Vecchio* in 1541 . . . and the *Ghetto Nuovissimo* in 1633."[16]

By the mid- to late 16th century, the ghetto housed between 2,000 and 3,000 Jewish persons, constituting between 1 and 2 percent of the Venetian population. It became an integral part of the city's social order, which consisted of "legally defined estates endowed with specific privileges, and . . . corporations with expressly declared rights and duties, specializing in particular fields of social and economic action." One such "corporation of specialists within this highly regulated society was the *Università degli Hebrei* . . . and the Jews could also be said to form an estate of outcasts, lower in status than all the recognized Christian orders [that is, noblemen, merchants, artisans, and clergy]."[17] During this time, the traditional occupations of Venetian Jews in pawnbroking services expanded to include local and international trade, ranging from trade in secondhand merchandise to extensive overseas import-export operations. There were also long-established Jewish physicians, scholars, teachers, and artists.

Different groups within the Jewish community specialized in different occupations. By the turn of the 17th century, the corporation of Jews in Venice comprised three Jewish "nations" (as they were termed). The oldest settlers were the Germanic and Italian Ashkenazic Jews who were concentrated in banking, pawnbroking, and secondhand trade. The other two groups, both of them Sephardic Jews, were occupied in international trading; these were the Levantines originating in the Ottoman lands, and the Ponetines, or "westerners," who came to Venice from Spain, Portugal, and the Low Countries.

The base component of group membership among Venetian Jews in the 14th- and 15th-century period of residential dispersion was a fused ethno-religious identity. Although the Judaic faith and social-political location in the host society remained largely undifferentiated, the deeply habituated *religious* component of this identity was experienced by its bearers as primordial or inescapably given. In contrast, the social (as in relations and exchanges) and cultural (as in interests and pursuits) dimensions of ethnic identity and membership of Venetian Jews in that period represented a blend of primarily Jewish components and, of lesser scope and impact but nevertheless notable, broader (Christian) society influences. This latter element of Venetian Jews' ethnicity, reasserted in their encounters with the local Christian society (its political authorities as well as economic and cultural actors and agencies) in which the Jews were subordinate and insecure players, had a constructed and situational rather than primordial character.

In comparison, while the still fused ethno-religious principle remained crucial to the later, ghetto-era ethnic identity and group membership of Venetian Jews, its social-cultural component (the familiar "sounds, colors, tastes, and odors" of everyday life in the shared space)[18] had also acquired a primordial character, which at the same time sustained or even enhanced the religious one. It was on the basis of this dual-anchor (Judaic religion as the fundament of their identity and social-cultural immersion in their own group), along with their relative security (thanks to legal provisions that affirmed ghetto residents' status as Venetian citizens and allowed for a large measure of self-government), that 16th- and 17th-century Jews in the city interacted with the outside society. In comparison with the era of residential dispersion, when the social pillar of Jews' ethno-religious identity and group membership was weaker and their civic-political security was notably less stable, the situational component of ghetto-era ethnicity of Venetian Jews considerably diminished in the overall constellation. Their ethnic identity and pursuits retained an admixture of the broader society's influences through cultural and social ties maintained with the city's Christian residents. But the constructed component of their ethnicity remained unavoidably in place in Jews' relations with the outside society: dominant Christians' continued perception of Jews as inexorable (if tolerated) "others" and the evident constraints to which they were subject as citizens could not but sustain in Jewish residents the urge to present themselves to their neighbors as law-abiding and loyal Venetians and, among themselves, to reiterate a strategy of self-representation that stressed the importance of stability and quiescence.

The changing circumstances of Venetian Jewish existence shaped their differently nuanced ethnicities in each of the two periods considered here. In the period of residential dispersion in the 14th and 15th centuries, the chief condition that shaped ethnic identity and group membership of Venetian Jews was the taken-for-granted integral place of religion in people's—Jews' as well as the surrounding Christians'— everyday lives. For both Jews and Christians, Judaism was also the distinguishing characteristic of Jewish group membership: Jews perceived themselves and were perceived by Christians in ethno-religious terms.

The second circumstance shaping Venetian Jews' ethnicity in the period of residential dispersion was the residential dispersion itself, combined with civic-political constraints imposed by the republic's authorities, such as a prohibition on the erection of synagogues and on the establishment of in-group organizations, both of which significantly impeded the social base of local Jews' ethno-religious membership. Moreover, periodic reassessment by the government of residential permission for the group, as well as the restrictions placed on Jews' economic pursuits, undermined their sense of stability. The residence permit (*condotta*), the (low) interest rate allowed to be charged in money-lending to Christians and the (high) taxes levied on Jews were periodically reassessed by the Venetian government. Moreover, in order to prevent close relations between Jews and Christians and to make the former clearly distinguishable from the latter, all Jews coming to the city were made to wear a yellow circle on their outer clothing. Although the Venetian government did not force Jews to accept baptism, as was the case in other Italian towns in the 14th and 15th centuries, Jews were not allowed to build synagogues or Jewish schools in the midst of Christian neighborhoods, lest these "contaminate Christianity with Judaism."[19]

The third important circumstance influencing the composition of 14th- and 15th-century Venetian Jews' ethnicity, and somewhat counterbalancing the official restrictions, was the relative tolerance and openness of Christian Venetians of the time, combined with the great appeal of their Renaissance culture to educated Jews. Renowned across Europe, Renaissance Venice's prominence in literature, arts, and science afforded a splendid opportunity for a flourishing Jewish literary culture, including the printing of Hebrew religious books, poems, scholarly inquiries, and other literary works. While directly inspired by the Jewish religious tradition, this growing literature, as well as musical and theatrical performance culture, was evidently influenced by Italian Renaissance trends and ideas. Venetian Jewish scholars' participation in scientific research was equally notable. Even though theological projects and artistic and scientific activities were mainly pursued by Jewish religious sages and scientists, and not by the representatives of commercial occupations, the latter were unavoidably affected by (Christian) Renaissance philosophical ideas, aesthetic tastes, and literary trends. The influence of the outside culture was also visible in the Jews' dress and manners, which followed the current fashion.

Venetian Jewish bankers' and merchants' daily social contacts included their co-religionists, naturally, but also Christian residents of Venice as well as visitors to the city. Relations with the Christians were primarily but not exclusively economic. Social contacts with non-Jews were facilitated both by the Jews' residential dispersion and by Christian Venetians' generally friendly attitude toward them. Thus, middle-class Venetian Jews met socially, attended cultural events, gambled, and even drank together with Christians—whom they resembled in comportment, manners, and local interests. Jewish merchants' familiarity with the Italian or, more precisely, Venetian language (among themselves they spoke a Judeo-Venetian dialect) was an important facilitator of these contacts.[20]

The fourth circumstance shaping ethnic identity and group membership of Venetian Jews in the residential dispersion era, underlying the above factors, was what Robert Bonfil has called "the basic ambivalence of the Jewish condition" in the city. From the beginning of their settlement in Venice, Jews received contradictory signals from the host society, its officialdom, and rank-and-file residents. On the one hand, they were welcomed to Venice—in fact, city authorities actively encouraged them to come, in order to provide specific functions needed for the city's social peace (money-lending to the poor), the wellbeing of its affluent classes (medical services) and economic growth (for traders)—and, as such, their lives and property were legally protected. On the other hand, they were constrained in their life options and treated as inferior outsiders whose fate as Venetians was not in their own hands.[21]

As noted, Venice's Christian residents were often friendly toward Jews, and this facilitated social and cultural contacts between the two groups. At the same time, Jews were perceived irrevocably as "others" by their Christian neighbors—in terms of religion, of course, but also commonly (as convincingly argued by Richard Sennett) as representatives of a different, lower, physical species.[22] Occasional attacks on Jewish persons and property, prompted by the anti-Jewish preachings of visiting friars, added to Jews' sense of insecurity.

We now consider the major factors in the surrounding society and among Jews themselves that shaped the Venetian Jews' ethnicity in the ghetto during the 16th and 17th centuries. These comprised four sets of circumstances, some of which were holdovers from the previous era, but which now came together in a new constellation that produced a qualitatively different outcome.

The first circumstance was the persistence of the fused, ethno-religious basis of Jews' identity and group membership, reflecting the traditionalism of their own lives and the endurance of the accustomed perceptions of Jews (and, for that matter, of other non-Christians residing in the city) by their Christian neighbors. The second circumstance introduced an important change in the functioning of this ethno-religious basis: the formation of the ghetto and its effects in the realm of legal protection and the relative civic autonomy of the Jewish community, and the impact of all this upon the social-cultural lives of its members.[23]

The Jews' existence in Venice in the ghetto era was subject to the same general principle as before: they were welcomed by the city's government as performers of important economic functions and as such they were protected by the law, yet their ultimate fate was outside of their control. But the institution of the ghetto introduced a crucial difference. First, in contrast to the earlier period of residential dispersion, the establishment of the ghetto allowed Jews to live in the city under an explicitly stated legal provision to this effect, which offered the Jewish community a new sense of stability. Second and importantly, like other occupational and religious corporations in the city, the *Università degli Hebrei* had a self-government that allowed the Jewish community a certain autonomy. Representing the three Jewish "nations" residing in the ghetto, the Jews' self-governing institution was responsible both for the maintenance of internal order and for the regulation of Jews' commercial activities. It also acted as a negotiator (with limited powers) of the terms of renewed charters and fiscal obligations of the Jewish community, apportioning payments and collecting them in the form of specific taxes.[24]

Permitted now to erect synagogues in the enclosure of their own neighborhoods, Venetian Jews built no less than eight houses of prayer by the mid-16th century, which also served as centers of religious education and talmudic study for the (male) residents. They were now able to pursue their religious practices in the open. They were also involved in diverse cultural activities. Several confraternities, or voluntary associations, served the social (including entertainment) and practical needs of the residents. Highly regarded printing houses produced books in both Hebrew and Italian (by the 16th century, bilingual competence became widespread in Jewish cultural and scholarly circles). Established in the previous era, medical studies gained popularity among middle-class Venetian Jews; the nearby Padua Medical School attracted a considerable number of Jewish students from Venice, many of whom were sons of affluent merchants.

Group social life intensified, compared with the earlier period of residential dispersion, as Jews were cramped into an overcrowded ghetto, sharing the same space and separated from others. Inside, social contacts of ghetto inhabitants took place primarily within the boundaries of the three nations: German/Italian, Ponetine, and Levantine.[25]

The third factor shaping the composition of Venetian Jews' ethnicity in the ghetto era was the sustained influence of the outside world through cultural and social contacts with the city's Christian residents. To be sure, the intensity of social and cultural exchange between ghetto residents and non-Jews outside had probably diminished overall in comparison with the earlier period. Moreover, intensified efforts of Catholic Counter-Reformation agitators to isolate the Jews, followed by heightened Christian fears of the "Jewish disease" during and after the Venetian plague in 1629–1631—and, more generally, the gradual decline of Venice as a cultural and economic center—further contributed to the weakening of social interactions between Jewish and Christian Venetians. Yet contact between the two groups by no means disappeared. It continued, first and foremost, in the economic realm, but also socially and during Christians' visits in the ghetto to attend cultural events such as public lectures of celebrated Jewish scholars, and musical or theatrical performances.

A new and important influence in the mid-16th century, not only on Jewish religious scholars but also on the larger population, was the study and public teaching of kabbalah, an esoteric interpretation of the Bible that emphasized inner spirituality as the means to grasp its true meaning. Interest in this new theosophical approach was actually shared by Jews and Christians, and scholars from both groups publicly exchanged ideas on the topic. Educated Jews and Christians keenly followed the polemics between mystics and rationalists (among the latter were two well-known Venetian rabbinical scholars, Leon Modena [1571–1648] and Simone Luzzatto [1583–1663]). These sustained contacts served as transmitters of outside influences into the Jewish society and, from there, into its members' ethnic self-perceptions and pursuits.[26]

The fourth important factor shaping the composition of ethnicity among Venetian Jews in the ghetto era was their situation as economically needed, legally protected, and socially tolerated, but nevertheless irrevocably inferior, "others." As before, the Jews' existence in the city was dependent on a charter periodically reissued by the Venetian government. Although it was never refused, its renewal invariably caused considerable apprehension in the Jewish community. Jews were also subject to several constraints on their economic activities: any attempt on their part to engage in unauthorized pursuits (for instance, handicrafts) was suppressed; nor were they allowed to hire Christian servants or to provide medical services to Christians (thus bringing to an end the golden age of Jewish medicine in Venice, and across Italy). Still, in comparison with the period of residential dispersion, when Venetian Jews were far more exposed to unpleasantness from the dominant society, the existence of the ghetto provided them a sense of togetherness and, with it, increased security.

German Jewish Socialists in Berlin at the Turn of the 20th Century and during the Interwar Period

During the last decades of the 19th century, native-born German Jews in Berlin— totaling about 45,000 in the year 1900, or about 2.5 percent of the total population of the city[27]—had witnessed a double transformation: the economic and political modernization of Germany, and the political emancipation of their own group. Largely urbanized and traditionally occupied in entrepreneurial pursuits, Jews were probably the main beneficiaries of the belated but rapid modernization of Germany's economy in the 1870s and 1880s, as their once marginal trades and professions became integral to developing capitalism. Germany's political unification in 1871 as a nation-state had been executed *von oben* (from above), and it retained old-regime elements such as the hegemony of Prussian Junkers, the feudal aristocracy, and monarchic rule. However, under the pressure of political liberalism as the doctrine of the rising German middle class, the political emancipation of the Jews, the so-called *Gleichberechtigung* introduced in the year of the country's unification, replaced their segregation (under special regulations dating back to the Middle Ages) with full civil rights and legal equality.[28]

German Jews' occupational structure during the Kaiserreich and later in the Weimar republic, especially in large urban centers such as Berlin, significantly differed from that of the rest of the population. Most of the Jews, more than 60 percent, were occupied in middle- to large-scale trade and banking, and nearly one third worked in professions, especially as lawyers and doctors, and in the so-called *freie Berufe* (free professions), which included artists, journalists, and writers. (They were, however, practically excluded from higher-level positions in the universities.) Hardly any German-born Jews were in the ranks of the industrial proletariat.[29]

The political emancipation of the Jews was founded on the idea of converting them into German citizens as individuals, not as Jews. This idea was keenly taken up by middle-class Jews who were eager to participate fully in German society. The earlier Haskalah and Reform philosophers had already elaborated a discourse of Jewish Germanness, and most middle-class urban Jews were now prepared to be *Deutsche Staatsbürger jüdischen Glaubens*—German citizens of the Judaic faith, fully German in public and Jewish at home. The increasingly aggressive German nationalism in the Weimar republic, and the spread of open antisemitism reflecting it, had inevitably undermined but did not eradicate the acculturated German Jews' sense of identification with and loyalty to their home country.[30]

It was against this backdrop that young Jewish socialists were raised during the late 19th century. Concentrated mostly in Berlin, they served as the intellectual leaders of the movement: journalists, organizers, theoreticians, propagandists, and teachers. Among the most prominent were Joseph Bloch, the brothers Heinrich and Adolf Braun, Gustav Landauer, Paul Singer, Emanuel Wurm, Georg Davidsohn, Max Kayser, and Wilhelm Dietz.[31] The present discussion of the ethnicity of the Berlin Jewish socialist intelligentsia[32] in the late 19th and early 20th centuries concerns only one fraction of this group, the so-called voluntaristic (as in dependent on human agency) revisionists, for whom the socialist project was a vision of a better society whose realization was contingent on the shared action of committed individuals.[33]

The multi-level constellation of ethnicity in the milieu of the German Jewish (revisionist) socialist intelligentsia appears even more complex than that of the Jewish Venetians four centuries earlier. For turn-of-the-20th-century Jewish socialists in Berlin, the German component of their identity was so solidly built into their (self-constructed) representations of themselves that it acquired a quasi-primordial character. The "quasi" qualification was imposed by the surrounding German society, whose recognition of native-born and assimilated Germans of Jewish origin as "their own" was uncertain: an economic downturn was enough for a rise in antisemitism.

The Jewish component of their identity (but not social membership) was not self-consciously recognized as such by Berlin Jewish socialists. It was given play, however, in their secularized messianic universalism, a disposition that had ethno-religious (Judaic) origins. Founded on the ethical imperative to "improve the world," this worldview can be related to their early-age socialization into the principles of Reform Judaism, which were later translated into the socialist project of justice and equality for all—a commitment that might be called a primordial impulse from a deeper-yet, or what Heinz Kohut called an "experience-near," layer of their shared life-orientations.[34]

In comparison, during the interwar period a new element in the composition of ethnicity of the same Berlin Jewish socialist intelligentsia had the effect, as if in a turned kaleidoscope, of changing its overall landscape. While they still considered themselves primarily German and still held a universalist vision of the future, their primary identities and concerns were accompanied by a development that Shulamit Volkov has called "dissimilation," the partial revival of Jewish interests and affinities among otherwise acculturated middle-class German Jewry.[35]

In the case of the socialist intelligentsia it meant, first, a recognition that Germany's (and, more broadly, Europe's) "Jewish question" was not, as they had believed earlier, a purely class (or economic) problem, but rather an ethnic-national (or cultural-political) issue that would not be resolved by a socialist transformation of society. Second and relatedly, it involved a new sympathy for (and in some instances, an identification with) the Zionist movement, which they had previously condemned. Under the new circumstances of the interwar period, Zionism could be seen as a legitimate mode of collective response to a persistent—indeed, increasingly ubiquitous—antisemitism, combined with a "cultural rapprochement" with lower-class immigrant Jews: the formerly despised *Ostjuden*, or East European Jews who had settled in Germany. These new concerns and sympathies contributed to a reorientation of Berlin Jewish socialists' universalism, from a resolutely post-ethnic emphasis to a recognition of multiculturalism or, to borrow from Michael Walzer, a recognition of a "reiterative universalism" that allowed for universal themes within particularist sets of ideas and modes of action as the basis for the better functioning of society.[36]

Two sets of circumstances were responsible for the composition of ethnic identity and participation among the turn-of-the-20th-century German Jewish intelligentsia in Berlin. The first was the economic, political, and cultural context of their upbringing, both that of the larger society and of their own families. We have already noted the parallel developments of economic advancement and political emancipation of German Jewry in the post-unification period and the accompanying process of cultural transformation. The notion of *Bildung*, an ethical development founded on reason and cultural elevation and aiming at the full realization of individual rights and potential, integral to German high culture since the late-18th century, was also the crucial component of German Jews' acculturation process. Indeed, middle-class Germans of Judaic faith upheld the *Bildung* ideal with neophyte passion. Combined with their *Besitz*, an accomplished economic status based on property and education, *Bildung* was seen as an assured means of integration into the German society; it was firmly expected to eventually annihilate whatever remnants of antisemitism, especially in the social sphere, were still harbored by their fellow Germans.[37]

The childhood and adolescent socialization of the socialist offspring of the affluent German Jewish middle class explains the deeply embedded and primary German component of their ethnicity. Their lack of interest in their Jewish origins, their general disaffiliation from the German Jewish community, and the universalist underlayer of their self-representations were the outcome of another major circumstance of their lives, namely, their double estrangement: from their own bourgeois families and a lifestyle that they considered to be philistine, and from the political situation in Germany, especially the rightward turn of the liberal parties in the 1880s that were co-opted into Bismarck's ruling clerical-conservative block.[38] Their involvement with socialism was a response to this combined alienation.

Another factor working to "naturalize" the socialist commitment of German Jewish intellectuals was what Michael Löwy has called an elective affinity between socialist ideology and the secularized, messianic universalism of biblical origin.[39] The universalist strand of the Jewish messianic tradition emphasized by Reform Judaism—in particular, its ethical call upon humans to persist in their efforts toward the improvement of the world, combined with a vision of the emancipation of all people—blended easily with socialist principles. "Secularization stripped away the theological husk, but preserved and transformed a core of [traditional Jewish] belief"; the main transformation was the abandonment of the particularistic strand in traditional (religious) Jewish messianism and the expansion of the universalist strand.[40]

Löwy distinguishes three levels, or degrees, of elective affinity. The lowest one, simple affinity, denotes "a spiritual relationship or a correspondence." The intermediate level implies "the *election*, the reciprocal attraction and active mutual choice of the two socio-cultural configurations." Finally, the highest degree of elective affinity between the two given phenomena represents "the articulation, combination or 'alloying' of partners [resulting] in various modalities of a union."[41] The Berlin Jewish intelligentsia's attraction to socialism corresponded with one of the two lower-level elective affinities suggested by Löwy, depending on the intensity of their rejection of the bourgeois lifestyles of the families in which they grew up.[42] Last and important, the camaraderie of colleagues preoccupied with similar issues—turn-of-the-20th-century Berlin was a vibrant center of multicultural and "multi-ideological" life and a mecca for socialists of different persuasions—further cemented their commitment.

The main implications of the German Jewish intelligentsia's adherence to socialist ideology were the enhancement of their secularism, that is, the programmatic abandonment of "the Judaic faith" addendum to their German identities, on the one hand, and, on the other, the adoption of a strong universalist or "post-tribal (ethnic)" orientation founded on the principle that "one could be a Jewish [Catholic, Protestant] socialist but not a socialist Jew [Catholic, Protestant]."[43] As ideologues of the socialist movement, Jews themselves formulated and propagated those directives.

Both Jewish and non-Jewish socialists condemned antisemitism, which not only increased as nationalist sentiments in the newly united Germany gained force and as the country's public opinion reacted with resentment to the economic and civic-political empowerment of Jewish citizens, but also acquired a new "scientific" form of genetically justified racism.[44] The same post-ethnic universalist principles that informed their creed made Jewish socialists believe that antisemitism, both in Germany and elsewhere, would be vanquished not by Zionism or other forms of ("tribal") Jewish solidarity but rather by working-class action and the "transformation" (according to moderates) or "abolition" (according to radicals) of the capitalist order.[45]

The emergence (as they were rarely if ever present before) of Jewish concerns and solidarities among German Jewish socialist intelligentsia in Berlin during the interwar period altered the composition of their ethnicity, bringing into it some "Jewish self-consciousness" as a situational component. Two sets of circumstances—one in the surrounding society, and the other in the response to it of Jewish socialists themselves—were responsible for this development. The former was a progressive deterioration of public life in Germany, specifically, the expansion and radicalization of the Right and the eventual disintegration of liberal parties, accompanied by a growing virulence of German nationalist antisemitism. Related to it, and probably more personally hurtful and alienating to Jewish socialists, were the increasingly frequent public expressions of antisemitism within the Social Democratic party. These were directed primarily at the East European *Ostjuden*, the wartime laborers and refugees who had settled in Germany, especially in Berlin, and who formed tight-knit ethno-religious communities. As noted by Peter Pulzer, the Social Democratic party "had little sympathy with the Jewish desire to survive as a community with a separate identity," and it collectively stigmatized East Europeans in public as "alien and suspicious elements."[46] At the same time, German-born Jewish socialist intellectuals were accused of being "pushy outsiders" who were trying to insinuate themselves into the workers' movement.[47]

As a result, it is possible to speak of a disillusionment on the part of these Jewish socialists with their taken-for-granted belief in the gradual disappearance of antisemitism. Together with their non-socialist fellow ethnics, they were bitterly disappointed to see that their cultural assimilation not only did not bring about their integration into German society but, on the contrary, had turned them into despised outcasts in the eyes of the increasingly popular nationalists. As socialists, they saw that instead of moving into the enlightened post-tribal society governed by universalist humanistic principles, Germany was turning into an aggressively exclusionary and even racist social order.

In response to these disappointments, without losing identification with their primordial *Deutschtum* (Germanness), a number of German Jewish socialist intellectuals, for example, Joseph Bloch, Eduard Bernstein, Julius Moses, and Oskar Cohn, developed a sympathy for or even a personal commitment to Zionism. In the previous era most of them, as we have seen, had vigorously opposed this movement as a misconstrued means of solving the "Jewish question," and a few who supported Zionism did so on behalf of the *Ostjuden* in order to "liberate the gentile [German] world from anti-Semitism."[48] Developments in Germany in the 1920s and 1930s persuaded many Jewish socialists that Zionism (in particular, that espoused by Poale Zion, a party that promulgated socialist Zionism) offered a legitimate means of resistance to the spreading trend of antisemitism and a reasonable alternative for Jews unwilling to have their socialist principles ruined by it.[49]

A parallel development in the orientations of the German Jewish socialist intelligentsia during the interwar period was their sympathetic interest in East European Jews living in Berlin. Considered "backward" and "embarrassing" by the established bourgeois German Jews and stigmatized as "troublesome aliens" by gentile Social Democrats, *Ostjuden* attracted Jewish socialists' sympathy as underdogs. The socialists were also intrigued by the East Europeans' solidly traditional Jewish lifestyle. Marginalized on all sides: not accepted as Germans by the Germans and cast as "outsiders" by their comrades in the socialist movement, a number of Jewish socialist intellectuals felt a wave of nostalgia while visiting the vibrant East European communities in the city.[50]

The emergence of these new elements in Jewish socialists' orientations—their acceptance of the bases and purposes of Zionism and their sympathetic recognition of their *ostjüdische* neighbors' distinct way of life—altered, as already noted, the character of their universalism (still an important component of their identities and concerns) by making it compatible with group particularisms in the form of multicultural society.

Contemporary Soviet/Post-Soviet Jews in Philadelphia and Tel Aviv

The Soviet/post-Soviet Jewish settlers in Philadelphia and Tel Aviv belong to the last wave of Jewish emigration from the Soviet Union/FSU in the late 1980s and early 1990s.[51] Emigrés in both groups originated from large cities in Russia and Ukraine, especially Moscow, Kiev, and Odessa.[52] They also had a similar educational and occupational profile upon leaving their home country: some 65 to 70 percent of the adults were professionals or upper-level, white-collar workers concentrated in technical occupations, engineering, or medical and other scientific research. Jews' high educational and occupational collective achievement (relative to Soviet national standards) did not prevent and perhaps even contributed to the enduring, deeply embedded resentment toward them on the part of the Russian/Ukrainian majority in their country of origin. Zigzagging (now neutral, now inimical) official policies toward the Jews added to their underlying insecurity. Both émigré groups considered here shared fused political-economic motivations for leaving Russia and cited family connections and social support networks as the main reason for settling in a particular destination country.[53]

Upon their settlement in either Philadelphia or Tel Aviv, however, the two groups' sociodemographic situation differentiated in at least three important aspects. First, numbering between 30,000 and 35,000 in the year 2000, the Philadelphian Russian Jewish immigrants constituted a tiny fraction of the city's total population of some 2.5 million. In stark contrast, the number of ex-Soviet fellow ethnics in Tel Aviv that year (from all emigration waves combined) was five times larger and constituted more than one-fourth of the city's population. Second, in comparison with the predominantly younger (middle-aged) Tel Aviv settlers, their counterparts in Philadelphia had a much larger proportion (more than a third) of elderly immigrants over 65 years of age. Finally, whereas immigrants in both destination sites initially experienced housing problems and considerable occupational skidding, the Philadelphians managed to recoup their status losses more quickly and more effectively than Soviet Jews who settled in Tel Aviv.[54] As we shall see, a combination of these and other differences has produced different compositions of ethnicities among former Soviet and post-Soviet Jewish emigrants in these two cities.

We begin with the Philadelphians. The core element of their ethnicity has been a primordial identification as Russian Jews, with an emphasis on the Russian component. Unlike the previously examined early 20th-century German Jews who viewed themselves as Germans, the majority of Russian Jews in the USSR/FSU, while thoroughly russified culturally, had their Jewish attribution imposed upon them by the surrounding society. If the collective experience of being unwanted in their home country constituted a negative component of Russian Jews' ethnic identity, a positive one was what Larissa Remennick has called "the spirit of excellence,"[55] or the drive toward individual achievement, socialized at home and reconstructed through in-group role models. In contrast with German Jewish socialists' secular universalism anchored in Judaic ethics, we may call this shared orientation of Russian Jews a secular particularism or the secularized version of the notion of the "Chosen People": founded on the belief and pride in "Jewish genius and achievement throughout history," and mobilizing group members to sustained efforts to make the best of their lives and to cope with hardships.[56]

After resettling in America and with the passage of time, there grew around this Russian-based core a newly constructed and gradually internalized layer of (American) Jewish ethno-religious identity and social membership, replacing the imposed "political Jewishness" of the home country. The immigrants' transplanted culture of achievement has blended very well with prevalent orientations in the American Jewish community and has facilitated their acculturation to it. To the mixing-and-blending of the "primordial" Russian Jewish and self-constructed American Jewish ethnicity was added an outer layer, as it were, containing elements of mainstream American cultural habits. The longer immigrants stayed in the host country, the more they identified as "Russian Jewish Americans." Two distinctive characteristics of the formation of this new ethnic configuration among Soviet/post-Soviet Jewish immigrants in Philadelphia should be noted: it occurred primarily in the private sphere, and the actors themselves eagerly participated in its development.

As in the case of émigrés to Philadelphia, the core component of ethnicity of the last wave of Russian Jewish settlers in Tel Aviv has been a primordial Russian cultural identity acquired through early socialization and sustained through their adult lives in the Soviet Union/FSU. Unlike the Philadelphian immigrants, however, for whom Russian attachments have been a private matter displayed only in their circle of acquaintances and who have gradually fused their Russian "core" with American Jewish and mainstream American components, Soviet/post-Soviet Jews in Tel Aviv have gone assertively public with their Russian heritage as members of a large ethnic minority in Israel.[57]

At the same time, the difficulties the immigrants have experienced in the receiver society, first with replicating and then with improving their socioeconomic status, have collided with the "spirit of excellence" cherished as their ethnic group's distinctive feature. Some enduring discontent with their personal situation in Israel and with aspects of Israeli society at large has tended to qualify or diminish their identification with Israel (elements of acculturation notwithstanding), which has further enhanced their Russian identity. And, unlike their Philadelphia counterparts who under the auspices of the American Jewish community have undergone a "religious conversion (return?)" to Judaism, Russian Jewish immigrants in Tel Aviv have remained by and large detached from religion except for minimal, selective, and situational practices. The character of Soviet/post-Soviet Jewish identities and group membership in Tel Aviv has mainly been Russian ethnic (not ethno-religious) and Russian Israeli ethnic-minority based.

Three major sets of circumstances have shaped the constellation of ethnicity among Russian Jewish immigrants in Philadelphia. First, its core Russian component, the outcome of their already noted profound cultural russification in the home country, has been sustained in their new American habitat by means of residential concentration in shared neighborhoods and intense social contacts with their fellow immigrants. The immigrants regularly use Russian in their homes and among friends and also prefer Russian-language media—as one respondent noted, "I rest in Russian, it is a comfort."[58] This linguistic preference-cum-practice has served further to reinforce the Russian basis of immigrants' identities and social relations.

Two related factors produce the second set of circumstances, which together have been responsible for the emergence of a new addition to immigrants' identities and participation as Russian *American* Jews. One of them is the immigrants' shared sense of *osvobozhdenie* (liberation) and *blagodarnost'* (gratitude) upon their arrival in America, a land in which they have found individual and collective security (*bezopashost'*) as Russian Jews. They also found opportunities to do what they want: "*Eta strana dla ludi, nie ludi dla strany*" (this country is for the people, not people for the country); "*my schastlivyi zdyes*" (we are happy here).[59] Such feelings, expressed by most of my respondents regardless of their sociodemographic differences, have made the immigrants eager to assimilate.

A related factor contributing to the transformation of ethnicity of Russian Jewish arrivals has been the sponsorship and expectations of the local American Jewish community. Philadelphian Jews who aided the newcomers often encouraged them to become "real Jews" and acted as role models in this regard. Because "Jewish" in the U.S. context connotes ethnic and religious affiliation both in the larger society and among American Jews themselves, the immigrants' incorporation into the American Jewish community—as a sub-ethnic path of integration into mainstream American society—has entailed their acquiring a religious identity and practices (usually non-Orthodox). In this case, too, immigrants have been eager to collaborate. Back in the home country, many of them note, Jewishness was ascribed to them by the surrounding society: "In Russia, I was a Jew because of discrimination. . . . In Russia, we were Jews because it said so in our passports." Whereas "here we feel we are Jews. We celebrate [Jewish] holidays, go to the synagogue, and give [charitable] donations."[60]

A third set of circumstances has been responsible for the private-sphere-only displays of Philadelphia's Russian Jewish immigrants' ethnicity. An important contributing factor has been the relatively small size of their group and its absorption into the established, high-status American Jewish community which, as their sponsor, initially took it upon itself to represent them in public. The preoccupation with making it in America materially and occupationally (the latter often requiring intensive retraining, not to mention the acquisition of English fluency), as well as the fact that a large proportion of the elderly have already withdrawn from active life, have also been responsible for Russian Jews' concentration on their private affairs. Finally, there is an underlying, historical condition contributing to their reluctance to get engaged in public affairs, Jewish or otherwise, apart from becoming naturalized (more than 80 percent of Philadelphia's Russian Jewish immigrants held American citizenship in the year 2000). In the USSR and later in the FSU, involvement in public matters was, first, impossible for rank-and-file citizens unless they were members of the *nomenklatura* (a pool of ranking Communist Party comrades judged trustworthy by its leaders), and second, and especially for unwelcome Jews, potentially dangerous to themselves and their families. Immigrants transplanted their deeply habituated preference for privacy from their home country to Philadelphia, where the above-noted circumstances of their lives have sustained this orientation.

A different constellation of factors has shaped the composition of ethnicity of Russian Jewish immigrants in Tel Aviv. First, the Tel Aviv settlers have shared with Russian Jews in Philadelphia the deeply habituated Russian cultural identities and practices transplanted from the sender country and sustained through residential concentration and intense social contacts with fellow émigrés. At the same time, both the host society and the in-group response to it are very different in Tel Aviv. Officially, Israel is characterized by a strict assimilationis ideology and policies. These have been met with opposition on the part of immigrants, who, having come from one authoritarian regime, are not eager to succumb to another; in this they have been encouraged by the fact that Israeli society "on the ground" exhibits a growing multiculturalism. Thus, although increasingly bilingual, immigrants have retained Russian as the main language of their mutual contacts and of their preferred media. They have also retained the Russian-style celebration of the (Christian) New Year with Christmas trees and *Dyed Mroz*, the secular (Soviet) version of Santa Claus. At the same time, the hegemony in Israel of the Orthodox branch of Judaism with its strict requirements for membership—although admittedly less pervasive in cosmopolitan Tel Aviv than in, say, Jerusalem—has turned the overwhelming majority of secular Russian Jewish immigrants away from religion.

Russian Jewish immigrants based in Tel Aviv by and large report less contentment with their lives than their counterparts in Philadelphia. In addition to difficulties with regard to housing conditions and occupational status, there are the additional stresses associated with Israel's continuous engagement in violent conflict with its neighbors. These causes for malaise have been accompanied by Russian Jewish settlers' shared sense of cultural superiority vis-à-vis the "Oriental" society to which they have transplanted themselves. A large (estimated 25–35 percent) proportion of non-Jews in the last wave of arrivals from the Soviet Union/FSU, along with sustained, intense ties with the home country (on the part of both non-Jewish and Jewish immigrants) have further contributed to the predominance of the Russian component of the immigrants' ethnicity.

One further factor shaping the ethnicity of Soviet/post-Soviet Jewish immigrants in Tel Aviv has been the large number and proportion of Soviet/post-Soviet immigrants both in the city and in the country at large. In the context of the multicultural character of Israeli society, this gives the Russian immigrant sector a sense of collective strength—a new development, considering their past insecure status in their home country. Their status as a recognized ethnic minority in Israel has, in turn, given the Russian component of immigrants' ethnicity a new role as a situational political tool to assert their group interests—a tool they have repeatedly used.

As we have seen, in contrast to the emerging Russian Jewish American ethnicity of Soviet/post-Soviet settlers in Philadelphia, that of their fellow émigrés in Tel Aviv has been a Russian Israeli ethnicity transformed through the incorporation of new ingredients: bilingualism and other elements of acculturation to the host society, and a sense of collective civic-political entitlement as an ethnic minority.[61]

Conclusion

The foregoing comparative examination of the three sets of cases of different forms and "contents" of ethnic identities and practices of Jews living in different times and places has been intended as an empirical demonstration of the proposed conceptualization of ethnicity as context-dependent, that is, changing in accordance with varying constellations of its contributing (primordial, constructed, and situational) elements. The diversity presented here would have been even greater and the ethnic compositions more complex had it also been possible to analyze their gender dependency across time and place. Likewise, more levels of complexity would be added by considering separately the ethnicity of each of the three "nations" that made up Venetian Jewry; the ethnic identities and group membership not just of the Berlin socialist intellectuals of bourgeois background, but also of German Jewish communists in Berlin; or the composition of ethnicity among, for example, Soviet/post-Soviet Jews who have resettled in Berlin, their third-largest post-migration concentration.

The purpose of this essay, however, has not been an encompassing coverage of the existing subgroup variations in the examined cases. It was obviously impossible given the limited scope of this analysis and also unnecessary. In addition to the empirical documentation of the conceptualization of ethnicity proposed here, the intended contribution of this comparative exercise has been to provide interested researchers a guiding framework for analyzing this phenomenon. This approach postulates a three-step analytic procedure. First, with the definitions of different mechanisms of ethnicity (primordial, constructed, situational) in hand, the researcher identifies the major sets of circumstances in the surrounding society and in the examined group that might have contributed to each of these components of the examined phenomenon, and in what specific ways. He/she may conclude that one or more of the definitional mechanisms are not present in the specific case. Next, the researcher examines possible impacts of home- and host-country traditions, behavioral patterns, and orientations on each of the identified components of ethnicity and locates them within the contributing larger-society and in-group contexts. The third step in the analysis informed by the conceptualization of ethnicity proposed here requires the researcher to check the effects of the changing larger-society and in-group circumstances (including newly emerging factors that were not on the original list of contributors identified in step 1) on the examined phenomenon and then appropriately readjust the constellation of ethnicity.

Notes

I thank David Ruderman, Benjamin Ravid, Larissa Remennick, Shulamit Volkov, Michael Brenner, and Evyatar Friesel for patiently answering my repeated inquiries regarding particular Jewish communities I chose to examine, and my husband, Willfried Spohn, for providing volumes of studies on the history of Jews in 19th- and early 20th-century Germany that were unavailable in the UK.

1. For overviews of the definitions of this term, see Steve Fenton, *Ethnicity* (Cambridge: 2003); John Hutchinson and Anthony Smith (eds.), *Ethnicity* (New York: 1996); Werner Sollors, *Theories of Ethnicity: A Classical Reader* (New York: 1996); and Richard Jenkins, *Rethinking Ethnicity: Arguments and Explorations* (London: 1997).

2. Clifford Geertz, *The Interpretation of Cultures* (New York: 1973), 259–260; on primordial ethnicity, see also Anthony Smith, *The Ethnic Origins of Nations* (Oxford: 1986).

3. On situational ethnicity, see Fredrik Barth (ed.), *Ethnic Groups and Boundaries: The Social Organization of Culture Difference* (London: 1969); Nathan Glazer and Daniel Moynihan, *Beyond the Melting Pot: The Negroes, Puerto Ricans, Jews, Italians, and Irish of New York City* (Cambridge, Mass.: 1975); on instrumental ethnicity, see Michael Hechter, *Internal Colonialism: The Celtic Fringe in British National Development 1536–1966* (Berkeley: 1975).

4. For classical representations of communities and traditions as constructed, or "imagined," see Eric Hobsbawm and Terence Ranger (eds.), *The Invention of Tradition* (Cambridge: 1983); Benedict Anderson, *Imagined Communities: Reflections on the Origin and Spread of Nationalism* (London: 1983); on the applications of this notion to the concept of ethnicity, see Werner Sollors, *The Invention of Ethnicity* (New York: 1989); G.M. Scott, "A Resynthesis of the Primordial and Circumstantial Approaches to Ethnic Group Solidarity: Towards an Explanatory Model," *Ethnic and Racial Studies* 13, no. 2 (1990), 147–171; and Marcus Banks, *Ethnicity: Anthropological Constructions* (London: 1996).

5. For elaborations of the notion of symbolic ethnicity, see Herbert Gans, "Symbolic Ethnicity: The Future of Ethnic Groups and Culture in America," *Ethnic and Racial Studies* 2, no. 1 (1979), 1–20; and Mary Waters, *Ethnic Options: Choosing Identities in America* (Berkeley: 1990).

6. Fenton, *Ethnicity*.

7. Raphael Patai, *Tents of Jacob: The Diaspora—Yesterday and Today* (London: 1971), 160.

8. David Myers, "'The Blessing of Assimilation' Reconsidered: An Inquiry into Jewish Cultural Studies," in *From Ghetto to Emancipation: Historical and Contemporary Reconsiderations of the Jewish Community*, ed. David Myers and William Rowe (Scranton: 1997), 17–36.

9. On the advantages of comparative analysis in social-historical studies, see Charles Ragin, *The Comparative Method* (Berkeley: 1987); and John R. Hall, *Cultures of Inquiry: From Epistemology to Discourse in Sociohistorical Research* (Cambridge: 1999).

10. For recent comparative studies of Jewish communities, see Pierre Birnbaum and Ira Katznelson (eds.), *Paths of Emancipation: Jews, States, and Citizenship* (Princeton: 1995); Todd Endelman (ed.), *Comparing Jewish Societies* (Ann Arbor: 1997); Noah Lewin-Epstein, Yaakov Ro'i, and Paul Ritterband (eds.), *Russian Jews on Three Continents: Migration and Resettlement* (Portland: 1997); Ewa Morawska, "Exploring Diversity in Immigrant Assimilation and Transnationalism: Poles and Russian Jews in Philadelphia," *International Migration Review* 38, no. 4 (2004), 1372–1412; and Larissa Remennick, *Russian Jews on Three Continents: Identity, Integration and Conflict* (New Brunswick: 2007); see also David Biale (ed.), *Cultures of the Jews: A New History* (New York: 2002).

11. Endelman (ed.), *Comparing Jewish Societies*, 13.

12. Studies on Soviet/post-Soviet Jews in Israel usually examine this group as a whole or else focus on immigrants who settled in the largest cities in that country. From available studies, I extracted information about Russian Jews in Tel Aviv, and I also checked with Larissa Remennick on the applicability of general findings reported in these studies to immigrants in Tel Aviv.

13. Morawska, "Exploring Diversity in Immigrant Assimilation and Transnationalism."

14. Only for a period of 15 years, from 1382 to 1397, were Jews as a collective permitted to live in the city.

15. The term *ghetto* originally referred to the foundry area in that location.

16. Benjamin Ravid, "The Venetian Government and the Jews," in *The Jews of Early Modern Venice*, ed. Robert Davis and Benjamin Ravid (Baltimore: 2001), 152. In order to prevent the mingling of Jews and Christians, the gates to the ghetto were closed at sunset and opened at sunrise by Christian guards, and all Jews were required to wear special headgear to distinguish them from Christian residents.

17. Brian Pullan, *The Jews of Europe and the Inquisition of Venice, 1550–1670* (New York: 1983), 146.

18. Robert Bonfil, "A Cultural Profile," in Davis and Ravid (eds.), *The Jews of Early Modern Venice*, 169–190.

19. David Malkiel, "The Ghetto Republic," in ibid., 118–142; Brian Pullan, "Jewish Banks and the Monti de Pietà," in ibid., 53–72; Robert Bonfil, *Jewish Life in Renaissance Italy* (Berkeley: 1994); Benjamin Ravid, "Between the Myth of Venice and the Lachrymose Conception of Jewish History: The Case of the Jews of Venice," in *Studies and Texts in Jewish History and Culture*, ed. Bernard Cooperman (Bethesda: 2000), 151–192; idem, "The Venetian Government and the Jews."

20. Cecil Roth, *The History of the Jews of Italy* (Philadelphia: 1946); Arthur Lesley, "Jewish Adaptation of Humanistic Concepts in Fifteenth- and Sixteenth-Century Italy," in *Essential Papers on Jewish Culture in Renaissance and Baroque Italy*, ed. David Ruderman (New York: 1992), 45–62; Alexander Altmann, "*Ars Rhetorica* as Reflected in Some Jewish Figures of the Italian Renaissance," in Ruderman (ed.), *Essential Papers on Jewish Culture in Renaissance and Baroque Italy*, 63–84; Marc Saperstein, "Italian Jewish Preaching: An Overview," in ibid., 85–106; Bonfil, *Jewish Life in Renaissance Italy*; Ravid, "The Venetian Government and the Jews."

21. Bonfil, *Jewish Life in Renaissance Italy*.

22. Richard Sennett, "Fear of Touching: The Jewish Ghetto in Renaissance Venice," in *Flesh and Stone: The Body and the City in Western Civilization*, ed. Richard Stone (New York: 1996), 212–251.

23. Scholars of Italian Jewish history differ on the issue of the impact of the ghetto on Jewish culture and social relations. My interpretation here follows those who argue that the effects of ghettoization on Venetian Jewry were not as culturally impoverishing and socially isolating as some (older-generation) historians have argued, and that this experience actually revitalized Jewish in-group life. For a critical overview of this debate, see David Ruderman, "The Cultural Significance of the Ghetto in Jewish History," in Myers and Rowe (eds.), *From Ghetto to Emancipation*, 1–16; and David Ruderman, "Cecil Roth, Historian of Italian Jewry: A Reassessment," in *The Jewish Past Revisited: Reflections on Modern Jewish Historians*, ed. David Myers and David Ruderman (New Haven: 1998), 128–142.

24. Cecil Roth, *History of the Jews in Venice* (New York: 1975); Pullan, *The Jews of Europe and the Inquisition of Venice, 1550–1670*; Bonfil, *Jewish Life in Renaissance Italy*; and Ravid, "The Venetian Government and the Jews"; on Venetian Jews' economic pursuits, the three nations and the operation of the "ghetto republic" in the 16th and 17th centuries, see Pullan, *The Jews of Europe and the Inquisition of Venice, 1550–1670*; Malkiel, "The Ghetto Republic"; Donatella Calabi, "The 'City of Jews,'" in Davis and Ravid (eds.) *The Jews of Early Modern Venice*, 31–52; and Benjamin Arbel, "Jews in International Trade: The Emergence of the Levantines and Ponentines," in ibid., 73–96.

25. Roth, *The History of the Jews of Italy*; idem, *History of the Jews in Venice*; David Ruderman, "The Impact of Science on Jewish Culture and Society in Venice," in *Essential Papers on Jewish Culture in Renaissance and Baroque Italy*, ed. David Ruderman (New York: 1992), 519–533; and Davis and Ravid (eds.), *The Jews of Early Modern Venice*.

26. See the works cited in the previous note.

27. Including the *Ostjuden*, the total number of Jews in Berlin in 1900 was 93,000 (based on Robert Wistrich, *Socialism and the Jews: The Dilemmas of Assimilation in Germany and Austria-Hungary* [Rutherford, N.J.: 1982], 59; Marion Kaplan [ed.] *Jewish Daily Life in Germany, 1618–1945* [Oxford: 2005], 176).

28. On the earlier attempts toward political emancipation of Jews in Germany, in 1815 and 1848, see George Mosse, *German Jews beyond Judaism* (Bloomington: 1985); idem, "Jewish Emancipation: Between *Bildung* and Respectability," in *The Jewish Response to German Culture: From the Enlightenment to the Second World War*, ed. Jehuda Reinharz and Walter Schatzberg (Hanover, N.H.: 1985), 1–16; Werner Mosse, "From *'Schutzjuden'* to *'Deutsche Staatsbuerger Juedischen Glaubens'*: The Long and Bumpy Road of Jewish Emancipation in Germany," in *Paths of Emancipation: Jews, States, and Citizenship*, ed. Pierre Birnbaum and Ira Katznelson (Princeton: 1995), 59–93; Wistrich, *Socialism and the Jews*.

29. Wistrich, *Socialism and the Jews*; Marion Kaplan, *The Making of the Jewish Middle Class: Women, Family, and Identity in Imperial Germany* (New York: 1991).

30. George Mosse, *Germans and Jews: The Right, the Left, and the Search for a "Third Force" in Pre-Nazi Germany* (New Haven: 1971); idem, *German Jews beyond Judaism*; Werner Mosse, "From *'Schutzjuden'* to *'Deutsche Staatsbuerger Juedischen Glaubens'*"; Reinharz and Schatzberg (eds.), *The Jewish Response to German Culture*. On the German Reform movement, see Michael Meyer, "Reform Jewish Thinkers and Their German Intellectual Context," in ibid., 64–84; Walter Grab and Julius Schoeps, (eds.), *Juden in der Weimarer Republik* (Darmstadt: 1998).

31. Peter Pulzer, *Jews and the German State: The Political History of a Minority, 1848–1933* (Detroit: 2003); Wistrich, *Socialism and the Jews*; Adam Weisberger, *The Jewish Ethic and the Spirit of Socialism* (New York: 1997).

32. The term *intelligentsia* refers here to educated people in the so-called free occupations or, to use Karl Mannheim's renowned coinage, free-floating intellectuals: journalists, writers, artists, unaffiliated (or semi-affiliated) scholars, party leaders, organizers, and propagandists (Mannheim, *Ideology and Utopia: An Introduction to the Sociology of Knowledge* [London: 1936]).

33. The limited scope of this essay does not permit examination of the configuration of ethnicity among members of the orthodox fraction, who adhered to Marxist-Leninist principles concerning the unavoidable historical-materialist forces of the communist revolution.

34. It should be noted here that a number of German Jewish historians remain unconvinced by the thesis of the Judaic origins of Jewish socialists' commitment to this universalist utopia. They do not, however, offer a satisfactory alternative explanation of the secular German Jewish intelligentsia's involvement in socialism/communism. I present this thesis here because I find it an intriguing parallel to Willfried Spohn's well-documented claim that, in the case of German social democrats of Protestant origin (and unbeknownst to the actors themselves), a secularized Lutheran representation of the relation between salvation and the world underlay their political attitudes (Spohn, "Religion and Working-Class Formation in Imperial Germany, 1871–1914," *Politics and Society* 19, no. 1 [1991], 109–132). See also Heinz Kohut, *The Restoration of the Self* (New York: 1977).

35. Shulamit Volkov, "The Dynamics of Dissimilation: *Ostjuden* and German Jews," in Reinharz and Schatzberg (eds.), *The Jewish Response to German Culture*, 195–211.

36. Michael Walzer, "Two Kinds of Universalism," in *The Tanner Lectures*, ed. Ronald Dworkin (Salt Lake City: 1990).

37. On the role of *Bildung* in German Jews' acculturation, see Mosse, "Jewish Emancipation"; Jacob Katz, "German Culture and the Jews," in Reinharz and Schatzberg (eds.), *The Jewish Response to German Culture*, 85–99; Kaplan, *The Making of the Jewish Middle Class*; Adam M. Weisberger, *The Jewish Ethic and the Spirit of Socialism* (New York: 1997).

38. On the double marginalization of Jewish socialists, see Wistrich, *Socialism and the Jews*; Weisberger, *The Jewish Ethic and the Spirit of Socialism*.

39. Michael Löwy, *Redemption and Utopia: Jewish Libertarian Thought in Central Europe* (Stanford: 1988); see also Weisberger, *The Jewish Ethic and the Spirit of Socialism*; Yuri Slezkine, *The Jewish Century* (Princeton: 2004); and Will Herberg, "Socialism, Zionism, and the Messianic Passion," *Midstream* 2, no. 3 (1956), 65–80.

40. Weisberger, *The Jewish Ethic and the Spirit of Socialism*, 115.

41. Löwy, *Redemption and Utopia*, 11.

42. For different formulations of the elective affinity thesis regarding German Jewish intellectuals' commitment to socialism, see Weisberger, *The Jewish Ethic and the Spirit of Socialism*; Slezkine, *The Jewish Century*; cf. Herberg, "Socialism, Zionism, and the Messianic Passion."

43. Pulzer, *Jews and the German State*, 153.

44. It perhaps bears noting that in the political context of the times, much of the socialist content of the right-wing Christian Social groups, later recovered via fascism, was being hijacked and realigned with nationalist-particularistic outlooks. The universalist perspective of the socialist intelligentsia might be also viewed as a reaction to this development. (I thank the anonymous reviewer of my essay for this observation.)

45. On German Jewish socialists' response to antisemitism in Germany and in Europe and their attitudes toward Zionism, see Mosse, "From *'Schutzjuden'* to *'Deutsche Staatsbuerger*

Juedischen Glaubens'"; Shlomo Na'aman, *Marxismus und Zionismus* (Gerlingen: 1997); Hans Bach (ed.), *The German Jew: A Synthesis of Judaism and Western Civilization 1730– 1930* (New York: 1984); Pulzer, *Jews and the German State*; and Wistrich, *Socialism and the Jews*.

46. Pulzer, *Jews and the German State*, 263.

47. It should be emphasized, however, that the attacks on Jewish socialist theorist-intellectuals as "divorced from the working-class practice" were more common in the orthodox communist camp than among revisionist socialists (cf. Mosse, *German Jews*, 67; see also idem, *Germans and Jews*; Pulzer, *Jews and the German State*).

48. Wistrich, *Socialism and the Jews*, 169.

49. On German Zionism and Jewish socialists' relations with this movement, see Stephen Poppel, *Zionism in Germany 1897–1933: The Shaping of a Jewish Identity* (Philadelphia: 1977); Wistrich, *Socialism and the Jews*; and Jehuda Reinharz, "The Zionist Response to Anti-Semitism in the Weimar Republic," in Reinharz and Schatzberg (eds.), *The Jewish Response to German Culture*, 266–293.

50. On increased interest in their Jewish origins among Jewish socialist intelligentsia in the interwar period, see Mosse, *Germans and Jews*; idem, *German Jews beyond Judaism*; Trude Maurer, "From Everyday Life to a State of Emergency: Jews in Weimar and Nazi Germany," in *Jewish Daily Life in Germany, 1618–1945*, ed. Marion Kaplan (Oxford: 2005), pt. IV, 271– 374; Pulzer, *Jews and the German State*; Volkov, "The Dynamics of Dissimilation"; Bach (ed.), *The German Jew*.

51. See Robert Brym, "Russian Anti-Semitism, 1996–2000," in *Jewish Life after the USSR*, ed. Zvi Gitelman, Marshall Goldman, and Morton Glanz (Bloomington: 2003), 99–116; Victor Zaslavsky and Robert Brym, *Soviet-Jewish Emigration and Soviet Nationality Policy* (London: 1983); Alfred Low, *Soviet Jewry and Soviet Policy* (New York: 1990); Mark Tolts, "The Post-Soviet Jewish Population in Russia and the World," *Jews in Russia and Eastern Europe* 52, no. 1 (2004), 37–63; on the volume and directions of post-Second World War emigration of Russian Jews, see Lewin-Epstein, Ro'i, and Ritterband, *Russian Jews on Three Continents*.

52. Although Soviet/post-Soviet Jewish émigrés originate from both Russia and Ukraine, because of the cultural russification of the latter, I refer to both groups jointly as "Russian Jews."

53. On the educational and occupational position and civic-political situation of Jews in the U.S.S.R. and the FSU, see Mikhail Chlenov, "Jewish Community and Identity in the Former Soviet Union," in *Jews in the Former Soviet Union: Yesterday, Today, Tomorrow*, ed. Shlomo Avineri, Mikhail Chlenov, and Zvi Gitelman (New York: 1997), 11–16; Zvi Gitelman, *A Century of Ambivalence: The Jews of Russia and the Soviet Union, 1881 to the Present* (New York: 1988); and Gitelman, Goldman, and Glanz, (eds.) *Jewish Life after the USSR*.

54. This difference in existential disappointments of transplantation was not limited to Philadelphia versus Tel Aviv, but rather reflects the disparity in immigration absorption capacities between the two receiver counties, the United States and Israel. The latter, much smaller in size than the United States and "burdened" with proportionately much larger numbers of immigrants to whom it offers extensive assistance in the settlement and initial integration process, has not been able to cope effectively with the challenge.

55. Remennick, *Russian Jews on Three Continents*, 191–192.

56. Ibid., 191.

57. It should be noted, however, that in an ongoing debate among Israeli scholars about patterns of incorporation of Soviet/post-Soviet Jews into Israeli society, this claim has been challenged by Dmitrii Shumsky, who argues that the Russian component of the émigré community has been overrated by the outsiders, whereas the sense of Jewishness shared by group members has been underestimated (Shumsky, "Etniyut veezrahut bitfisat hayisreelim harusiyim," *Teoriyah ubikoret* 19 [2001], 17–40).

58. Morawska, "Exploring Diversity in Immigrant Assimilation and Transnationalism."

59. Ibid., 1386–1387.

60. Ibid., 1388. It should be noted that the majority of Russian Jewish immigrants in Philadelphia attend religious services only on special occasions such as high holidays, circumcisions, bar/bat-mitzvahs, and the yahrzeits of their relatives.

61. Information about the (non-)integration of Russian Jewish immigrants in Tel Aviv has been compiled from Remennick, *Russian Jews on Three Continents*; idem, "Transnational Community in the Making: Russian Jewish Immigrants of the 1990s in Israel," *Journal of Ethnic and Migration Studies* 28, no. 3 (2002), 515–530; author's correspondence with Larissa Remennick, January 2008; and from studies by Majid Al-Haj, *Immigration and Ethnic Formation in a Deeply Divided Society: The Case of the 1990s Immigrants from the FSU in Israel* (Leiden: 2004); Daniel Levy and Yfaat Weiss (eds.), *Challenging Ethnic Citizenship: German and Israeli Perspectives on Immigration* (New York: 2002); Alek D. Epstein and Andrey V. Fedorchenko (eds.), *Mass Migration and Its Impact on the Israeli Society* (Jerusalem: 2000); Tamar Horowitz, "The Integration of Immigrants from the Soviet Union: Four Scripts of Integration," in *Politics and Identities in Transformation: Europe and Israel*, ed. Shlomo Avineri and Werner Weidenfeld (Berlin: 2000), 59–70; Gila Menachem and Idith Geijst, "Language and Occupation among Soviet Immigrants to Israel in the 1990s," in *Language, Identity and Immigration*, ed. Elite Olshtain and Gila Horencyk (Jerusalem: 2000); Eliezer Ben-Rafael, Elite Olshtain, and Idith Geijst, "Identity and Language: The Social Insertion of Soviet Jews in Israel," in *Immigration to Israel: Sociological Perspectives*, ed. Elazar Leshem and Judith T. Shuval (New Brunswick: 1998), 333–356; and Eva Etzioni-Halevy, "Collective Jewish Identity in Israel: Towards an Irrevocable Split?" in *Jewish Survival: The Identity Problem at the Close of the Twentieth Century*, ed. Ernest Krausz and Gitta Tulea (New Brunswick: 1998), 65–76.

Communism and the Problem of Ethnicity in the 1920s: The Case of Moissaye Olgin

Tony Michels
(UNIVERSITY OF WISCONSIN, MADISON)

During the 1920s, thousands of American Jews joined the Communist party and allied organizations. The party's Jewish Federation, its Yiddish-speaking section, claimed around 2,000 members, or 10 percent of the party's overall membership in mid-decade, yet that figure hardly conveys the extent of Jewish involvement with Communism during the 1920s.[1] A significant number of Jews also joined the party's English- and Russian-speaking units. Moreover, Communism's influence among Jews extended far beyond party organizations. The Communist Yiddish daily, *Di frayhayt*, enjoyed a reputation for literary excellence and reached a readership of 20,000–30,000, a higher circulation than any other Communist newspaper, including the English-language *Daily Worker*. Jewish Communists built a network of summer camps, schools, cultural societies, theater groups, choirs, orchestras, and even a housing cooperative in the Bronx, all of which encompassed tens of thousands of Communist party members, sympathizers, and their families. Finally, Communists won a strong following among Jewish workers in the needle trades and came close to capturing control of the International Ladies Garment Workers Union (ILGWU) in the mid-1920s.[2] Viewed through the lens of immigrant Jewry, then, Communism's golden age was not the Great Depression but rather the preceding decade. To be sure, Jewish Communists were in the minority, but they were far from isolated. As their numbers grew, Communists had reason to believe they represented the vanguard of Jewish labor.

Communism's popularity among immigrant Jews was extraordinary in the context of the conservative 1920s. In a decade characterized by isolationism, nativism, and labor retrenchment, Communism made little headway among workers of other racial, religious, or ethnic groups. The only foreign language federation larger than that of the Jews was that of the Finns, which claimed around 7,000 members in 1924. However, the organizational strength of the Finns was undercut by their demographics. The total Finnish immigrant population in the United States numbered only 150,000 in 1920, around one-fifteenth the size of immigrant Jewry. Furthermore, Finns were geographically isolated as compared with Jews.[3] Whereas Finns lived mainly in rural mining areas of the upper Midwest, Jews concentrated in major cities, where they often comprised a plurality and even, in certain places and times, a majority of party members.[4] In New York, Jews comprised the city's largest ethnic group, numbering 1.75 million, or almost 30 percent of the city's population. Jewish workers also dominated New York's clothing industry, the city's primary manufacturing industry, which gave them a strategic economic position. For those reasons, Communist party leaders viewed Jewish workers, who were already highly organized into pro-socialist unions such as the ILGWU, as an important entryway into organized labor as a whole.[5] As Nathan Glazer noted in his 1961 study, *The Social Basis of American Communism*, "no detailed understanding of the impact of Communism on American life is possible without an analysis of the relationship between American Jews and the American Communist Party."[6]

The special attraction of Communism for immigrant Jews cannot be understood apart from ethnic—that is, Jewish—group concerns. Many individuals became supporters of Soviet Russia not only because they viewed it as a beacon of social progress, but also because they believed the Bolshevik government could provide solutions to urgent Jewish problems, starting with the very survival of the Jewish people. The mass slaughter of Jews by counterrevolutionary forces during the Russian civil war convinced many Jews in the United States that the Bolsheviks' triumph was an existential necessity. The social, economic, and cultural reconstruction of Russian Jewish life provided additional evidence, in the eyes of many, that Communism had significantly improved the lives of Jews. Thus, immigrant Jews in the United States perceived their interests tied to Soviet Russia to a degree unmatched by almost any other immigrant group (the Finns, again, can be considered an exception). Regarding domestic issues, many immigrants viewed the American Communist movement as a force capable of reinvigorating socialism and also of advancing Yiddish culture in opposition to the prevailing "bourgeois" culture of the American middle class.[7] From that perspective, Communism appealed to "the Jewish masses" in both ethno-cultural and class terms.

Yet Communism also posed a challenge to a coherent Jewish ethnicity. Communists in the 1920s held that Jewish workers belonged to the general proletariat and therefore must not make common cause with middle- or upper-class Jews. Jewish employers were to be regarded as enemies, Gentile workers as allies. Communists were not, of course, the first political grouping to reject the idea of Jewish unity. Jewish socialists of all stripes had advanced a class-based perspective since the late-19th century. Communists, however, injected a spirit of heightened militancy at a time when many Jewish socialist and labor leaders had already moderated their early refusal to participate in Jewish communal affairs.[8] The Communists' class-war position should not be disregarded as a mere theoretical construct. It had actual ramifications at a time when Communists enjoyed significant support among Jewish workers who, in the 1920s, still comprised a majority (albeit a shrinking one) of employed Jews in New York. The large and violent Communist-led strikes of the mid-1920s demonstrated the continued salience of class conflict and political radicalism during the Jazz Age.[9]

Communism's popularity among Jews suggests the need to reappraise American Jewish ethnicity, especially in relation to politics, during the 1920s. Historians of that decade have stressed the attraction of the Democratic party to middle-class Jews, thereby marking a transition from the political and class divisions of the pre-First World War era to a new era of liberal consensus within an increasingly native-born and economically prosperous Jewish community.[10] To be sure, the shift toward liberalism was extensive, but it should not be considered the only trend of the 1920s. Rather, two divergent trends can be detected: a dominant trend toward the liberal center and a secondary one toward the radical Left. In other words, the politics of American Jews was more internally conflicted and unstable than is often recognized. While many Jews sought to create a "type of ethnicity consonant with American middle-class values," as Deborah Dash Moore has argued, Communists and their sympathizers revolted against society's dominant institutions and rejected any notion of Jewish group unity.[11] Deep rifts thus persisted both among Jews and between Jews and the larger society.

Moreover, ethnicity served as a point of conflict within the Communist movement itself. Most immigrant Jewish Communists, specifically those who were Yiddish-speaking, participated in self-defined Jewish organizations and maintained a collective identity as Yiddish-speaking Jewish workers. Put simply, they viewed themselves as both Jews and Communists. By contrast, those who were American-raised and English-speaking did not usually define themselves as Jewish Communists, but rather as Communists who happened to be of Jewish parentage. Such individuals, in keeping with most party leaders, typically looked askance at separate ethnic or foreign language organizations of any kind. Communist leaders tolerated separate ethnic organizations mainly because immigrants comprised around 90 percent of the party's membership, not to mention the majority of the country's industrial work force. Still, to see intrinsic value in separate ethnic organizations was considered an expression of "bourgeois nationalism." The party wanted immigrant members to learn English and leave foreign language organizations as quickly as possible. Insofar as Communists viewed ethnicity as a problem to be overcome, they fitted comfortably into the prevailing climate of "100 percent Americanism." To be sure, they were opposed to the term's bigoted overtones, but nonetheless favored cultural assimilation.

How, then, did Yiddish-speaking Communists negotiate between ethnic ties and pressures to assimilate? That question can be explored through the case of Moissaye Olgin. During the 1920s, Olgin emerged as the leading figure within the Jewish Communist movement, widely admired by Yiddish-speaking workers as much as, or more so, than any general secretary of the party.[12] Highly educated and prominent in certain American intellectual circles, Olgin was a versatile writer, editor, lecturer, translator, and novelist fluent in English, German, Russian, and Yiddish. His expertise in Russian affairs earned him a place in the party's upper (albeit not its highest) echelon, a position few other ethnic-based Communist leaders, Jewish or not, attained. It was a sign of Olgin's importance that, when he died in 1939 at the age of 67, some 45,000 people attended his funeral in Manhattan, according to the *New York Times*.[13]

In 1917, nobody, least of all Olgin himself, would have predicted his future role as a Jewish Communist leader. He had originally opposed the Bolshevik seizure of power, and although he would grow more sympathetic to the Soviet government within the year, he opposed the creation of the American Communist party in 1919.

Not until December 1921, in the wake of a trip to Soviet Russia, did Olgin forge a political alliance with the Communist party, and not until 1923 did he identify himself wholeheartedly as a Communist. Olgin, in other words, did not undergo a sudden conversion. He took short steps and made the required compromises along the way, a trajectory that provides a window onto the larger political trend.

A devotee of Yiddish culture and the Bolshevik revolution, Olgin faced dilemmas shared by an entire generation of Jewish Communists. Their efforts to develop a distinct ethnic sphere within the larger Communist movement met with opposition from party leaders who wanted Jews and all immigrants to Americanize as soon as possible. On the one hand, the size and scope of the Jewish Communist movement grew throughout the 1920s. On the other, party leaders sought to curtail the organizational and cultural autonomy of Jews and other ethnic groups as much as possible. Ethnicity thus served as a source of both solidarity and division within the Communist movement, just as class politics, in its Communist form, crosscut and destabilized Jewish ethnicity on the whole. By retracing Olgin's steps toward Communism, this essay explores the divisive role of ethnicity during the 1920s.

By the time Olgin immigrated to the United States in 1914, he had been active in the Bund (General Alliance of Jewish Workers in Lithuania, Poland, and Russia) for more than a decade. A staunch Yiddishist, Olgin not only affirmed the Bund's program calling for "national cultural autonomy" in a future revolutionary Russia, but also championed a cultural renaissance in the Yiddish language. He urged party intellectuals to speak Yiddish rather than Russian in their private lives, formulated guidelines on how to write Yiddish correctly, advocated for Yiddish children's schools, wrote frequently on Yiddish literature and, despite his atheism, argued for celebration of Jewish religious holidays on the grounds that even a secular culture required hallowed rituals.[14] In New York, Olgin continued his identification with the Bund by joining the Jewish Socialist Federation (JSF), the Socialist party's Yiddish-speaking section that was founded and led mostly by Bundists who had immigrated to the United States in the years following the 1905 Russian Revolution. The émigré Bundists established the JSF on the familiar principle that Jewish workers possessed specific "Jewish national" interests that were best represented by a Jewish socialist organization. The JSF acted as a quasi-political party, formally attached to the Socialist party (along with other foreign language federations), but autonomous in its internal affairs. Not long after Olgin settled in New York, he joined the JSF's national executive committee and became an editor of its weekly newspaper, *Di naye velt*. He also joined the staff of the *Forverts*, the most widely read Yiddish daily in the U.S., which bolstered Olgin's prominence in Jewish public life. As a popular Yiddish journalist and JSF leader, Olgin appeared at numerous mass meetings during the tumultuous years in and around the First World War.

Yet even as Olgin immersed himself in the world of immigrant Jewry, he moved beyond it with apparent ease. In 1915, he enrolled in Columbia University, where he earned a Ph.D. in economics two years later.[15] In November 1917, he published his dissertation under the title *The Soul of the Russian Revolution*, a 400-page history of the Russian revolutionary movement up to March 1917.[16] Olgin's timing could not have been better. While interest in Russian affairs ran high after the tsar's overthrow, English-speaking Americans knew little about the country: the differences between

Mensheviks and Bolsheviks or Socialist Revolutionaries and Social Democrats eluded even many radicals. As both veteran revolutionary and newly minted scholar, Olgin became a recognized expert in Russian affairs, and his book received favorable reviews in important liberal magazines such as the *Nation* and the *New Republic*, as well as in the *New York Times*.[17] He published a second book in early 1918, a translated collection of articles by Leon Trotsky, whom he had met several times in Europe and New York.[18] In the following year, he joined the faculty of the New School for Social Research as a lecturer in Russian history.[19] In 1920, he published a third book, the highly regarded *A Guide to Russian Literature*.[20] Olgin also lectured frequently[21] and authored articles on Russian politics and literature for scholarly and popular publications.[22]

Thus, in a remarkably brief period, Olgin attained considerable recognition in both the immigrant Jewish community and the larger, English-speaking society. A number of his peers had managed the crossover to English, but those who did so either stopped writing in Yiddish or expressed no special commitment to its future. Olgin, by contrast, maintained an ideological devotion to Yiddish even as his stature grew in English-speaking intellectual circles. Few, if any, Russian-born Jewish intellectuals managed to bridge the Yiddish- and English-speaking worlds in the same way. It was a balance Olgin would always seek to maintain, even after he became a Communist.

As mentioned, Olgin at first opposed the Bolshevik seizure of power. Like most Bundists (and the Mensheviks with whom they were allied), Olgin considered Russia unprepared for socialism in 1917. War and revolution had left the country in chaos, and its situation would worsen if the Bolsheviks insisted on pushing forward. On occasion, Olgin described Vladimir Lenin as a demagogue who enchanted the masses with baseless promises of land redistribution and worker's control of factories. At other times, he characterized Lenin as a deluded idealist, "a man who sees life only from the angle of his own ideas. . . . Ignoring the most striking facts, or interpreting them away, [is] a peculiarity of Lenine's mind," Olgin wrote in the *New York Times* in December 1917.[23] Lenin, he believed, was an authoritarian fanatic who would bring harm to the people he claimed to represent.

During 1918, however, Olgin's hostility to the Soviet government weakened and eventually turned into sympathy. At a large public gathering in Cooper Union in January 1919, he expressed dismay over the course of the revolution, but added, "I must say that the Bolsheviki were the only ones who introduced order out of chaos." He denounced foreign military intervention against Soviet Russia and called on western governments to begin economic assistance at once.[24] (This position provoked a rebuke from George Kennan, the most prominent commentator on Russian affairs in the United States.[25]) By 1920, Olgin praised the Bolshevik revolution in the most ebullient terms. "We are now living through the springtime of humanity," he declared in the JSF's weekly, *Di naye velt*, "and its name is—socialism. It is here, springtime, it has already come. . . . Let the weak-hearted be afraid. Let the weak-headed see no other way. Let them be afraid of the first messengers of the socialist order. . . . Let them look at the newborn child of the future and shrug: 'Is this socialism? Is this what we have waited for so many years?'. . . Those who have eyes to see and the intellect to understand will not be afraid of the venom from enemies, of the despair of supposed friends."[26]

Thus within two years, Olgin went from viewing the Bolsheviks as a destructive force to celebrating them as architects of a glorious new society. This turnaround occurred against the backdrop of the Russian civil war. Amid the fighting, counterrevolutionary armies slaughtered anywhere between 50,000 and 200,000 Jews and beat, robbed, or raped tens of thousands more.[27] Well aware of the anti-Jewish bloodbath underway, Olgin came to view the Red Army as the sole force capable of restoring order and protecting Jews. The choice seemed clear to Olgin, as well as to thousands of other immigrant Jews: either Bolshevism or death.

Despite Olgin's growing sympathy for the Soviet Union, he opposed the creation of the American Communist party in the summer of 1919. This occurred several months after the establishment of the Communist International (Comintern) in March of that year. At its founding, the Comintern instructed socialists abroad to purge moderate elements from their respective parties in preparation for imminent revolution. In response, an insurgent left wing formed within the Socialist party and gained ground until the Socialist party leadership expelled it in June. (The American Communist party was actually the outcome of a merger of two breakaway factions, the Communist party and the Communist Labor party.) America's newborn Bolsheviks incensed Olgin, who believed they had lost touch with reality. "The young men of this group," Olgin wrote in the *Forverts*, "live in a little world created in their own imagination where everything is as they like it to be. The workers are united, classconscious, organized, and armed. Only one thing remains to be done: begin the final conflict."[28] Olgin thus drew a sharp distinction between the Bolshevik revolution and those who wished to reenact it on American soil, a position that might seem inconsistent, considering that the Comintern had encouraged the creation of the American Communist party in the first place, but which nonetheless contained an internal logic. From Olgin's perspective, Bolshevik tactics and programs were appropriate for Russia but should not be applied to the United States, where entirely different conditions prevailed.

This was not an idiosyncratic position at the time. Most Jewish socialists—intellectuals, union leaders, and political activists alike—shared Olgin's perspective around 1919–1920. Abraham Cahan, for instance, disdained the American Communist party but praised Soviet Russia in fulsome terms. As he wrote in one editorial, "We have criticized them [the Bolsheviks], some of their utterances often irritate us, but who can help rejoicing in their triumph? Who can help going into ecstasy over the Socialist spirit with which they have enthroned the country, which they now rule?"[29] For a time, Cahan even refused to print criticism of the Soviet government, something he impressed upon the Menshevik and Bundist leader, Raphael Abramovitsh, when they met in Germany in 1920. When Abramovitsh tried to inform Cahan of the "Red Terror," he reportedly covered his ears and cried out, "Don't destroy my illusions; I don't care to listen."[30] Cahan, like Olgin, distinguished between Communists at home and those abroad, opposing the former but championing the latter.

Although Olgin had no desire to join what he regarded as a deluded sect, his admiration for the Bolshevik revolution grew stronger with each passing year. His sixmonth trip to Soviet Russia between 1920 and 1921 marked an important turning point.[31] Olgin traveled extensively and met a wide range of people, from workers to opposition leaders to government officials. The trip served to intensify his ardor for the revolution. For all its persistent difficulties, he reported, the revolution had brought major improvements in the lives of the masses. They had gained access to education and the arts, dominated the instruments of government, and were taking control of factories and land. The common man, Olgin announced in the *New Republic*, "has come to the top. He is a new man. Everything is done in his name and for his welfare. In principle he is the master. He enjoys the fruit of the revolution, no matter how irksome his everyday existence may be."[32] To be sure, Olgin recognized that myriad problems existed. "There is hunger in Russia," he acknowledged. "There is no personal liberty in Russia. . . . There is no political freedom in Russia. . . . There is no equality in. . . Russia. . . . There is corruption in Russia."[33] Nonetheless, Olgin believed the Bolsheviks were not to blame for problems that resulted from war, counterrevolution, and external aggression. In any event, the Bolsheviks had made great strides in the construction of socialism, even if they had (regrettably) used some heavy-handed measures in the process. Whatever mistakes the party had made, Olgin assured readers, it would soon correct. Bolsheviks, as he described them, were dedicated, capable, principled, and practical. By contrast, Olgin dismissed the government's left-wing opponents—the Mensheviks and Socialist Revolutionaries—as lacking practical experience and a viable program. Free elections, he believed, would inevitably cause increased instability.[34]

Olgin did not address the subject of Jews in his series for the *New Republic*, whose readers were mostly American-born Gentiles. But he published a longer (and heavily promoted) series in the Yiddish *Forverts* that delved into the revolution's impact on Jews, a subject of immediate importance to the newspaper's readers.[35] Olgin acknowledged that, in certain respects, Jewish economic fortunes had declined because of the suppression of commercial trade. Still, he made it clear that Jews overall had benefited from the revolution. First and foremost, the Red Army had rescued Jews from horrific violence, about which Olgin reported in some detail. He recounted the case of a 25-year-old man who had been snatched up by a group of soldiers, shot twice in the arm, tortured, ridiculed, and held captive for five days until he escaped.[36] In another incident, a woman had been taunted and beaten by a jeering crowd in a town square. Such information weighed heavily on Olgin, himself a native of the Ukraine, where most of the killing took place. Soon after his return from Russia, Olgin published a Yiddish booklet in tribute to his *shtetl*, in which he described a lost world rich in values and traditions: respect for learning over wealth, an ethos of mutual responsibility, and genuine piety.[37] As his series for the *Forverts* made clear, Olgin's bereavement was offset by an equally profound faith in the revolution's promise to build a new and better world. The revolution offered redemption, not only of the Jews, but of all oppressed peoples.

Beyond ensuring the physical survival of Jews, the revolution transformed Jewish cultural, economic, and communal life in positive ways, according to Olgin. In his profile of Orshe, a small city in White Russia, he hailed the reconstruction of its 20,000-member Jewish community. Yesterday's traders, shopkeepers, and bookkeepers had found a new sense of purpose in building socialism, he reported. Workers no longer had to suffer bosses. Jewish cultural life flourished. The city boasted a Jewish youth club, several Jewish children's homes, two evening schools for adults, two amateur Yiddish theater groups, a choir, and a workers' library in Yiddish. Remarkably, the government had opened a "people's university" in which Yiddish literature was taught in the Yiddish language. Branches of the Bund and the Marxist-Zionist party, Poale Zion, continued to function, thereby indicating the survival of independent Jewish politics. And although a significant amount of antisemitic feeling persisted among the Gentile population, the government suppressed it. "We don't care if they like us," one man told Olgin, "we just want rights, equal rights."[38] In an article titled "The Bolshevik Rabbi," Olgin described his visit to a shul in Minsk, where the rabbi delivered a Friday-evening sermon praising the government and urging members of the congregation to organize collective farms and factories. Even Orthodox Jews, readers of the *Forverts* were meant to understand, supported the Bolshevik revolution.[39]

Among the notable aspects of Olgin's trip were meetings with old comrades who now occupied important positions in the Soviet government. One such person was a former Bundist named Max Goldfarb who, in New York, had worked as the *Forverts*' labor editor. Goldfarb returned to Russia in June 1917 and seems to have joined the Bolsheviks two or three years later, perhaps following the Bund's split into pro- and anti-Communist factions. By the time Olgin encountered Goldfarb in Moscow in 1921 the latter had changed his last name to Petrovsky and now served as the director of all officer training schools for the Red Army.[40] Petrovsky/Goldfarb invited Olgin to attend a graduation ceremony presided over by the Red Army commander, Leon Trotsky, who was already familiar to Olgin from his stay in New York during early 1917. At one point during the ceremony, a former tsarist general dismounted his horse and saluted Petrovsky and Trotsky as they inspected the troops. That was an astounding sight—there, in Red Square, stood a former pillar of the old regime now subordinated to a former Yiddish journalist from New York, who himself served under another revolutionary Jew. In that moment, Olgin witnessed a world turned upside down, one where the Jews had finally landed on top.[41]

Olgin returned to the U.S. in the spring of 1921 enamored of the Bolsheviks. He was not yet ready to join the Communist party, which he continued to view as a deluded sect, but he grew increasingly critical of the Socialist party. He and other Jewish Socialist Federation leaders, such as Yankev Salutsky, implored the Socialist party to join the Communist International, which they believed could invigorate their party with a badly needed fighting spirit. When their efforts failed, Olgin and Salutsky called on the JSF to break from the Socialist party, which the federation elected to do during a special convention in early September. The *Forverts* promptly fired Olgin and other staff writers who voted in favor of the split. Over the following three months, the JSF steered an independent course and attempted to rebuild the organization. But in November, an opportunity arose that would result in a merger with the Communist party.[42]

In the fall of 1921, the Comintern concluded that revolution was no longer an immediate prospect in the United States and, on that basis, ordered the American Communist party to create a new, aboveground party in alliance with non-Communists. This provided an opening to the JSF and like-minded organizations (such as the Finnish Socialist Federation) that had broken with the Socialist party over the previous two years. Olgin and Salutsky represented the JSF at the negotiating table. Olgin was amenable, but as the negotiations proceeded, Salutsky came to suspect the Communists of acting in bad faith. He believed the party had no intention of creating a truly independent party, but rather aimed to dominate the proposed new party. Shortly before an agreement was reached, Salutsky called a meeting in Olgin's apartment to convince the other non-Communists to back out of the proposed merger. However, neither Olgin nor most of the others present could be persuaded. According to Salutsky's retrospective account, Olgin viewed a merger with the Communists as a means to remain connected to Soviet Russia. "What the hell do you want with this business?" Salutsky claims to have asked Olgin during the negotiations. "I want to be free to come to Russia," was Olgin's reply.[43] Salutsky went along with Olgin and the majority of other non-Communist delegates; it seemed too late to turn back.

Olgin and Salutsky led the JSF into a new organization, named the Workers Party (WP), which was supposed to be independent of the underground Communist party. Although affiliated with the Comintern, the Workers Party was not designated as its official representative in the United States (that status was reserved for the Communist party). Olgin did not define himself as a Communist at the time of the merger. He was what Communists derisively called a "centrist," that is, someone who had taken the correct step of aligning with the Communists, but was not yet willing to convert to Communism. Whatever their differences, Olgin believed that centrists and Communists could cooperate in order to achieve shared goals. In a pamphlet published in early 1922, he promised readers that the Workers Party would not be the Communist party under a new name. There could be no room for an underground, conspiratorial party in the United States, he wrote. As long as the social revolution remained a distant prospect, the Workers Party would play primarily an educational role, propagating a militant brand of socialism so as to prepare workers for their historic task. The party's newly created Jewish Federation would ensure a "pure, sustainable, serious spirit in the Jewish labor movement" by fighting against the "cheap, watered-down, formless, hurrah-socialism" espoused by the *Forverts* and other "official socialists" who led the movement.[44]

Olgin's pamphlet neglected to mention several important details that would suggest his optimism was premature. He failed to acknowledge that a precarious balance of power existed within the Workers Party and its Jewish Federation. The federation was governed by an 18-member executive committee divided equally between Communists and centrists. This deprived Olgin's camp of a free hand in organizational affairs, contrary to what his pamphlet implied. As long as the power-sharing arrangement held, the centrists needed to secure the assent of the Communists. Furthermore, Communists were allocated a slight majority of seats on the Workers Party's Central Executive Committee (CEC), so that they controlled the party as a whole, thereby strengthening the position of Communists inside the Jewish Federation.

A final problem ignored by Olgin was the relationship of the underground Communist party to the Workers Party. Olgin and Salutsky expected the Communist party to dissolve itself altogether after the establishment of the Workers Party, so that the latter would supersede the former. Yet it soon became clear that the Communists intended to maintain the underground party ("Number One," as they called it), which would secretly control the Workers Party ("Number Two"). In the words of one leader, the Workers Party would function, not as an independent party, but as the "transmission apparatus between the revolutionary vanguard of the proletariat [the Communist party] and its less conscious and as yet non-revolutionary masses."[45] The historian

Theodore Draper maintains that Olgin and Salutsky were aware of the Communists' intentions when they agreed to the merger, but this seems unlikely.[46] Both men had always opposed the existence of an underground party and would continue to do so after the foundation of the Workers Party. It seems more likely that the two men were given reason to believe that the underground party would soon be dissolved, although no formal promise had been made. In any case, the status of the underground party was left unresolved at the time of the merger in December 1921. Olgin evidently believed that differences of opinion between the Communist and non-Communist camps would be worked out amicably and that Communists would honor the terms of the merger.

Unresolved matters notwithstanding, the creation of the new Jewish Federation brought one important tangible benefit: the publication of a new Yiddish daily, *Di frayhayt*. Olgin co-edited the newspaper with Shakhne Epshteyn, who, like Olgin, was a former member of the Bund, a staff writer at the *Forverts*, and a national leader of the old JSF. Unlike Olgin, however, Epshteyn was a full-fledged Communist. He had spent four years in Soviet Russia, where he had served in a number of official positions, including the directorship of the state-owned Yiddish publishing house. In mid-1921, the Comintern sent Epshteyn back to New York to edit the Communist party's new Yiddish weekly newspaper, *Der emes* (named after the Moscow daily), which positioned Epshteyn to become co-editor of *Di frayhayt*, representing the Communist faction of the Workers Party.[47]

Although Epshteyn was a Communist and Olgin a centrist, the two were compatible as editors. They shared a love of Yiddish literature and agreed that *Di frayhayt* should provide a forum not merely for radical politics but also for Yiddish letters. In the premier issue, dated April 2, 1922, the editors promised "to bring about a revolution, not only in economic, social, and political concepts of Jewish workers, but in their outlook toward questions of culture." Other staff members expressed similar sentiments. According to Tsivion (Ben Tsien Hofman), another former Bundist who, with Olgin, had been expelled from the *Forverts* in September 1921, "a true Yiddish labor newspaper must be particularly interested in enriching and refining Yiddish literature and art, as well as in developing the literary and artistic tastes of the Jewish masses." Morris Vintshevsky, the venerable "grandfather of Jewish socialism," wanted *Di frayhayt* to "give the Jewish worker a daily treasure of principled articles . . . and true literature."[48] Such sentiments highlighted *Di frayhayt*'s intention to be a new kind of Yiddish daily, one committed equally to radical socialism and Yiddish culture.

Olgin and Epshteyn defined *Di frayhayt* in opposition to the *Forverts*. While they acknowledged the *Forverts*' important role in building the early Jewish labor movement, they accused it of betraying its legacy. The problem with the *Forverts* was that it sacrificed socialist principles and literary standards for commercial success (a long-standing accusation by Yiddishist and left-wing intellectuals). According to one early *Di frayhayt* editorial:

> For material success, [*Forverts*] sacrificed spiritual success. Instead of educating the masses in a truly cultural manner, in a truly revolutionary way, to awaken in them the most beautiful and best feelings and aspirations, it stooped to their level, to their crude instincts. . . . [I]n the chase after material success, striving to become a man of substance

with a ten-story brick house, the *Forverts* did not become the organ of the conscious labor movement, but the street paper of the rabble, of the marketplace.... [I]t has not wanted and does not want to notice that the popular reader, which it created, has outgrown it, has become penetrated with an entirely different spirit and has taken to demanding not fantasies but true revolutionary enlightenment, true education.[49]

As it turned out, *Di frayhayt* did not pose much of a threat to the *Forverts*. Its circulation initially ran in the tens of thousands whereas the *Forverts'* soared past 200,000. Still, the upstart daily outclassed the *Forverts* in the literary realm. *Di frayhayt* assembled the most impressive stable of journalists and creative writers in the Yiddish press. Outstanding essayists included Kalman Marmor, A. S. Zaks, "Liliput" (Gavriel Kretshmar), Vintshevsky, Tsivion, Olgin, and Epshteyn. Poets and prose writers included Moyshe Leyb Halpern, Mani Leyb, Moyshe Nadir, Yosef Opatoshu, H. Leyvik, Ayzik Raboy, and Dovid Ignatov, writers previously associated with the experimental literary group known as *Di yunge*. These writers did not necessarily think of themselves as Marxists, let alone Communists, but what they found in *Di frayhayt* was a respect for artistic seriousness combined with the readership and financial reward of a daily newspaper.[50] In the words of one staff member, joining *Di frayhayt* was a form of "penance" for his "sin" of writing for the *Forverts*.[51]

Di frayhayt's existence, however, was imperiled from the start. In addition to chronic financial difficulties, a fierce struggle between Communists and centrists raged over control over the newspaper and the Jewish Federation as a whole. Communists faulted *Di frayhayt* for paying too much attention to Yiddish culture, allegedly at the expense of working-class interests. "The struggle against the Forward," Alexander Bittelman, a founder of the Communist party, declared, "must be ... on the basis of communist principles. We fight the Forward not merely and mainly because it is not a decent literary paper, but because it serves the reactionary and socially treacherous union bureaucracy."[52] A proper Communist paper, according to Bittelman, should not seek to advance Yiddish culture but rather function as the Yiddish mouthpiece of the party.

Tensions came to a head in October, when three members of the Jewish Federation's executive committee defected from the Communist faction, thus tipping the balance of power in favor of the centrists. Bittelman's group demanded a return to the *status quo ante* but Olgin and the centrist faction refused. Bittelman and the executive committee's other five Communists resigned in protest and enlisted the support of the Workers Party's highest authority, the Central Executive Committee. Controlled by the Communists, the CEC naturally ruled in favor of Bittelman's group. It demanded not only restoration of the lost seats to the Communist faction, but also the installation of a representative to be selected by the CEC. Furthermore, the CEC ordered the Jewish Federation to turn over half of *Di frayhayt*'s ownership to the Workers Party. In response, Salutsky wanted the Jewish Federation to withdraw from the Workers Party immediately, but Olgin and most of the federation's leaders wanted to reach a negotiated settlement. Olgin and another member of the Jewish Federation leadership, George Vishnak, negotiated with the CEC on behalf of the Jewish Federation, while one of Salutsky's supporters went on a speaking tour in preparation for a possible split. The Jewish Federation was scheduled to decide the question at its national convention scheduled for December 20.[53]

As negotiations dragged on, the Jewish Federation came under intense pressure to comply with the CEC's ruling. The December 9 issue of *The Worker*, the party's English-speaking organ, published a statement by the CEC condemning the Jewish Federation for disrupting party unity:

> A faction of the Executive Committee of the Jewish Federation is endeavoring to disrupt the Jewish Federation and to bring disorganization in the ranks of the Party. This faction led by Olgin, Hoffman [Tsivion], Wishnak, and others . . . has become drunk with the power which the Party membership has permitted them to wield. After months of violation of Party discipline this group has openly defied the authority of the highest party authority and has issued a call for a convention of the Jewish Federation after the Administrative Council of the Party had set the date for the convention of the Federation. . . . these Centrists, the Olgins and Hoffmans, etc. have shown by their methods of conducting the struggles of the Workers' Party that they are not Communists . . . The Centrist disruptionists have singled out for their attack the Communist Party of America. In the character of this attack they again expose themselves as Centrists, as men who have no understanding of Communist principles or willfully ignore facts in order that they may make an argument.[54]

A week later, all of the party's foreign language federations, which represented some 90 percent of the total party membership, published a statement in *The Worker* criticizing the Jewish Federation for disrupting party unity. None other than the Comintern's Secretary, Grigorii Zinoviev, wired a cable ordering the Jewish Federation to obey the CEC. "We decisively condemn [the] frivolous breach of discipline against [the] Central Committee of the Workers Party," Zinoviev wrote. "We request [that] all Jewish branches and members carry out decisions of [the] Central Committee . . . to reestablish unity[,] otherwise [the] Central Committee [will] have to carry out energetically immediate disciplinary measures against leaders of revolt."[55] The Comintern and the entire Workers Party stood against the Jewish Federation.

As late as December 19, Olgin and Vishnak refused to back down. Yet, at the last minute, they suddenly relented. They agreed to restore the balance of power on the Jewish Federation's executive committee, to allow Bittelman to assume leadership of the federation, and to turn over full ownership of *Di frayhayt*—not merely 50 percent, as originally demanded—to the Workers Party.[56] It is not clear what happened behind closed doors. Melech Epstein, a member of the Communist faction at the time, later claimed that Olgin was bought off by the promise of sole editorship of *Di frayhayt*. In this regard, it is worth noting that, by this time, Shakhne Epshteyn had fallen out of favor with the Communist leadership; this may have been a signal to Olgin that he could become *Di frayhayt*'s sole editor-in-chief.[57] Another factor influencing Olgin's decision may have been the Communist party's recent decision, on Comintern orders, to dissolve itself as an underground organization and merge fully into the Workers Party. Considering that the existence of the underground party had been one of Olgin's chief grievances, the Comintern's decision may have made Olgin more amenable to the Workers Party's Central Executive Committee's demands.

Whatever motivated Olgin, his concessions did not stop the infighting. Factional struggles continued into 1923, as Communists and centrists jockeyed for position inside the Workers Party. The fighting grew so fierce within the Jewish Federation that Olgin felt compelled to resign from *Di frayhayt* in the spring. The Workers Party's CEC installed a new editor, Benjamin Gitlow, to supervise *Di frayhayt* and to make sure it would be "more working class" and "less devoted to literary affairs." An American-born Jew, Gitlow was "not at home in the Yiddish language and had no qualifications as a writer in this field," in the words of Communist leader James Cannon.[58] Gitlow was instructed, as he himself writes in his memoir, to "watch over every line the writers wrote, give attention to the raising of money . . . and convince the membership [of the Jewish Federation] that the paper was not being destroyed through the changes made by the Central Executive Committee of the Party." Thus *Di frayhayt*, a newspaper regarded for its high literary standards, passed into the hands of a "commissar" who had little knowledge of, or regard for, Yiddish.[59]

One might wonder why Olgin did not quit the Workers Party altogether in 1923. He had already resigned from *Di frayhayt*—and by this time, the Workers Party had fallen under full Communist control. Before the year was over, the party had given up any pretense of political independence and had become recognized by the Comintern as its "official section" in the United States. Centrists were co-opted or expelled, or else resigned from the party. Tsivion, for instance, quit and returned to the *Forverts*.[60] Not long afterward, Salutsky was expelled for violating party discipline. Under the name J.B.S. Hardman, Salutsky started an English-language magazine, the *American Labor Monthly*, and continued to serve as the educational director of the Amalgamated Clothing Workers of America.[61] Yet Olgin chose to remain loyal to the Workers Party and defined himself henceforth as a Communist without reservation or qualification. He did not make a dramatic final decision but assumed gradually a new political identity as he came to accept Communist control of the Workers Party.

Why did Olgin take that small, but important, final step toward Communism? The question can be answered, in part, by considering Olgin's options. Tsivion's path back to the *Forverts* could not have appealed to him, as it would have required pleading for forgiveness from Cahan and accepting a subordinate position under his notoriously imperious editorship. Assuming Cahan would have permitted Olgin's return, this would have involved an embarrassing loss of status in Olgin's eyes. A respected intellectual with a doctorate from a prestigious university, Olgin could have only cringed at the thought of returning to the *Forverts*, where he would have little hope of ever becoming its editor-in-chief. At the same time, he could not have considered Salutsky's turn to English-language journalism a desirable choice. Whereas Salutsky harbored no special affection for Yiddish, Olgin loved the language too much to abandon it. Thus Olgin's attachment to Yiddish kept him from moving completely to the English press, while his own status as an intellectual leader, achieved in part by his English-language journalism, prevented him from returning to a second-rung position at the *Forverts*.

Furthermore, had Olgin quit the Workers Party, he would have necessarily severed a direct link to Soviet Russia, an unthinkable sacrifice. Whatever frustration he might have felt toward the Workers Party, Olgin had lost none of his ardor for the Russian Revolution, "the greatest event in the history of the working class and in the history of the world."[62] Olgin understood that if he wanted to stay directly connected to Soviet Russia, he needed to remain a member of the Workers Party. Standing on the outside as a sympathizer would not do. During his first trip to Soviet Russia, Olgin had witnessed firsthand the sad fate of anti-Bolshevik revolutionaries—some of them former friends and comrades—who had been swept aside by events. Olgin did not want to end up like them, as he had made clear in his articles for the *Forverts* and the *New Republic*.[63] Not only was he a true believer in the revolution, but his status in the party's upper echelon rested on his expertise in Russian affairs, for instance, as editor of the party's Russian-language daily, *Novi Mir*, and as American correspondent for *Izvestia*. And, unlike Salutsky/Hardman, Olgin could not count on an institutional base of support outside of the Workers Party. He had no union position waiting for him. If Olgin wanted to be "free to come to Russia," as he reputedly told Salutsky in 1921, he needed to stay with the Workers Party. This benefit would be confirmed in 1924 when Olgin was sent to Moscow as a delegate to the Comintern's fifth congress. Four years earlier, Olgin had traveled to Soviet Russia as a sympathetic reporter; now he returned in an official capacity to deliberate Comintern policy with revolutionaries from around the world. The contrast could not have been lost on Olgin, who surely relished his new role.[64]

Finally, and perhaps most important, Olgin's move to Communism should be viewed against the backdrop of developments outside the party. By 1923, Communists had gained much ground in the Jewish labor movement's major organizations. They formed a powerful bloc, known as *Di linke* (the Left), which flourished beyond the narrow precincts of the Workers Party. Di linke consisted of two main elements. One comprised post-1905 immigrants (mostly, but not only, former Bundists like Olgin and Bittelman), who founded the first Jewish Communist organizations between 1919 and 1922. The other, perhaps larger, element was made up of young immigrants who came to the United States in the years immediately following the First World War. A significant number of the postwar immigrants—who totaled 250,000 between 1919 and 1924—had been active in Russian Jewish revolutionary parties, especially the Bund and Poale Zion or their respective youth organizations. Others came without political affiliations but had been radicalized during the years of war, revolution, and pogroms.[65] Great admirers of the Bolsheviks, the new arrivals came in a mood of revolutionary fervor. In their eyes, the established Jewish socialist and labor organizations appeared staid and bureaucratic, a perception even some Socialist party stalwarts shared. As Nokhum Khanin, leader of the Jewish Socialist Farband, wrote in 1926:

> We have ceased thinking of ourselves as leaders of a great people's movement. We have become practical businessmen . . . We have thought we could achieve everything with a little money and that inspiring the masses is superfluous. We have ceased being the center around which people could warm themselves, and therefore people have turned away from us. We have been left to ourselves. I maintain that Communism or Communist influence among Jewish workers is a protest against our coldness, a protest against our "practicality". . . . The masses have seen in the Communist movement an idealistic, sincere, relationship to the workers and their struggles.[66]

A similar sense of dissatisfaction pervaded Di linke. Few of its adherents actually joined the Workers Party, but *linkistn*, or leftists, looked to the party for leadership and joined myriad organizations founded by party members.[67] Within Di linke, Communists defined the discursive terrain, operated as a disciplined group, and could always invoke the authority and prestige of Moscow when needed. Yet Di linke formed a broad enough arena to accommodate various elements: Communists, Bundists, Marxist-Zionists, Yiddishists and, in the words of one Yiddish cultural activist in Chicago, those "searching for . . . a spiritual roof over their heads."[68]

Di linke found its strongest base of support in the garment unions, in particular the International Ladies Garment Workers Union. In the ILGWU's 1924 election, Di linke won control of three New York locals, which comprised a remarkable 70 percent of the union's membership in that city. In the following year, it gained control of the New York Cloak Makers Joint Board, a stronghold of ILGWU membership. (Di linke would be largely defeated within the ILGWU by 1927, after it badly mishandled the cloakmakers strikes of the previous year, but its demise could not have been predicted just a year earlier.) Di linke also won full control of the Furriers Union and made additional gains in locals of other important unions.[69] Within the Arbeter Ring fraternal order, linkistn seized control of 26 out of some 30 Yiddish children's schools in New York, the Arbeter Ring center in Harlem, and the Kinderland summer camp. Linkistn also controlled 64 Arbeter Ring branches, with a membership of about 7,000, and were influential in many others. Eventually, in 1930, members of Di linke would break away from the Arbeter Ring to form the rival International Workers Order.[70]

While linkistn threatened to overturn the established leadership in the Jewish labor movement, they also formed dozens of new organizations with a strong cultural bent. In the Bronx, there was the Young Workers Union of Writers, which sponsored literary readings and lectures on literature and art in addition to publishing a successful journal called *Yung kuznye*, and ultimately evolved into the proletarian writers association known as *Proletpen*.[71] Readers of *Di frayhayt* formed a Yiddish choir, the Frayhayt Gezangs Fareyn, numbering 288 members in New York alone (other branches were established in a number of other cities, including New Haven, Philadelphia, Pittsburgh, Newark, Cleveland, Toronto, and Montreal).[72] The Arbeter Teater Klub, an amateur Yiddish theater group, offered lessons in theater history, organized group discussions and, in 1925, spearheaded the creation of the Arbeter Teater Farband (ARTEF), representing 133 organizations.[73] In that year, Communists also founded the Jewish Workers' University for the purpose of developing a "Jewish workers' intelligentsia." The school offered a two-year curriculum (three for teachers) in "general sciences and problems of the labor movement" that included courses in Jewish history, the Yiddish language, and Yiddish literature. Three hundred students were enrolled as of 1927.[74] There were many other Communist-oriented initiatives, groups, and organizations: art centers, workers clubs, summer camps, a cooperative housing venture in the Bronx, an agency to support Jewish colonization in the Soviet Russia, and so on. Much of what was fresh and energetic in American Yiddish culture during the 1920s occurred within the realm of Di linke.

Di linke provided an expansive organizational and social framework congenial to Olgin. The Workers Party may have been small and faction-ridden, but Di linke was large and effective. As a writer, cultural activist, educator, and political spokesman, Olgin found an enthusiastic reception within Di linke, an arena where he could pursue his love of Yiddish culture and radical politics while remaining connected to the party and Moscow.

Yet Di linke did not provide complete insulation from disagreeable party policies. In 1925, the party instituted a policy of "Bolshevization" that delegitimized the idea of separate ethno-cultural spheres and sought to minimize them within the Communist movement. Implemented on instructions from the Comintern for the purpose of creating a centralized "monolithic" party, to quote James Cannon, Bolshevization formally disbanded all of the party's foreign language sections. Members were transferred to either factory- or neighborhood-based party units. Within those units, immigrants were allowed to join foreign language "fractions" affiliated with a corresponding national "bureau" responsible for transmitting party policies to immigrant members; these fell under strict party control. All the while, party leaders urged immigrants to "Americanize" and learn English as soon as possible.[75] For those, like Olgin, who believed in the importance of Yiddish culture as an expression of Jewish working-class life, Bolshevization could only be seen as a threat. Jewish Communists already had to contend with party leaders, Jews among them, who regarded Yiddish culture as a distraction from genuine revolutionary work, an impediment to Americanization, and a potential conveyor of Jewish nationalism. Even before Bolshevization was implemented, the party refused to allow the publication of a Yiddish-language "youth newspaper" and, as already noted, had reprimanded Olgin and his allies for devoting too much space to Yiddish culture in *Di frayhayt*.[76] Yet Bolshevization formalized and intensified preexisting efforts to diminish the role of ethnicity in the Communist party.

In the wake of Bolshevization, Olgin needed to justify Yiddish cultural activity—indeed, Jewish organizations of any kind—more than before. In 1926, he started editing a new political-cultural magazine called *Der hamer*, which did not fall under direct control of the Workers Party, although it did clearly identify with the party. On its pages, Olgin dared not challenge Bolshevization or Americanization directly. Instead, he criticized the general idea of "assimilationism," which he attributed primarily to the Jewish labor movement's non-Communist leaders, the so-called "official socialists." Olgin acknowledged that "some" Communists mistakenly favored cultural assimilation, but the real culprits were old-guard socialists, such as Abraham Cahan, who promoted English, opposed Yiddish schools for children, and showed insufficient respect to the Yiddish language and literature. Lest Olgin expose himself to criticism by party members, he denounced Jewish nationalists who upheld the value of Yiddish culture as a thing unto itself and who spoke in terms of Jewish group unity, rather than proletarian solidarity. A correct Communist position, Olgin argued, rejected both assimilationism and nationalism in favor of a pragmatic approach: whatever produced the "best social result" should be considered the best policy. Olgin claimed that "intensive cultural work" in Yiddish was necessary because "the masses hunger for education in the broad sense of the word." In his reasoning, "[t]he more left-wing the worker, the more the desire for culture." Yiddish culture did not distract from revolutionary political work; the two, in fact, reinforced one another. Failure to recognize that fact, Olgin warned, would impede Communism's advance among Jewish workers. Remarkably, Olgin did not appeal to Lenin's authority for validation. He invoked the needs of Jewish workers whose "hunger" for Yiddish culture provided its own justification.[77] Yet *Der hamer*'s numerous articles on Yiddish cultural life in Soviet Russia implied that the magazine's perspective was altogether in line with Moscow's.[78]

Compared to Olgin's writings from his pre-Communist years, his defense of Yiddish culture during the 1920s was rather mild, but pre-Communist antecedents could be detected. A contemporary reader familiar with the Bund's history would have noticed in Olgin's essays hints of the old Bundist concept of "neutralism," formulated two decades earlier. Neutralism held that Jews existed as a Yiddish-speaking nation for the time being and therefore Jewish workers possessed national cultural interests that needed attention. But neutralism disavowed any subjective desire to maintain the Jewish nation and Yiddish culture for their own sake. Ironically, Olgin had opposed neutralism during the 1900s in favor of a more outspokenly nationalist perspective.[79] However, in his incarnation as a Communist, Olgin fell back on the neutralist argument in order to justify Yiddish cultural work as perfectly consonant with Communist ideology and Workers Party policy. From reading Olgin's articles in *Der hamer*, one would not know that Workers Party leaders stated otherwise.

The balance Olgin struck between party imperatives and Jewish goals did not survive the decade. In 1929, he resumed editorship of *Di frayhayt*, now renamed *Di morgn-frayhayt*, shortly after the party adopted an ultra-militant program in the wake of Stalin's consolidation of power[80] and became even more heavy-handed in its approach to matters of Jewish concern. The most damaging incident involved Zionism. In August, American Yiddish newspapers reported the outbreak of widespread violence in Palestine perpetrated by Arabs against Jews, both Zionists and not. In the words of historian Anita Shapira: "These [riots] constituted a new phenomenon. For the first time, the Jewish community of Palestine found itself caught up in a wave of violent disturbances that swept with a fury through Jewish settlements and neighborhoods throughout the length and breadth of the country."[81] *Di morgn-frayhayt* originally used the word "pogrom" to describe the violence, implying that they contained an inexcusable, antisemitic character. However, in response to criticism of *Di morgn-frayhayt* from party leaders, Olgin quickly put forward a different interpretation. The "events in Palestine," he stated, actually amounted to "a mass revolt against imperialist domination."[82]

This change of position failed to satisfy party leaders, who viewed it as too soft on Zionism. "We sharply condemn the position of our Communist Jewish daily, the Morning Freiheit, as absolutely opportunist and hardly, if at all, different from the stand of the Jewish nationalist, Zionist and the capitalist press," the party secretariat declared. Accordingly, it forced Olgin to publish a declaration, which stated, in part: "The establishment of a Jewish country in Palestine is the fig leaf of British imperialism in its land-grabbing aggression in this part of Asia. And the Zionist movement is willingly and knowingly lending itself to this mission. . . ." Several days later, in an attempt to stave off further criticism, Olgin printed even more strident denunciations of "Zionist-Fascists." A public rally organized by *Di morgn-frayhayt* for the purpose of denouncing Zionism was a further attempt to establish the newspaper's credibility within the party.[83]

Di morgn-frayhayt's position on the violence in Palestine provoked a furious reaction in immigrant Jewish communities around the United States. Every Yiddish newspaper condemned *Di morgn-frayhayt*; newspaper vendors in New York City refused to handle it for five days or more; businesses stopped purchasing advertisements; the Communist-controlled Furriers Union suffered a large-scale defection of members that almost destroyed the union; in Chicago, a riot almost broke out at *Di morgn-frayhayt*'s local office; in Cleveland, Jewish Communists could not find a hall willing to rent to them; the Yiddish Writers' Union expelled *Di morgn-frayhayt*'s staff members; a host of acclaimed Yiddish poets and writers resigned from the newspaper; and in New York, a panel of distinguished Yiddish scholars presided over a mock trial in front of 2,500 people, which found Olgin and his colleagues guilty of "willfully and maliciously falsifying the news from Palestine."[84] The large-scale backlash almost bankrupted the newspaper.[85]

The scandal surrounding *Di morgn-frayhayt* in 1929 marked an ironic turnaround for Olgin. Ten years earlier, the slaughter of innocent Jews during the Russian civil war had impelled Olgin toward a sympathetic view of the Bolsheviks. In 1929, however, Soviet orders pressured Olgin to justify violence against the Jews of Palestine. A similar dynamic would repeat itself over the following decades. At certain moments, the Soviet Union and the American Communist party appeared as protectors of the Jews. This held true during the Second World War and Israel's War of Independence, when the Soviet Union briefly changed its traditional anti-Zionist position and vigorously supported the establishment of the state of Israel. In the face of systematic extermination by Nazi Germany during the early 1940s and Arab military efforts to abort the establishment of the state of Israel in 1948, many thousands of Jews viewed the Soviet Union as a heroic defender of their people. And yet, in other instances—the German-Soviet non-aggression pact (1939), Stalin's suppression of Yiddish culture, and the party's antisemitic purges in the early 1950s—the Soviet Union betrayed Jewish hopes and expectations.[86] The contradictory roles played by the Soviet Union as rescuer of Jews at certain points and their persecutor at others made for a fraught relationship between Jews and Communism.

Olgin's trajectory toward Communism encapsulated the larger narrative of the Jewish relationship with Communism, revealing the particular attraction Communism held for Jews and the problems faced by Jewish Communists in trying to reconcile ethnic and political loyalties. Olgin gravitated to the Communist party out of a genuine belief in the Bolsheviks as the only force capable of halting the chaos of the civil war period, rescuing Jews from widespread slaughter, and implementing a socialist order. Almost immediately from the moment Olgin struck an alliance with the Communists, he discovered that his political goals did not coincide with his Yiddish cultural goals, that revolution and ethnicity could not be combined easily. Nonetheless, Olgin remained in the party, indeed became a respected figure within it, because disagreeable party policies were offset by the vibrant cultural atmosphere and militant activism fostered by Di linke, which provided something of an alternative arena for Olgin—distinct from the party yet still closely connected to it. Ultimately, however, party policy narrowed whatever latitude Olgin enjoyed during the mid-1920s, and he chose to accept party discipline rather than leave the party. By 1929, after the riots in Palestine, Olgin found himself out of step with the vast majority of immigrant Jewish public opinion. He could no longer plausibly claim that Communism represented the best interests of the Jewish working class. The opposite now seemed to be true in the eyes of most immigrants.

The large number of Jewish Communists and Communist sympathizers, and the profound disillusionment in Soviet Russia and its American followers, cannot be understood apart from the ethnic dimension. Communism appealed to many Jews for reasons of ethnicity and, consequently, served to differentiate Jews in a decade when American society had generally moved in a conservative direction. At the same time, Communism posed a problem for ethnicity in its insistence on Americanization and in its opposition, in principle, to ethnic group autonomy, let alone separateness. As large numbers of immigrant Jews rallied behind Communism, and as many Jews started to react against it, a stable ethnicity characterized by a set of coherent political and cultural goals continued to elude Jews during the 1920s.

Notes

1. Of those listed in 1924, 1,368 were current in their party dues. See Records of the Communist Party of the United States in the Comintern Archives (Fond 515), microfilm edition compiled by the Library of Congress and the Russian State Archive of Social and Political History (Tamiment Library copy) (henceforth: Tamiment), reel 29, delo [file] 446. During the decade, Jews may have comprised as much as 15 percent of the party's membership. See Theodore Draper, *American Communism and Soviet Russia* (New York: 1960), 191.

2. Arthur Liebman, *Jews and the Left* (New York: 1979), 305–325.

3. Fifty-two percent of the Finns lived in the copper-mining regions of Michigan and Minnesota. See Peter Kivisto, *Immigrant Socialists in the United States: The Case of Finns and the Left* (Rutherford, N.J.: 1984), 72. On similarities and differences between Finnish and Jewish Communists, see Paul C. Mishler, "Red Finns, Red Jews: Ethnic Variation in Communist Political Culture during the 1920s and 1930s," *YIVO Annual* 22 (1995), 131–154.

4. In Los Angeles, according to a 1929 report in *The Communist* by Jack Stachel, Jews made up 90 percent of the party's membership; see Nathan Glazer, *The Social Basis of American Communism* (New York: 1961), 220, n. 1. In Chicago, Jews were the party's largest foreign language group, comprising 22 percent of party members in that city. Randi Storch, *Red Chicago: American Communism at Its Grassroots, 1928–1935* (Urbana: 2007), 40.

5. Thus the party's Central Executive Committee stated in 1922 that establishing a strong base of support among Jews was "an absolute condition for the development of our influence among other sections of the organized working class." (Tamiment, "Report on the United States of America," Communist Party Records, reel 10, delo 162 [p. 107].) On the role of Jewish-led garment unions, specifically the Amalgamated Clothing Workers, as a source of support for Communism, see James R. Barrett, *William Z. Foster and the Tragedy of American Radicalism* (Urbana: 1999), 126–128.

6. Glazer, *The Social Basis of American Communism*, 131. Jews accounted for up to half the membership of the Workers Party in the early 1920s. The Workers Party, controlled by the underground Communist party in 1921–1922, became the official name of the Communist party for a brief period starting in 1923. See Auvo Kostianen, "For or Against Americanization? The Case of Finnish Immigrant Radicals," in *American Labor and Immigration History, 1877–1920s: Recent European Research*, ed. Dirk Hoerder (Urbana: 1983), 261.

7. Bat-Ami Zucker, "American Jewish Communists and Jewish Culture in the 1930s," *Modern Judaism* 14 (1994), 175–185.

8. Jonathan Frankel, *Prophecy and Politics* (Cambridge: 1981), 453–547.

9. Joseph Brandes, "From Sweatshop to Stability: Jewish Labor between Two World Wars," *YIVO Annual of Jewish Social Science* 16 (1976), 49–67; John Holmes, "American Jewish Communism and Garment Unionism in the 1920s," *American Communist History* 6, no. 2 (2007), 171–195; Irving Howe, *World of Our Fathers: The Journey of East European Jews to America and the Life They Found There* (New York: 1976 [rpt. 1993]), 330–341; Stanley Nadel, "Reds Versus Pinks: A Civil War in the International Ladies Garment Workers Union," *New York History* 66 (1985), 60–61; Robert D. Parmet, *The Master of Seventh Avenue: David Dubinsky and the American Labor Movement* (New York: 2005), 31–53. As one contemporaneous observer noted: "The needle-trade unions have been the chief American center of the world-wide struggle between left and right unionists." (Nathan Fine, "Left and Right in the Needle-Trade Unions," *Nation* [4 June 1924], 640.)

10. Henry L. Feingold, *A Time for Searching: Entering the Mainstream, 1920–1945* (Baltimore: 1992), 125–154, 189–224; Liebman, *Jews and the Left*, 357–443; Deborah Dash Moore, *At Home in America: Second Generation New York Jews* (New York: 1981), 201–232.

11. Moore, *At Home in America*, 4.

12. See, for instance, the short story collection about Olgin by Shloyme Davidman, *Gey in folk mit Olgin's vort!* (New York: 1954).

13. *New York Times* (27 Nov. 1939), 14; Statement of the National Committee, Communist Party of the U.S.A., "Moissaye Joseph Olgin," *The Communist* (Dec. 1939), 1138–1139. Olgin's picture adorned the masthead of the Yiddish Communist daily *Di morgn-frayhayt* (originally *Di frayhayt*) from his death in 1939 until the newspaper went under in 1989.

14. See, for instance, the following articles by Olgin: "Di yidishe shprakh un unzer privatlebn," *Fragn fun lebn* (1911), 39–49, reproduced in *Never Say Die: A Thousand Years of Yiddish in Jewish Life and Letters*, ed. Joshua Fishman (Hague: 1981), 551–564; "Di alte un naye yontoyvim," *Di yidishe arbeter velt* (22 April 1910), 4; "Vi men darf nit shraybn yidish: notitsn far a lezer," *Di yidishe velt* 1, no. 1 (Jan. 1915), 43–53 (for abridged version, see *Di pen* 57 [Winter 1998], 57–62).

15. M. Olgin, *Amerike* (New York: 1941), 103–124.

16. Moissaye J. Olgin, *The Soul of the Russian Revolution* (New York: 1917).

17. *Nation* (6 Dec. 1917), 638–639; *New Republic* (22 Dec. 1917), 220–221; *New York Times* (13 Jan. 1918), 14. According to the economist Isaac Hourwich, *The Soul of the Russian Revolution* was "surely the best" recent book to appear on the Russian Revolution. See Hourwich's review in *Di tsukunft* (Aug. 1918), 494.

18. Leon Trotsky, *Our Revolution: Essays on Working-Class and International Revolution, 1904–1917*, collected and translated by Moissaye J. Olgin (New York: 1918). See reviews in *New York Times* (17 Feb. 1918), 62 and *Nation* (21 March 1918), 327.

19. *New York Times* (30 Sept. 1919), 20.

20. Clarendon Ross, "A Handbook of Russian Literature," *New Republic* (24 Nov. 1920), 334; Jacob Zeitlin, "A Guide to Russian Literature," *Nation* (18 Sept. 1920), 327–328.

21. For reports on Olgin's lectures, see Phebe M. Bogan, "Notes and News," *Hispania* 7, no. 5 (Nov. 1924), 335; Lewis S. Feuer, "American Travelers to the Soviet Union, 1917–1923: The Formation of a Component of New Deal Ideology," *American Quarterly* 14, no. 2 (part 1) (Summer 1962), 128.

22. See, for instance, the following articles by Olgin: "The Intelligentzia and the People in the Russian Revolution," *Annals of the American Academy of Political and Social Science* 84 (July 1919), 114–120; "Maxim Gorky," *New Republic* (18 Jan. 1919), 333–334; "A Wounded Intellect: Leonid Andreyev (1871–1919)," ibid. (24 Dec. 1919), 123–124; "A Sympathetic View of Russia," ibid. (26 May 1920), 426; "A Flashlight of the Russian Revolution," ibid., (27 July 1921), 250–251.

23. Moissaye J. Olgin, "Bolsheviki's Chief," *New York Times* (2 Dec. 1917), 21. "Lenine" is Olgin's spelling of the name in this article, which originally appeared in the December issue of *Asia*. Also see Olgin, "Lenin's program," *Forverts* (18 Nov. 1917), 9.

24. "Plea for Economic Aid to the Russians," *New York Times* (20 Jan. 1919), 6.

25. George Kennan, "The Bolsheviki and Their Apologists," *New York Times* (23 Jan. 1919), 12.

26. [no first name noted] Olgin, "Der yontev fun friling un frayhayt," *Di naye velt* (30 April 1920), 3.

27. Oleg Budnitskii, "Jews, Pogroms, and the White Movement: A Historiographic Critique," *Kritika: Explorations in Russian and Eurasian History* 2, no. 4 (Fall 2001), 751.

28. Olgin, "An oysgetrakhte velt," *Forverts* (7 June 1919), 3.

29. Quoted in Theodore Draper, *The Roots of American Communism*, (New York: 1957), 110.

30. Quoted in Melech Epstein, *Profiles of Eleven* (Detroit: 1965), 103. According to Peysekh Novik, a *Forverts* staff member in 1920, Abramovitsh complained to him repeatedly about Cahan's refusal to print his articles on Soviet Russia (Tamiment, tape-recorded interview with Novick). Cahan would change his position on the Soviet Union by 1924, if not sooner.

31. For a thorough account of Olgin's trip, see Daniel Soyer, "Soviet Travel and the Making of an American Jewish Communist: Moissaye Olgin's Trip to Russia in 1920–1921," *American Communist History* 4, no. 1 (2005), 1–20.

32. Moissaye J. Olgin, "Mechanics of Power in Soviet Russia," *New Republic* (15 June 1921), 70.

33. Ibid., 68.

34. Moissaye J. Olgin, "A Study in Dictatorship," *New Republic* (29 June 1921), 132–137.

35. Soyer, "Soviet Travel and the Making of an American Jewish Communist," 9–10.

36. Olgin, "Olgin shildert di shreklekhste pogrom-stsenes, vi a korbn hot es far im dertseylt," *Forverts* (15 May 1921).

37. M. Olgin, *Mayn shtetl in Ukrayne* (New York: 1921).

38. Olgin, "A yidishe shtot unter di Sovetn regirung," *Forverts* (9 July 1921).

39. Olgin, "A rov a Bolshevik halt a droshe in a Minsker shul," *Forverts* (11 Sept. 1921).

40. Later in the decade, Goldfarb/Petrovsky was appointed head of the Comintern's Anglo-American secretariat, where he played a significant role in the formation of its policy on "the Negro Question." He eventually changed his name again, to A.J. Bennet and served as a Comintern agent in England. See Draper, *American Communism and Soviet Russia*, 168; Zvi Gitelman, *Jewish Nationality and Soviet Politics: The Jewish Sections of the CPSU, 1917–1930* (Princeton: 1972); Mark Solomon, *The Cry Was Unity: Communists and African Americans, 1917–1936* (Jackson, Miss.: 1998), 68–91.

41. Olgin, "A parad fun royte soldatn in Moskve," *Forverts* (2 June 1921); Danyel Tsharni, *A yor tsendlik aza* (New York: 1943), 292–293. Also see Olgin, "A yid, Goldberg, komandevet iber hunderter rusishe generaln," *Forverts* (23 April 1921); and Soyer, "Soviet Travel and the Making of an American Jewish Communist," 17–18.

42. For more detailed accounts, see Y. Sh. Herts, *Di yidishe sotsyalistishe bavegung in Amerike* (New York: 1954), 188–198; Tony Michels, *A Fire in Their Hearts: Yiddish Socialists in New York* (Cambridge, Mass.: 2005), 228–238.

43. Transcribed interview with J.B.S. Hardman (Salutsky) (23 June 1962), 58, Tamiment, J.B.S. Hardman Collection, box 38, folder F-399.

44. M. Olgin, *A proletarishe politishe partey* (New York: 1922), 61.

45. Alexander Bittelman quoted in Draper, *American Communism and Soviet Russia*, 174.

46. Draper, *The Roots of American Communism*, 449, n. 23.

47. Gitelman, *Jewish Nationality and Soviet Politics,* 261–262, 278 n. 130; K. Marmor, "Funem 'Emes' tsu der 'Frayhayt'," *Di morgn-frayhayt* [(22 April 1932), found in Yivo Institute, RG 205, folder 378.

48. "A bagrisung fun M. Vintshevsky," *Di frayhayt* (2 April 1922), 1.

49. "Der 25-yoriker yubileum fun 'Forverts'," *Di frayhayt* (23 April 1922), 4.

50. The editors also instituted a modernized orthography that omitted certain silent letters and consonants meant to imitate German spelling and avoided the practice, common in the *Forverts*, of substituting English words for Yiddish. Both policies were meant to show respect for the Yiddish language. See Michels, *A Fire in Their Hearts*, 240.

51. "Lilliput" [Gavriel Kretshmar], "Aroys fun golus," *Di frayhayt* (2 April 1922), 3, 7.

52. Quoted in Melech Epstein, *The Jew and Communism*, 1919–1941 (New York: 1959), 108.

53. Ibid., 100–112; Michels, *A Fire in Their Hearts*, 244–246.

54. Statement by the Central Executive Committee of the Workers' Party, *The Worker* (9 Dec. 1922), Tamiment, Noah London Collection.

55. Zinoviev to Ruthenberg, n/d, Tamiment, reel 8, delo 147.

56. "Conditions of Agreement" (signed by Olgin, Vishnak, and six others), Tamiment, reel 17, delo 115; Michels, *A Fire in Their Hearts*, 238–248.

57. Exec. Sec'y, CP to Sec'y, Jewish Federation, 1 Nov. 1922; Exec. Sec'y (?) to Jewish Bureau, 13 Nov. 1922; J. Miller, Exec. Secretary to Secretary, Jewish Federation, 20 Nov. 1922; Arkadieff [Epshteyn] to CEC of the CP, 23 Dec. 1922, Tamiment, reel 7, delo 115.

58. James Cannon, *The First Ten Years of American Communism: Report of a Participant* (New York: 1962), 108.

59. Benjamin Gitlow, *I Confess* (New York: 1940), 160.
60. Dr. B. Hofman [Tsivion], *Komunistn vos hobn oyfgegesn komunizm* (New York: 1923); idem, *Far 50 yor* (New York: 1948), 335–346; Tsivion to Olgin, n.d., Bund Archives, ME-40; Cahan to Tsivion, 29 Oct. 1923, ibid.
61. In December 1922, Salutsky had invited Olgin to join the *American Labor Monthly*, but Olgin wished to evaluate the "tone" of the magazine before accepting the invitation. See Olgin to Salutsky, 28 Dec. 1922, Tamiment J.B.S. Hardman Collection, box 3, folder 5.
62. Moissaye J. Olgin, "The Mad Dog of Menshevism," English trans. of an article appearing in the American, Russian-language Communist daily *Novi Mir*, dated 27 Jan. 1925, Tamiment, reel 21, delo 365.
63. Olgin, "Di umgliklekhe 'Menshevikes'," *Forverts* (30 May 1921); Soyer, "Soviet Travel and the Making of an American Jewish Communist," 18–19.
64. With regard to Olgin's trip, Melech Epstein writes: "The men in the Kremlin knew Olgin from the time of their exile abroad, and Zinoviev and the others took him in hand. Highly flattered by the special attention of the mighty, Olgin returned a faithful toer of the line." Epstein, *The Jew and Communism*, 119.
65. Epstein, *The Jew and Communism*, 197–201; Kenneth Kann, *Joe Rapoport: The Life of a Jewish Radical* (Philadelphia: 1981), 20–87; Max Perlov, "A tsurikblik tsu di tsvantsiker yorn," *Di pen* 4 (1994), 23–26; Yankev Rot, *Tsvishn sotsyalizm un tsienizm* (Tel Aviv: 1996), 131–157.
66. N[okhum] Khanin, *Der veker* (6 March 1926), quoted in Herts, *Di yidishe sotsyalistishe bavegung in Amerike*, 264.
67. In the 1924 presidential election, for instance, the Poale Zion-Left created a formal alliance with the Workers Party. Minutes of General Executive Committee (WP), 9 July 1924, Tamiment, reel 18, delo 276; Minutes of Executive Council (WP), 29 Sept. 1924, ibid., reel 20, delo 303; M. Bzshoza to Central Executive Committee (WP), 5 Oct. 1924, ibid., reel 25, delo 389; Workers Party of America, Decisions of the CEC, 6 Oct. 1924, ibid., reel 24, delo 365.
68. *Dos naye vort* 2 (Nov. 1924), 9 (Tamiment reel 25, delo 390).
69. Epstein, *The Jew and Communism*, 122–143; J.B.S. Hardman, "The Needle-Trades Unions," *Social Research* 27, no. 3 (Autumn 1960), 342–343; Nadel, "Reds Versus Pinks," 60–61.
70. Epstein, *The Jew and Communism*, 144–150; Liebman, *Jews and the Left*, 310–321.
71. Perlov, "A tsurikblick tsu di tsvantsiker yorn," 25–26; Dovid Katz, "Introduction," in *Proletpen: America's Rebel Yiddish Poets*, ed. Amelia Glaser and David Weintraub, trans. Amelia Glaser (Madison: 2005), 3–29.
72. *Frayhayt gezang fareyn un mandalin orkester* (Dec. 1924), YIVO, RG 1400, box 6A, folder 13; *Gezang un kamf: yorbukh fun dem yidishn muzikalishn arbeter farband* (1928), ibid., box 7, folder 17.
73. Edna Nahshon, *Yiddish Proletarian Theatre: The Art and Politics of the ARTEF, 1925–1940* (Westport, Conn.: 1998), 13–58.
74. *Ershter friling yontef: Yidisher arbeter univerzitet* (April 1927), YIVO, RG 1400, box 11, folder 34.
75. Glazer, *The Social Basis of American Communism*, 46–70; Liebman, *Jews and the Left*, 492–497. James P. Cannon, "The Bolshevization of the Party," *Workers Monthly* 4, no. 1 (Nov. 1924), 34–37; John Pepper, "Problems of the Party—IV: Be American!" *The Worker* 6, no. 276 (26 May 1923), 5.
76. Minutes of the National Exec. Committee, Young Workers League, Sept. 1923, Tamiment, reel 16, delo 240; Minutes of the Central Exec. Committee (WP), 3 May 1924, ibid., reel 18, delo 276.
77. Ed. [Olgin], "Unzere kultur-oyfgabn," *Der hamer* (May 1926), 18; idem, "Di arbet fun di yidishe komunistn in Amerike," ibid. (Dec. 1927), 26–27; idem, "Tsvishn undz geredt," ibid. (Aug. 1928), 64.
78. See, for instance, K. Marmor, "Yidishe visenshaftlekhe forshungen in Sovetn-farband," *Der hamer* (Dec. 1926), 54–56; M. Levitan, "Yidisher shul boy in der Sovetn republik," ibid. (Nov. 1926), 48–51.

79. M. Olgin, "Naye natsyonale shtrebungen bay yidishe sotsyalistn," *Di yidishe arbeter velt* (28 April 1911), 5. "[We] are convinced," Olgin writes, "that [Jewish workers] require a separate Yiddish culture. . . . [W]e want to awaken the masses and help raise them to a higher political level of economic and intellectual life."

80. Randi Storch, "'The Realities of the Situation': Revolutionary Discipline and Everyday Political Life in Chicago's Communist Party, 1928–1935," *Labor: Studies in Working-Class History of the Americas*, 1, no. 3 (Fall 2004), 19–44. Storch argues that the party demonstrated a small measure of flexibility at the local level, even during the restrictive "Third Period" between 1928 and 1935.

81. Anita Shapira, *Land and Power: The Zionist Resort to Force, 1881–1948* (Stanford: 1999), 174.

82. Ed. [Olgin], "Kegn vemen protestirn?" *Di morgn-frayhayt* (28 Aug. 1929), 4. See also Meylekh Epshteyn [Melech Epstein], "Di tsienistn kenen zikh nit aroysdreyen," *Di morgn-frayhayt* (28 Aug. 1929), 4; Dovid Magievitsh, "Der emes vegn di gesheenishn in Palestine," *Di morgn-frayhayt* (30 Aug. 1929), 5.

83. Epstein, *The Jew and Communism*, 225–226.

84. "Find Reds Falsified News of Palestine," *New York Times* (23 Sept. 1929), 20.

85. Epstein, *The Jew and Communism, 1919–1941*, 223–233. Epstein (see n. 79) was a staff member of *Di frayhayt* at the time of the scandal.

86. Paul Buhle, "Jews and American Communism: The Cultural Question," *Radical History Review* 23 (Dec. 1980), 21–31; Liebman, *Jews and the Left*, 501–535.

Ethnic Group Strength, Intermarriage, and Group Blending

Joel Perlmann
(LEVY ECONOMICS INSTITUTE OF
BARD COLLEGE)

The value of ethnicity as an analytic concept will depend on the kind of society under study. In this essay, I limit attention to immigrant societies such as the United States. However, even within immigrant societies it is important to distinguish between groups that the host society has or has not severely racialized or otherwise rigidly isolated, for example through legislation. For the groups that have not been severely racialized, such as the European immigrants to the United States, the utility of ethnicity as a concept depends upon generational status. Although it is conceivable that ethnic ties might strengthen across generations—that something in the nature of social relations between groups in a society might retard patterns of assimilation—it would be hard to point to instances of such a pattern in the American experience.

Many would wish for a more complicated and subtle treatment of the continuum from non-racialized ("ethnic") to severely racialized groups. For example, Victoria Hattam recently stressed the extent to which the concept of ethnicity was conceived in opposition to the concept of race. She observes that it might well have been healthier for American society had the concept of ethnicity been applied to all groups, rather than applied in a way that suggests that some groups (races) differed biologically from others in important ways, whereas among ethnic groups, differences were designated as cultural. Still, it is possible to see the issue differently, to suggest that those who formulated the concept of ethnicity did so not because they necessarily believed that racial differences were in fact rooted in biology, but merely because they were observing the social beliefs and behaviors of the mainstream toward the racialized. My point is not to argue against Hattam that the thinkers she describes necessarily held this weaker position, although some may have, but rather to argue that this weaker position is a useful way for us today to describe the continuing utility of the ethnicity concept. That is, the concept has value for describing the non-racialized, or more weakly racialized, distinctions among peoples—in the American context, those distinctions involving Europeans then and now (Madison Grant and company notwithstanding) and perhaps most Asians and Hispanics now. Since this essay is bound up in particular with themes of intermarriage and with mixed- versus single-origin offspring, this distinction between racialized and ethnicized groups is especially useful, for one of the clearest markers of the former is that marriages across the divide are rare.[1]

Yet even if we accept this usage for the concept of ethnicity, the concept of generation is itself problematic. As applied to the first generation—the immigrant—the concept is relatively clear, although a moment's reflection will reveal the marginal case of the young child brought from one country to another. Not for nothing have the sociologists begun to refer to such people as the "1.5 generation," or even, in connection with the very youngest and the nearly adult immigrant children respectively, as the "1.75" or "1.25" generation. Such terminology might lead us to refer to the children of the 1.5 generation as . . . perhaps the 2.5 generation? Still, the concept of generation works fairly well for the first generation, and also for the second generation. The great majority of immigrants (at least adult immigrants, the "true" first generation) have married other immigrants from the same country of origin (not least because many came as married couples). Consequently, the American-born child of two immigrant parents from the same country of origin is the simple, and usually dominant, type of second-generation member. Nevertheless, there are messy cases at the margin: the native-born child of immigrants from two different countries of origin (of a Polish immigrant mother and an Italian immigrant father, for example), or of one immigrant and one American-born individual (from the same or from a different country of origin).

By the third (or occasionally the fourth) generation, the messy cases have become the norm: the complexity inherent in the concept of generation is likely to characterize the majority, and not merely a minority. For it is in the third generation that the *majority* of offspring of European immigrant groups in 19th- and 20th-century America typically came to have mixed ethnic origins. This domination of third-generation mixed origins in turn rested on substantial earlier second-generation out-marriage. I have done extensive research on the Italians, the largest of the immigrant groups in the early 20th century, and one that was culturally isolated and geographically concentrated. Yet even among the Italians, a substantial minority—about a third—of the second generation married outside the group. As a result, about half of the third generation of Italian Americans were of mixed origin—part Italian and part something else.[2]

How does it come about that when a third of the group out-marries, half of the children in the next generation are of mixed origin? Table 1 shows the relevant factors. We can appreciate the key point by following the row in bold. Imagine that we start with 1,000 second-generation Italians, and an out-marriage rate of 33 percent. The rest who in-marry, 670 of the 1,000, marry each other and form 335 couples. The 330 who out-marry form just about the same number of couples, by drawing in partners from other groups. Now the children of the next generation are produced by the family units, and the third who out-marry produce fully half the couples involving second-generation Italians—and therefore half the children in the third generation. True, another factor also determines the number of single and mixed offspring: the fertility rates of the two kinds of couples. However, fertility differences between single- and mixed-origin families are likely to be much less significant than the level of intermarriage in the second generation in determining the proportions of the third-generation offspring who will be of single and mixed origins.

Ethnic Group Strength, Intermarriage, and Group Blending 51

Table 1. The Dynamic of Out-marriage in Producing Offspring with Mixed Origins: Hypothetical Examples Starting with 1,000 Second-Generation Members of an Ethnic Group

Assumed rate of out-marriage	Of 1,000 second-generation members			Ethnic origin of couples formed		
	IN-marry	OUT-marry	Total	Single (=.5b)	Mixed (=c)	% Mixed
a	b	c	d	e	f	g
10%	900	100	1,000	450	100	18
25%	750	250	1,000	375	250	40
33%	**670**	**330**	**1,000**	**335**	**330**	**50**
50%	500	500	1,000	250	500	67
67%	330	670	1,000	165	670	80
75%	250	750	1,000	125	750	86
90%	100	900	1,000	50	900	95

Notes: Given *equal* fertility rates in single- and mixed-origin families, the percentage of mixed-origin children in the next generation will equal the percentage of mixed couples (column g).

Given modestly *lower* fertility rates in mixed-origin as opposed to single-origin families, the percentage of mixed-origin children will be modestly lower than the percentage shown in column g.

However, only if the fertility rate in mixed-origin families is *no more than half* the rate of single-origin families (an unlikely outcome) will the percentage of mixed-origin children (column g) fail to exceed the percentage of out-marriage in the parents' generation (column a).

All this matters to the concept of ethnicity, and especially to the notion of ethnicity as being embedded in time, because it is generally harder for ethnicity to remain a strong force in a mixed- as opposed to a single-origin family. We all can probably think of exceptions to this generalization, but these do not challenge the generalization itself. Whatever force ethnicity does have in the mixed-origin family tends to be diluted across the allegiances of the two parents. Moreover, because the two parents do not share this feature of their lives, they are less likely to stress either ethnic heritage quite as much in their family interactions. Of course, the very fact that parents of different ethnic origins consider marrying each other in the first place suggests that the process of ethnic assimilation had been well underway in their lives even before they became a couple. After all, they found they could share a life with someone from another group. In that sense, intermarriage itself is an outcome of assimilatory developments. But the point I am stressing here is that intermarriage is also a background factor that accelerates assimilatory developments within the family; at the same time, the demographic dynamics described in Table 1 typically make those developments dominant in the group as a whole by the third generation.

Mixed origin also complicates generational standing. Thus, if a second-generation son of Italian-immigrant parents marries a native-born American woman of native-born parents, their child will be third-generation Italian on the father's side. Through the mother, however, that same child might be, say, fourth-generation German and also sixth-generation Irish. These complex roots on the mother's side are hidden by the description "native-born of native parentage," but they may be known, or known in part, to the mother and to her offspring.

To repeat: it is in the third generation that the majority of offspring of descendents of European origin are generally typified by mixed ethnic origins. I offer this observation not as a theoretical necessity but as an empirical observation of American patterns.

With these considerations as background, we can turn to the ways in which demographic processes, over time, condition the viability of ethnicity; my focus is on Europeans in America, but at least some of these considerations will hold more widely. Insofar as the processes of intermarriage contribute to demographic change and to further assimilation, we should not be surprised that ethnicity is so bounded in time, so much a function of the generational standing since immigration, and in particular so likely to be a first- and second-generation phenomenon. Nevertheless, there are also countervailing demographic patterns that support ethnic continuity.

Consider again the dynamics shown in Table 1. We observed earlier that these dynamics create a large *percentage* of descendents with mixed origins by the third generation. Now consider these descendents in terms of their absolute *number* by the third generation. In all likelihood, there are a great many more third-generation descendents than there were immigrant grandparents. So it is possible that even as the single-origin descendents have become a decided minority among all descendents in an ethnic group, the absolute number of those single-origin descendents may remain high for a long time. In fact, it is plausible that even in the third or fourth generation, the single-origin descendants may be more numerous than the immigrant forebears in their grandparents' or great-grandparents' generation. This large number of single-origin descendents may be crucial to explaining how a group continues to command adherents even as single-origin descendents become a minority among all descendents of that group.

Table 2 provides a crude model of such a process. The rates for out-marriage and fertility are simply illustrative, but they are not unrealistic illustrations. The model shows that substantial numbers of single-origin descendents may be produced through several generations even as these descendents form a decreasing proportion among all descendents of the particular immigrants we are following. In Table 2, the number of third-generation single-origin descendents (1,435) exceeds the number of original immigrants that produced them (1,000); of course the number of third-generation, mixed-origin individuals is higher still (2,366). The single-origin descendents are likely to be concentrated in particular cities and neighborhoods, increasing the likelihood that they will continue to be involved with their ethnic origins. Of course, the number of such single-origin individuals cannot remain large indefinitely; eventually the rapidly declining *percentage* with single origins will overcome the impact of population growth. The example in Table 2 is crude in that it does not take into account at least two important factors: people who do not marry at all, and children who die before reproducing. But crude efforts to take account of these factors for the Italians of 1910 suggest that the force of the example is in the right direction: generally, fertility could plausibly produce twice as many descendents in the third generation as among the immigrant grandparents (see Appendix); and in some groups, a higher rate of fertility resulted in notably more grandchildren than that estimate. Consequently, even if only half the third-generation members are of single ethnic origin, the absolute number of those third-generation members will be as large as the number of their immigrant grandparents. There will still be many cultural forces working on these descendents to make them members of the American

Table 2. A Crude Model for the Size of Ethnic Generation in the Context of Out-marriage and Population Growth: Hypothetical Data Starting with 1,000 Immigrants from One Country of Origin

Generation	Out-marriage rate for single-origin individuals	Nature of couples produced			Average number of children per couple	Total N	(next gen=)	Children in the *NEXT* generation, by origin type			
		Single-origin	Mixed-origin	% Mixed	N			Single-origin	Mixed-origin	Total	% Mixed
	a	b	c	d	e	f		g	h	i	j
1) 1,000 immigrants	10%	450	100	18	3.4	2nd		**1,530**	340	1,870	18
2) Second generation	33%	513	845	62	2.8	3rd		**1,435**	2,366	3,801	62
3) Third generation	55%	323	3,155	91	2.2	4th		**710**	6,941	7,651	91
4) Fourth generation	70%	107	7,438	99	2.2	5th		**234**	16,364	16,598	99

Notes: The model assumes that fertility rates in single- and mixed-origin couples are equal and all individuals marry.

Calculations for:

Column b:

Row 1 1000 * (1-a) * 0.5

Row 2 (cell g, row 1) * (1-a) * 0.5

Row 3 (cell g, row 2) * (1-a) * 0.5

Row 4 (cell g, row 3) * (1-a) * 0.f

Column c:

Row 1 1000 * a

Row 2 (cell g, row 1) * a + (cell c, row 1) * (cell e, row 1)

Row 3 (cell g, row 2) * a + (cell c, row 2) * (cell e, row 2)

Row 4 (cell g, row 3) * a + (cell c, row 3) * (cell e, row 3)

Column g:

b * e

Column h:

c * e

mainstream; at the same time, at least one critical demographic factor, that of growing up in a mixed-origin family, will not be contributing to their cultural shifts—suggesting that, if it were a matter of sheer numbers of descendents, ethnicity could well hang on strongly through the third generation and probably beyond.

However, the formulation in the preceding paragraph ignores one important feature of the demographic realities, which works to radically reduce the impact that sheer number of single-origin offspring will have on the force of ethnic life. That factor is connected to childbearing: the children and grandchildren of a particular mother are likely to be born across a surprisingly wide range of years. And so, while the numbers of single-origin, third-generation descendents may be large, the power of their numbers for group cohesion and survival will be diluted, since their birth years extend across many more years than do those of their immigrant grandparents. We like to think of a generation as comprising something like 25–30 years across time—from the birth of the parent to the birth of the child. In fact, however, the ages at which a mother gives birth to her children varies and has always varied widely.

In order to appreciate the point, consider the mothers of the second- and third-generation Irish and Germans in the 19th century and of Italians in the 20th. The ages at which those mothers gave birth are shown in Table 3. The point is simple, but it bears stressing: the entire range covers fully 35 years, from about 14 to 49. Of course, far fewer children were born at the extreme ages, such that we can account for all but about 10 percent of the relevant births in each generation by focusing on mothers aged 19 to 38. But this restriction still leaves us with a range of 20 years during which a child could have been born to a given mother. The bottom rows of Table 3 show that we cannot further restrict the range of mothers' ages at birth of their children without excluding large proportions of those children. Note, moreover, that this wide range of birth years characterizes both the immigrant mother and the second-generation mother. Consequently, a randomly chosen third-generation child of an immigrant grandmother—for example, a German grandmother herself born in 1835, who arrived in 1856—could have been born across a period of some 25 years. This statement actually defines about four-fifths of the randomly chosen third-generation descendants of that immigrant forbearer (.9 of the third-generation children born to .9 of the second-generation children born to immigrants of age x arriving in a given year y); the other fifth were born across an additional 45 years of time.[3] It is hard to demonstrate how all this works out in an elegant graph using real data; nevertheless, Fig. 1 takes us farther than would have been possible before the recent creation of giant, digitized public-use samples that are now available for the entire range of American history since 1850.[4] Thus the presentation here is novel.

Novel, but alas still not all we would need to adequately relate patterns of arrival and later births. The case of the 19th-century Germans highlights the problem. The German immigration continued at a high level across many decades, and it had numerous peaks and valleys. Add to this the fact that the descendents of an immigrant woman arriving in the United States in a given year were born across the wide range of years that have just been described. The upshot is that it is hard to find much connection between particular years of immigrant arrivals and particular years of third-generation births in the German figures.

Table 3. Mother's Age at the Birth of Second- and Third-Generation Children: Examples from Census Data, 1880–1960

Mother's age at child's birth	Second-generation children			Third-generation children		
	Irish	German	Italian	Irish	German	Italian
	1880	1880	1920	1910	1910	1960
	% of children born to mothers of age						
14	0.1	0.2	0.2	0.0	0.1	0.1
15	0.2	0.2	0.4	0.1	0.2	0.1
16	0.4	0.4	0.8	0.2	0.4	0.3
17	0.6	0.7	1.5	0.4	0.7	0.4
18	1.1	1.3	2.7	1.3	1.7	0.9
19	1.6	2.1	3.6	1.6	2.4	1.9
20	2.4	3.1	4.8	2.6	3.6	3.2
21	3.0	3.8	5.4	3.3	4.9	4.3
22	3.7	4.5	5.7	4.1	5.6	5.6
23	4.6	5.0	6.0	4.9	6.2	6.2
24	4.9	5.3	5.9	5.1	6.2	7.1
25	5.4	5.4	6.0	6.2	6.3	7.3
26	5.6	5.5	5.8	6.3	6.4	7.5
27	5.6	5.4	5.5	5.9	6.1	7.3
28	6.1	5.4	5.1	6.2	5.8	6.9
29	5.6	5.0	4.8	6.2	5.6	6.7
30	5.8	5.0	5.4	6.1	5.1	5.9
31	5.5	4.7	4.1	5.2	4.5	5.4
32	5.2	4.6	4.0	5.3	4.0	4.8
33	5.3	4.4	3.7	4.5	3.8	3.9
34	4.6	4.1	3.3	4.4	3.4	3.6
35	4.2	3.8	2.8	3.8	2.8	2.5
36	3.7	3.5	2.6	3.5	2.8	2.0
37	3.2	3.1	2.2	2.7	2.4	1.8
38	2.8	2.9	1.9	2.4	2.1	1.4
39	2.2	2.4	1.6	2.1	1.9	1.0
40	1.9	2.2	1.2	1.5	1.6	0.7
41	1.4	1.8	0.7	1.4	1.1	0.5
42	1.1	1.4	0.9	1.0	1.0	0.3
43	0.8	1.1	0.5	0.6	0.5	0.2
44	0.5	0.7	0.4	0.4	0.3	0.1
45	0.4	0.5	0.2	0.2	0.2	0.1
46	0.3	0.3	0.1	0.1	0.1	0.0
47	0.2	0.2	0.1	0.1	0.1	0.0

(*continued*)

Table 3. (continued)

Mother's age at child's birth	Second-generation children			Third-generation children		
	Irish	German	Italian	Irish	German	Italian
	1880	1880	1920	1910	1910	1960
	% of children born to mothers of age					
48	0.1	0.1	0.1	0.1	0.1	0.0
49	0.1	0.1	0.0	0.0	0.0	0.0
All ages, 14–49	100.0	100.0	100.0	100.0	100.0	100.0
Ages 19–38	88.7	86.4	88.6	90.3	90.0	95.2
Most births in a 10-year range (shaded)	54.9	51.3	55.6	57.4	58.1	65.9
Most births in a 5-year range (dark-shaded)	28.7	27.0	29.5	30.7	31.2	36.1

Sources: IPUMS 1880, 1910, 1920, and 1960 (1 percent samples of the U.S. decennial censuses); NAPP 1880 (100 percent of the decennial census); see also n. 4.

We can do better with the famine Irish of the mid-19th century. The concentration of so many more Irish immigrants during the famine years of 1847–1854 shows up in dramatic clarity in the first-generation figures, and is clearly reflected in the second- and third-generation figures as well. However, the swollen population figures that capture the birth of the second- and third-generation descendants of the famine Irish do not come in a narrow range of years. While their parents may have arrived over an eight-year period, the children of the famine Irish were born over a much wider period, and thus the graph line of their births is elongated, rising less dramatically than that showing immigration arrival figures. If we assume that most of the famine Irish who would produce American-born children came in their teens and 20s, then we would expect the second generation to start building toward a peak during the decade after 1850. This is about what we do find: the number of second-generation births exceeds 75,000 beginning in 1856 and exceeds 100,000 beginning in 1860—and continues to exceed 100,000 annual births for 17 years, and 75,000 annual births for fully 30 years. The third generation rises to its peak roughly 25 to 30 years after that of the second generation, with third-generation births exceeding 100,000 annually between 1887 and 1910—a period of 24 years. We cannot be sure that all these newborns were in fact the grandchildren of immigrants who arrived in the eight years of the famine; some may be the grandchildren of later arrivals. Likewise, some grandchildren of the famine years' immigrants were born earlier or later than the 24-year period to which I call attention. Nevertheless, the distinctively high level of births during those years allows us to be confident that most of the births are in fact the grandchildren of those who arrived in the peak immigration years.

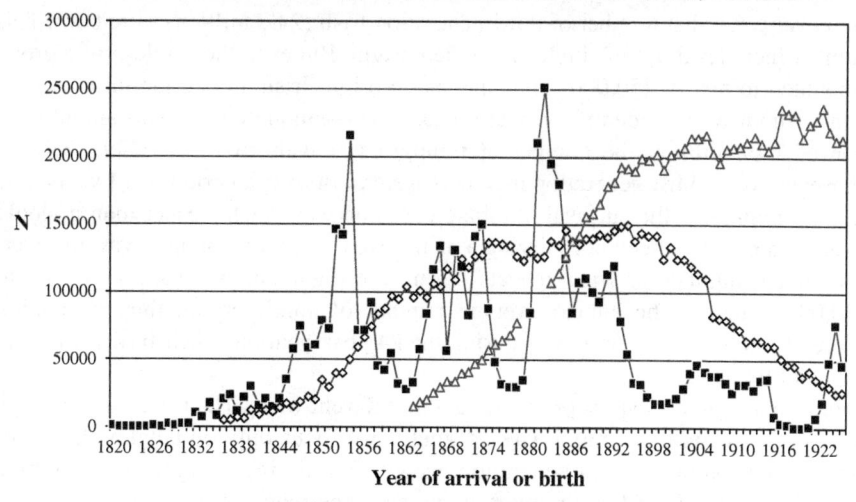

The Germans: Immigrants, Second and Third Generations, 1820-1925

a ■ German Immig. ◇ 2nd gen. △ 3rd gen.

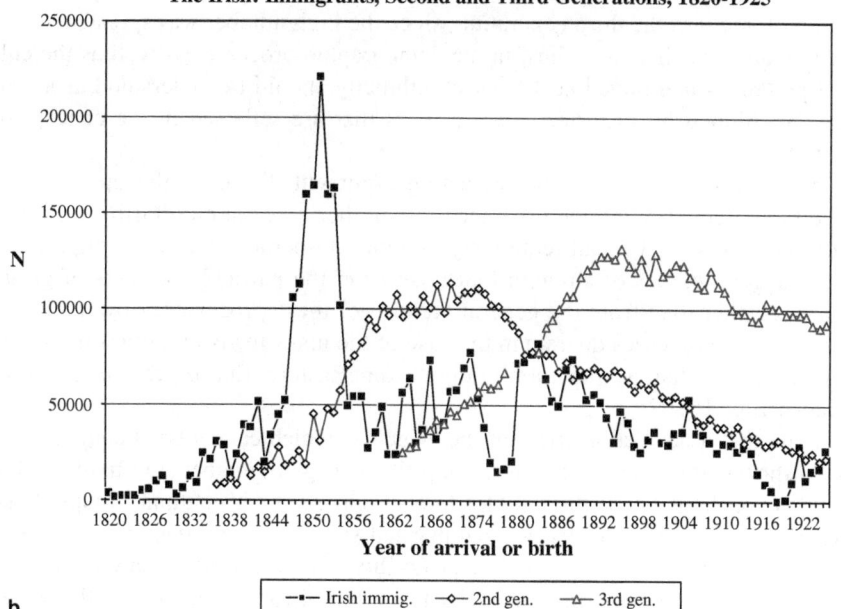

The Irish: Immigrants, Second and Third Generations, 1820-1925

b ■ Irish immig. ◇ 2nd gen. △ 3rd gen.

Source for Figures 1a and 1b: For second- and third-generation data, see note to Table 3. Immigrant arrival data from *Historical Statistics of the United States* (see n. 11), vol. 1, Part A, Table Ad 1-2.

Between 1847 and 1854, 1.19 million Irish arrived; between 1887 and 1910 alone, well over twice that number of third-generation Irish (2.87 million) were born. This number includes those of single and mixed origin. But even the single-origin group amounted to nearly 750,000. Thus the single-origin Irish among the third generation—whom we can identify in these peak years—amounted to a substantial fraction of 1.19 million, the number of immigrant arrivals two generations earlier.[5] However, these third-generation members were born over a period of 24 years, and so their impact on the survival of ethnic cohesion was much weaker than it would have been had they been born during a mere seven years. Put another way, the average annual number of Irish arrivals during the eight famine years amounted to 150,000, whereas the annual average number of single-origin, third-generation descendents of these immigrants during the 24 peak years for their births was only about a fifth as great.

In sum, the demographic processes cut in different ways. The large out-marriage rates in the second generation suggest that if we focus only on neighborhoods of ethnic cohesion in the third generation, we will be missing a larger story of ethnic assimilation that is in fact the more dominant experience of the grandchildren of immigrants. At the same time, the actual number of single-origin descendents was generally large, at least through the third generation. But this large absolute number of single-origin descendents could not do much to propel ethnic allegiances as a strong force into the third generation, since the high number was spread across a wide range of birth years. Thus, in the demographic processes as well as the cultural processes mentioned at the outset, ethnicity should be understood as a process conditioned by historical time in ways that are reflected in the concept of generation.

And what of the Jews? The preceding argument discusses the operation of these three demographic factors—fertility, mother's age at childbirth, and intermarriage—in ways we can tentatively assume to operate on every group, albeit with varying degrees of strength that arise from the particular aspects of group histories rather than from the general features of these processes. How, then, did these general processes operate in the case of the mass Jewish immigration to the United States, that is, the immigration from Eastern Europe during the four decades after 1880?

I think that a detailed analysis of the evidence, which cannot be attempted here, would show that two of these factors—fertility and age of mother at birth of child—would not be dramatically different for Jews as opposed to other ethnic groups. To be sure, to the extent that Jewish women married somewhat later than did women of various other immigrant groups, or that fertility was restricted for any number of reasons in the immigrant and especially the second generation, we will find some Jewish distinctiveness. I would expect that generally this distinctiveness would result in a lower level of fertility, and might also result in a narrower range of mother's age at childbirth. But these restrictions probably would have the effect of placing the Jews in the lower middle rather than at the upper end of immigrant groups; that is, Jews may turn out not to resemble Italians and Poles so much as later-arriving Germans or Scandinavians.[6]

The greatest Jewish distinctiveness is likely to be found in the lower rate of immigrant and second-generation out-marriage. Here we have to take into account the ambiguous application of the categories "immigration," "ethnicity," and "religion" to Jews. When a second-generation East European Jew marries the descendant of a German Jew, we are likely to regard the result as in-marriage. We do so because the Jewish group is partly defined by religion and because to some degree the Jewish groups of different European countries can be considered part of one people, one ethnic group (using the term very loosely) in Europe. In any case, even if we did not consider this marriage pattern to be in-marriage, the Jewish intermarriage rate will probably turn out to be lower than the intermarriage rate of other groups in the first and second generations. Certainly the Jewish rate is much lower when we do count marriage to any Jew as in-marriage.[7]

However we choose to define the Jewish ethnic categories, the intersection of religion and ethnicity also operate to reinforce the divide between Jews and others. Thus, for example, even if we chose to think of American Jews ca. 1925 as comprising two ethnic groups, German and East European, we would still note that, for both these ethnic groups, religion and ethnicity worked to keep them apart from Christian Americans—even if religion and ethnicity operated somewhat differently in the two Jewish ethnic groups. We might quibble over whether distinct forms of Jewish religion joined ethnicity to keep the two Jewish ethnic groups somewhat apart from each other; however we decide to formulate this matter, our sturdier conclusion about the division of Jews from Christians, resting on both factors, would remain unaffected.

Among the three demographic factors I have discussed, then, two of them (fertility, and perhaps also a somewhat narrower distribution of mothers' ages at childbirth) may have worked to mildly reduce Jewish numbers, in contrast to how they operated for other groups. But the most important factor, numerically, was probably the lower out-marriage rate.

In consequence, we might ask whether the historical experience of a lower out-marriage rate for the first two or three generations after immigration—for the better part of a century, in other words—may continue to affect the nature of the group in coming generations. My hunch is that any such effects will be modest. If they do exist, the place to look for them may be in the substantial build-up of Jewish institutional entities that a longer period of in-marriage probably helped create. Institutional strength, created over a long period, may in turn have a modest effect in stimulating the interest of those of mixed origins in their Jewish origins and in things Jewish.

Such considerations carry us well beyond the demographic factors themselves. And the sort of fuller analysis that will need to include such considerations will also want to take into account, for any group and for the Jews in particular, other social characteristics of the specific migration stream that do not directly influence the numerical base "at risk" for ethnic involvement across the country as a whole, but which nevertheless influence an individual's likelihood of ethnic involvement—characteristics such as geographic, educational, and economic mobility.

Appendix: Estimating Net Reproduction Rates for Two Immigrant Groups

The Net Reproduction Rate (NRR) is meant to describe the number of daughters who will replace one mother. For Italian immigrant women in 1910, it was roughly 2.6 (the calculations are explained below). Because I am relying heavily on the conveniently available work of demographers associated with the 1910 U.S. census,[8] I cannot include NRR estimates for the 19th-century Irish and Germans, although I do discuss other aspects of their demographic patterns in the main body of this essay. In addition, I cannot include NRR estimates for the second-generation Italian women. However, even if the second-generation NRR was much lower than the first, the product of first- and second-generation NRRs very likely reached 2.0 among the 1910 Italian women and their daughters.[9]

The NRR is calculated from the Total Fertility Rate (TFR), "a weighted sum obtained by adding together the age-specific fertility rates for each [typically five-year] cohort . . . [It] indicates the average number of children born to each 1,000 women at all childbearing ages." In calculating the NRR, the TFR is limited to female births (roughly .49 of all births), and limited further to include only those females who "survive to an age at which they can bear at least one daughter."[10] I used life tables indicating the probability of female survival until age 25 to meet this second limitation.[11] The 1910 TFR per 1,000 Italian immigrant women is 6,930. The 1910 white female life table survival to age 25 is .82; but a child mortality index for births to Italian immigrant mothers that year stands at 1.25 times those in the society generally;[12] I applied that correction factor to the 1910 life table survival probabilities for age 25, thus estimating the relevant survival rate to be $1- [1.25*(1-.82)] = .78$. Thus the 1910 estimate for the NRR per 1000 Italian immigrant women was calculated as $6930*.49*.78 = 2632$.

Notes

1. Victoria Hattam, *In the Shadow of Race: Jews, Latinos and Immigrant Politics in the United States* (Chicago: 2007), esp. 75–76. Hattam highlights a related issue, irrelevant to the present argument but likely of interest to readers of this annual—the fact that many of those who crafted the concept of ethnicity were Jews interested in Jewish affairs. She refers to them as "Zionists," as at least some of them were; but what is more relevant is their broader emphasis on Jewish cultural survival.

2. Joel Perlmann, "Demographic Outcomes of Ethnic Intermarriage in American History: Italian Americans through Four Generations" (Levy Economics Institute of Bard College Working Paper No. 312) (Aug. 2000), online at www.levy.org/pubs/wp312.pdf (accessed 4 Aug. 2010).

3. A refined model would need to exclude those children born to such a mother before her arrival in the host society; thus in the preceding example, the German woman born in 1835 would not have been able to have American-born children until age 21.

4. These are known as the IPUMS (Integrated Public Use Microdata Samples) and each includes at least 1 percent of the American population in each census year. However, the figures from the 1880 census do *not* come from the IPUMS datasets but rather from a new project

administered by the population center at the University of Minnesota (which also created the IPUMS). This new project, known as the NAPP (North Atlantic Population Project), includes a machine-readable dataset of the *entire population* from the census of 1880—the complete census record for some 50 million Americans, as well as the entire 1880 populations of several other countries. See Steven Ruggles, J. Trent Alexander, Katie Genadek, Ronald Goeken, Matthew B. Schroeder, and Matthew Sobek, *Integrated Public Use Microdata Series: Version 5.0* (Minneapolis: 2010).

5. Note that the method here differs from that used earlier, for Table 2 and for the Appendix. There, I attempted to estimate net reproduction rates, whereas here I am graphing the actual number of second- and third-generation children found in various censuses.

6. The Appendix estimates a net reproduction rate for Italian immigrant women in 1910 to be 2.6; using the same sources and methods discussed there, the comparable estimate for East European Jewish women is 1.8. For both Scandinavians and Germans, it is 1.6.

7. On the rates of American Jewish intermarriage across the 20th century, see, for example, Sidney Goldstein, "Profile of American Jewry: Insights from the 1990 National Jewish Population Survey," *American Jewish Yearbook 1992* (New York: 1992), 77–173. For the impact on offspring, see Joel Perlmann, "The American Jewish Periphery: An Overview" (Levy Economics Institute of Bard College Working Paper No. 473) (August 2006), online at www.levy.org/pubs/wp_473.pdf, Table 2 (accessed 4 Aug. 2010).

8. Susan Cott Watkins (ed.), *After Ellis Island: Newcomers and Natives in the 1910 Census* (New York: 1994), 378, 384 (Tables B1 and B2).

9. Using Watkins (ed.), ibid., one cannot estimate the NRR for second-generation Italians. However, for second-generation Irish and Germans that year, I estimate .9 and 1.3 (calculated in the Appendix). Even if the relevant Italian rates had been as low as .8, the product of first- and second-generation NRRs would still have reached 2.0.

10. Jay Weinstein and Vijayan R. Pillai, *Demography: The Science of Population* (Boston: 2001), 137, 142.

11. Susan Carter, et al. (eds.), *Historical Statistics of the United States: Earliest Times to the Present* (New York: 2006), vol. 1, part A, series Ab793.

12. Watkins (ed.), *After Ellis Island*, 378.

Talking Jewish: The "Ethnic English" of American Jews

Sarah Bunin Benor and Steven M. Cohen
(HEBREW UNION COLLEGE-JEWISH INSTITUTE OF RELIGION)

Research on ethnic groups in the United States has pointed to language as an important element of ethnic distinctiveness.[1] Immigrants and other non-native English speakers may use their native languages alone or in conjunction with English, and those who learn English may speak it with influences from their native language in their accent and grammar. But even in families that have been using English for several generations, Americans of African, Latin American, and Native American descent continue to distinguish themselves linguistically through qualitative and quantitative differences in grammatical structures, pronunciations, and words.[2] To what extent do American Jews follow this pattern? What peculiarities of verbal communication exist, if at all, among Jews? How do such linguistic markers vary according to communication networks and social contexts? What do these markers tell us about social and religious differences among Jews and between Jews and other Americans? This paper explores these questions using data from a large-scale survey we conducted in 2008.

The presence and persistence of a Jewish version of "ethnic English" would be somewhat surprising for a number of reasons. First, it has been about a century, and four to five generations, since the peak of the massive migration of East European Yiddish-speaking Jews to the United States. In the interim, Jews have become fluent in American language and culture. Like other immigrant groups, Jews underwent substantial linguistic, cultural, and social assimilation. They achieved the highest rates of educational attainment of any veteran American religious or ethnic group, surpassing even such socially prestigious groups as the Episcopalians.[3] They dispersed geographically and underwent massive integration of their social networks, marked by deep declines in both in-group friendship and in-group marriage.[4]

Another reason that a distinct Jewish English, reserved for in-group communication, would be surprising is that many Yiddish-origin words have become part of the general American lexicon. As our data suggest, terms such as "klutz," "kvetch," "shpiel" and "mazel tov" are widely known among American non-Jews, with words such as "maven," "mensch," and "shmutz" not far behind.

Third, not all Jews in America are descended from Yiddish-speakers. Before, during, and after the massive East European migration, Jewish immigrants also entered the United States from Central and Western Europe, the Balkans, and the Middle East. These immigrants spoke German, Hungarian, Ladino (Judeo-Spanish), Arabic, and other languages. More recently, American Jewry has absorbed immigrants who speak several other languages, including Russian, Farsi (Persian), Israeli Hebrew, Latin American Spanish, and French. Although the preponderant element is still of East European descent, American Jewry is actually quite heterogeneous. What kind of common linguistic idiosyncrasies could possibly characterize such a linguistically diverse ethnic group?

Based on these considerations, one might think it unlikely that Jews today would use nonstandard grammar, accented English, or distinctive words. At the same time, some degree of linguistic distinctiveness of Jews is to be expected. Jews in the aggregate remain socially cohesive and culturally distinct in several ways. Compared to other "white" immigrant groups, Jews display distinctive patterns of residence, employment, education, social class composition, family formation, and politics.[5] For example, Jewish voters are disproportionately affiliated with the Democratic party and express liberal views on a number of social issues. While there are of course rural Jews, working-class Jews, and Jewish Republicans, the trends are overwhelmingly in certain directions.

Of course, Jews are also religiously distinct. The majority of American Jews have some religious education, including at least minimal exposure to liturgical Hebrew. Although weekly synagogue attendance remains low, the majority of American Jews do participate at least a few times a year in religious ritual in which Hebrew plays a prominent role.[6] Moreover, despite the diversity of geographic origins, Eastern Europe looms large in the Jewish imagination, as we can see in the popularity of "Jewish" foods such as gefilte fish and blintzes, as well as in the revival of klezmer music. It is possible that Yiddish-inflected speech has gained some currency even among Jews with no Yiddish-speaking ancestry. Finally, many Jews have some connection to the state of Israel, both in their ideological attachments and, more concretely, in visits they have made. The modern Hebrew spoken there may have an impact on the speech of American Jews.

In short, we have several reasons to believe that American Jews might have distinctive linguistic practices. They are connected biographically or culturally to three linguistic domains that have the potential to leave marks: East European Yiddish, modern Israeli Hebrew, and the lexicon of the religious Jew: the Hebrew/Aramaic literature of Jewish biblical and rabbinic liturgy. In addition, we might expect that Jews, like members of other minority groups, would be motivated to tailor their speech patterns as they align themselves with some people and distinguish themselves from others.[7]

In this paper, we look closely at the use of Hebrew and Yiddish words (such as *macher*, *keppie*, *shmutz*, *davka*, and *balagan*), as well as Yiddish-origin syntactic constructions (such as "she has what to say" and "are you coming to us for dinner?"). As we will show, Jews talk to each other in ways that significantly differ from their communications with non-Jews. We found numerous words used by large numbers of Jews and only small numbers of non-Jews, including *nu, macher, naches, bashert, keppie,* and *heimish.*

We may take this research question a step further: if linguistic features serve to distinguish Jews from others by delineating or reflecting social boundaries that circumscribe the Jewish population, they may also serve to differentiate Jews internally. That is, Jews with different social and religious orientations may distinguish themselves from one another by means of differential use of certain linguistic items.

We began this research with several hypotheses concerning which Jews would use more Hebrew- and Yiddish-origin words and constructions. We expected more distinctive in-group language among Jews who are more religiously observant, Jews who have more Jewish friends, Jews who have spent more time in Israel, and Jews who are closer to the generation of immigration. Given the concentration of these and other factors among the Orthodox and the semi-segregated communities they inhabit, we also hypothesized that Orthodox identity per se might exert an additional impact upon language use. In fact, our hypotheses turned out to be correct: all of these factors correlate with knowing and using distinctively Jewish linguistic elements.

To be sure, not all features bear identical relationships with their underlying predictors. Thus, one additional task of this research is to discern different clusters of Jewish linguistic features that may relate differently to the following factors: generation since immigration; Israel travel; religious engagement; in-group friendship; and Orthodox identity. Some Jews may understand the sentence, "*Davka,* a *macher* like you shouldn't be *staying by* a *kvetch* like him"; but depending on their histories and social identities, it may turn out (and it does) that some Jews use some of these words and syntactic constructions while others use others.

Although the questions of Jewish/non-Jewish difference and intra-Jewish difference are interesting in their own right, our purpose is to go beyond making a descriptive contribution. We also seek to demonstrate the validity and usefulness of the analysis of sociolinguistic variation as a way of exploring the past and present of American Jewry.[8]

Since the early studies in the 1960s, Jews have been only marginally present in research on sociolinguistic variation.[9] William Labov's study of the Lower East Side included detailed linguistic analysis of 45 Jewish participants (23 Orthodox and 22 Conservative or Reform, all native English-speakers), compared with Italian Americans, African Americans, and others.[10] He found that Jews had slightly different pronunciations of certain vowels, such as the "a" in "bad" and the "o" in "coffee." Jews were also compared with members of other ethnic groups in studies of vowel pronunciation in Boston, Grand Rapids (Michigan), and Montreal, and similar ethnic differences were found there.[11] These studies focused only on vowel pronunciation, as that has been the main focus of research on sociolinguistic variation.

A few studies have looked at other elements of Jews' language, such as the use of Hebrew and Yiddish words,[12] the pronunciation of Hebrew words,[13] the pronunciation of /t/ at the end of words,[14] and aggressive or argumentative discourse styles.[15] All of these previous studies of Jews and language necessarily used a small sample, never larger than a few dozen participants. We set out to add to this foundation of research by investigating Jewish language use on a much larger scale.

As this previous research shows, the ideal way to analyze language variation is to provide individuals with microphones, record them in a variety of situations, transcribe their speech, and analyze it at the micro-level. The problem with this technique is that it is extremely time consuming. If we wanted to analyze the language use of 20,000 Jews, we would need to spend several years following people around with microphones and even more time analyzing the recordings. A more practical way to obtain sociolinguistic data on a large scale is through a questionnaire.

While a few studies have used this method fruitfully,[16] it is still not common in sociolinguistics, because individuals' actual language use may differ from their reported language use. They may not be sure whether they pronounce the Festival of Booths as "SUK-kiss" or "soo-COAT," or they may believe it is better to say "synagogue" even though they usually say "shul." They may assume that they use "macher" and "shpiel," but an actual analysis of their speech might indicate that they do not. In short, the survey method may be quite good in capturing attitudes about language, but it is not a completely accurate representation of individuals' language use. Despite these limitations, we believe that a survey can give us valuable information about correlations between reported language use and social dimensions. Based on our observation of Jewish language use in situ, we believe that the results we found in the survey do represent actual trends.

Method

In the summer of 2008, we fielded a web-based survey, using the online survey tool www.SurveyMonkey.com. We e-mailed invitations to participate in "The Survey of American Jewish Language" to 326 of Benor's acquaintances, as well as to several e-mail lists of Jews and linguists (numbering more than 1,000), and we invited recipients of our invitation to pass it on to Jews and non-Jews in the United States and Canada. By the end of November 2008, nearly 44,000 respondents had completed the questionnaire. The data set upon which this analysis is based consists of 31,500 respondents, divided between 25,611 Jews and 5,889 non-Jews. We restricted this sample to current U.S. residents who grew up in the United States or Canada (we received responses from around the world; less than 1 percent of the respondents grew up in Canada), and who spoke only English before the age of 15.

In every respect, this is a non-random sample. We had little influence on who received the secondary or subsequent invitations, and no way of determining the proportion of invitees who actually responded. Because so many of the initial invitees were Jewish and many of the non-Jewish respondents received the survey invitation from a Jewish acquaintance, the sample of non-Jews includes an overrepresentation of non-Jews with Jewish friends. In comparing the characteristics of the Jewish members of the sample with the 2001 National Jewish Population Survey (NJPS),[17] we find several variations. This sample underrepresents those in the 18–34 age range and overrepresents those in the age range of 55–74. Also overrepresented are women, the married, and the highly educated (that is, those with graduate degrees). There is also overrepresentation of those who claim moderate to high levels of attachment to being Jewish or who possess several characteristics indicative of Jewish engagement, including affiliation with a synagogue or having spent time in Israel. At the same time, the sample's distributions of denominational identity and childhood Jewish schooling are very similar to those found in the 2001 NJPS.

These patterns lead us to believe that, among both Jews and non-Jews, we attracted a sample that uses distinctively Jewish linguistic features somewhat more than the respective universes from which they were drawn. That said, we note that our analysis relies upon comparisons across various clusters of Jewish linguistic elements and upon relationships between social dimensions (for instance, friendship patterns or synagogue attendance) and linguistic patterns (use of certain types of words and phrases). Such relationships tend to be less sensitive to sample bias, and we have tried to limit our substantive inferences to major tendencies in the data analysis. In any event, these results need to be treated with some caution owing to the voluntary nature of the sampling and the resultant biases that emerged.

The Measures

The first analysis we conducted correlates whether the speaker is Jewish with his or her use of Hebrew and Yiddish words and Yiddish-influenced grammatical constructions. The independent variable here is based on the question: "Do you consider yourself Jewish?" The options were "yes," "no," "I was raised Jewish, but I don't consider myself Jewish now," and "I was not raised Jewish, but I have some Jewish heritage." Those giving "yes" answers were distinguished from all the others.

The subsequent analysis of intra-Jewish variation looked at a number of social and religious variables. After extensive preliminary analysis, we selected five social dimensions (independent variables) with the greatest impact on the likelihood of using a variety of Jewish linguistic features (dependent variables). When several conceptually related measures were available, we settled on the single measure that best captured the predictive power of a specific domain. One reason to focus on a single measure within a possible cluster of alternatives is that, in multiple regression analysis, the inclusion of several empirically related indicators dilutes the apparent impact of the domain from which they are all drawn. For example, ritual practice, synagogue attendance, and denominational identity (Orthodox, Reform, Conservative, etc.) all relate to the domain of religiosity; including all such measures would dilute the apparent effect of religiosity. We selected synagogue attendance to represent the domain of Jewish religious engagement because of its greater predictive power than the alternatives. The *Synagogue Attendance* measure codes respondents according to the frequency of attendance at Jewish religious services, aside from life-cycle events: never (22 percent), high holidays (17 percent), a few times a year (25 percent), monthly (14 percent), and several times a month or more (24 percent), coded 0 to 4.

We call the second independent variable *Generational Cohort*, a measure that combines generational status and age in equal proportion. There are empirical and theoretical reasons for combining these two variables. First, age and generation are highly correlated in this sample ($r = 0.49$), as in the American Jewish community. Second, Jews of a given age are likely to interact with members of a certain generational cohort even if they themselves are generationally linked to a different cohort. On the basis of the birthplace of the respondents' parents and grandparents (United States/Canada or elsewhere), we created a five-point generational status variable that ranged from the children of two immigrant parents to those whose parents and all four grandparents were born in North America. We created a seven-point age scale for age categories ranging from 18–24 to 75+. We divided each of these two components by the respective number of categories (five for generation, seven for age) and totaled the two components. The lowest values on the resulting index are those with the most "advanced" generational status (entirely North American ancestry for at least two generations) and most youthful age (18–24); the other extreme are those aged 75 or older who are the children of two immigrant parents.

Jewish Friends also combines two items that are highly correlated (r = 0.40). We asked about the proportion of close friends (currently) who are Jewish and about the proportion of close Jewish friends who "are highly engaged in Jewish life." The response categories for the two questions were the same: none, some, about half, most, all or almost all. We assigned them interval codes and totaled the two items to form the single two-item index that measures the presence of Jewish friends, particularly those highly engaged in Jewish life.

The *Israel Visits* measure consists of two items: number of visits to Israel, and time spent there. The resultant scale had four options: none (36 percent), one (26 percent), two (11 percent), three or more (17 percent), or "lived there for 10 months or more" (10 percent).

Finally, *Orthodox Identity* is a dichotomous (0/1) measure to indicate those who self-identified as Orthodox (including modern Orthodox and "Black Hat") in terms of their current denomination (8 percent of the respondents), or not.

Our dependent variables consist of indices that draw upon questions regarding the use of certain words and constructions in respondents' speech. The questions about Hebrew and Yiddish words allowed for respondents to indicate whether they use the word with all speakers or only with Jews; the questions about Yiddish-influenced grammatical constructions simply asked if they use the phrase at least occasionally. For purposes of scale construction, we re-coded the items as dichotomies, distinguishing those who use each element from those who do not.

The following analysis utilizes five indices of selected linguistic features. We constructed the indices initially on the basis of a factor analysis, allowing us to determine which items empirically cluster together. We then made some adjustments to our scales in accordance with an analysis of the individual items and their relationships with the independent variables, including their use by non-Jews (see Table 1 below). The sorting-out process produced the following five indices:

Jewish Yiddish
1. *nu* (well?)
2. *macher* (big shot)
3. *bashert* (predestined match)
4. *takeh* (really)
5. *naches* (pride)
6. *heimish* (homey)

We call this scale "Jewish Yiddish" because it consists of Yiddish words largely unused by the vast majority of non-Jews even in this voluntary sample—on average, only about 7 percent of the non-Jews use the words in this scale.

Crossover Yiddish
1. *mensch* (good person)
2. *maven* (expert)
3. *mazel tov* (congratulations)
4. *kvetch* (complain)
5. *shmutz* (dirt)
6. *keppie* (head, usually in child-directed speech)
7. *I don't know from that* (I don't know about that; cf. Yiddish *ikh veys nisht fun dem*, where *fun* means both "from" and "about")

The Crossover Yiddish scale includes items that are used more frequently by the non-Jewish respondents than the Jewish Yiddish items, but not as frequently as "klutz" and "enough already."

Yinglish
1. "She *has what to say*" (has something to say; cf. Yiddish *hot vos tsu zogn*)
2. "She's staying *by us*" (at our place; cf. Yiddish *bay undz*)
3. "Are you coming *to us* for dinner?" (to our place; cf. Yiddish *tsu undz*)
4. "What do we *learn out* from this?" (learn, derive; cf. Yiddish *oyslernen*)

The Yinglish scale, as we call it, consists of four phrases bearing the influence of Yiddish syntax (with critical elements italicized). The critical elements are all direct translations from Yiddish syntax and, while perhaps understandable in English, are hardly characteristic of U.S.-born American English-speakers.

Israeli Hebrew
1. *yofi* (nice, great!)
2. *balagan* (mess, bedlam)
3. *yallah* (come on, let's go)
4. *ahalan* (hi)

The Israeli Hebrew scale consists of four words currently used in Israeli Hebrew. *Yallah* and *ahalan* are originally from Arabic, and *balagan* is originally from Russian and Yiddish.

Yeshivish
1. *chas v'shalom* (equivalent of "God forbid")
2. *leyn* (chant from the Torah)
3. *drash* (sermonic commentary)
4. *moadim l'simcha* (times of gladness—holiday greeting)
5. *hameyvin yavin* (those in the know will understand)
6. *kal vachomer* (a fortiori, all the more so)
7. *davka* (particularly)
8. *lav davka* (not necessarily)
9. *l'chatchila* (ab initio, before the fact)

The Yeshivish scale consists of words from Yiddish, Hebrew, and Aramaic that refer to religious concepts or terms used in rabbinic discourse. The term "Yeshivish," stemming from the name of the institution of traditional Jewish learning, is commonly used in the Orthodox community to refer to English that is highly influenced by Yiddish and the rabbinic lexicon.[18]

As we will demonstrate, not all distinctive Jewish linguistic features are created equal. With respect to the independent variables, each scale presents a different pattern or a distinctive set of relationships with generational cohort, Jewish friends, Israel visits, synagogue attendance, and Orthodox identity.

Findings

In answer to our first question—what peculiarities of verbal communication exist, if at all, among Jews?—we present a selection of words and expressions that were asked in our questionnaire of both Jewish and non-Jewish respondents, listing the percentage of Jews and non-Jews who report using each item. We incorporated most, but not all, of these items into the five linguistic indices we constructed. In addition, several words asked only of Jewish respondents (facilitated by the ability of the survey program to filter selected questions) were included in the Yeshivish index.

Several observations can be made about the use of these words and expressions among Jews and non-Jews. First, we find considerable variation among the items. More than 90 percent of the Jews in this sample use the terms *kvetch*, *mensch*, *klutz*, and *mazel tov*. At the same time, hardly any use the word *ahalan* (the Arabic-derived word used in colloquial Israeli Hebrew for "hi"), and almost as few use the expression, "What do we *learn out* from this?"

In addition, the items used most frequently by Jews are used relatively frequently by non-Jews, whereas the items less frequently used by Jews are hardly used even by the non-Jews who voluntarily participated in this study. Thus, of the group of items used by 75 percent or more of the Jews (appearing in the upper part of Table 1), the frequency of use among non-Jews ranges from 44 to 96 percent. In contrast, in the next group of items in Table 1, those used by 57 to 71 percent of Jews, the frequency of use among non-Jews ranges only from 6 to 12 percent. Thus, Jews' distinctive lexicon is larger, embracing Yiddish-derived words and syntax as well as words derived from contemporary Israeli Hebrew, the liturgy, and Jewish text study. At the same time, we also see that some items seem to have been absorbed into general American English (especially "klutz"), with more non-Jews reporting use of certain Yiddish-derived expressions ("enough already," "money shmoney") than Jews.

To answer our second question—in what ways does the use of distinctive language vary among American Jews?—we performed regression analyses for each of the five scales of Jewish linguistic features. We explored how each is associated with generational cohort, Jewish friends, Israel visits, synagogue attendance, and Orthodox identity. Table 2 presents the results of those analyses.

For readers unfamiliar with multiple regression analysis, we offer the following explanation. The numerical entries in Table 2 represent the predictive power of each independent variable controlling for all of the other independent variables, that is to

Table 1. Use of Words and Expressions in American English by Jewish and Non-Jewish Respondents (entries are percentages and are ordered in descending order for the Jewish respondents)

Word or expression	Non-Jews	Jews
mazel tov	66	98
klutz	96	98
mensch	48	93
kvetch	58	92
shmutz	54	85
shpiel	66	83
Enough already!	86	81
maven	44	75
naches	9	71
macher	9	68
bashert	6	66
nu?	12	65
heimish	6	59
keppie	6	57
Are you coming to us for dinner?	8	34
I don't know from that.	20	30
tachlis	3	26
Money, *shmoney*.	39	26
She's staying by us.	10	23
I'm living here 10 years already.	13	23
takeh	1	22
yofi	1	22
balagan	1	20
yalla	2	17
davka	1	17
chas v'shalom	3	15
I want that you should see this.	14	12
She has what to say.	8	12
Such a nice car he drives.	14	10
What do we learn out from this?	4	8
ahalan	1	5

say, holding the others constant. A high number indicates that the independent variable is strongly predictive of that dependent variable. We also report the explained variance (or the R-square) for each model. This statistic tells us the extent to which all five independent variables, taken together, can accurately predict the given dependent variable (that is, each of the five scales of Jewish linguistic features). In a perfect model, R-square would be 1.00.

Talking Jewish: The "Ethnic English" of American Jews

Table 2. Regression Analyses for Five Scales of Jewish Linguistic Features

	Jewish Yiddish*	Crossover Yiddish	Yinglish	Israeli Hebrew	Yeshivish
Generational cohort	0.34	0.14	–0.09	–0.13	–0.07
Jewish friends	0.24	0.20	0.16	0.10	0.10
Israel visits	0.16	0.00 (n.s.)	0.06	0.54	0.32
Synagogue attendance	0.14	0.05	0.05	0.07	0.26
Orthodox identity	0.00 (n.s.)	–0.07	0.11	0.05	0.22
Adjusted R-square	0.31	0.08	0.07	0.41	0.44

Population: U.S. and Canadian-born Jews, age 18+, living in the United States. Minimum N=24,644. Entries are unstandardized regression coefficients. All relationships are statistically significant at the p<.01 level unless otherwise indicated.

*As a reminder, we summarize the scales here:

Jewish Yiddish = Yiddish words used by many Jews but by few non-Jews; for instance, *nu, bashert*.
Crossover Yiddish = Yiddish terms used by many Jews and by some non-Jews; for instance, *mazel tov, maven*.
Yinglish = English-language phrases with syntax influenced by Yiddish; for instance, *"staying by us."*
Israeli Hebrew = Hebrew words used in English speech; for instance, *yofi, balagan*.
Yeshivish = Words used in traditional religious circles; for instance, *drash, davka*.

Reading down the first column of entries, generational cohort emerges as the strongest predictor (coefficient = 0.34) of *Jewish Yiddish*, words much more common among Jews than non-Jews. In addition, we find that Jewish friends, Israel visits, and synagogue attendance also exert noticeable effects. In more colloquial terms, the frequency with which respondents report using such words as *naches, heimish*, and *bashert* rises with age and generational proximity to the immigrant generation. It also rises with the number of Jewish friends, the frequency of synagogue attendance, and having a history of visits to Israel.

The moderate to strong relationships with generational cohort, Jewish friends, synagogue attendance, and Israel visits testify to the power of social networks in influencing both the knowledge of distinctive Jewish language and the readiness or opportunity to use such language. The results say, in effect: if you are older and closer to the immigrant generation, and if you have many Jewish friends, go to synagogue frequently, and repeatedly visit Israel, then you are the type of person who has had the opportunity to pick up many Hebrew and Yiddish words, and you have the circle of friends and associates who are also likely to use and understand them.

This summary statement applies only to words that have largely remained embedded within the Jewish population. It does not apply as readily to those words that have managed to "escape" to the wider American population. The patterns of association of the independent variables with what we call *Crossover Yiddish*—words that are more widely used by non-Jews—differ strikingly. In fact, the relationships for these words with the independent variables are much weaker, meaning that given the same information, it is much harder to predict who uses (or doesn't use) Crossover Yiddish than to predict who uses (or doesn't use) Jewish Yiddish. We find that the independent variables explain nearly four times as much variance for Jewish Yiddish as they do for Crossover Yiddish (R-square =.31 for Jewish Yiddish versus .08 for Crossover Yiddish).

For Crossover Yiddish, the strongest predictor is Jewish friends, followed by generational cohort. Synagogue attendance and Israel visits exert hardly any influence, and Orthodox identity actually has a negative correlation; that is, Orthodox Jews are less likely than non-Orthodox Jews to use words such as "maven" and "shpiel." When we look at words that have been picked up by non-Jews, we see that participation in Jewish religious life and even Jewish social circles are not as critical for predicting who uses these words.

What is most interesting here is that even those variables with the strongest relationships with Crossover Yiddish evidence weaker relationships than we saw with Jewish Yiddish. A prime example is generational cohort, with a regression coefficient of 0.34 for Jewish Yiddish and only 0.14 for Crossover Yiddish. In other words, advancing birth cohort and generation from immigration are associated with rather significant drops in the use of words such as *nu* and *bashert*, but they have a smaller impact on the frequency of the use of words such as *maven* and *shmutz*, which have entered the larger American lexicon.

The conclusion we draw is that, in the case of words that are used by sizable numbers of other Americans, the frequency of use hardly varies among American Jews, as opposed to non-Crossover words. If you don't have to be Jewish to say "mazel tov," then among Jews, you don't have to be very Jewishly engaged (or have a very Jewishly identified social circle) to say "mazel tov" or other words that have crossed over into the larger culture. The density and nature of Jewish social circles affect how frequently Jews use the words from the internal Jewish lexicon, but such traits hardly predict the Jew who will use those words that are generally known and available to non-Jewish Americans.

Quite another pattern can be seen with respect to our third scale, *Yinglish*, denoting the use of Yiddish-influenced syntax in English. Here, the major predictor is Jewish friends, with Orthodox identity exerting a small impact as well. One other statistical relationship with respect to Yinglish is noteworthy: the reversal of the relationship with generational cohort. We have a small but significant negative coefficient (- 0.09), which takes on greater significance when seen in contrast with the positive coefficient that emerges in the analysis of Jewish Yiddish (0.34). Whereas Jewish Yiddish declines with the advance of birth cohort and generation (this is the significance of a positive coefficient), the opposite is true, albeit to a lesser extent, with respect to Yinglish. In other words, younger Jews and those generationally farther removed from immigration are actually more likely to use Yiddish-influenced syntax than their elders and those closer to the immigrant generation—a reversal of the pattern for Yiddish words in general.

We can only speculate on the reason for this reversal. Of note is the slight positive effect of Orthodoxy (0.11), which explains part, but not all, of the tendency for younger age and more advanced generation to be associated with greater use of Yinglish. Phrases such as "are you staying by us?" and "what do we learn out from this?" are common in Orthodox circles but uncommon among children of Yiddish-speaking immigrants. These Yiddish-influenced phrases have become a marker of Orthodox identity, and Jews who become Orthodox as adults often incorporate them into their linguistic repertoire.[19]

The negative coefficient for generational cohort is likely related to the growth of Orthodoxy in the American Jewish population; younger Jews are more likely to be Orthodox. In our non-random sample, Orthodox respondents constitute 4 percent of Jews aged 65 and over, but fully 15 percent of those aged 18–34. In addition, our data suggest that young Orthodox Jews are more likely than their Orthodox elders to have Orthodox friends. We asked respondents to estimate the number of their close Jewish friends who "are highly engaged in Jewish life." While 54 percent of the Orthodox respondents aged 65+ said that most of their Jewish friends are highly engaged Jews, the number grew with youthfulness, such that fully 80 percent of Orthodox Jews aged 18–34 made such a claim. Over time, Orthodox Jews are both growing in numbers and increasingly enclosed within social circles of other Jews sharing their commitment to Jewish engagement. Consistent with this explanation, we also find that having Jewish friends, particularly those engaged in Jewish life, is the strongest predictor of the use of Yinglish.

A related yet distinctive fourth pattern of relationships emerges when we look at the factors associated with *Israeli Hebrew*. Of relevance here is the fact that, in recent years, many young Jews have chosen to spend either a semester or a year in Israel between the ages of 14 and 25. This includes very significant numbers of Orthodox young people who spend a year following the end of high school in yeshiva programs in Israel, as well as non-Orthodox Jews who attend college or post-college year-abroad programs in Israeli universities and other institutions. Although these American students tend to interact mostly with other Americans during their stay, they are also exposed to Hebrew-speaking Israelis and to Americans who are proficient in Hebrew. It is no surprise, then, that Israel visits exerts a powerful impact upon the use of Hebrew words (coefficient = 0.54, the largest in the table).

As with Yinglish, and unlike Jewish Yiddish, the use of Israeli Hebrew is more common among youthful cohorts and those farther removed from the generation of immigration (note the coefficient of - 0.13). This is related not only to the growing popularity of visits to Israel, but also to the increasing importance of Israeli Hebrew in American Jewish education. When we look at respondents' reported proficiency in spoken Hebrew, we see a striking age trend. Among Jews aged 18–34, 52 percent say they understand at least some spoken Hebrew, compared with only 15 percent of Jews over the age of 74. Based on these trends, we can predict that Israeli Hebrew will likely continue to have an impact on the distinctive English of American Jews.

Turning to the final linguistic scale, *Yeshivish*, we see the best overall fit of the model (R square =.44), meaning that the independent variables in combination do a better job of predicting the use of terms such as *chas v'shalom* and *davka* than the other scales. This scale represents a group of words from Yiddish and from textual Hebrew/Aramaic that are commonly used by Orthodox Jews. But as the regression analysis shows, it is not just Orthodox identity that has an impact on the use of these words. Synagogue attendance has an even greater impact, and Israel visits still more. It is not surprising that Jews who attend religious services regularly and who spend time in Israel (often in religious-oriented programs) are more likely to learn words in the religious domain: these are contexts in which such words are likely to be used more frequently. In addition, Jews who are Orthodox, attend religious services regularly, and/or spend time in Israel are also likely to have strong language skills in the domain of biblical and rabbinic text study. There are strong correlations between all of these variables and respondents' self-ratings of their proficiency in biblical Hebrew and talmudic Aramaic. Tables 3 and 4 give examples of the correlations between textual language proficiency and the use of linguistic features.

While synagogue attendance and Israel visits have strong effects, and Jewish friends has a moderate effect, we see that generational cohort has a slight negative effect. As with the Yinglish and Israeli Hebrew scales, Yeshivish words are more commonly used by younger Jews than by Jews closer to the generation of immigration. This scale offers more evidence for a trend toward more distinctive language use among younger, and especially Orthodox, Jews as well as others highly engaged in Jewish religious life. It also offers suggestive sociolinguistic evidence for the observation that Orthodox Jews have been "sliding Right," that is, becoming stricter in their observance, more socially insular, and more culturally distinct from their non-Jewish neighbors.[20]

In sum, this analysis points to a number of different types of Jewish linguistic features that correlate with different types of Jewish engagement. The five scales and five independent variables that we have identified offer a glimpse into the linguistic diversity of American Jews, but they only begin to touch upon what may be called the mapping of the Jewish sociolinguistic terrain.

Table 3. Correlation between Jews Reporting Comprehension of Biblical Hebrew and Use of the Phrase "Chas V'Shalom"

Biblical Hebrew comprehension	% who use "chas v'shalom"	N
Excellent	71	991
Good	52	2139
Fair	24	3823
Poor	8	8023
None	4	9460

Table 4. Correlation between Jews Reporting Comprehension of Talmudic Aramaic and Use of the Phrase "Kal Vachomer" ("All the More So")

Talmudic Aramaic comprehension	% who use "kal vachomer"	N
Excellent	82	94
Good	69	434
Fair	45	1,397
Poor	15	3,426
None	1	18,705

Conclusion

Do American Jews speak differently from their non-Jewish neighbors? According to our analysis of the use of Yiddish and Hebrew words and phrases in a nonrandom sample of American Jews and non-Jews, the answer is yes. We found that most of the items we tested are much more common among Jewish respondents. In addition, we found what seems to be a trend toward more distinctive language use among younger Jews: age and generation have a negative effect on many of the linguistic items we tested. An entire century after the massive wave of immigration from Eastern Europe, American Jews seem to be increasing their use of some distinctive linguistic features.

The age trend is not the only evidence for increasingly distinct language on the part of some American Jews. We asked the survey's Jewish respondents: "In the past 10–15 years, would you say that the number of Yiddish-derived and Hebrew-derived words you use within English speech has increased, decreased, or remained the same?" Fifty-one percent responded "increased a lot" or "increased a little," and only 7 percent responded "decreased a little" or "decreased a lot." Many Jews are now using Hebrew and Yiddish words for things they used to refer to in English, such as *shul* for synagogue and *balagan* for "mess." And a sizable percentage of Jews have more opportunities to use religious-oriented words such as *leyn* and *chas v'shalom*, as they are participating more in home-based Jewish ritual and in synagogue-based communities.[21] At the same time as fourth- and fifth-generation American Jews remain integrated socially and culturally in American society, many Jews are distinguishing themselves religiously and linguistically from their non-Jewish neighbors.

Among Jews, our analysis identifies a number of social and religious characteristics that predict greater use of various distinctive linguistic features, including age, percentage of friends who are engaged in Jewish life, visits to Israel, synagogue attendance, and Orthodox identity. A common thread connecting these social variables is associations. In synagogue holiday celebrations, on Israel programs, and in Orthodox communities, Jews come into contact with Jews of similar backgrounds and orientations. When they speak, they can use certain types of Jewish words and expressions and expect that their interlocutors will understand and reciprocate with similarly distinctive language.

Sometimes these contexts of interaction serve as opportunities for language learning. A recent college graduate who spends a year in Jerusalem studying at the Pardes Institute of Jewish Studies may learn some Israeli Hebrew and a good deal of textual Hebrew and Aramaic and may begin to incorporate many of those words into his English speech. A middle-aged Jew who begins to attend her Reconstructionist synagogue more frequently may learn to refer to chanting Torah as *leyning* and to the sermon as the *drash*. And a pensioner who moves to a retirement community may hear Yiddish words such as *naches* and *heimish* from his new friends, and he may begin to incorporate them into his own speech. The social variables we discuss in this paper represent not only factors correlating with linguistic distinctiveness but also opportunities for language socialization.

It is important to note that the distinctively Jewish linguistic features we have observed and tested are mostly at the surface level of lexicon, rather than at the structural level of syntax and phonology. This fact differentiates Jewish American English from African American English, Latino English, and other ethnic varieties that make ample use of distinctive grammar and pronunciation. At the same time, there is some evidence that Jews around the country are more likely than their non-Jewish neighbors to use elements of a New York accent,[22] distinctive patterns of discourse,[23] and intonation influenced by Yiddish and Talmud study.[24] These non-lexical areas of language call for further research.[25]

The use of particular linguistic features is often a conscious act of identity. Individuals of every ethnic group regularly make decisions about which pronunciations, grammatical structures, and words to use, and these decisions enable them to construct their identity in relation to their ethnic group, other ethnic groups, and various subgroups. Jews are no exception. They use words and expressions from Hebrew and Yiddish not only to indicate that they are Jews, but also to indicate that they are certain types of Jews. These sociolinguistic decisions are meaningful in consort with other symbolic practices, including associations, religious and social activities, dress and hair styles, culinary habits, home decoration, and musical preferences. By looking in depth at language and other cultural practices, we can gain a better understanding of contemporary American Jews.

Notes

We gratefully acknowledge the assistance of Judith Veinstein, Marion Lev Cohen, and Roberta Benor, as well as the editors of this volume. Our thanks also to the dozens of people who helped us refine the survey tool and to the tens of thousands of survey respondents.

1. For overviews, see Rosina Lippi-Green, *English with an Accent: Language, Ideology and Discrimination in the United States* (London: 1997); Joshua Fishman (ed.), *Handbook of Language and Ethnic Identity* (New York: 2001); Carmen Fought, "Ethnicity," in *Handbook of Language Variation and Change*, ed. J.K. Chambers, Peter Trudgill, and Natalie Schilling-Estes (Malden, Mass.: 2002), 444–472; idem, *Language and Ethnicity* (Cambridge: 2006); Janina Brutt-Griffler and Catherine Evans Davies (eds.), *English and Ethnicity* (New York: 2006); Walt Wolfram and Natalie Schilling-Estes, *American English*, 2nd ed. (Oxford: 2008).

2. For black English, see, for example, William Labov, *Language in the Inner City: Studies in the Black English Vernacular* (Philadelphia: 1972); John Baugh, *Black Street Speech: Its History, Structure and Survival* (Austin: 1983); John R. Rickford, *African American Vernacular English: Features, Evolution, Educational Implications* (Oxford: 1999); John Russell Rickford and Russell John Rickford, *Spoken Soul: The Story of Black English* (New York: 2000); Lisa Green, *African American English: A Linguistic Introduction* (Cambridge: 2002).

For Latin-American English, see, for example, Anna Celia Zentella, *Growing Up Bilingual* (Malden, Mass.: 1997); Carmen Fought, *Chicano English in Context* (New York: 2003); Norma Mendoza-Denton, *Homegirls: Language and Cultural Practice among Latina Youth Gangs* (Oxford: 2008).

For Native American English, see, for example, William L. Leap, *American Indian English* (Salt Lake City: 1993); Natalie Schilling-Estes, "Constructing Ethnicity in Interaction," *Journal of Sociolinguistics* 8, no. 2 (2004), 163–195.

3. See, for example, Pew Forum on Religion & Public Life, "U.S. Religious Landscape Survey" (Philadelphia: 2008), online at http://religions.pewforum.org/reports (accessed 9 Nov. 2009).

4. Steven M. Cohen, *Religiosity and Ethnicity: Jewish Identity Trends in the United States* (New York: 2002); idem, *A Tale of Two Jewries: The "Inconvenient Truth" for American Jews* (New York: 2006).

5. Steven M. Cohen and Charles S. Liebman, "Understanding American Jewish Liberalism," *Public Opinion Quarterly* 61, no. 3 (Fall 1997), 405–430; Steven M. Cohen, *Religion and the Public Square: Attitudes of American Jews in Comparative Perspective* (New York: 2000); Calvin Goldscheider, *Jewish Continuity and Change: Emerging Patterns in America* (Bloomington: 1986); Tom Smith, *Jewish Distinctiveness in America: A Statistical Portrait* (New York: 2005).

6. Pew Forum on Religion & Public Life, "U.S. Religious Landscape Survey."

7. The current trend in sociolinguistics is to view language use not only as reflecting social categories but also as helping to constitute them. See, for example, Robert B. Le Page and Andrée Tabouret-Keller, *Acts of Identity: Creole-Based Approaches to Language and Ethnicity* (Cambridge: 1985); Penelope Eckert, *Linguistic Variation as Social Practice* (Oxford: 2000); Nikolas Coupland, *Style: Language Variation and Identity* (Cambridge: 2007); Mary Bucholtz and Kira Hall, "Language and Identity," in *Companion to Linguistic Anthropology*, ed. Alessandro Duranti (Oxford: 2003), 369–394.

8. For an accessible introduction to sociolinguistics, see Ronald Wardhaugh, *An Introduction to Sociolinguistics* (Oxford: 1986). For a more comprehensive account, see Chambers, Trudgill, and Schilling-Estes (eds.), *Handbook of Language Variation and Change*.

9. See David L. Gold, "Jewish Intralinguistics as a Field of Study," *International Journal of the Sociology of Language* 30 (1981), 31–46; idem, "Jewish English," in *Readings in the Sociology of Jewish Languages*, ed. Joshua A. Fishman (Leiden: 1985), 280–298. Cf. Anna Verschik, "Jewish Russian and the Field of Ethnolect Study," *Language in Society* 36 (2007), 213–232.

10. William Labov, *The Social Stratification of English in New York City* (Washington, D.C.: 1966).

11. Martha Laferriere, "Ethnicity in Phonological Variation and Change," *Language* 55, no. 3 (Sept. 1979), 603–617; Rebecca Knack, "Ethnic Boundaries in Linguistic Variation," in *New Ways of Analyzing Sound Change*, ed. Penelope Eckert (New York: 1991), 251–272; Charles Boberg, "Ethnic Patterns in the Phonetics of Montreal English," *Journal of Sociolinguistics* 8, no. 4 (Oct. 2004), 538–568.

12. Sarah Benor, "Yavnish: A Linguistic Study of the Orthodox Jewish Community at Columbia University," *Iggrot ha'Ari: Columbia University Student Journal of Jewish Scholarship* 1, no. 2 (1998), 8–50; idem, "Loan Words in the English of Modern Orthodox Jews: Hebrew or Yiddish?" in *Proceedings of the Berkeley Linguistic Society's 25th Annual Meeting, 1999*, ed. Steve S. Chang, Lily Liaw, and Josef Ruppenhofer (Berkeley: 2000), 287–298; idem, "Second Style Acquisition: The Linguistic Socialization of Newly Orthodox Jews" (Ph.D. diss., Stanford University, 2004); Cynthia Goldin Bernstein, "Representing Jewish Identity through English," in Brutt-Griffler and Davies (eds.), *English and Ethnicity*, 107–129; Ayala Fader, "Reclaiming Sacred Sparks: Linguistic Syncretism and Gendered Language Shift among Hasidic Jews in New York," *Journal of Linguistic Anthropology* 12, no. 1 (2007), 1–22.

13. Benor, "Second Style Acquisition"; Aliza Sacknowitz, "Linguistic Means of Orthodox Jewish Identity Construction: Phonological Features, Lexical Features, and the Situated Discourse" (Ph.D. diss., Georgetown University, 2007).

14. Sarah Bunin Benor, "Sounding Learned: The Gendered Use of /t/ in Orthodox Jewish English," in *Penn Working Papers in Linguistics: Selected Papers from NWAV* 29, ed. Daniel Ezra Johnson and Tara Sanchez (Philadelphia: 2001), 1–16; idem, *"Talmid Chachams and Tsedeykeses*: Language, Learnedness, and Masculinity among Orthodox Jews," *Jewish Social Studies* 11, no. 1 (2004), 147–170; Erez Levon, "Mosaic Identity and Style: Phonological Variation among Reform American Jews," *Journal of Sociolinguistics* 10 (2006), 185–205.

15. Deborah Tannen, "New York Jewish Conversational Style," *International Journal of the Sociology of Language* 30 (1981), 133–149; Deborah Schiffrin, "Jewish Argument as Sociability," *Language in Society* 13 (1984), 311–335.

16. Sylvie Dubois and Barbara Horvath, "When the Music Changes, You Change Too: Gender and Language Change in Cajun English," *Language Variation and Change* 11 (1999), 287–313; Sylvie Dubois and Negan Melançon, "Cajun Is Dead—Long Live Cajun: Shifting from a Linguistic to a Cultural Community," *Journal of Sociolinguistics* 1 (1997), 63–93;

Charles Boberg, "The North American Regional Vocabulary Survey: Renewing the Study of Lexical Variation in North American English," *American Speech* 80, no. 1 (2005), 22–60.

17. Laurence Kotler-Berkowitz, Steven M. Cohen, Jonathon Ament, Vivian Klaff, Frank Mott, and Danyelle Peckerman-Neuman, *The National Jewish Population Survey 2000–01: Strength, Challenge and Diversity in the American Jewish Population* (New York: 2003).

18. See Chaim Weiser, *Frumspeak: The First Dictionary of Yeshivish* (Northvale: 1995); Benor, "Second Style Acquisition."

19. Benor, "Second Style Acquisition."

20. Samuel Heilman, *Sliding to the Right: The Contest for the Future of American Jewish Orthodoxy* (Berkeley: 2006).

21. On newly Orthodox Jews, see Benor, "Second Style Acquisition," and references there. On non-Orthodox Jews becoming more engaged in religious life, see Paula Amann, *Journeys to a Jewish Life: Inspiring Stories from the Spiritual Journeys of American Jews* (Woodstock: 2007) and references there.

22. Knack, "Ethnic Boundaries in Linguistic Variation"; Laferriere, "Ethnicity in Phonological Variation and Change."

23. Tannen, "New York Jewish Conversational Style"; Schiffrin, "Jewish Argument as Sociability."

24. Benor, "Second Style Acquisition"; Samuel Heilman, "Sounds of Modern Orthodoxy: The Language of Talmud Study," in *Never Say Die! A Thousand Years of Yiddish in Jewish Life and Letters*, ed. Joshua A. Fishman (The Hague: 1981) 227–253.

25. In a paper geared toward a general audience, we report survey results about these linguistic features. See Sarah Bunin Benor and Steven M. Cohen, "Survey of American Jewish Language and Identity," Hebrew Union College—Jewish Institute of Religion, 2009," online at http://www.bjpa.org/Publications/details.cfm?PublicationID=3874 (accessed 8 Feb. 2010).

Old Casks in New Times: The Reshaping of American Jewish Identity in the 21st Century

Bethamie Horowitz
(NEW YORK UNIVERSITY)

Recently, the novelist Zadie Smith wrote about the advantages of "speaking in tongues," noting that, in their daily lives, large numbers of people "conjure contrasting voices and seek a synthesis between disparate things."[1] She described her realization that in the era following the election of Barack Obama, she feels more comfortable moving between the several identities that make up her own experience, and greater latitude in traversing the various settings and relationships in her life. She no longer feels that her background is at odds with mainstream social expectations. This previously alienating condition of mixed and multiple identities now turns out to hold great promise, at least in America.

Many American Jews will recognize this as familiar territory. In countries all over the world, Jews have long known the experience of being part of one's country while also feeling distinct from and not entirely embraced by the larger society. Yehudah Halevi wrote about living in the West while longing for the East; centuries later, Y.L. Gordon admonished readers to "be *a Jew in private* and an individual in public"—an example of the ongoing challenge for Jews in the modern period to figure out the interface between one's Jewishness and its status in the societal mainstream.

"Difference," that is, Jewishness, was traditionally regarded as a liability, a sociological fact that shaped the contours of identity dynamics at the individual level. The major change in contemporary America is that there is no longer a social stigma attached to being Jewish. At this point in American history, it is striking to look back and discover that, in 1937, Mordecai Kaplan observed that "the average Jew today is conscious of his Judaism as one is conscious of a diseased organ that gives notice of its existence by causing pain."[2] Yet by 2004, Joseph Lieberman, a self-avowed observant Jew, was the Democratic party's candidate for vice president of the United States. Over the course of the 20th century, the social boundaries defining the American mainstream shifted dramatically, and Jews, along with Italians, Irish, and other "white ethnics," became incorporated into the American establishment.[3]

Some of the changes are obvious, especially in popular culture, as any TV fan can attest. When Jerry Seinfeld went on the air in 1990, he was clearly Jewish (and "New Yorkish") without really talking about it. In presiding over *The Daily Show*, which many young Americans use as their main source of commentary about the news of the day, Jon Stewart is comfortably and proudly Jewish in public.

"Jewish," in fact, has become something of a plus, an accepted and even admired status rather than a social liability. Although this does not in itself contribute to "preventing intermarriage," it does account for the growing numbers of people with Jewish ancestry who have not tried to make that ancestry disappear, in contrast to the older pattern of Jews "marrying out" in order to escape the confines of being Jewish.

Yet admiration and acceptance pose a major challenge to what has been the standard Jewish "operating system" built on a set of premises that grew out of different societal conditions. For this reason, it makes sense to consider the state of contemporary Jewish identity. When being Jewish is no longer a stigmatized and (wholly) negative category in the eyes of the broader society, what becomes of the individual's Jewish identity? What is the "shelf life" of the individual's Jewish self-consciousness in this multicultural era in which Jews as a social category in America have largely come to be considered as part of the (white) mainstream?[4]

In this essay, I examine the relationship between ethnicity and identity, both as concepts and as phenomena, with special reference to the Jews in the United States. I begin by offering a brief semantic history of the terms, as "Jewish identity" has a particular usage that both intersects with and diverges from the general course of "ethnicity" or "identity"—both of which have also been changing. In particular, I consider the relationship between (structural) external markers of Jewish group or category membership or descent, on the one hand, and the internal experience of self-identity, attachment, and commitment, on the other.

Setting the Terms

No one talks about *Jewish identity* today without also being concerned about its retention. In other words, in contrast to words such as "ethnicity" or "identity" (and religion), under whose auspices the particular story of the Jews typically gets subsumed in the social sciences, "Jewish identity" is an insider term that is laden with various agendas, interests, politics, and worlds of discourse. This lends it a parochial cast from the point of view of mainstream American social science. The impression is probably reinforced by the fact that much research about American Jews has been commissioned by the American Jewish communal-organizational world, which typically tilts its research questions toward communal concerns without necessarily interfacing with the wider conversations about ethnicity and religion in America. The upshot is that the study of Jews and their identities has been part of an internal conversation within the organized Jewish community, impelled by underlying existential concerns such as "keeping Jews Jewish" (in the sense of not disappearing demographically; retaining connection to Jewish life and practice).[5] Not surprisingly, the Jewish agenda and the sociological investigation have often diverged.

This was not always the case. There was a time when studying Jews in America was a cutting-edge undertaking in sociology. During the foundational period of American social science in the first part of the 20th century, Jewish immigrants and their children, along with their Italian and Irish counterparts, figured significantly in scholarship about assimilation and acculturation.[6] Yet by mid-century, the data proxies of "mother tongue" and "country of birth" that were once used to identify the descendents of those European immigrants in the U.S. census had ceased to apply. This, coupled with the fact that the U.S. census has not tracked religion, meant that Jews and other European immigrant groups fell off the grid of mainstream sociological inquiry, even though Jews have figured into studies of religion. However, sociological interest in religion was minimal until the religious resurgence in the latter part of the 20th century.

In its American usage, "ethnic," the linguistic seed for ethnicity, started off as a way of referring to another's immigrant background or country of ancestry. That is to say, it was "a polite term referring to Jews, Italians, Irish and other people considered inferior to the dominant group of largely British descent."[7] For each ancestry group, "ethnic" conjured up specific accents, foods, linguistic usages, and so on. For Jews, "ethnic" can refer to the culture of Jewishness as distinct from its rigorously religious expression. In this context, ethnic means cultural or secular, evoking such things as Woody Allen, Yiddish, and bagels and lox, as opposed to any kind of religious definition.

The term *ethnicity* first appeared in the mid-20th century, and it was widely used by the early 1970s to refer to a range of minority groups in an increasingly plural/diverse American society.[8] Today, in the United States, everybody is asked to designate an ethnicity, which has come to be understood as some amalgam of race, class, and language. Official forms and applications routinely include a question about one's ethnicity, the answer to which is expected to be White, African American, Native American, Hispanic, Asian, or Other.[9] Just as *ethnic* took on a new linguistic shape in yielding the term *ethnicity*, so the underlying phenomenon morphed into something new, in part reflecting changing historical manifestations, along with different ideas and ideologies about the outcomes of assimilation and acculturation for minority groups.[10]

Along with this new inflection of ethnicity, the valence of Jewishness itself has changed. Consider the case of American Jews: when faced with today's routine ethnicity question, under what circumstances, if any, does one write that one is Jewish? When applying for some kind of quota-related opportunity, one might feel that ethnicity-*race* trumps ethnicity-*religion*, and so one might answer "white," or "black" or even "Jewban," in the words of a Cuban Jewish acquaintance. The decision with regard to which terminology to use is highly dependent on the immediate context, in addition to one's own psychic disposition or sense of "people-consciousness."[11] At the very least, there is a question of one's ethno-racial *background* (however one construes this) and the "face" one chooses to show about oneself; these are also related to a subjective component, one's *foreground*. Under what conditions, if any, does one's sense of connection to being Jewish get highlighted? These kinds of complex questions arise in trying to understand the relationship between ethnicity and identity among contemporary American Jews.

And *identity*? Here the story of the concept is even more complex. The word identity has two almost opposite meanings in English. On the one hand, there is identity in the sense of "*individuality*, self, selfhood; personality, character, originality, distinctiveness, singularity, uniqueness." Simultaneously, the term is also understood to mean "*congruity*, congruence, sameness, oneness, interchangeability; likeness, uniformity, similarity, closeness, accordance, alignment."[12] Identity's dual quality—denoting uniqueness of the self as differentiated from others and the connection between the individual and others—makes it distinctly socio-psychological in nature, as it necessarily involves an interface between the individual and the shared collective.

The term itself has been in wide use over the past century, beginning in psychology and sociology and extending across the humanities and social sciences.[13] Almost as a matter of course, the review articles that have appeared in recent years have included a sentence in which the author remarks on the sheer volume of writing that radiates from this term.

In 1989, the psychologist Roger Brown was able to write: "Identity is a concept no one has defined with precision, but it seems we can move ahead anyway, because everyone roughly understands what is meant."[14] This shift from Brown's relative clarity about the phenomenon and his sense of shared enterprise among scholars, to a situation in which researchers almost stagger from the sheer volume of material, deserves comment. In the past twenty years, there has been a surge in the number of new terms related to identity, including social, collective, or group identities (for instance, national and transnational identities), whereas the individual aspect has been captured by terms such as personal, self, and core identities, agency, narrative, consciousness, and the self in its various forms—multiple, partial, and possible[15]—to name just a few. The proliferation of new forms of identities mirrors the changes arising from our expanded mobility across multiple contexts, including wide-ranging webs, networks, and cross-cutting circles.[16] The world has become more complex, and along with that, the self has become more entangled. Consequently, we are in the process of developing new ways of managing these new realities, which results in phenomena such as "multiple selves."

In these new conditions, it makes sense to reconsider the shape and dynamics of identity and of Jewish identity. In the past, when being Jewish was considered a significant difference, the issue of joining versus remaining distinct was largely experienced as a forced choice. Difference was a liability, and in that context, Jewishness was seen as alien and other. Joining the mainstream relegated one's Jewishness to a private (and, for some, a hidden) sphere. If, today, difference (or at least certain forms of it) has become a neutral or even an admirable quality, the dynamics are shifting, and thus our notions of what goes into the forming of Jewish identity are in need of an update.

The new dynamics involve several related elements:

- The *opportunity structure* for social identities—the extent to which having a group identity is a good thing. For instance, being a "hyphenated American" (Irish-American, Italian-American, African-American, Asian-American, etc.) has become very acceptable in American life.
- *Jewishness as a social category*. How is Jewishness viewed by the societal mainstream, and through this, what are its limits and possibilities?
- *The individual's role in forming the Jewish self*. Is the fact that a person has a Jewish background psychologically significant to the person? Where does being Jewish figure in with other aspects of the self? How much does self-consciousness come into play?

I shall highlight the role of *Jewishness as a social category*, along with the attendant *opportunity structure* for social identities, since both play a significant role in defining and structuring individual choices in addition to affecting the "shelf-life," or persistence, of Jewishness among individuals.

I begin with a brief review of how some key Jewish historians of the modern period have understood the issues and dynamics related to being Jewish in various European countries, where Jewishness meant difference. Although the European Jewish experiences of becoming citizens and joining the emerging nation-states have taken on a canonical status in the thinking about contemporary Jewish identity, their applicability to the case of Jews in America needs to be (re)evaluated. America, for its part, represents a different set of possibilities. As one of the main groups comprising the European immigration to America at the turn of the 20th century, Jews figured significantly in the large literature about how immigrants ("foreigners") and their descendents became American, and in that process also transformed the American mainstream.

Finally, after considering these two contexts, I look at the current thinking about Jewish identity and "multiple selves" (the current formulation of the concept formerly known as identity), and discuss what is worth studying in the lives of Jews and the ways in which they relate to their Jewishness in light of current social/societal conditions.

The Modern Self and Modern Jewish Identity

Although the modern period yielded both the *self* and *Jewish identity*, these two literatures have not been linked. However, they deserve to be connected, since Jews were "there" at the outset and can be viewed as pioneers in the experience of coping with multiple identities.

The modern self was first conceptualized by Enlightenment philosophers, notably John Locke, who in 1694 added a chapter to the second edition of his *Essay concerning Human Understanding*. Locke viewed the individual's perception, reflection, and experience as forming the basis for knowing and action. In contrast to the notion of the individual's soul as given by God, the new social conditions of what we now called modernity necessitated that individuals participate in the forming of themselves. The *self* became a project of the individual.[17]

In contrast, the modern *Jewish self* emerged from a different configuration, and serves a different function. When historians write about pre-modern society, they do not write about the identity of the individual. For instance, in writing about educational practices in traditional (pre-modern) 14th-century Germany and France, Ivan G. Marcus describes the interplay between Jewish civilization and the Christian world:

> ... Jews remain[ed] firmly planted within a single identity as Jews by combining early and contemporary Jewish symbols with contemporary non-Jewish symbols and rites to support their own cultural identity as Jews. They often did this through rituals or narratives that denied or even mocked the competing stronger ideology of Christianity in medieval Europe.[18]

The clearly delineated social and cognitive boundaries between Jews and Christians and their respective worlds predominated. Individuals did not have to figure out their place (as Jews or as Christians) because they knew where they stood in that regard. To speak of an individual's "Jewish identity" in this situation makes little sense, because being Jewish was a constant that was not affected by one's predilections (unless one converted out, which meant leaving Jewish society and civilization).

The political emancipation of the various Jewish populations into the emerging nation states of Europe in the 18th and 19th centuries connected these formerly separate worlds under one overarching heading (the nation), leaving individual Jews to navigate the differences. From a socio-psychological perspective, Jewish identity emerged as a feature of the individual because there had been a shift away from an all-encompassing, one-and-only environment to a more complex situation in which people could move between various social roles and their correspondingly varied cultural assumptions. Moreover, each individual had to navigate the boundaries between these worlds, since lines of distinction were no longer self-evident or fully structured. As Todd Endelman notes:

> Judaism was no longer an all-embracing, self-sufficient civilization; it was reduced to a system of religious observances and beliefs. Jews who embraced European modes of thought and behavior no longer defined their lives in exclusively Jewish terms. They rearranged their personal priorities in such a manner that their Jewishness came to occupy only a segment of their personal identity.[19]

In other words, Judaism had functioned as a stand-alone social system before Jews became citizens in modern nation-states, at which point the category of Jew remained one of *difference* from the national mainstream. Being German was deeply intertwined with being Lutheran, just as being French was tied to being Catholic; Jews (and other religious minorities) deviated from this shared background. For Jewish individuals, being Jewish remained a marked condition that raised persistent questions about the authenticity of their connections to the nation. On the Jewish side was the question of being Jewish enough. Hence the impetus for the motivation to "prove" the worthiness of oneself and one's group. These were the basic structural-social-cognitive underpinnings at the beginning of "Jewish identity."

The concern about the Jewish identity of the individual did not emerge as an issue until "Jewish" became a distinct category within a larger whole, and the boundary between Jewish and national became traversable. At that point the individual faced the "bifocal" experience of being at once a Jew and a national. Thus the idea of the *self* as compared to the *Jewish self* had different social origins and dynamics, with one more focused on the individual person, and the other necessarily involving both the individual person as well as the individual as identified by others as a Jew, in a time and place where being a Jew was to be Other.

For Jews (and other ethnic and religious minorities), one's essential difference was always in view (by others) and thus the possibility of forming the self was not wholly in one's control. The self as somehow "othered" creates the basis for "dual consciousness" in that it produces a disjunction between people's views of themselves and their aspirations and how they are seen, categorized, and delimited by others.

In America, where Jewish integration into the societal mainstream has been more complete than in the various European cases, Jewish identity has had a different trajectory. Writing about England but noting that this also held true for the case of Jews in North America, Endelman has noted some of the socio-structural features that laid the groundwork for these different trajectories:

> [T]here were no communal institutions to monitor effectively the social behavior of Jews who settled there. There was no legally recognized Jewish communal organization to which all Jews were required to belong, as was the case elsewhere in Europe. Voluntarism was the only organizing principle of Anglo-Jewish communal life. Those who uprooted themselves to migrate to England were coming to an under-developed Jewish community in a country that graces its inhabitants an extraordinary degree of personal freedom.[20]

Although there were many social distinctions in America, *e pluribus unum* was the ethos of the nation—the many becoming one. This was explicitly tied to the religious toleration in the founding documents of the state. Yuri Slezkine has described the American "national religion" as being more accommodating to multiple "others" than those of European nations:

> [The European] model with its tribal descent built into the new states meant that one could not be a good German or Hungarian without worshipping the national canon. This was the real new church.... It was possible [however] to be an American "of the Mosaic faith" because the American national religion was not based on tribal descent and the cult of the national soul....[21]

Sociologists have kept tabs on this leveling out of difference. American sociologists have written extensively about the acculturation and integration of European immigrants in the early 20th-century American context. Here ethnicity—a property of the group related to its cohesion—takes center stage in the analysis of assimilation, whereas identity (of individuals) has been viewed as a sidebar to the larger story of how the immigrants and their descendents fared, as a group, in becoming American.

In sociological discourse, ethnicity has come to be equated with group *distinctiveness* in comparison with other ethnic groups, and scholars have devised a whole range of empirical indicators or proxies of group integration and socioeconomic attainment measured at the *aggregate* level. These include residential clustering or "spatial assimilation" (looking at the ethnic composition of locales inhabited by members of different ethnic groups), language ("mother tongue" spoken at home by children of immigrants), occupational status, educational attainment, income levels, and finally, social networks (percentage of social ties with members of one's own or other groups in various domains) and intermarriage (religion of spouse). The waning of sociological distinctiveness is seen as an index of integration and non-discrimination. And indeed that is largely what has happened.

In contrast to ethnicity, *ethnic identity* refers to a *person's self-perception of being a member of an ethnic group*. In the bumpy ride from distinctiveness to assimilation and incorporation, the concrete ethnicity of old immigrant neighborhoods gave way over the course of time to what Herbert Gans has termed "symbolic ethnicity," by which he means an individual, idiosyncratic ethnic identity that has no institutional underpinning.[22] As ethnicity dissipates, individual-level ethnic identity—expressed episodically in relation to changing circumstances—is all that remains. Gans looked at the relationship between declining social distinctiveness and an individual's experience of ethnic attachment. His thesis is that as "hard ethnicity" dissipates, so too does ethnic identity weaken. It becomes activated only intermittently, and in symbolic, "costless" ways as opposed to actually affecting the daily set–up of one's life. According to a study by Richard D. Alba, this has been the pattern among "white ethnics" such as Italians, Poles, and Irish, who arrived in America at roughly the same point in history. At the same time, Alba's study indicates that the group distinctiveness of Jews remains.[23]

The comparative frame with its focus on structural distinctiveness has a number of advantages when it comes to looking at the process of assimilation into America, namely, letting us understand more about the American societal context and identifying the factors that help or inhibit assimilation. The attention has been on *what happens around the boundaries* and the process of incorporation, whereby the boundaries between minorities (immigrant groups) and the mainstream change from bright to blurred.[24] Do people cross the bright, clearer boundaries between enclave and mainstream and, if so, in what domains and under what circumstances? Do the boundaries begin to soften and blur and eventually change? These questions are critical when the framing question is about the possibility of equal treatment or equal chances, irrespective of one's ethnic origins.

Yet understanding the Jewish case solely on the basis of what happens at the boundaries is not sufficient to account either for the persistence of Jewish ethnicity (distinctiveness) or for changes in the internal landscape of what Jews and Jewishness mean to Jews themselves. In terms of getting a handle on the American *Jewish* experience, the comparative frame simplifies the story too much to allow us to follow the more interesting developments inside the group. Neither ethnicity in the comparative mode nor religion (by itself) has done an adequate job in capturing Jewish inner dynamics and their particular emotional glue.

One would have to conclude that ethnicity as defined by sociologists does not fully account for the persistence of ethno-*religious* groups such as Jews or Armenians. Jews have been compared to Italians and Poles[25] who arrived in America in the same time period. Yet in the ensuing decades, as these immigrant groups became "white," the social boundaries between white American Catholics and Protestants receded more than the boundary separating Jews and Christians. When we add in the history of trauma and oppression and the attendant historical consciousness that developed, the notion of group persistence gains more traction.

When we look at the case of the Jews from the point of view of religion, the comparative social scientific treatment has proved to be limiting in other ways. The markers used for religion do not capture the ethno-religions effectively, such that Jews wind up looking much less "religious" than people of other religions. Barry Kosmin and Ariela Keysar have been documenting the growing proportion of Jews who say they have *no religion*, and indeed they do not, at least not in the Christian-centric ways in which religion has been defined in terms of faith and church-going.[26]

Meanwhile, in political analyses, Jews always register as much more liberal than their socio-structural counterparts (as per Milton Himmelfarb's old saw: they earn like Episcopalians but vote like Puerto Ricans). Jewish political liberalism, along with the Jews' engagement with social justice and philanthropy, leads us back to having to take "culture" into account, because defining ethnicity as being solely about maintaining distinctiveness (at the boundaries) has not been sufficient for decoding Jewish socio-ethnic and religious practice.

Socio-psychological Analysis of Identity/Jewishness

When prejudice and intergroup relations were major concerns within American social psychology, group identity was explored in terms of ethnocentrism and group chauvinism, as part of the effort to understand intergroup conflict and cooperation. (The question was how to ameliorate these tendencies). In the period around the Second World War, the plight of Jews motivated some influential research and theorizing. Two main subjects of inquiry concerned the authoritarian and prejudiced personalities, on the one hand, and the consequences of being a member of a stigmatized or victimized group, on the other hand. With regard to the latter issue, Kurt Lewin wrote an essay in 1939 that was titled "When Facing Danger." This was followed by another essay in 1940 titled "Bringing Up the Jewish Child" and a 1941 piece titled "Self-Hatred among Jews." These writings addressed the strategies for creating a sense of well-being in Jewish individuals, given their group's highly victimized status.

American Jews aren't writing essays like that anymore: Jewish self-hatred is part of a broader ethnic style that is rapidly being phased out and now appears as dated as Jewish men named Sylvan, Mortimer, and Lionel. In this context in which being "Jewish" is no longer a denigrated or negatively freighted characteristic—where it may not even be readily detectable from the outside—what happens to the Jewishness of individuals? Put somewhat differently, the attention has shifted from social barriers that make it hard to be a Jew to questions about the nature of the "Jew within." One noticeable expression of this shift was the changing terminology in the Jewish communal-organizational world in the late 1980s, where the challenge to *Jewish survival* was reformulated as that of assuring *Jewish continuity*, the latter being an expression of anxiety about collective disappearance due to disinterest and disinclination among individuals rather than concern about threats to the physical well-being of the group.

The sense of difference due to being "too Jewish" has declined, in part because Jews are less different, and also because contemporary America relates to difference in new ways. At the same time, there are other things that increase the sense of otherness and difference, pulling Jews together. The significant place of the Holocaust in Jewish identity remains: even those who do not consider Jewishness to be particularly significant in their own lives are haunted by the fact that it happened and that Jews were killed because they were Jews.[27] Although most American Jews did not directly experience the Holocaust, the proliferation of museums, courses, and books (in addition to findings from surveys and interviews) attests to its influence on Jewish identity, though the effects of this awareness are not uniform.

Steven Cohen and Arnold Eisen have written that "the principal authority for contemporary American Jews . . . has become the sovereign self."[28] In describing the historical shift from "living Jewishly" out of a sense of inherited obligation to being the author of one's own life, they highlight the significance of individual autonomy in making choices about one's Jewish life:

> ... if those we interviewed are and seek to be autonomous, sovereign selves, who carefully weigh every commitment they make and no less carefully guard their options for transferring commitments as they please, they are only exhibiting in the Jewish realm attitudes and behaviors which are demanded of them in every other realm of contemporary American life.[29]

Although against the backdrop of centuries of Jewish history this shift from obligation to autonomy is noteworthy, within the context of our contemporary times, the emphasis on *sovereignty* overstates the case. It makes it seem that people are the masters of their fate, that they can, on their own, choose any direction in life, and ignores the various elements that play a determinative role in shaping choice one way or another. As Mary Douglas noted, we need "a stricter discussion of how choice is possible" in our current context.[30]

The central challenge in postmodern times is to examine the ways in which people's supposedly autonomous actions are embedded in relationships and contexts, and to consider the various elements that come into play in arriving at a choice. Put another way, there is room for a more critical, nuanced examination of the interaction between individual *agency* (and related capacities) and the *structures* and relationships that make choices and journeys possible. We need to examine the notion of choice more closely, to explore the dynamic interplay between the individual actor and the social context that enable or inhibit choice or its foreclosure. A more dynamic socio-psychological consideration of "Jewish identity" would keep both of these elements, both individual agency and social structure, in view.

This brings us squarely into the realm of psychology, where there are numerous ideas about the elements that shape who and how we become. Psychologists have understood identity as a process as much as a structure. In my own writing about contemporary Jewishness, I chose the word *journey* rather than path to capture the serendipitous quality that comes through when we look at people's lives, their Jewish connections and their other commitments, over time.[31]

But when the props and background scenery are changing—when the rise of Islamic fundamentalism, the fallout of the current situation of Israel, the new views of Zionism, and the election of a half-black president all have as yet unknown impact on Jewish self-identity—the mapping of identity journeys becomes less evident, and the old shibboleths, in all likelihood, no longer apply.

Notes

My thinking about identity in general and Jewish identity in particular has benefited from my working on the "Choosing to Teach" study, sponsored by the Mandel Center for Studies in Jewish Education at Brandeis University; I am grateful to Sharon Feiman Nemser for her support. Charles Kadushin's friendship, and steady willingness to read and critique my work, has been especially helpful.

1. Zadie Smith, "Speaking in Tongues," *New York Review of Books* (26 Feb. 2009), 41–43.
2. Mordecai Kaplan, *The Meaning of God in Modern Jewish Religion* (New York: 1937), 92–93.
3. Richard D. Alba and Victor Nee, *Remaking the American Mainstream: Assimilation and Contemporary Immigration* (Cambridge, Mass.: 2003).
4. This has happened as American Jews have come to be viewed as part of the "white" mainstream. Note, however, that the racial-ethnic composition of American Jewry is becoming more diverse. See Diane Tobin, Gary A. Tobin, and Scott Rubin, *In Every Tongue: The Racial and Ethnic Diversity of the Jewish People* (San Francisco: 2005).
5. In part, this is due to cracks in the data infrastructure undergirding the field. Studying Jews depended on the availability of adequate data sources. By mid-century when most Jews had resided in America for three generations or more, tracking them using foreign ancestry as a proxy for Jewish descent was no longer possible. Sociologists sought other routes, and in 1970, the National Jewish Population Survey (NJPS) was established by the Jewish Federations to serve the needs of the Jewish communal-organizational world as well as those of sociologists and demographers.
6. For instance, Louis Wirth's *The Ghetto* (1928), a significant contribution coming out of the Chicago school of sociological inquiry. In the middle decades of the 20th century, the American Jewish Committee supported studies of the Jews of "Lakeville" by Marshall Sklare and Joseph Greenblum. In addition, it sponsored the research leading to the publication of the *Studies in Prejudice* series, the first volume of which was *The Authoritarian Personality*, authored by T.W. Adorno, Else Frenkel-Brunswik, Daniel J. Levinson, and R. Nevitt Sanford (New York: 1950).
7. Thomas Hylland Eriksen, *Ethnicity and Nationalism: Anthropological Perspectives* (London: 1993), 4.
8. *The Oxford English Dictionary*'s 1972 supplement cites David Riesman as first using the term ethnicity in 1953—cited in Nathan Glazer and Daniel P. Moynihan (eds.), *Ethnicity: Theory and Experience* (Cambridge, Mass.: 1975), 1.
9. The U.S. decennial census now includes a question relating to ethnicity, but not religion. The Canadian census includes both.
10. Alba and Nee, *Remaking the American Mainstream*; Richard D. Alba, *Ethnic Identity: The Transformation of White America* (New Haven: 1990), 24, 318–319.
11. The view of Jewishness as a racial quality has certainly changed from the 19th- and 20th-century conceptions documented by Macy Hart in S*ocial Science and the Politics of Modern Jewish Identity* (Stanford: 2000).
12. Definitions are taken from *Concise Oxford Dictionary* (2004) and *Concise Oxford Thesaurus* (2002).
13. Historian Philip Gleason wrote about the semantic and intellectual roots of "identity" in his essay "Identifying Identity: A Semantic History," *Journal of American History* 69, no. 4 (1983), 910–931.
14. Roger Brown, *Social Psychology: The Second Edition* (New York: 1989), 551. Concurring with Brown's view are Richard D. Ashmore and Lee Jussim ("Introduction: Toward a Second Century of the Scientific Analysis of Self and Identity," in *Self and Identity: Fundamental Issues*, ed. Richard D. Ashmore and Lee Jussim [New York: 1997]):

> [Self and identity] point to large, amorphous, and changing phenomena that defy hard and fast definitions, although individual researchers and practitioners of particular definitions do operate according to widely accepted and operational definitions . . . there is not a single self or identity construct/variable. Instead there are a wide variety of self-and identity-related phenomena and terms to label these (p. 5).

15. On the concept of "possible selves," see Hazel Markus and Paula Nurius, "Possible Selves," *American Psychologist* 41, no. 9 (Sept. 1986), 954–969, who note that:

> Possible selves derive from representations of the self in the past and they include representations of the self in the future. They are different and separable from the current or

now selves, yet are intimately connected to them. Possible future selves, for example, are not just *any* set of imagined roles or states of being. Instead they represent specific, individually significant hopes, fears, and fantasies (p. 954).

16. Georg Simmel, "The Metropolis and Mental Life," in *The Sociology of Georg Simmel*, ed. Kurt Wolff (New York: 1950), 409–424. See also Daniel V.A. Olson, "Fellowship Ties and the Transmission of Religious Identity," in *Beyond Establishment: Protestant Identity in a Post-Protestant Age*, ed. Jackson Carroll and Wade Clark Roof (Louisville: 1993), who notes:

> The difference between contemporary subcultures and the preindustrial community lies in the greater freedom of moderns to choose which elements of their identity they will emphasize in the construction of their personal networks and the degree of their involvement in subcultures based on those identities. Moderns are freer to shape their personal networks and thus their own identity (p. 36).

17. See Kurt Danziger, "The Historical Formation of Selves," in Ashmore and Jussim (eds.), *Self and Identity*, who writes: "Not only were individuals separated from their social identities, but that separation was accelerating at a time when the hold of theologically-based notions of personal identity was also beginning to weaken" (p. 141). Philip Gleason, citing Robert Langbaum, notes that "identity did not take on psychological connotations until empiricist philosophers called into question what he calls 'the unity of the self.' The unity of the self was not a problem so long as the traditional Christian conception of the soul held sway. . ." (Gleason, "Identifying Identity: A Semantic History," *The Journal of American History* 69, no. 4 [March 1983], 911). See also Jerrold Siegel, *The Idea of the Self: Thought and Experience in Western Europe since the Seventeenth Century* (Cambridge: 2005).

18. Ivan G. Marcus, "Honey Cakes and Torah: A Jewish Boy Learns His Letters," reprinted in *Judaism in Practice: From the Middle Ages through the Early Modern Period*, ed. Lawrence Fine (Princeton: 2001), 116–117.

19. Todd M. Endelman, *The Jews of Georgian England 1714–1830: Tradition and Change in a Liberal Society* (Philadelphia: 1979), 118–119.

20. Ibid., 119.

21. Yuri Slezkine, *The Jewish Century* (Princeton: 2004), 67.

22. Herbert J. Gans, "Symbolic Ethnicity: The Future of Ethnic Groups and Cultures in America," *Ethnic & Racial Studies* 2, no. 1 (Jan. 1979), 1–20.

23. Richard D. Alba, *Ethnic Identity: The Transformation of White America* (New Haven: 1990); Mary C. Waters, *Ethnic Options: Choosing Identities in America* (Berkeley: 1990).

24. Alba and Nee, *Remaking the American Mainstream*.

25. For instance, see Matthew Frye Jacobson, *Special Sorrows: The Diasporic Imagination of Irish, Polish, and Jewish Immigrants in the United States* (Cambridge, Mass.: 1995).

26. Barry A. Kosmin and Ariela Keysar, *Religion in a Free Market* (Ithaca: 2006).

27. Bethamie Horowitz, "Connections and Journeys: Assessing Critical Opportunities for Enhancing Jewish Identity" (report to the Commission on Jewish Identity and Renewal, UJA-Federation of New York), online at www.jewishdatabank.org/Reports/Connections_And_Journeys_2003rev.pdf (p. 69).

28. Steven M. Cohen and Arnold M. Eisen, *The Jew Within: Self, Family and Community in America* (Bloomington: 2000), 184.

29. Ibid., 40.

30. Mary Douglas made this comment in her critique of the overly stereotyped notion of the autonomous modern self in "The Effects of Modernization on Religious Change," originally published in *Daedalus* (Winter 1982) and reprinted in a special edition of *Daedalus* ("Three Decades of *Daedalus*") (Summer 1988), 457–484, online at www.jstor.org/stable/20025187 (accessed 19 Nov. 2009); quote appears on p. 481.

31. Horowitz, "Connections and Journeys."

Jews and the Ethnic Scene: A Multidimensional Theory

Uzi Rebhun
(THE HEBREW UNIVERSITY)

This essay presents a multidimensional theoretical approach to the study of contemporary Jewish ethnicity, based on existing literature and my own analysis of demographic and sociological data. The empirical evidence has led me to the conclusion that the study of Jewish ethnicity should mainly concern itself with three different (albeit complementary) dimensions: *time*, *space*, and *sub-identity*. Each of these can be treated and assessed in different ways. Furthermore, within each possible combination of the three dimensions, the patterns of Jewish identification vary in form and content. Although the various components of Jewish identification operate together and are strongly interrelated, some of these components play a more important role than others in determining the strength of group commitment and thus contribute differently to the overall consciousness of ethnic and religious identity.

These insights have methodological implications for social research on Jews. In addition, because Jews in the diaspora have often been ahead of other ethnic and religious groups in adjusting to the social and cultural patterns of the majority population—whether as immigrants who arrived only recently in the host country, or as later-generation descendants of immigrants—the observations presented in this essay may also aid in the crystallization of more general theoretical insights on ethnicity and group boundaries.

Conceptions of Time and Ethnicity

Time is the passage from an earlier to a later period. It is not a one-step move from one date to another, but rather a continuum that reflects (among other things) the ideological, social, and cultural processes affecting all aspects of group and personal life, including ethnicity.[1] It can be argued that, over time, the behaviors of different actors in a given society become more uniform; groups that initially differed from one another in accordance with their various ethnic orientations tend to become more similar. To be sure, this observation runs counter to the current emphasis on a multicultural model that provides legitimacy for distinctive ethnic patterns.[2] I would argue, however, that such patterns are largely manifested in intermittent and symbolic expressions such as the celebration of major holidays.[3]

Time, in this sense, is also associated with changes in the status of minorities in the surrounding environment, the degree of their acceptance by the host population, and the extent to which they acquire social equality. Under circumstances of freedom and integration, the members of a given ethno-religious group may come to identify themselves first as members of the civic nation—for instance, as Germans or as Americans—and only then as members of a specific ethnic or religious subgroup. This, in turn, may influence ethnic patterns in the direction of weakening group identification in the public sphere, leaving it to be expressed mainly inside the home or in limited social venues.[4]

It should be noted, however, that the social and cultural mainstream into which minority groups incorporate is not homogenous. Rather than evolving toward uniformity, many western societies, each within its own specific context, have accommodated a blend of cultural elements, traditions, and faiths. More specifically, the mainstream has expanded to incorporate elements of the minorities' cultures. Such an expansion may blur the borders between ethnic groups, a process that is furthered by structural assimilation in residential neighborhoods, educational and occupational attainment, and mixed marriages.[5]

The reaction to such macro-level changes is largely associated with another aspect of time, namely generational status. The distinctive patterns of an ethnic group, which are largely maintained by the first generation, are likely to become blurred by the time of the second or third generation. Such distancing from the immigrant generation weakens the group's concentration in ethnic residential and occupational niches and its distinctive cultural patterns (including, in particular, language), and it is also likely to generate families of mixed ethnic origins. The pace of these processes varies among groups according to educational and occupational qualifications and in light of opportunities for absorption.[6] Nevertheless, the effect of generational status on ethnicity is not determined solely by the distance from the immigrant generation: it is also influenced by the influx of new immigrants of similar ethnic background. Such new immigrants bring with them authentic ethnic behaviors and cultural elements that may strengthen interest in and sympathy toward the group's heritage on the part of later generations. These new immigrants can both enhance the distinctive ethnic identity of the veteran members and contribute to their ethnic cohesion. This is true for such contemporary cases as Israeli Jewish immigrants to the United States and Soviet Jewish immigrants living in Germany.[7]

In the individual sphere, time attests to age and different demographic and social characteristics. The importance of ethnic identity and its translation into distinctive behavioral patterns is not constant throughout the life cycle. Fluctuating periods of high and low ethnic identification are strongly associated with marital status and the presence of children at home, and identity may regain strength at older ages.[8] The relationships between family characteristics and ethnicity are not uniform and may develop in numerous directions. One salient example is that of interfaith marriage: on the one hand, marriage between people from different religions or ethnic groups may weaken distinctive identity and diminish expressions of specific group belonging;[9] on the other hand, it may enhance the aspiration of a partner to exhibit his or her group identity as a contrast to that of the other spouse.[10]

The Role of Space

To a large extent, the spatial dimension of ethnicity is also multilayered. It reflects general local influences, be these ideological, social, or cultural, as well as the nature of ethnicity as perceived in the society at large. This dimension emphasizes the paramount importance of the local context in shaping ethnic identity. It is true that the role of place has recently been somewhat undermined in light of processes connected with modernization, especially globalization and its accompanying "flattening" of the globe (in the sense of rapidly transmitted information and patterns of behavior). Accordingly, the similarity between groups may expand beyond the borders of a given country or area. The spread of ethnic patterns is further accelerated by international migration and the direct transmission of cultural elements, or by other types of cultural importation such as those resulting from long stays in another country. Hence, it can be argued that the role of the actors, namely of specific ethnic groups, is declining. Nevertheless, empirical investigations of ethnicity in general—and Jewish identity in particular—point to the significance of the local context, whether historical or contemporaneous.[11] In fact, there seems to be an interplay between general global influences and more local events.

Space is also the immediate area of residence. As Louis Wirth suggested:

> If you would know what kind of Jew a man is, ask him where he lives; for no single factor indicates as much about the character of the Jew as the area in which he lives. It is an index not only to his economic status, his occupation, his religion, but also to his politics and his outlook on life and the stage in the assimilative process that he has reached.[12]

Thus, for example, the religious and ethnic identification of Jews in Philadelphia differs from that of Jews in Boston, and Jews in both these northeastern U.S. communities are significantly more committed, ethnically and religiously, than their counterparts in Los Angeles.[13]

With regard to international migration, the spatial dimension involves the ethnic status of the immigrants in their new environment. In the case of Jews, immigrants who operate as members of a minority at origin (Jews in the diaspora) and move to their national country (Israel) experience a change in status as they become part of the majority population, whereas those who move from one diaspora country to another maintain their minority status. Still another group undertakes a reverse process, trading their majority membership (in Israel) to minority status abroad. More precisely, in their new country they have a "double ethnicity," as they are both Jews and Israelis. These two components of ethnicity do not contradict one another, yet over time it is anticipated that the Jewish component will strengthen while the Israeli component will decline.[14] In any event, majority or minority status, and the transition from one to the other, involves the need to reshape the meaning of ethnic identity and the identificational patterns derived from this.

Related to space in a somewhat different way are population size and ethnic density. A large mass of people of similar ethnic belonging is likely to exhibit a confident ethnic identity both in formal and informal intra-group relationships and in social and political activities. Ethnic concentration is especially important in conditions of minority status: the larger the group, the more likely it is that intrinsic characteristics will be strengthened at the expense of ties with the surrounding majority population.[15] Ethnic mass is also an important tool for asserting a particular group's interests, as is the case with Soviet Jewish immigrants in Israel.[16]

Inclusive Ethnicity and Sub-identities

Depending on circumstances, ethnicity can be either inclusive or exclusive. A group behaves in an inclusive way when it takes care of "its own," often in the context of political activity. Historically, Jews who were active in various political movements often viewed their involvement as a way to secure or enhance the status of their fellow Jews, and the liberal orientation of a majority of American Jews today is often attributed to the practical realization that Jews generally have done better in societies in which social and economic mobility was determined by achievement and where discrimination was legally forbidden.[17]

Ethnic exclusivity, in contrast, entails subdivisions or stratification, which keep "fellow ethnics" within more narrowly circumscribed subgroups. High levels of international migration of members of an ethnic group from different areas of origin to a given location give rise to a need to define and discover sub(exclusive)-identities within the broad ethnic entity. Definitions of separate or newly developing sub-ethnicities may sometimes appear to be arbitrary and have relatively little basis in previously acknowledged sub-identities. An example of the latter would be the rise of neo-ethnic labels such as "Mizrahi"—a category that did not exist prior to the 1950s.

It follows that ethnic identity should be investigated not merely as a unique inclusive identity (which, to some extent, it may be) but rather as an amalgamation of sub-identities, each of which stems from a separate historical and cultural experience and contributes to the function of sub-ethnicity within the overall cultural-religious makeup. Obviously such an approach is especially appropriate for investigation of a majority population in which sub-ethnicity is a decisive identifying factor (as is the case, for example, with Jewish sub-ethnicity in Israel). But it might also be adopted in other instances such as France since the mid-20th century.[18]

Analysis of sub-identities within broader ethnic groups also makes sense when we look at individuals or family units. The family and communal base are paramount factors in determining the social standing of the individual, and this reflects to no small extent the genealogical ties of Jews originating in specific areas. The prioritization of the private sphere might later have been accelerated within the context of modernization in both western and Mediterranean societies. The process of modernization may be seen as the separation and redefinition of functional components that were all previously part of one undefined whole: the separation of the idea of "religion" from nationality, for instance, is a product of the modern western world, and one may similarly observe distance between the individual and community, family, and religious faith, among other things. One of the consequences of such separation is that religious activity is observed, if at all, on select occasions or in particular institutional settings.

In this context, several identities, or even mixed identities, are sustainable. A growing number of Americans report multiple ethnicities in the decennial census. This is further reflected in multiple screening questions in studies aimed at identifying members of specific ethnic or religious groups, including surveys of the Jewish population.[19] From this standpoint, the developments of the last several decades, especially in the United States, are to some extent akin to those of Europe in the emancipation era, which also provided conditions conducive to navigating between different identities. In any event, Jewish ethnicity today is but one component of a larger sociocultural puzzle.

Yet, unlike early modern times, the current compartmentalization of sub-identities penetrates as well into the realm of religion. Together with an increased emphasis on individualism and self-fulfillment, multiculturalism provides opportunities for interfaith connections, including familial frameworks, and the evolution of a primary religious identity alongside another religious belonging. Such mixed identities blur the boundaries and extend the degree of diversity within minority populations. At the same time, multiculturalism can introduce new barriers. People with multiple identities may associate their religious beliefs with a variety of behaviors, thus detaching themselves from a coherent ethno-religious framework. In the Jewish context, the development of multiple ethno-religious identities (which include, but are not limited to, a Jewish component) is especially significant with regard to the state of Israel, which under the Law of Return allows people of paternal Jewish origin, who might not define themselves (nor are they legally defined) as Jewish, to immigrate and acquire citizenship. Clearly, the line that was once drawn around a simple definition of ethnicity and religion has been breached, and the penetration of other ethnic elements encourages mixing in the religious sphere.

Measuring Jewish Identification

Ethnic and religious identity is the individual's self-concept of his or her group-belonging and the value and emotional significance attached to it.[20] This subjective identity, in terms of "self-reported statements or placement in social categories"[21] as compared with objective/normative definitions, can be either public identity, namely, one's perception of identity in the public square, or self-identity, reflecting one's perception of social attachments.[22] An individual's identity is determined by the continual interplay between primordial (or ascribed) affinities, on the one hand, and patterns absorbed from the proximate social environment, on the other.[23] The manifestation of group consciousness or identity evolves from the gradual merging of various individual identifications and behaviors.[24] Thus, different self-definitions of group belonging or family background reflect the nature of ethno-religious commitment as translated into beliefs, attitudes, values, rituals, and other distinct group behaviors.[25] To a large extent, this approach treats "identity" as a cognitive-ideological phenomenon, whereas "identification" is given a more tangible-behavioral meaning.[26]

I suggest looking at the array of group identifications in a two-dimensional manner (Fig. 1), where one dimension expresses the mode of identification and the other expresses the locus, or environment, in which the identification takes place. The identificational mode is composed of attitude and behavior, whereas the locus of identification distinguishes between the private and the public sphere. Hence, we

	Mode of identification	
Locus of identification	Attitude	Behavior
Private	Importance of identity; general issues A	Rituals; ethnic culture; visits to holy sites B
Public	C Groups boundaries; collective memory; ethnic cohesion	D Membership; voluntarism; networks; philanthropy

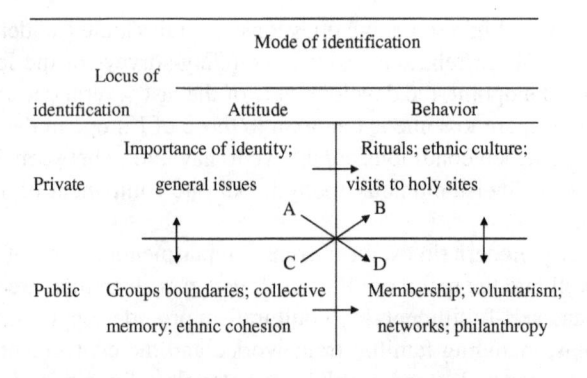

Figure 1. The dual dimensions of group identification: locus and mode

have four quadrants of group identification for the combination of each of the categories in the mode and the locus of identification. Strong relations between the four quadrants are illustrated by the arrows. According to the attitude/behavior theory, there will be strong relationships between quadrants A and B and between quadrants C and D; thus there are relationships within the same locus as well as between different loci (as shown by the diagonal arrows between quadrant A and quadrant D and between quadrant C and quadrant B).[27] There are also strong internal ties between the two categories of the locus of identification, namely, between the private and the public spheres, regarding both attitudes (quadrants A and C) and behaviors (quadrants B and D). These latter effects are bi-directional.

Each of these quadrants is composed of many specific elements. Most are manifestly "Jewish," but some (for instance, attitudes toward general social and political issues) may (directly or indirectly) reflect an older set of Jewish values or may be the product of minority-status considerations. Quadrant A, dealing with attitudes in the private sphere, includes group belonging and attitudes on general matters—for instance, the importance a person attaches to ethno-religious or national identity (Jewish/Israeli); to relationships with group members who live in other countries; to ethnic residential concentration; to endogamous marriage on the part of offspring; or to political orientation. Quadrant B, which pertains to behaviors in the private sphere, includes religious rituals, consumption of ethnic culture, and visits to holy sites. Quadrant C, representing attitudes connected with the public sphere, comprises such matters as group boundaries (for instance, "who is a Jew" or who should be covered by the Law of Return), collective memory (for instance, with respect to the Shoah), concern for safety of the group (for example, an individual's perception of antisemitism), and ethnic cohesion, as well as more general attitudes concerning the separation between religion and state or social justice. Quadrant D, pertaining to behaviors in the public sphere, includes membership in religious and ethnic institutions, voluntary activities, philanthropy, participation in informal social networks of ethnic peers, and the like.

Behaviors can be distinguished not only on the basis of the private versus the public sphere. A further two-dimensional classification (Fig. 2) characterizes behaviors according to their essence and intensity. The essence of behavior can be either religious or ethnic

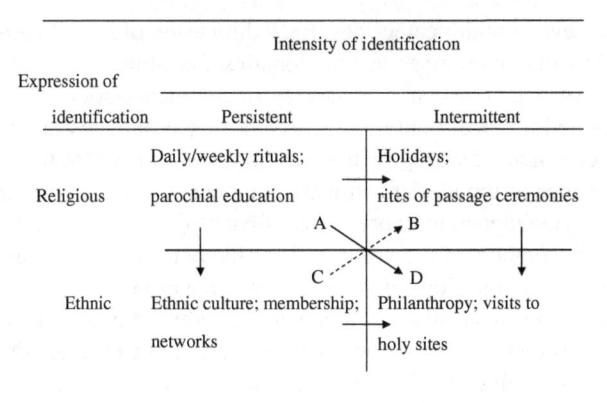

Jews and the Ethnic Scene: A Multidimensional Theory 97

	Intensity of identification	
Expression of identification	Persistent	Intermittent
Religious	Daily/weekly rituals; parochial education	Holidays; rites of passage ceremonies
	A ↘ ↗ B	
	C ↙ ↘ D	
Ethnic	Ethnic culture; membership; networks	Philanthropy; visits to holy sites

Figure 2. The dual dimensions of group behavior: expression and intensity

(with the latter including as well communal and cultural patterns), whereas intensity can be either ongoing behaviors that occur in daily life or else intermittent behaviors generally associated with the observance of major holidays or rites of passage. Once again, there are strong relationships between the different quadrants, and it may especially be assumed that persistent behaviors affect intermittent behaviors and that the religious expressions of identification can predict ethnic expressions. Although these relationships are mainly horizontal or vertical, it stands to reason that there are also some diagonal effects—certainly between persistent religious behaviors and intermittent ethnic behaviors and, to a lesser extent, between persistent ethnic behaviors and intermittent religious ones.

The specific components of each of the quadrants of behavioral patterns are those that were outlined earlier with regard to behaviors in the private versus the public sphere, but here they are distinguished according to the two dimensions of essence and intensity. Accordingly, ongoing rituals associated with dietary laws (kashruth) or the enrollment of children in parochial schools (in the diaspora context) will be placed in quadrant A, whereas the celebration of major holidays (for instance, Yom Kippur, Hanukah, Passover) or the rites of passage connected with a bar- or bat-mitzvah are assigned to quadrant B. Quadrant C, persistent ethnicity, comprises behaviors such as membership in group organizations, affiliation with informal social networks of ethnic peers, and consumption of ethnic culture. Quadrant D, intermittent ethnic patterns, includes, among other items, philanthropy and visits to holy sites. To be sure, the distinction between quadrants is not always clear-cut or significant. Group patterns might at the same time have religious and ethnic meanings, and one can decide whether to practice them regularly or only intermittently. For some, "synagogue membership" and the variables associated with it are connected to the synagogue's being perceived as a place of worship reflecting a religious way of life; for others, the synagogue is primarily regarded as a place for social gatherings or as a locus of identity with the organized local community. (This, of course, can determine the frequency of synagogue attendance.) Similarly, the intensity of voluntary activities varies from ongoing involvement to occasional activity.

Taken together, the various components of Jewish identification, both attitudinal (cognitive) and behavioral (regardless of essence and frequency of practices), can be classified into several major categories. Each dimension of identification, either attitudinal or behavioral, comprises several domains. For attitudes, the domains include collectiveness (group cohesion), cosmology (theological outlook), and attitudes on general social and political matters; for behaviors, the domains include rituals, culture, history, community, segregation, education, and attachment to homeland.[28] The extent of relevance of the identificational components varies across time and space. Likewise, the actual/apparent expressions of each of the practices may not be uniform among all members of the group and are likely to reflect the influences of specific experiences and traditions of subgroups by area of origin.

Given this abundant array of components of ethno-religious identification and strong internal correlations, the importance, or weight, of each component for assessing the overall strength of Jewish identification may be different. I would argue that behaviors attest more strongly to group commitment than do attitudes. Similarly, persistent (rather than intermittent) behaviors contribute more significantly to the feeling of group belonging and group cohesion. While researchers will agree less on the hierarchy of the private versus the public sphere of group identification as well as on the hierarchy of the essence of identification—namely, religious versus ethnic practices—many empirical studies nevertheless lead to the conclusion, even though not decisive, that patterns of Jewish identification in the public sphere hold greater weight than those in the private sphere, and that religious involvement outweighs ethnic or community involvement.[29]

Discussion

The significance of time largely supports the view of constructivism or situationalism, according to which ethnicity reflects a social process rather than being a cultural given, depending on the "logic of the situation and the characteristics of the persons interacting."[30] Similarly, the spatial dimension, in its various aspects, emphasizes the need to understand group identity as a social construction determined by local context and related factors. Over time, ethnicity loses some of its primordial attachments, rendering it more fluid and more dependent on constructed elements.

Nevertheless, ethnicity also has an important primordial intrinsic power. While variable forms of ethnicity may be observed among any number of group affiliates, many others maintain common normative group behaviors over a long time and across space. This is especially salient in regard to religious elements, but it is also seen in ethnic and communal activities without which the group could not ensure its internal cohesion, whether locally or globally.

The three-dimensional look at ethnicity is summarized in Fig. 3. The vertical axis (T) expresses changes in ethnic identity over time, be these macro-level trends on the general scene, changes in generational status, or differing stages of a person's life cycle. The horizontal axis (S) represents the distribution of a given population across space and the importance of place in shaping distinctive patterns of group belonging. Each ethnic population—for instance, Jews—comprises many subgroups (SG) that differ in specific historical experience or contemporary adjustments and mingling of ethnic identity; even within a given geographic location, the ethnic group is characterized by

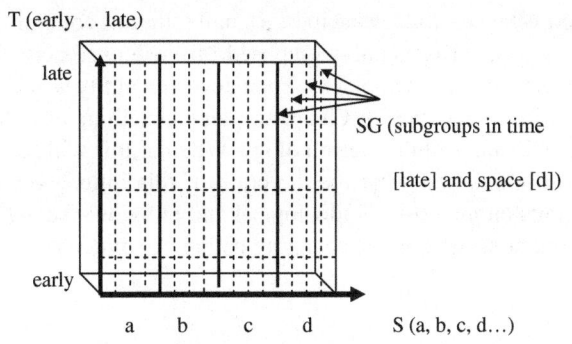

Jews and the Ethnic Scene: A Multidimensional Theory 99

Figure 3. Schematic description of factors involved in ethnic identity

internal variations of its subgroups. Thus, the nature of group identity depends on some kind of combination of time, which can range from an early to a later period ($T_{e=early...l=late}$); space, corresponding to the number of places in which members of the group live ($S_{a,b,c...}$); and the specific patterns of subgroups within the broad ethnic identity in each time (t) and space (s) ($SG_{t,s}$).

Ideological and social developments enhance, and do not weaken, the wish of people to express ethnic self-identity in an increasingly varied range of behaviors. Yet the multiple and mixed nature of ethnic identity renders more difficult the recognition, definition and, accordingly, the measure of ethnic identity and identification. The combination of an increasing tendency to express ethnic identity in some form, on the one hand, and the various possibilities for a single or multiple identity, on the other, suggests that the study of ethnicity in general, and that of Jews in particular, will need to adopt a split approach that examines specific sub-identities, in lieu of studying any targeted ethnic population as one homogenous group. Analysis of broadly defined ethnic categories may mask important internal variations and subgroup uniqueness.

Moreover, in light of the partly but nonetheless significant situational nature of ethnicity, the study of Jews cannot remain wedded to traditional approaches, but should instead adopt a wider and more dynamic approach both for defining and allocating the target population and for measuring group identification. Doing so would reveal a paradox. As suggested above, social research should direct attention to trends over time and variations across space, alongside examining how religious and ethnic identification differ between subgroups within a given population sharing ethnic and religious identity. Yet to the extent that patterns of identification are not uniform along these dimensions, it is difficult to ensure a comprehensive comparative examination. This is an important issue in the social scientific study of Jews, and also in the more general field of ethnic studies, and it is one that requires further methodological and conceptual considerations.

Meanwhile, the largest Jewish community in the diaspora, namely North American Jewry, is facing a major change in the ethnic profile of its surrounding general environment. A recent influx of immigrants, along with internal demographic processes, is likely to transform non-Hispanic whites into a minority among the U.S. population. (This is also the case for some major metropolitan areas in Canada.)

Under such circumstances, the Jews will be a small religious component of an ethnic-racial minority in a majority mainly composed of those once classified under such rubrics as Hispanics, Asians, and blacks. Their Jewish identity will be subordinate to two major identities: American (or Canadian), and something else that may or may not conflate "racial" and "ethnic" terminology. Whether this will have any influence on Jewish commitment, and what the direction of this influence will be, depends among other things on macro-level ideological and individual social characteristics, on inter-group relations, and on the changing nature of ethnicity.

Notes

1. For a comprehensive discussion on the meaning of time, see Andrew Abbott, *Time Matters: On Theory and Method* (Chicago: 2001).
2. Nathan Glazer, *We Are All Multiculturalists Now* (Cambridge, Mass.: 1997).
3. Grace Davie, "Religion in Europe in the 21st Century: The Factors to Take into Account," *European Journal of Sociology* 47, no. 2 (2006), 271–296; Herbert Gans, "Symbolic Ethnicity and Symbolic Religiosity: Towards a Comparison of Ethnic and Religious Acculturation," *Ethnic and Racial Studies* 17 (1994), 577–592.
4. Steven M. Cohen, *Religious Stability and Ethnic Decline: Emerging Patterns of Jewish Identity in the United States* (New York: 1998); Uzi Rebhun, "Jewish Identification in Contemporary America: Gans's Symbolic Ethnicity and Religiosity Theory Revisited," *Social Compass* 51, no. 3 (2004), 349–366.
5. Richard Alba and Victor Nee, *Remaking the American Mainstream: Assimilation and Contemporary Immigration* (Cambridge, Mass.: 2003); Andreas Wimmer, "The Making and Unmaking of Ethnic Boundaries: A Multilevel Process Theory," *American Journal of Sociology* 113, no. 4 (2008), 970–1022.
6. Ariela Keysar, Barry A. Kosmin, and Jeffrey Scheckner, *The Next Generation: Jewish Children and Adolescents* (Albany: 2000).
7. Uzi Rebhun and Lilach Lev-Ari, *American Israelis: Migration, Transnationalism, and Diasporic Identity* (Leiden: 2010); Julius H. Schoeps, "Russian-Speaking Jews and Germany's Local Jewry," in *Transnationalism: Diasporas and the Advent of a New (Dis)Order*, ed. Eliezer Ben-Rafael and Yitzhak Sternberg (Leiden: 2009), 295–302.
8. Rebhun, "Jewish Identification in Contemporary America"; Uzi Rebhun and Shlomit Levy, "Unity and Diversity: Jewish Identification in America and Israel, 1990–2000," *Sociology of Religion: A Quarterly Review* 67, no. 4 (2006), 391–414.
9. Uzi Rebhun and Sergio DellaPergola, "Heibetim soziyodemografiyim vezehutiyim shel nisuim me'uravim bekerev yehudei arzot habrit," in *Eros eirusin veisurim: miniyut umishpahah bahistoriyah*, ed. Israel Bartal and Isaiah Gafni (Jerusalem: 1998), 369–398.
10. Sylvia Barack Fishman, *Double or Nothing? Jewish Families and Mixed Marriage* (Waltham: 2004); Keren McGinity, *Still Jewish: A History of Women and Intermarriage in America* (New York: 2009).
11. Ira M. Sheskin, *How Jewish Communities Differ: Variation in the Findings of Local Jewish Population Studies* (New York: 2001).
12. Louis Wirth, "The Ghetto," *American Journal of Sociology* 33 (1927), 68.
13. Uzi Rebhun, "Geographic Mobility and Religioethnic Identification: Three Jewish Communities in the United States," *Journal for the Scientific Study of Religion* 34, no. 4 (1995), 485–498. See also Ewa Morawska's discussion of Soviet Jewish immigrants in her essay in this symposium, "Ethnicity as a Primordial-Situational-Constructed Experience: Different Times, Different Places, Different Constellations," 16–19.
14. Rebhun and Lev-Ari, *American Israelis*.

15. Bernard Lazerwitz, J. Alan Winter, and Arnold Dashefsky, "Localism, Religiosity, Orthodoxy, and Liberalism: The Case of Jews in the United States," *Social Forces* 67, no. 1 (1988), 229–242; Jonathan Rabinowitz, "The Paradoxical Effects of Jewish Community Size on Jewish Communal Behavior: Intermarriage, Synagogue Membership and Giving to Local Jewish Federations," *Contemporary Jewry* 10, no. 1 (1989), 9–15.

16. Morawska, "Ethnicity as a Primordial-Situational-Constructed Experience," 16–19.

17. Michael Waltzer, "Is Liberalism (Still) Good for the Jews?" *Moment* (March 1986), 13–19.

18. Dorris Bensimon and Sergio DellaPergola, *La population juive de France: sociodemographie et identité* (Jerusalem: 1984); Sergio DellaPergola and Uzi Rebhun, "Heibetim stoziodemografiyim udfusei hizdahut shel yehudim sefaradim veashkenazim bearzot habrit bishnat 1990," in *Hevrah vetarbut: yehudei sefarad leahar hageriush,* ed. Michel Abitbol, Yom Tom Assis and Galit Chazan-Rokem (Jerusalem: 1997), 105–135).

19. See, for example, Charles Kadushin, Benjamin T. Phillips, and Leonard Saxe, "National Jewish Population Survey 2000–01: A Guide for the Perplexed," *Contemporary Jewry* 25 (2005), 1–32; Benjamin Phillips, "Numbering the Jews: Evaluating and Improving Surveys of American Jews" (Ph.D. diss., Brandeis University, 2006); Uzi Rebhun, "Similarities and Dissimilarities in National and Community Surveys: The Case of American Jews," in *Papers in Jewish Demography 1993*, ed. Sergio DellaPergola and Judith Even (Jerusalem: 1997), 55–78.

20. Benjamin Beit Hallahmi, *Prolegomena of the Psychological Study of Religion* (Lewisburg: 1989); Simon Herman, *Jewish Identity: A Social Psychological Perspective* (Beverly Hills: 1977); Henri Tajfel, *Human Groups and Social Categories: Studies in Social Psychology* (Cambridge: 1981).

21. Arnold Dashefsky and Howard M. Shapiro, "Ethnicity and Identity," in *Ethnic Identity in Society*, ed. Arnold Dashefsky (Chicago: 1976), 5.

22. Daniel R. Miller, "The Study of Social Relationships: Situation, Identity, and Social Interaction," *Psychology: A Study of a Science*, vol. 5, ed. Sigmund Koch (New York: 1963), 639–737.

23. Herman, *Jewish Identity*; Harold R. Isaacs, "Basic Group Identity: The Idols of the Tribe," in *Ethnicity: Theory and Experience*, ed. Nathan Glazer and Daniel P. Moynihan (Cambridge, Mass.: 1975), 29–52.

24. Erik H. Erikson, *Childhood and Society*, 2nd. ed. (New York: 1963); idem, *Identity: Youth and Crisis* (New York: 1968).

25. Michael A. Hogg and Dominic Abrams, *Social Identification: A Social Psychology of Intergroup Relations and Group Processes* (New York: 1988).

26. Mordechai Bar-Lev and Peri Kedem, "Ahdutiyut umuvhanut bahizdahut uvazehut hayehudit vehaziyonit shel hastudent hayisreeli," in *Heibetim bahinukh*, ed. Yehudah Eisenberg (Ramat Gan: 1986), 155–177.

27. On the attitude/behavior theory, see Martin Fishbein and Icek Ajzen, *Belief, Attitude, Intention and Behavior: An Introduction to Theory and Research* (Reading, Mass.: 1975).

28. See, for example, Sergio DellaPergola, Shlomit Levy, Uzi Rebhun, and Dalia Sagi, "Patterns of Jewish Identification in the United States, 2001", in *Theory and Construction and Multivariate Analysis: Applications of Facet Approach*, ed. Dov Elizur and Eyal Yaniv (Tel Aviv: 2009), 305–318; Uzi Rebhun, "Jewish Identity in America: Structural Analyses of Attitudes and Behaviors," *Review of Religious Research* 46, no. 1 (2004), 43–63.

29. Sergio DellaPergola, "Jewish Identity/Assimilation/Continuity: Approaches to a Changing Reality," in *Cadernos de Lengua e Literatura Hebraica* (São Paulo: 2001), 17–51; idem, "Jewish Assimilation/Continuity: Three Approaches," *Proceedings of the Latin American Jewish Studies Association Conference* (Mexico City: 1995).

30. Andreas Wimmer, "The Making and Unmaking of Ethnic Boundaries: A Multilevel Process Theory," *American Journal of Sociology* 113 (2008), 977.

The Utility of the Concept of "Ethnicity" for the Study of Jews

Riv-Ellen Prell
(UNIVERSITY OF MINNESOTA)

The early 21st century is an apt time to reconsider the utility of the concept of ethnicity for the study of Jewry. The imprecision of the term, which might well serve the study of a group as complex as the Jews, might at the same time render it unable to account for what it claims to describe.

The study of ethnicity in North America, the area I know best, engendered particularly creative scholarship in the last third of the 20th century. A variety of scholars conceptualized the term in a dynamic or a social constructivist manner and offered powerful interdisciplinary studies that cut across the humanities and social sciences. The concept of ethnicity was thoroughly deconstructed and historicized, to the extent that it is now difficult to regard it as a neutral term of scholarly discourse.

In North America, at least, the term's intellectual history inextricably linked it to the concept of race.[1] Which groups in America were called "races" and which were called "ethnics"; whether ethnics had a race or whether people of color had an ethnicity; and why ethnicity was not even a common term until the 1940s—all of these issues underline the political nature of the term. The fact that Americans of European descent were transformed over time from being members of races to being "ethnics" reveals the centrality of racial politics to systems of classification.

The concept of ethnicity was first associated with a group of Jewish intellectuals in the 1920s and 1930s. This group, including among others Horace Kallen and Julius Drachsler, used the term to describe Jews as a group that shared cultural rather than racial traits. Political scientist Victoria Hattam argues that they linked Jewishness to culture and language in order to separate it from the immutability of race. This, after all, was a period in which race science and eugenics dominated the public discourse, a time when Americans were obsessed with the notion of the inferiority both of the non-native-born and of native-born men and women of color. In the midst of pitched battles over immigration, worthiness for citizenship, and the question of who belonged in America, the concept of ethnicity became not only a model for pluralism, but a defense against the racialization of Jews. In light of this history, the persistence of ethnicity as a mode of analysis underscores the need to make clear what exactly is being described.

Beyond the racially freighted world of American immigration politics, what ethnicity as a conceptual category attempts to capture is ambiguous. The anthropologist Richard Jenkins' careful rethinking of the concept of ethnicity demonstrates that scholars from Max Weber on argued that shared descent (the concept that precedes the notion of ethnicity) did not "cause" political action; what was more likely was that group identification was an outcome of shared action and political interests. Yet the question of what it is that causes or reflects cultural difference remains a matter of debate.[2]

Most recently, Eli Lederhendler has argued in a similar vein that Russian Jewish immigrants in the United States coalesced around an urban industrial economy that restructured the meaning of social capital. The social capital they acquired in America shaped the character of their mutual connections and cleavages; he finds this social analysis preferable to the more ambiguous terms connected to ethnic history that focus on culture.[3]

It is tempting simply to set aside the term "ethnicity" in order to avoid its distractions. But that does not solve the problem. How to describe Jews' relationship to one another as well as their ideas about that relationship is no less complex than the history of the ethnicity concept. The essays in this symposium attempt to capture something about how various strands of Jewishness—language, connection, and identity, among others—are realized. They describe ethnicity variously as a source of cohesion, identity, group boundaries, and distinctiveness. They present ethnicity both diachronically and synchronically, each of them pointing to a different set of problems for analysis. In short, for historians and social scientists of Jewry, ethnicity is indispensable and problematic, freighted with political baggage and intellectually challenging. My comments address three of the essays that seek to rethink how to study ethnicity in all of its complexity.

Joel Perlmann, himself a significant contributor to the scholarship on the historical formation of issues of race and ethnicity in the United States, makes an important contribution to the discussion of ethnicity by addressing issues of temporality for groups he characterizes as "weakly racialized"—that is, those that were once distinct but that are increasingly integrated into the larger society through intermarriage. Perlman finds that people of color have been less likely to intermarry than are people who are seen and who see themselves as "white." His demographic analysis focuses on the waning of ethnic connection over time, as men and women marry across groups and their children have multiple group connections. He assumes that ethnicity is most powerful among the offspring of endogamous marriages. He also demonstrates that single-origin descendents remain numerous through the third generation.

Perlmann points as well to a demographic reality that "works to radically reduce the impact that sheer number of single-origin offspring will have on the force of ethnic life"—the fact that the offspring of any group of mothers are born over a wide range of years, and thus the possibility of group cohesion is diluted. In fact, in the cases Perlmann presents of 19th-century Irish and German and 20th-century Italian immigrants to the United States, a large number of single-origin descendents failed "to propel ethnic allegiances as a strong force into the third generation."

Although Perlmann argues that ethnicity is a "process" that is "conditioned by historical time in ways that are reflected in the concept of generation," he offers important observations about Jewish distinctiveness beyond the obvious point that the Jews' rate of out-marriage was much lower in the first few generations after immigration. He suggests that non-demographic factors may play a significant role in "affecting the nature of the group" in subsequent generations. For example, Jews' ongoing ethnic attachments led them to create elaborate communal institutions over an extended period of time, which may have sparked an "interest in Jewish origins and things Jewish" among those of "mixed origins." He also notes that ethnic "involvement" might well be attributed to various forms of mobility, including geographic and economic.

Perlmann links communal institutions to the reproduction of ethnicity, but he is less precise about what defines that sort of ethnicity. For Perlmann, there is a significant difference between "cohesion," "allegiance," and "ethnic involvement." The terms are progressively less concrete and move from the possibility of behavioral measures to attitudes that ultimately might be quite individual and even interior, from group attachments to the realm of identity. How institutional frameworks might work to create that identity is not his concern. But his observations are important for the questions that he raises: What does ethnicity mean when a temporal dimension is added and analysts can begin to think in terms of less and more? What do institutional frameworks do, particularly when they are frequently bound to particular generations' visions of Jewish ethnicity? Do institutional structures tend to outlast particular definitions of ethnicity?

Bethamie Horowitz argues that Jewish ethnicity is not well explained or analyzed by conventional sociological categories. The persistence of Jewish ethnicity, which she defines in sociological terms both as "distinctiveness" and as the more difficult to define "meaning" or "experience," leads her to argue that Jews are not best understood either as a "religion" or as comparable to other ethnic groups. She argues that the study of Jewish ethnicity should focus on "inner dynamics" in order to understand the "emotional glue" of Jewish ethnicity. Horowitz turns to a socio-psychological framework to examine "Jewish identity" as a term of greater salience than the social distinctiveness implied by ethnicity. What psychology offers is the opportunity to examine the relationship between individual agency (the choice-making element in the construction of identity) and the structures in which choice is embedded.

Perlmann and Horowitz both identify unpredictable interventions—institutions, mobility, "personal journeys"—that account for a persistence in some aspects of Jewish ethnicity. Each of them works to complicate the concept in order to capture some Jews' ongoing investment in their Jewishness even in the absence of certain classical features of ethnic relations or identity such as boundaries. Perlmann's analysis points to institutional infrastructures whereas Horowitz emphasizes personal choices embedded in social relationships; both see a broad range of dynamics at work in Jewish ethnicity.

Ewa Morawska's contribution offers a model for the study of Jewish ethnicity that focuses on comparison across time and space among Jews. She does this by means of two significant modes of analysis. She first casts the project as one that embeds Jewish experience in historical surroundings, looking at comparisons among Jews rather than between Jews and non-Jews. Because she is interested in the "context-dependent and changing character of Jewish ethnicity," Morawska places her emphasis on the "receiver" society to which Jews will have to respond as they articulate social boundaries and "common descent." This approach focuses on flexibility in what constitutes Jewish ethnicity, how it changes over time, the centrality of actors and, most important, its context. The model allows for comparison of different forms that Jewish ethnicity has taken and for understanding why these forms came about. Morawska draws her examples largely from the work of other scholars and acknowledges that the absence of information related to gender (and, one might add, other forms of differentiation) is a significant limitation. Nonetheless, her approach is truly promising.

Certainly this work is responsive to Bethamie Horowitz's concern about the need for flexible definitions of Jewishness and to Joel Perlmann's interest in nondemographic factors that shape persistent identity among Jews. As with any work of comparative sociology, Morawksa's essay argues for the structural features that will best explain, or at least capture, these processes.

Morawska's context-dependent approach employs a second mode of analysis that I find more challenging. She draws on the work of another scholar, Steven Fenton, who transformed the debates about ethnicity that emerged in the late 20th century, to which I referred at the outset, by constructing a set of "ideal types" of ethnicity. In employing this scheme, Morawska takes a look at the broad, sometimes mutually contradictory, categories of "primordialism," "social construction," and "contingency" to analyze how Jews will experience each of them within a given host society or particular historical circumstances. She defines primordial attachment as the "givens" of social existence that create an "absolute" tie between group members. The "social construction" view of ethnicity casts it as specific to particular contexts and dynamic, but less instrumental than the last category, something that is dynamic and will change over time. The final formulation of ethnicity is one that views the ties as "contingent on circumstances" and thus highly flexible. Group members "use" these ties for specific purposes. The change in experiences of Jewish ethnicity will emerge and differ from various times and places depending on how these ideal types are actually experienced, and Jews will experience some versions of all ideal types depending on the circumstances.

One of the most productive outcomes of late 20th-century work on ethnicity was the end of dualistic thinking that pitted ethnicity as primordial against ethnicity as socially constructed; in the end, there were no credible holdouts for primordialism as an analytic framework. The question, then, is why these particular categories should be employed as ideal types. What is the relationship between them, and how, in this case, do Jews experience their identities or group within the "home country"? Rendering such dynamic notions as "construction" or "situational" or "instrumental" as transparent "mechanisms" or "types" that can be compared and contrasted is not entirely convincing to me. Taking the felt experience of primordialism, labeling it as an approach to ethnicity, and then reshaping it as an ideal type may not produce as dynamic and context-specific approach to ethnicity as would be ideal.

The devil is in the details, and Ewa Morawska is clear that she is most interested in the model that she has advanced, which certainly offers an interesting vision for comparative study. By necessity, the sweeping generalizations of a comparative sociology must brush against the demands of a more fine-grained analysis of culture and cultural history. My concern is to caution scholars to tread carefully in the use of ideal types whose intellectual baggage is considerable and whose notions are anything but transparent. These concepts do not readily lend themselves to typological thinking; they may render comparison—presumably an important goal—overly challenging.

These articles on ethnicity underline a dilemma for scholars. I would argue that, while Bethamie Horowitz and Joel Perlmann continue to use the concept, they do so somewhat ambiguously, as they are interested in explaining a set of experiences that falls outside reigning models and ideas about ethnicity. There is some sort of Jewish persistence that is interesting to understand under the banner of identity or attachment. Similarly, Ewa Morawska attempts to avoid some of the ambiguities of the concept by focusing on how Jewish experience is embedded in historical surroundings and to use that as the basis of comparison within her model. For all three scholars, the utility of the concept for Jews is not questioned; they rather seek to redefine it and find new approaches to it.

And yet the ambiguity and complexity of the concept continues to raise the question of its utility. As ethnicity is continually unpacked, reapplied, and renegotiated methodologically and conceptually, one wonders if there are other questions to be considered in analyzing Jewish experiences. The remaining underlying task is to arrive at a viable definition of what it is that research on Jewish ethnicity seeks to establish. If the questions driving the study of contemporary Jewry outside of Israel focus primarily on the persistence of feelings of attachment to an identity, and not necessarily even a group, then, as Horowitz argues, they may be grounded increasingly in social psychology. If the questions concern group boundaries, solidarity, or shared action, then they might best be linked to larger notions of common political or economic interests. The best antidote to the imprecision of the concept of ethnicity is greater precision in defining the research questions and never assuming Jews' connections to one another.

Careful analysis of the ways in which "race" and "ethnicity" have emerged as forms of social categorization that imply one another suggests that any study of Jews should involve a thorough investigation of the underlying assumptions of what are ostensibly neutral terms. Each of the papers in this symposium engages key aspects of social identity—language, group attachment, personal identity, and social boundaries, among others. Following Ewa Morawska's lead, it is important to understand how they relate to one another, and what their significance is. Only by asking those foundational questions will we understand those key assumptions.

How to separate the intellectual history of the concept from its utility as a lens for analysis underlines the richness and the challenge of studying Jews.

Notes

1. Matthew Frye Jacobson, *Whiteness of A Different Color: European Immigrants and the Alchemy of Race* (Cambridge, Mass.: 1998); David Roediger; *Working toward Whiteness: How America's Immigrants Became White: The Strange Journey from Ellis Island to the*

Suburbs (New York: 2005); Victoria Hattam, *The Shadow of Race: Jews, Latinos and Immigrant Politics in the United States* (Chicago: 2007); Thomas A. Guglielmo, *White on Arrival: Italians, Race, Color, and Power in Chicago, 1890–1945* (Oxford: 2003); Eric Goldstein, *The Price of Whiteness: Jews, Race, and American Identity* (Princeton: 2006).

2. Richard Jenkins, *Rethinking Ethnicity: Arguments and Explorations* (London: 1997).

3. Eli Lederhendler, *Jewish Immigrants and American Capitalism 1880–1920: From Caste to Class* (Cambridge: 2009).

Ethnicity and Beyond

Jonathan D. Sarna
(BRANDEIS UNIVERSITY)

Ethnicity had nothing to do with Jews prior to the 1930s. The classical meaning of the term "ethnic," according to the *Oxford English Dictionary*, is "one who is not a Christian or a Jew." Ethnics, the *OED* continues, were Gentiles, heathens, and pagans—not Jews. At different times in America, Jews were described as a "nation," a "society," a "people" and (most commonly) a "race."[1] For more than 250 years, though, no Jews in America ever considered themselves, or were considered by others, to be "ethnics."

The word ethnic, and its cognates, took on new meaning in Nazism's shadow. With the politicization of the term "race" and the discrediting of "racial science," liberal social scientists searched for new ways to describe "a group of people differentiated from the rest of the community by racial origins or cultural background, and usually claiming or enjoying official recognition of their group identity."[2] In their influential book, *We Europeans: A Survey of 'Racial' Problems* (1935), biologist Julian S. Huxley and anthropologist Alfred C. Haddon urged that "the term race as applied to human groups should be dropped from the vocabulary of science." In its place, they advocated for "ethnic group" or "people."[3]

Early users of these new terms employed them much the way "race" had once been used: to denote a primordial tie that group members shared in common. In response to Hitler, and in line with the teachings of anthropologists, they may have looked to culture rather than biology to explain the origin of ethnic differences. But they scarcely doubted that ethnicity reflected history and shaped destiny. As Tony Michels demonstrates in his fascinating essay in this symposium, this was the case even among Jewish Communists. They did not know the word "ethnicity" and they certainly eschewed religion. But for all their attention to class, they continued to harbor deep emotional attachments to their fellow Jews. They looked to common descent and culture as the basis for Jewish identity and as a marker of social boundaries. That explains why, when *Di morgn frayhayt*, under pressure from Communist party officials, stridently attacked Zionism following the 1929 Hebron riots, "the large-scale backlash [among readers] almost bankrupted the newspaper."

The belief that ethnicity was innate—that even the most assimilated of Jews harbored within them some kind of *pintele yid*, a dormant Jewish homunculus waiting to burst forth—lived on for many decades. But as Lila Corwin Berman has recently reminded us, conversions to Judaism raised a daunting challenge to the view that ethnicity was primordial. The widely publicized 1956 conversion of actress Marilyn Monroe, in particular, pointed to a much more volitional definition of ethnicity. If, after all, the "American body" (symbolized by the erotic Monroe) could be Judaized, then Judaism was obviously much more determined by consent than descent, and ethnicity was not destiny after all.[4]

It took time before this new view of ethnicity took hold. Indeed, the publication of Nathan Glazer and Daniel P. Moynihan's *Beyond the Melting Pot* (1963) and Michael Novak's *The Rise of the Unmeltable Ethnics* (1972) provided fresh ammunition to support the view that ethnicity was destiny. Politically speaking, these scholars argued, once an ethnic, always an ethnic. Nevertheless, a growing volume of contrary evidence, coupled with an ideological distaste for determinism of any sort, soon swept the old consensus aside. Books like Werner Sollors' *The Invention of Ethnicity* (1989) and Mary Waters' *Ethnic Options: Choosing Identities in America* (1990) implied that ethnicities were either selected or invented; they were not innate.

This new view of ethnicity as volitional and contingent meshed nicely with facts on the ground in Jewish life. Everywhere, it seemed, non-Orthodox converts to Judaism, children of intermarried Jewish fathers (patrilineal Jews), people descended from 15th-century forced converts to Christianity on the Iberian peninsula (*anusim*), Ethiopian Falash Mura, and others sought recognition as Jews on the basis of their having *freely chosen* Judaism. Where "citizenship" in the Jewish people had once overwhelmingly depended on having been born into the Jewish "race" through a Jewish mother, now a much broader definition was advocated. Hundreds of thousands of people worldwide today self-identify as Jews, and seek to have others identify them as Jews, based on their belief that identity should be volitional. They hope that the boundaries of (Orthodox) Judaism will someday be opened wide enough to receive them.

Ewa Morawska, in her essay here, complicates contemporary reinterpretations of ethnicity by arguing, following Steven Fenton, that "changing constellations of primordial, circumstantial and constructed components . . . make up ethnic practices and identities." She views Jewish ethnicity as "a hybrid creation" composed of elements that are in some cases timeless and universal, and in others, time-dependent and context-dependent. In passing, she reminds us that the sub-ethnic components of ethnicity—those that distinguish Russian Jews from German Jews, or even Russian Jews in Philadelphia from their counterparts in Tel Aviv—are deeply significant, even if historically contingent. The "ethnicization" process that melts immigrants into ethnics tends to erode sub-ethnic categories among succeeding generations. Even once highly significant sub-ethnic designations, such as "Galician Jew," have disappeared over the course of time.

Morawska's understanding of ethnicity is informed by historical examples and by recent work on immigrants from the former Soviet Union. Bethamie Horowitz, however, reminds us that Jewish ethnicity in the United States operates within a strikingly different context than was true even a generation ago. Three differences seem to me particularly important.

First of all, the nation's values have changed. Neither endogamy nor the maintenance of ethnic identity is high on the current American scale of values. Indeed, the current president of the United States, Barack Obama, projects through his own life's story a sense that mixed and multiple identities "hold great promise" and that ethnicity, even as it contains primordial elements, is to a considerable degree constructed. With an African father who was, in his words, "black as pitch," and an American mother who was "white as milk," Obama is himself the product of a mixed marriage. He experienced "a variety of cultures in a climate of mutual respect" while growing up in Hawaii, and over time, he assumed an African American identity, though it was not one that he was born into. He is, in short, the poster child for freedom of choice in both marriage and matters of identity.[5]

The second great change in the American context, related to the first, is the normalization of intermarriage. In the 1950s, most Americans married people of their own kind: "birds of a feather," the saying went, "flock together." Endogamy rates for Protestants, Catholics, Jews, African Americans, Asian Americans, and white people were all extraordinarily high. Today, by contrast, marriages across ethnic, religious, and racial lines are culturally celebrated, in many circles, and have become commonplace. Swedish, Norwegian, German, Italian, and Irish Americans all experience intermarriage rates in excess of 60 percent. Among Catholics, intermarriage rates among young people exceed 50 percent. In the much smaller Greek Orthodox Church, by the early 1990s, fully two-thirds of all marriages involved a partner who was not Greek Orthodox. Asian Americans and African Americans have likewise witnessed dramatic upswings in intermarriage. "Nearly half of recent marriages for U.S. born Asian-Americans have been to non-Asian White Americans," according to an account published in 2002, whereas marriages between blacks and whites multiplied seven-fold between 1960 and 1993.[6] Jews have been greatly affected by this cultural transformation. Roughly half of all Jews in America today marry individuals not raised as Jews, and some say that there are now more intermarried than in-married families in the community. Since, as Joel Perlmann reminds us in his essay, "it is generally harder for ethnicity to remain a strong force in a mixed than in a single-origin family," ethnic ties are weakening. An increasing number of young people are, in Sylvia B. Fishman's phrase, "Jewish and something else."[7]

Third, both American society and American Jewish society have become culturally far more heterogeneous and pluralistic. Foreign-born immigrants to the United States have literally changed the complexion of the country; the largest groups of immigrants come from Latin America, China, the Philippines, India, and Vietnam. The Jewish community has similarly been transformed, seemingly overnight, from a homogeneous community of white European origin to a much more heterogeneous community embracing a full range of races and colors. Intermarriages, conversions, interracial adoptions, and immigration have brought about these changes, which are especially prevalent within the Reform movement but are now also visible wherever Jews gather in numbers.[8] Gone are the days when savvy Jews could look at a crowd and, at a glance, pick out "members of the tribe" on the basis of their looks alone. Today, appearance plays a much smaller role in Jewish ethnicity than it did even one generation ago.

What continues to hold Jews together in the wake of these seismic changes? Sarah Bunin Benor and Steven M. Cohen suggest in their innovative discussion here that patterns of speech play some role. "American Jews speak differently from their non-Jewish neighbors," they conclude, and the *younger* they are, the more they want to distinguish themselves linguistically from their neighbors—perhaps because the younger they are, the more likely they are to be Orthodox. Like head coverings and "Star of David" necklaces, "talking Jewish" in the way that Benor and Cohen describe helps to distinguish as Jews those who in so many other ways closely resemble their non-Jewish neighbors.

Jews also turn to genetics to validate who they are. Harkening back to the idea that Jewishness is innate, they point to studies that provide a biological basis for Jewish intelligence ("Jewish intelligence is simply a compensatory genetic error linked to other genetic diseases").[9] Or they study the "Cohen" gene that supposedly demonstrates priestly continuity. Or they point to Jewish genetic diseases that likewise are said to show that, at the DNA level, Jews form a single biological family. Jews may appear more variegated and diverse, but these genetic studies imply that in terms of the fundamental building blocks of life, they are as interrelated as ever they were.[10]

Lastly, Jews point to behaviors that define them distinctively as Jews. Studies of Jewish habits, political behaviors, and attitudes in the United States suggest that, as a group, Jews differ from other Americans in terms of their "high level of and interest in education and learning," their commitment to the values of individual freedom and choice, their support for liberal values such as minority rights and social justice, their "urban orientation," their child-rearing practices, and their "skepticism about the military." Yet for all of this emphasis on "Jewish distinctiveness in America," these same studies reveal that on fully 88 percent of all issues examined, Jews differ little or not at all from their neighbors, ethnicity notwithstanding.[11]

Against this complex and changing background, a collection of essays on "ethnicity and beyond" could scarcely be more timely. The word "ethnicity," unknown prior to the 1930s and ubiquitous in the 1970s, has lost much of its cachet in recent years, but the idea that Jews are still *somehow* distinctive continues to muster strong support. What that "somehow" is, and whether it will suffice to sustain Jewish group loyalties in the 21st century, remains to be seen.

Notes

1. Eric L. Goldstein, *The Price of Whiteness: Jews, Race, and American Identity* (Princeton: 2006).
2. "Ethnic," *Oxford English Dictionary Online*, http://dictionary.oed.com (accessed 14 Feb. 2010).
3. Julian S. Huxley and Alfred C. Haddon, *We Europeans: A Survey of 'Racial' Problems* (London: 1935), 107–108.
4. Lila Corwin Berman, *Speaking of Jews: Rabbis, Intellectuals and the Creation of an American Public Identity* (Berkeley: 2009), 167.
5. Barack Obama, *Dreams from My Father: A Story of Race and Inheritance* (New York: 1995), 10, 23–25; *Honolulu Star Bulletin*, (8 Feb. 2007), online at archives.starbulletin.com/2007/02/08/news/story02.html (accessed 15 Feb. 2010).
6. Jonathan D. Sarna, "Intermarriage in America: The Jewish Experience in Historical Context," in *Ambivalent Jew: Charles Liebman in Memoriam*, ed. Stuart Cohen and Bernard Susser (New York: 2007), 125–133.
7. Sylvia B. Fishman, *Jewish and Something Else: A Study of Mixed-Married Families* (New York: 2001).

8. Diane K. Tobin, Gary Tobin, and Scott Rubin, *In Every Tongue: The Racial & Ethnic Diversity of the Jewish People* (San Francisco: 2005).

9. Sander Gilman, "Bell Curve to Bell Jar," *Tablet* (12 June 2007), online at tabletmag.com/life-and-religion/2394/bell-curve-to-bell-jar/ (accessed 2 Aug. 2010), paraphrasing Gregory Cochran, Jason Hardy and Henry Harpending, "Natural History of Ashkenazi Intelligence," online at homepage.mac.com/harpend/.Public/AshkenaziIQ.jbiosocsci.pdf.

10. Sander Gilman, "Bell Curve to Bell Jar"; David B. Goldstein, *Jacob's Legacy: A Genetic View* (New Haven: 2005); Jon Entine, *Abraham's Children: Identity and the DNA of the Chosen People* (New York: 2007).

11. Tom W. Smith, *Jewish Distinctiveness in America: A Statistical Portrait* (New York: 2005), 33, 53 (online at www.ajc.org/atf/cf/%7B42D75369-D582-4380-8395-D25925B85EAF%7D/JewishDistinctivenessAmerica_TS_April2005.pdf).

Essay

German Jewish Interwar Migration in a Comparative Perspective: Mandatory Palestine, the United States, and Great Britain

Hagit Lavsky
(THE HEBREW UNIVERSITY)

In the conclusion of his book *Branching Out: German-Jewish Immigration to the United States, 1820–1914* (1994), Avraham Barkai compared the profile of German Jewish immigrants in the United States to the Jewish population that remained in Germany. Barkai found great similarity in the patterns of social, political, and economic behavior of the two communities, despite the change in environment and context. He claimed, in addition, that German Jews—more than other minorities—maintained their distinctive character, though he added that further comparative studies in this area were needed.

Apart from the comparison between emigrants and those who stayed behind, a systematic comparison of different groups of German Jewish emigrants is called for in order to establish whether differences in the timing of migration had any effect on the characteristics of the emigrants and on their patterns of absorption in the receiving countries. Research on Jewish migration has so far concentrated primarily on the histories of the emigrating communities in their countries of destination, generally in isolation from one another.[1] This emphasis is partially related to the prevailing approach that views Jewish migration mainly as an involuntary movement propelled by economic and/or political persecution.[2] Consequently, social science-based questions concerning the decisions of individuals and families with regard to whether, when, and where to migrate (given both their demographic and socioeconomic situations and the existing conditions in their countries of origin and in the prospective destinations) have rarely been addressed by students of modern Jewish migration. Likewise, very little attention has been paid to the possible effects that the timing of migration and the choice of destination might have had on the social profile of the migrating groups and on their functioning within their new host societies.[3]

In this essay, I will touch upon some of these hitherto neglected questions in the context of the interwar migration of German Jews. For its inner periodization (namely, periodization according to factors relevant specifically to German Jews), I adopt the distinction suggested by Doron Niederland between voluntary emigration from the Weimar republic (1920–1932); the movement of emigrants in the years 1933–1938, which was still free, though propelled by urgent, albeit indirect, push factors and constrained by limited options; and the refugee stream from late 1938 until early 1941.[4]

Drawing on a number of existing studies as well as relevant archival sources, I will sketch out the basic contours of Jewish emigration from Germany to the three major overseas destinations—Mandatory Palestine, the United States, and Great Britain— and then proceed to compare these parallel but quite distinct immigrant streams. Focusing on the migrants' social profiles, their patterns of adjustment, the roles they played in their new host countries, and the extent to which they preserved their common character as German Jews, I will offer a typology of three different German Jewish destinies.

World Jewish Migration between the Wars

The post-First World War era was marked by growing restrictions on immigration imposed by countries that, prior to the war, had served as major destinations for emigrants from Eastern and Southern Europe—the main sources of Jewish migration in the decades up to 1914. In the United States, which received approximately two thirds of the mass European emigration prior to the First World War, a largely unrestricted immigration policy was replaced by immigration quotas aimed at preserving the prewar ethnic composition of the American population. These quotas, mainly affecting the inflows from Southern and Eastern Europe, were first introduced in 1921 and became much more rigid in the legislation of 1924. Likewise, Britain, although not a major immigration country, tightened its prewar (1905) restrictions on the entrance of foreigners by means of the Aliens Act of 1919.[5]

Palestine, in contrast, with its emerging potential for political and economic development under the British Mandate, became a favorable destination for Jewish migrants as early as the 1920s. It remained relatively open to Jewish immigration until the second half of the 1930s. At that point, in the wake of the outbreak of the Arab revolt in 1936 and the ensuing political unrest, the British government replaced the previous system of economic criteria as a basis for granting entry to Jewish immigrants; the new restrictions placed a cap on the number of Jews to be allowed to enter Palestine.[6] During the first half of the 1930s, however, Palestine was an attractive option for Jewish migrants. Following the recovery of the local economy from the downturn of 1926–1927 and from the aftermath of the violent outbursts against Palestinian Jews in 1929, the country entered a phase of economic prosperity and a relatively stable political atmosphere that lasted until the mid-1930s. It was precisely at that time that the United States, Britain, and many other countries were struggling with the Great Depression, attempting, among other means, to limit the entry of people into their severely damaged economies, and in turn losing much of their attractiveness as potential destinations in those years.

Table 1. The Share of Palestine and the United States as Destinations for Jewish Migration, 1920–1939

Period*	Worldwide total of migrating Jews	Palestine total	% of total	United States total	% of total
1920–1931	733,000	115,000	15.7	360,000	49.1
1932–1935	249,000	161,000	64.7	14,000	5.6
1936–1939	246,000	86,000	35.0	81,000	33.0
1920–1939	**1,227,000**	**362,000**	**29.5**	**455,000**	**37.1**

*Periodization dictated by changes in the status of Palestine as a destination compared with the United States.
Sources: Calculations (in round figures) based on Moshe Sicron, *Immigration to Israel 1948-1953* (Jerusalem: 1957), statistical supplement (Tables A1, A5); Jacob Metzer, *The Divided Economy of Mandatory Palestine* (London: 1998), 66 (Table 3.1). Both sources include American data.

Consequently, the proportional share of Palestine in receiving Jewish international migration grew significantly, from 16 percent in 1920–1931 to 65 percent in 1932–1935 (see Table 1). In numerical terms, out of a total of 733,000 internationally migrating Jews in the period 1920–1931, 115,000 immigrated to Palestine (of whom 48,300 arrived in 1924–1925 alone), compared with 360,000 who immigrated to the United States; in the four-year period of 1932–1935, the number of Jewish olim, or immigrants to Palestine, hit a record number of 161,000. In late 1935, a depression, subsequently aggravated by the Arab revolt of 1936–1939, altered the economic and political atmosphere, and the new Mandatory immigration restrictions added another factor to the downturn. In the period of 1936–1939, some 86,000 immigrants reached Palestine, constituting only 35 percent of total world Jewish migration in this period. These numbers were only slightly larger than those of Jewish immigration to the United States during the same time (81,000). Palestine's position deteriorated further in the spring of 1939 with the issuance of the British White Paper that restricted total Jewish immigration to Palestine (not to exceed 75,000 over a five-year period and then to cease, for all intents and purposes). However, at this juncture—which followed the Anschluss of Austria in March 1938, the annexation of the Sudetenland in October 1938, the Kristallnacht pogrom of November 1938, and the occupation of Czechoslovakia in March 1939—the United States and Britain introduced new regulations that somewhat eased the entry of refugees into their countries. Consequently, the bulk of the Jewish refugee emigration from Central Europe by the end of the 1930s and the beginning of the 1940s reached the shores of Britain and the United States rather than Palestine.

Interwar German Jewish Population and Emigration: An Overview

According to the German census of 1925, the number of Jews in the country totaled about 564,000. Thereafter, the number of Jews in Germany declined steadily, mainly because the community was relatively aged and had a death rate higher than its birthrate (conversions and other forms of withdrawal from the community did not exhibit an increase during the Weimar era and thus did not contribute appreciably to the demographic decline).[7] The post-First World War economic instability of the Weimar republic was another factor responsible for the population decline; during this period, tens of thousands of Germans, including some 35,000–40,000 Jews, emigrated.[8] Of the estimated 517,000 Jews who lived in Germany in January 1933,[9] more than 31 percent were over 40 years old, and by June 1933, out of about 500,000 Jews, the proportion older than 40 had increased to 48 percent.[10] As shown in Table 2, most German Jews were engaged in commerce, with only a minority in professions. Despite the pace of economic mobility, only a small proportion was able to climb the occupational ladder and reach its highest echelons. The bulk of German Jews during this period were small merchants or white-collar wage-earners.[11]

The Nazi seizure of power caused a significant upsurge of Jewish emigration. More than half (270,000) of the German Jewish population of early 1933 left Germany between 1933 and 1941, as shown in Table 3. The yearly estimates in this table do not reflect the real turning points—the first wave of emigration from Nazi Germany occurred in 1933, whereas a second, smaller upheaval followed the passage of the Nuremberg Laws of September 1935 and lasted through March 1936, causing a further aging of the German Jewish population (by 1941, some 45 percent of German Jews were older than 45).[12] During this period, the majority of the emigrants went to neighboring West and East European countries. In the following two years, the outflow slowed somewhat. But 1938 marked a new turning point: between 39,000 and 40,000 Jews left Germany during that year,[13] with the exodus intensifying following the Kristallnacht pogrom. More than half of the total emigration from Nazi Germany between 1933 and 1941—150,000 out of 270,000 individuals—left after mid-November 1938.[14]

Table 2. Demographic and Occupational Profile of German Jewry, June 1933

Age[a]		Occupation[b]	
Age groups	%	Branch of employment	%
0–15	16.5	Business	61.3
16–24	11.7	Industry	23.1
25–39	23.9	Professions & services	13.9
40–59	31.5	Agriculture	1.7
60 and over	16.3		
	100.0 (n= 499,800)		**100.0 (n = 248,000)**

[a] Calculated on the basis of Herbert A. Strauss, "Jewish Emigration from Germany: Nazi Policies and Jewish Responses (I)," *Leo Baeck Institute Year Book* 25 (1980), 318 (Table 3a).

[b] Avraham Barkai, "Bevölkerungsrückgang und wirtschaftliche Stagnation," in *Deutsch-jüdische Geschichte in der Neuzeit*, vol. 4, ed. Avraham Barkai and Paul Mendes-Flohr (Munich: 1997), 40; Michael Traub, *Die jüdische Auswanderung aus Deutschland: Westeuropa, Übersee, Palästina* (Berlin: 1936), 10–11, 14–17.

Table 3. Jewish Emigration from Nazi Germany

Year	Estimated Number of Emigrants		
1933	38,000 (*37,000)		
1934	23,000		
1935	20,000 (*21,000)		
1933–1935		81,000	
1936	25,000		
1937	23,000		
1933–1937		129,000	
1938	40,000		
1939	78,000		
1938–1939		118,000	
1933–1939			247,000
1940	15,000		
1941	8,000		
1933–1941			270,000
1942–1945	8,000		
1940–1945		31,000	
1933–1945			278,000

Sources: Yearly estimates and causes summarized by Wolfgang Benz in *Handbuch der deutschsprachigen Emigration 1933–1945*, ed. Claus-Dieter Krohn, Patrick von zur Mühlen, Gerhard Paul, and Lutz Winckler (Darmstadt: 1998), 5–16. Slightly different estimates found in Strauss, "Jewish Emigration (I)," 326 (Table 7), indicated by *.

German Jewish Immigration to Palestine

Among the Jews emigrating from Germany during the Weimar era, some 3,300 immigrated to Palestine, most of them during the peak years of the Fourth Aliyah (1924–1925) (see Table 4).[15]

Doron Niederland has demonstrated the lack of evidence for the widespread assumption that Zionist ideology was the only (or even the major) motive underlying aliyah, pointing instead to economic push and pull factors, particularly with regard to the timing of the move. However, it is important to differentiate the impact of economic factors on various sectors of German Jewry. Among the push factors was the galloping inflation of 1922–1923, which affected mostly white-collar wage-earners—members of this sector, including students, constituted the majority of the Zionist membership. A second, and contrasting, push factor was the deflation of 1925–1926, which affected mainly small businesses in which Jews in general were extensively represented: more than 60 percent of Jewish breadwinners were merchants.[16] Among the pull factors was the early to mid-1920s prosperity in Palestine, which, as has been seen, coincided with the transition from inflation to deflation in Germany. This situation made Palestine particularly appealing for Jews who were most likely to be hurt by the German inflation—among them, students abandoning academic studies in the face of dim prospects for white-collar employment in the public sector. Since many Zionists belonged to this

Table 4. Jewish Immigrants to Palestine from Weimar Germany, by Year

Year	Number of Immigrants
1920–1921	360
1922	44
1923	149
1924	480
1925	963
1926	325
1927	84
1928	87
1929	201
1930	138
1931	122
1932	353
1920–1932	**3,306**

Source: Doron Niederland, *Yehudei germanyah—mehagrim o pelitim? 'Iyun bidfusei hahagirah bein shetei milhamot ha'olam* (Jerusalem: 1996), 26.

group, it is quite difficult to separate ideological from material motivations in moving to Palestine. It seems, however, that potential immigrants of Zionist inclination took both economic and ideological considerations into account when they decided to acquire new skills and know-how that possibly could be applied in Palestine.

Table 5 points to some of the distinctive socioeconomic characteristics of German Jewish immigrants to Palestine during the Fourth Aliyah. This group was made up mainly of young, unmarried, educated, and professionally trained people. A significant number of them were active members of Zionist organizations, which prepared them professionally, either as individuals or as groups, for the needs of Palestine. Among them were the pioneers and founders of the kibbutzim Ein Harod, Yagur, and Beth Zera; the graduates of the Blau-Weiss youth movement, who set up cooperative workshops for construction and carpentry in Jerusalem and Tel Aviv; the architects Richard Kaufmann and Lotte Cohn; and the first scholars of the Hebrew University (inaugurated in 1925): Gershom Scholem, Shlomo Dov Goitein, Avraham Halevi Fränkel, and Yitzhak Fritz Baer. In addition, there were a number of people who were key Zionist functionaries: Arthur Hantke and Julius Berger, the directors, respectively, of the Palestine Foundation Fund (Keren Hayesod) and the Jewish National Fund (Keren Kayemet) in Jerusalem; and Georg Landauer, the head of the Jewish Agency's labor department and later the head of the Palästinaamt (the extension of the Jewish Agency's immigration department) in Berlin. Once in Palestine, these immigrants joined the select group of dedicated German Zionists who had settled in the country before 1914 and who played a pioneering role both in cultivating professional skills in the realms of medicine, education, and agronomy and in creating the institutional linkages between the World Zionist Organization and Palestine. Among these earlier settlers were Arthur Ruppin, the founder of the Zionist Palestine Bureau (and later head of the Zionist settlement department); Arthur Biram, founder of the

Table 5. Demographic and Occupational Profile of German Jewish Immigrants to Palestine, 1923–1924

Marital status	%	Occupation	%
Unmarried	71.4	Professional/services	31.1
Married	24.5	Agriculture	28.7
Unknown	4.1	Industry	26.6
		Business	13.6
Total	100.0 (n = 476)	Total	100.0 (n = 376)

Source: Based on partial data in Central Zionist Archives (CZA), S6/4878, S4/16, S4/26/1.

Reali high school in Haifa; the agronomist Selig Soskin; and the physician and agronomist Wilhelm Brünn.

As noted, the peak year for German Jewish immigration to Palestine during this decade was 1924–1925. Although the worsened economic climate in Palestine at the end of the 1920s led to a temporary sharp drop in the number of German Jewish immigrants, those who had arrived earlier in the decade would later be instrumental in shaping the patterns of organization, absorption, and integration of a large influx of emigrants from Nazi Germany.

Even before Adolf Hitler's rise to power, the German Zionist movement had affected the patterns of aliyah both by preparing its members for it and by playing a leadership role in the Zionist integration and settlement project.[17] Prominent figures already living in Palestine directed the Central Bureau for the Settlement of German Jews in Palestine, which was founded in 1933.[18] In the first years of the Nazi regime, the international Jewish response focused on Palestine as a safe haven for persecuted Jews. Palestinian Jewry had already acquired an official status as an autonomous national community under the British Mandate—the "National Home"—whereas the Jewish communities in Britain and the United States did not enjoy this kind of status in their respective countries. But the most decisive advantage of Palestine in the early to mid-1930s was its renewed economic prosperity at a time when most of the West was still suffering from the Great Depression. The transfer (*ha'avarah*) agreement between the Zionist leadership and the Nazi government, which allowed Jewish emigrants to transfer a considerable part of their wealth to Palestine in the form of imported German goods, was another factor favoring Palestine over Britain or the United States as a destination of choice. Likewise, the Central British Fund, created in 1933 to support German Jewish emigration and resettlement in general, put Palestine at the top of its agenda and laid the basis for a special Zionist settlement apparatus (the aforementioned Central Bureau) aimed specifically at German Jews.[19]

During the late 1920s and early 1930s, German Jews who had a relatively large amount of capital could consider a variety of emigration options. For those who did not have considerable possessions, the possibility of immigrating to Britain or to the United States was virtually nil—but in the case of Palestine, there was a limited opening based on British Mandate immigration regulations at that time. According to these regulations, apart from "capitalists" possessing a minimum of P 1,000 (Palestine pounds, equivalent to sterling, or English pounds), who could freely enter Mandate

Palestine, there was an additional quota of Jewish immigrants. The exact quota, known as a "schedule," was set twice a year by the Mandatory government's immigration department in accordance with its estimates of the economic absorptive capacity of Palestine. The Jewish Agency's immigration department was in charge of the allocation of certificates according to detailed prerequisites that were meant to ensure the economic absorption of the immigrants. This department, in turn, coordinated its efforts via the "Palestine Offices" located throughout Europe—in Germany, the office was located in Berlin—which were run by the Zionist movements and their affiliated political parties and youth movements.[20] Following the rise of the Nazi regime, the Zionist movement in Germany was joined by new supporters motivated by the desire to acquire immigration certificates (the first to receive certificates were veteran Zionist activists or those who had undergone pioneer training). Joining one of the Zionist movements, it was felt, was tantamount to attaining a place on the waiting list.

As is shown on Table 6, some 53,200 German Jews immigrated to Palestine between 1933 and 1941. This figure accounted for 19.7 percent of the total German Jewish emigration of 1933–1941 (270,000). Of this total, more than 30,000 had arrived in Palestine by the end of March 1936. With the assistance of world Jewish immigration organizations such as the Central British Fund and the Central Bureau for the Settlement of German Jews in Palestine, the country attracted people who had never identified themselves with Jewish nationalism of any kind. At the same time, it

Table 6. Jewish Emigration from Nazi Germany to Palestine, 1933–1941

Year / Period	From Germany Total	To Palestine	% of Total
1933	38,000	7,600	20.0
1934	23,000	9,800	42.6
1935	20,000	8,600	43.0
1933–1935	**81,000**	**26,000**	**32.1**
Feb. 1933–March 1936	**93,000**	**31,000**	**33.3**
1936	25,000	8,700	34.8
1937	23,000	3,700	16.1
1938	40,000	4,800	12.0
1939	78,000	8,500	10.9
1933–1939	**247,000**	**51,700**	**20.9**
1940	15,000	900	6.0
1941	8,000	600	7.5
1933–1941	**270,000**	**53,200**	**19.7**

Sources: Table 3 (for yearly emigration from Germany); Herbert Strauss, "Jewish Emigration from Germany: Nazi Policies and Jewish Responses (II)," *Leo Baeck Institute Year Book* 26 (1981), 346 (Table 1); Traub, *Die jüdische Auswanderung aus Deutschland*, 10–11, data for the period ending March 1936; *Aid to Jews Overseas: Report of the Activities of American Jewish Joint Distribution Committee for the Year 1936* (New York: 1937); *Aid to Jews Overseas: Report of the Activities of AJJDC for the Year 1937* (New York: 1938); *Aid to Jews Overseas: Report of the Activities of AJJDC for the Year 1938* (New York: 1939); *Report of the Executives of the Zionist Organisation and of the Jewish Agency for Palestine, submitted to the 21st Zionist Congress and the 6th session of the Council of the Jewish Agency at Geneva, Elul, 5699, August, 1939* (Jerusalem: 1939).

Table 7. Demographic and Occupational Profile of German Jewish Immigrants to Palestine, 1933–1938

Age	%	Occupation	%
0–20	31.4	Business	26.1
21–40	44.6	Professions & services	24.4
41–50	9.8	Industry & transportation	18.3
51–60	7.8	Agriculture	17.4
61 and over	5.2	Unskilled	5.3
Unknown	1.2	Unknown	8.5
Total	100.0 (n = 40,061)	Total	100.0 (n = 13,000)*

Source: Calculated from Yoav Gelber, *Moledet hadashah: 'aliyat yehudei merkaz eiropah uklitatam, 1933–1948* (Jerusalem: 1990), 57, 59 (based on statistical survey by the Jewish Agency).
*Comprising mainly males, not including children, elderly, and tourists.

is reasonable to assume that those thousands who decided to join the Zionist Organization—even if their decision was based solely on a belief that membership would enhance their chances to emigrate—were not totally estranged from Judaism.[21]

From Table 7, we learn about the high proportion (more than 30 percent) of children and youth among those immigrating to Palestine during this period. The proportion of adults over the age of 50 was remarkably small, whereas the share of younger adults (aged 21–40) was close to 45 percent. Statistics tabulated by the Jewish Agency indicate a particularly high rate of young adult immigrants during the period 1933–1935, ranging between 48 and 51 percent. These proportions did not represent the aging profile of German Jewry, as shown on Table 2. On the whole, the selective profile of immigration to Palestine was largely due to British and Zionist immigration policies: the criteria set by the authorities could most readily be met by younger age cohorts who responded to the pull factors of Palestine. Since Palestine absorbed the greater part of its German Jewish immigrants during the earlier half of the 1930s, the youthful pattern observed among the immigrants of 1933–1935 was generally applicable to the entire immigration cohort of the 1930s.

In striking contrast with the occupational structure of Jews in Germany (Table 2), about 75 percent of the German Jewish adult immigrants to Palestine in the 1930s were active breadwinners (as against less than half of the Jewish population of Germany). This fact reflects both the relatively younger profile of the immigrants as well as the partial entry of women into the Palestine labor market after preparing themselves in Germany for their new lives in Palestine. Half of the breadwinner immigrants had entered the country as "capitalists" possessed of resources worth a minimum of P£1,000. No less than 26.1 percent of the immigrants were in business; 24.4 percent were professionals, mainly in the fields of medicine (9 percent), education (3.5 percent), and law (3.2 percent); 18.3 percent were entrepreneurs in industry and transportation; and 17.4 percent were farmers and agricultural trainees (having participated in the Zionist pioneering [*hakhsharah*] program).[22]

German Jews immigrating to Palestine until 1939 (ca. 52,000) accounted for about 21 percent of the 247,000 immigrants of the Fifth Aliyah (1932–1939; see Table 1).

Beginning in 1938, an additional 13,000 German-speaking immigrants arrived from Austria and Czechoslovakia, which swelled the ranks of the "German" groups from 21 to more than 26 percent of the overall aliyah of the 1930s, raising the proportion of the German-speaking sector in the Jewish population of Palestine from 2 percent at the beginning of the 1930s (3,500 people out of a total of 175,000) to about 15 percent (68,500 out of 449,500) by the end of the decade. About 75 percent of the immigrants from Germany settled in urban areas, mainly Haifa, Tel Aviv, and, to a lesser extent, Jerusalem, while some 25 percent settled in rural areas.[23] This urban-rural mix was essentially identical to that of the general Jewish population of Palestine (73.3 percent of the Jews resided in urban localities in both 1931 and 1946).[24] A distinct feature of the German Jewish settlement pattern was its concentration in certain localized urban areas, among them Ben Yehuda Street (Tel Aviv), Rehavia (Jerusalem), and Ahuzah (Haifa), which became known as *yekke* (the nickname for German Jewish) neighborhoods.

The spatial concentration of immigrant groups—enabling them to benefit from a close social network as well as reducing the pressure to adjust to a new environment and language—is a well-known phenomenon. However, it was particularly striking with regard to the newcomers from Germany. In addition to the general factors shaping the enclaves of immigrants in receiving countries, the "German-specific" pattern may have reflected a high language barrier, cultural differences, and mutual, rooted resentments that distanced the "snobbish" German Jews from the rest of Palestinian Jewish society and led to their self-imposed relative isolation.

German Jews' snobbery was, in large measure, a function of their unusually high level of educational attainment. Already in the 1920s, the German Jewish olim were distinguished by their high proportion of individuals with academic training.[25] Many young immigrants had just made their first steps in their academic careers. Nonetheless, they played a decisive role in building the infrastructure for the evolving academia of the Yishuv, including such institutions as the Hebrew University (which, as a result, became the world center for Jewish studies), the Technion, and the Sieff (later Weizmann) Institute. Aiding these young intellectuals was the fact that German institutions of higher learning were accorded great prestige in the Yishuv. Indeed, during the Weimar era, German academia was the intellectual habitat not only for the German-born, but also for an entire generation of students and young scholars originating in Eastern and Central Europe; almost all of the Jewish academics involved in Palestine's intellectual and scientific life had been trained in German universities.[26]

Central European immigrants (not just those from Germany) also made their mark in cultural production and consumption. The Philharmonic Orchestra, for instance, was founded in 1936, when the level of German immigrants to Palestine had reached a point at which there was a sufficient audience for such an enterprise. In addition, the immigrants' demand for design and aesthetic standards in production and marketing gave a crucial push to the development of new specializations, such as lithography and metal work, which were introduced at the Bezalel Art Academy. The immigrants also contributed significantly to an array of musical activities in the areas of education, performance, distribution, and consumption.[27]

Among the olim was a high percentage of teachers and physicians. Palestine was probably the preferred destination for German Jewish professionals with a background in Jewish education. German Jewish educators founded some of the most prominent religious (and also secular) schools in the Yishuv: Hugim and Leo Baeck in Haifa, Tikhon Hadash in Tel Aviv, and Ma'aleh and Horev in Jerusalem.[28] German Jewish physicians, for their part, had a major role in modernizing the Yishuv's health care system. German Jewish immigrants were also responsible for introducing innovations in social work, psychology, and psychiatry; as a result, Palestine was boosted to the level of the most advanced European professional standards in these fields.[29]

In at least one instance, however, efforts at modernization proved to be a failure. Germany was the cradle of the Liberal and Reform movements, and German Orthodoxy had developed the neo-Orthodox "Torah im Derech Eretz" movement, which sought to combine tradition with modern intellectual and cultural European trends. These religious innovations did not find an appreciable echo in Palestine, which continued to be dominated by East European and Sephardic religious traditions. To be sure, a number of small Orthodox and Liberal congregations were established in the three main cities, but these had virtually no followers apart from the German olim.

In contrast, the German Jewish input in the realm of production, marketing, and consumption patterns significantly modified Palestine's business culture, which heretofore had been shaped, on the one hand, by the East European legacy and, on the other, by its Oriental environment. German immigrants introduced such innovations as department stores, delicatessen shops, coffee shops, and artistically designed shop windows. They were also pioneers in the development of tourist services (hotels and pensions), financial markets (banks), architectural design and aesthetic standards in domestic life, and even new branches of industry, most notably pharmacology.[30]

Finally, German Jews made significant contributions in the area of agriculture. During the 1930s, the Yishuv had more people working in agriculture than did any other Jewish community worldwide. The immigration and absorption system established by the Jewish Agency prioritized the value of pre-immigration occupational and vocational training, and it particularly encouraged agricultural training, in accordance with Zionist ideology and settlement policy. Consequently, a large number of olim in general—and among them, many German immigrants—identified themselves as agricultural laborers or as trained farmers. German Jewish immigrants to Palestine introduced new branches of agriculture such as egg production and were also responsible for innovating cooperative frameworks within the realm of private farming settlements (for instance, Ramot Hashavim's marketing cooperative).[31] Such changes could be readily implemented because Jewish agriculture in Palestine had already reached a level of development that allowed for, and even demanded, further improvements. Some of these improvements were inevitable, perhaps, but the influx from Germany served as a significant catalyst for change.

As noted, a considerable part of the immigration to Palestine was an organized enterprise. The newcomers were assisted by an elaborate apparatus—the Central Bureau for the Settlement of German Jews, along with the Central British Fund (coordinated with the Jewish Agency), which aided in the financing of the immigrants' move to Palestine and their settlement enterprises, particularly those in the rural sector. These agencies were run by German Jewish compatriots (among them, Arthur Ruppin, Martin Rosenblüth, and Georg Landauer) and were largely the product of prior efforts made by the early immigrants of the 1920s. In addition, anticipating the new wave, the early immigrants had founded a landsmanschaft known as Hitahdut Olei Germanyah (Association of Immigrants from Germany [HOG]) in 1932, whose main purpose was to foster the integration of the newcomers as individuals into the social and cultural life of the Yishuv.[32]

By and large, the developing economy of Jewish Palestine was in a position to absorb this new immigrant wave. Although the immigrants experienced a moderate deterioration in their living standards, those who came during the first wave of 1933–1935 were able to bring with them a considerable part of their capital, and there was a demand in Palestine for their skills and professions. On the whole, their economic and cultural contributions were recognized and appreciated.[33] At the same time, Central Europeans arriving in Palestine during the 1930s experienced a fair measure of culture shock in their encounter with the (for them) strange mixture of Oriental and East European civilization, which struck them as inferior to their own culture.[34] This may have offset, to some degree, the comparative economic advantage they enjoyed, and may have contributed to their distinctive organizational behavior.

German Jews in Palestine were sometimes caught in a dilemma regarding their public role. Earlier immigrants, especially those with a Zionist-movement background, tended to integrate more readily into the Yishuv's public culture. They accepted the norms established by an East European-dominated Zionist political elite. With the self-confidence of insiders, bolstered perhaps by their sense of cultural superiority, they were fully prepared to play an active role in public affairs. However, cultural estrangement and the language barrier prevented German Jewish political leaders from fully integrating into the existing political system.[35] Although many of them had learned some Hebrew before immigrating, the language barrier was often an insurmountable obstacle, even for veteran Zionists. Kurt Blumenfeld, for instance, the former chair of the Zionistische Vereinigung für Deutschland, was essentially deprived of his main leadership tool—his celebrated oratorical skills in German— once he had relocated to Palestine. To some extent, German Zionist leaders were also outside of the political mainstream in Palestine. In general, they were much less partisan than their East European counterparts; they prioritized achieving broad consensus and avoiding party divisions. Most of them had left-liberal leanings in the realm of economic and social policy and a moderate attitude with regard to Arab-Jewish relations. Many of them were members of, or supported, Brit Shalom (Peace League), an organization that sought paths to a peaceful reconciliation with the country's Arabs, with a view toward establishing a bi-national state of Jews and Arabs.[36]

Not being comfortable with the existing political parties and the dominant political culture, the German immigrant community published from 1933 on a German newspaper called *Mitteilungsblatt* (Newsbulletin) and a decade later founded its own political party, Aliyah Hadashah (New Immigration). This ethnic-based party, led by Felix Rosenblüth (later Pinhas Rosen, the first Israeli minister of justice), represented the moderate pro-leftist tendency of German Zionism; although it existed for barely six years, its offspring, the Progressive party, played a fairly significant role in Israeli politics during the first decade of statehood.[37] On the whole, though, German olim, despite their successful economic and cultural integration, were hindered both by their distinctive political heritage and by their problems in language adjustment from exerting much impact on the political system or the political life of the Yishuv.

German Jewish Immigration to the United States

We have discussed how the post-First World War economy pushed many Germans to emigrate. At first, the chief destination for Jews and non-Jews alike was the United States. While the inflation during 1922–1923 hit mainly those dependent on salary and rent income, the deflation of 1925–1926 affected mainly small businesses in which Jews were extensively represented (we recall that more than 60 percent of Jewish breadwinners were in business occupations). Immigrants to the United States thus came mainly from the ranks of business people and, in particular, members of the younger generation who saw no future for themselves in Germany.

The U.S. Jewish community at this time numbered approximately 4,000,000; during the 1920s, it absorbed 360,000 additional Jewish immigrants (see Table 1). Among them were some 7,300 German Jews, whose arrival peaked at almost 2,000 entries in 1923–1924.[38] The newcomers were quite different from German Jews who had come to the United States in the 19th century, some of whom had experienced a dynamic rise into the upper middle class, and quite a few of whom had become bankers, industrialists, prominent lawyers, and large-scale entrepreneurs, such as Louis D. Brandeis, Felix Frankfurter, Louis Marshall, Julius Rosenwald, Jacob Schiff, and Felix M. Warburg.[39] The new immigrants of the 1920s encountered a different America and experienced significant occupational and economic obstacles. Nevertheless, many of them pursued successful professional careers, notably in medicine, while others found their opportunity in such fields as communication and the arts.[40] Overall, however, their impact on the occupational and economic profile of American Jews was muted.

German Jewish immigrants in the post-First World War period were also quite active in terms of constructing the infrastructure for the later arrivals of the 1930s, which included numerous mutual aid societies such as the Prospect Unity Club, the Deutsch-jüdischer Club (German-Jewish Club) and (in 1926) the German-Jewish Center in New York.[41]

We have only partial data relating specifically to immigrating German Jews—as distinguished from Germans, on the one hand, and "Hebrews," on the other. There is also a dearth of data distinguishing between Germany and Austria. Between 1933 and 1941, the United States granted immigrant visas to 129,600 people from Germany and Austria.[42] These accounted for more than a quarter of the 500,000 refugees fleeing from Nazi rule.[43] Of the Germans and Austrians, 81,500 (or 68 percent) were self-identified as Jews by religion. According to Maurice Davie and Samuel Koenig, a majority of the remainder were so-called "non-Aryan Christians," namely, Jews by racial descent according to the Nazi definition, who were not characterized as "Hebrews" by U.S. immigration authorities.[44]

Between February 1933 and March 1936, the United States received only 9,500 of the total of 93,000 emigrants from Germany.[45] Most immigrants from Central Europe (both Jews and non-Jews), entered from the end of 1938 onward. Those who immigrated earlier were almost exclusively from Germany, and they came in moderate numbers, rising from 1,200 in 1933 to about 12,000 in 1937. With the arrival of 18,000 additional newcomers by the middle of 1938, German immigrants totaled about 46,000,[46] of whom more than half (about 27,000) were estimated to be Jews.[47]

According to U.S. immigration quotas as amended in 1929, it was legally possible to admit 25,557 German immigrants per year. Until 1938–1939, the quota was not filled, both because of the many rules limiting the categories of those eligible for a visa, and because of various bureaucratic obstacles put into practice by the American consulate in Berlin. This situation changed in the wake of the events of 1938, which took such a toll on German and Austrian Jews. Although the quota laws were not altered, a new category—refugees—was introduced, and this circumvented many of the existing limitations and obstacles in granting visas.[48]

During the period 1933–1935, the United States received less than 12 percent of the German Jewish emigration; through 1938, the total was 16 percent (Table 8). In 1938, 40,000 Jews left Germany (Table 3). The exodus intensified after the Kristallnacht pogrom, when U.S.-bound immigrants accounted for a major share of the total: between 1938 and 1941, some 55,000 Jewish refugees from Germany and Austria entered the United States.[49] This post-1938 influx can undoubtedly be considered a refugee migration, as reflected by the high proportion of older adults as compared to the arrivals of 1933–1938 (see Table 9), indicating the lack of age selectivity among the Jewish immigrants of the latter years.

The professional composition of those immigrating to the United States was at first disproportionately weighted toward academics, artists, and scientists. Special arrangements were often made to enable them to enter the country and to obtain employment at academic institutions or in consulting positions for the government or industry.[50] Of about 2,000 university professors fleeing Central Europe, two thirds resettled in the United States.[51] This occupational structure later changed dramatically. In 1938, only 1,109, or about 6 percent, were professionals, academics, or artists (see Table 9 and the notes there).[52]

Although, as mentioned, it is difficult to determine precisely the proportion of German Jews among total European Jewish immigration to the United States over the

Table 8. Jewish Emigration from Germany to the United States in Selected Periods, 1933–1941

Period	From Germany[a] Total	To the U.S.	% of Total
1933–1935	81,000	9,500[b]	11.7
1933–1938	169,000	27,000[c]	16.0
1938–1941	141,000	55,000[d]	39.0
1933–1941	270,000	82,000[e]	30.4

a See Table 3.

b Traub, *Jüdische Auswanderung*, covering February 1933-March 1936, based on official German sources.

c Werner Rosenstock, "Exodus 1933–1939, a Survey of Jewish Emigration from Germany," *Leo Baeck Institute Year Book* 1 (1956), 376; Herbert A. Strauss, "The Migration of Jews from Nazi Germany," in *Jewish Immigrants in the Nazi Period in the USA*, vol. 1, *Archival Resources*, ed. Steven W. Siegel (New York: 1978), xx.

d Based on HIAS material, YIVO, RG 245.4.5 MF 15.12 V-I, II (Table titled "Jewish Immigrant Aliens Admitted from July 1st 1933 to June 30, 1943 by Last Permanent Residence, Including Austria from 1937/8").

e Ibid., amended by adding half the number of the previous fiscal year to cover calendar years. Though Austria is included, it is estimated that Austrian immigrants account for only a small portion of the total.

Table 9. Demographic and Occupational Profile of Central-European Immigrants to the United States, 1933–1945

Age / Period	% 1933–1938	% 1939–1941	Occupation*	%
0–20	30.0	18.0	Business	58.5
21–50	55.0	51.0	Professions	38.0
51+	15.0	31.0	Industry	3.5
Total:	100.0 (n = 27,000)	100.0 (n = 55,000)	Total	100.0

*The available data do not allow for a systematic breakdown of the occupational structure to subperiods. However, partial data available in the following sources indicate that the greater portion of academics (5,400) and artists (2,700) included in the "professions" category came during the early 1930s.

Sources: YIVO, Chamberlain Collection (RG 278), Box 2, Folder 31 and Box 4 (Table titled "Immigrant Aliens or Newcomers Admitted to the United States for Permanent Residence, Who Gave Germany as Their Last Permanent Residence, Years Ended June 30, 1935, 1936, 1937, 1938, by Sex, Age, etc., as Specified"); The Academic Assistance Council Annual Reports 1934, 1935; Harold Fields, *The Refugees in the United States* (New York: 1938); Leo Grebler, "German-Jewish Immigrants to the United States during the Hitler Period" (1976), LBINY, ME 716, MM 29; Maurice R. Davie and Samuel Koenig, *The Refugees are Now Americans* (New York: 1945). The great majority of the immigrants from Central Europe were Jews; consequently, social and demographic surveys relating to the immigrants generally apply to Jews specifically.

entire period, it may be assumed that Central European Jewish immigrants (including Austrian and Czech nationals) constituted the majority of the "Hebrew" immigration to the United States between 1933 and 1941. Taking the figure of 129,000 as a reasonable upper limit for the Central European Jewish immigration during this period,[53] it may be inferred that this influx added only slightly more than 3 percent to the existing American Jewish population of 4,000,000 (in 1933).

What was the qualitative impact of the Jewish immigration of the Nazi era? It should be reiterated that a large German presence in American Jewry was established during the 19th century, although German Jews' share in the American Jewish population was later minimized by the massive immigration of East European Jews from 1880 to 1914. Nevertheless, German Jews significantly shaped certain areas of American Jewish life, notably in the realm of liberal religious trends and the Jewish philanthropic and welfare organizations. Jews of German background maintained their hegemonic position in national Jewish affairs until after the First World War. By the 1930s, however, leadership positions were increasingly occupied by well-established Jews of East European origin.[54] Given this background, the impact of the immigration from Nazi Germany on both the American Jewish community and on its German-origin component was rather limited. The new immigrants arrived at a time when the American Jewish populace was already dominated by East European Jews; moreover, American Jewry had long since adopted various German Jewish cultural and religious patterns.

German Jewish immigrants tended to concentrate mainly on the East coast, half of them in New York City. On the West coast, Los Angeles became the main center, though there was considerable dispersal to other communities, large and small, around the country.[55] Although the immigrants did not usually concentrate in specific neighborhoods, there were a few exceptions: Manhattan's Washington Heights ("Frankfurt on the Hudson"), which was made up mainly of Orthodox Jews who came from southern Germany during the late 1930s (this group did not include the cultural and economic elite of German Jewry and thus did not become the center of New York German Jewry); the middle-class area around Eustaw Place and Druid Hill Park in Baltimore; and various other clusters within walking distance of Orthodox synagogues.[56]

Central European academics, intellectuals, and artists were active in all disciplines, introducing notable innovations and in some fields contributing greatly to the upgrading of American arts and sciences. In some professions, however, the United States proved less welcoming. Under pressure from powerful professional associations, the authorities imposed strict requirements for studies and examinations as prerequisites for authorizing immigrant physicians to practice medicine. Many of the doctors who immigrated to the United States were too old to cope with these requirements and thus had to adjust to other available jobs or to abandon employment altogether.[57]

In the Jewish religious context, the arrival of the newcomers was barely noticeable. The Conservative and Reform movements were already well established, along with their respective educational systems. Newcomers could easily find synagogues suitable to their tradition and could send their children to public or existing Jewish day schools. There were, however, differences in customs, liturgy, and manners between German and East European Orthodox congregations. There were cases in which a rabbi from Germany formed an independent congregation for his fellow refugees—Simon Schwab of Ischenhausen, for instance, who moved to Baltimore and took up the post of rabbi of Congregation Shearith Israel, which soon became the center of German Jewish observant refugees who gravitated to the neighborhood of this "Glen Avenue shul."[58]

Although the German Jewish immigration to the United States included some of the most integrated and prosperous members of the German Jewish community, these arrived, for the most part, at the end of the 1930s. At that stage, they were forced to leave behind most, if not all of their possessions, which left them at a material disadvantage.[59] Easing their resettlement and integration was the fact that America was, after all, a classic immigration country. Moreover, its already existing Jewish community was quite well organized to welcome the newcomers.[60] The immigrants were thus accepted as full citizens and as another legitimate (albeit not new) sector in America's already heterogeneous society.

Interestingly, the Central European immigration was dealt with by public bodies—the first time in its history as an immigration absorptive country that the United States established such mechanisms under government auspices. In 1933, the United States participated in founding the Intergovernmental High Commission for Refugees Coming from Germany. In 1934, the National Coordinating Committee was established by the Joint Distribution Committee (JDC), at the suggestion of the State Department, in order to coordinate the work of affiliated private agencies; and in the spring of 1938, President Franklin D. Roosevelt established the President's Advisory Committee on Political Refugees, under the chairmanship of James G. McDonald, to serve as a liaison between private American agencies and the Intergovernmental Committee on Refugees that was created at the Evian Conference in July 1938.[61]

On the basis of being recognized as deserving of special treatment, the newcomers readily constituted landsmanschaft-type organizations, building on already existing groups and institutions. German Jewish clubs, and various associations that were founded in the 1920s, served as models for the establishment of similar institutions during the 1930s (among them, the German Jewish Clubs in Los Angeles and New York that were founded in 1933 and 1934, respectively) to promote the economic, social, and cultural integration of the newcomers. Membership, however, totaled only a few thousand, and these clubs lasted only for a few years.[62] The American Federation of Jews from Central Europe was established only in 1941.[63] New immigrants also founded a German-language periodical, *Aufbau*, which was one of several German-language publications, and created their own cultural institutions.

Alongside these sectoral activities, many members of the refugee influx actively sought to join veteran American organizations and institutions, acquire the English language, and mix socially and professionally with non-immigrants. Younger immigrants and women, in particular, succeeded in learning the ropes. This was atypical for immigrants and refugees, comparatively speaking. The devotion, persistence, and systematic strategies employed by the immigrants to attain civic integration may have had their roots in German cultural models; but these patterns could also have been based on their high professional level, the familiarity some of them already had with English and with other features of American culture, and the fact that many of them chose to settle down in established American neighborhoods rather than in tight immigrant clusters.[64] In general, the new immigrants from Germany did not add any particular novelty to American Jewish life; their contribution to America's social, intellectual, and cultural spheres was of a broad and universal nature rather than being distinctly German Jewish.

German Jewish Immigration to Great Britain

Prior to the 1930s, Britain did not experience large-scale German Jewish immigration. During the 19th century, a relatively small number of German Jewish and non-Jewish scientists and financial and industrial entrepreneurs entered Britain as immigrants.[65] Britain and British Jewry were hardly prepared, therefore, when German Jews tried to enter in large numbers during the Nazi period.

British policy on refugee immigration was based on legislation dating from the 1905 Aliens Act, the Aliens Restriction Act of 1919, and the ensuing Aliens Order of 1920. In addition, the earlier unconditional right of asylum was severely limited in 1926. From that year, aliens could enter the country only temporarily, unless they were granted a permit from the Ministry of Labour and had some visible means of support. This legislation, originally renewable annually, determined Britain's severely restrictive immigration policy during the Great Depression years. The government reacted to the early outrages of the Nazi regime by confirming that Britain was not a country of immigration, citing the country's already large population, high unemployment levels, and an ostensible fear of aggravating local antisemitism.[66]

Thus, in the early phase of the Jewish outflow from Nazi Germany, Britain played a very minor role, receiving only 4,000 German Jews out of the total emigration of 81,000 in the years 1933–1935 (Table 10).[67]

The picture, however, changed substantially in 1938 following the Anschluss and the Kristallnacht pogrom. In response, the British government created several new categories for immigration: holders of U.S. visas for transmigration while awaiting inclusion in future U.S. quotas; domestics hired by private families; holders of permits for vocational training in England (mainly in industry); Home Office special work permits, and "Blue Cards" (for those over 60 years old whose support was guaranteed by private or other agencies).[68]

Estimating the number of German Jews who immigrated to Britain in those later years is complicated, since a high percentage of trans-migrants left Britain before or during the Second World War in the wake of the special agreement made by the British government to allow American visa-holders to enter Britain for a temporary stay. Similarly, official statistics did not distinguish between tourists and immigrants. In view of these constraints, the following estimates seem to be the most reliable. About 73,000 Jews appear to have arrived in Britain from Germany and Austria, alongside 10,000 from Czechoslovakia, between 1933 and 1941, making a total of 83,000 Jewish immigrants from Central Europe. The great majority of this movement took place after 1938 and included 9,000–10,000 children who were brought to Britain via an operation known as the *Kindertransport*.[69] (Table 10 estimates the numbers of German refugees alone, excluding the Austrian and Czech refugees who accounted for a large part of the inflow during the period 1938–1941.)

As shown in Table 10, until 1938, Britain received only 10,000 German immigrants.[70] During the 18-month period between the annexation of Austria in March 1938 and the outbreak of the war, some 60,000 refugees came to Britain, only half of them from Germany, and the rest from Austria.[71] It turns out that the Austrian refugees accounted for more than a third of the total Central European refugee population.[72] Of the immigrants from Germany, estimated to have totaled about 63,000, 45,000 were Jews, and the majority of them—about 35,000—came between late 1938 and 1941.[73]

Of all the Central Europeans who came and stayed in Britain, about 20,000 re-emigrated during or after the war (13,000 to the United States; 1,200 to Palestine) and others—mainly

Table 10. Jewish Emigration to Great Britain from Germany, 1933–1941

Period	From Germany	To Britain	
	Total		% of Total
1933–1935	81,000	4,000	4.9
1933–1938	169,000	10,000	5.9
1939–1941	141,000	35,000	24.8
1933–1941	270,000	45,000	16.7

Sources: For total emigration from Germany, see Table 3. For Great Britain, we lack yearly statistics, so they are calculated here on the basis of the following sources: Traub, *Die jüdische Auswanderung aus Deutschland*, covering February 1933-March 1936 (based on official German sources); Central British Fund Report for 1939, WLL MF. 318/109; Rosenstock, "Exodus 1933–1939," 376; A.J. Sherman, *Island Refuge: Britain and Refugees from the Third Reich, 1933–1939* (London: 1973), statistical appendix; *AJR Information* 6 (June 1946). Strauss, "Jewish Emigration (I)," 354–355, cites slightly different numbers. There is a lack of absolute consistency between the various sources in numbers and periodization. Usually "1933–1938" applies to April 1933 through October 1938 and "1933–1936" covers the first quarter of 1936, whereas "1938–1939" refers to November 1938 through August 1939.

non-Jewish political refugees—were later repatriated.[74] It is estimated that about 50,000 of the total settled permanently in Britain.[75]

Demographic information tends to be scanty in the British case. Immigrant authorities registered immigrants by their entrance categories, and the only systematic statistics we have were compiled by the Jewish Refugees Committee (German Jewish Aid Committee), which left out those who did not require assistance. However, the majority of the Jewish immigrants did apparently register with the Committee, and thus its reports may serve as good approximations. Evidently, the early emigration was mainly made up of young people and those able to transplant their professional skills.[76] Although the great majority came after 1938, we assume that the age composition was largely affected by the high percentage of the 10,000 children of the *Kindertransport*. Thus, despite the overwhelming numerical weight of the later arrivals (including a large number of adults over the age of 50), the overall proportion of those over 50 was actually lower among the immigrants to England than among German Jewry on the eve of emigration. It is also the case that not much can be said about the immigrants' occupations. Statistics for 1933–1934 show that among some 4,000 immigrants, almost half were academics, students, or professionals (Table 11).[77] Those who reached Britain in the late 1930s and early 1940s possibly worked at a variety of occupations.

The 83,000 Central European Jews who reached British shores after Hitler's rise to power were actually the only Jews immigrating to Britain in those years. Their substantial number added 28 percent to the 300,000 Jews already residing in the country. Even if we consider only the 40,000 to 50,000 who remained in Britain, they represent a significant increase of 17 percent.

These immigrants concentrated mainly in London, where they gathered in the northwest sections of the city: Hampstead, Belsize Park and their vicinity. There they were able to patronize their own shops, bakeries, restaurants, and coffee shops, creating and

Table 11. Demographic and Occupational Profile of German Jewish Immigrants to Great Britain

Age Groups, 1933–1934		Age Groups, 1939		Occupation, 1933–1934		Entrance Permits, 1939	
Age	%	Age	%	Branch	%	Category	%
0–20	14.5	0–20	12.5	Business	18.0		
21–50	78.3	21–50	62.9	Professions	47.0	Transit migrants	19.0
50+	7.2	50+	24.6	Services	21.6	Vocational training	15.0
				Industry	6.2	Domestics	27.0
				Unknown / unskilled	7.2	Work permits	39.0*
Total	100.0 (n = 4,055)	Total	100.0 (n = 4,333)	Total	100.0	Total	100.0

*Apart from those with domestic or vocational training permits.

Source: Calculations based on partial data in Jewish Refugee Aid Committee Reports, 1933–1935, 1939, WLL, CBF.

preserving an island of German Jewish social and cultural life. They also established the Belsize Square Liberal synagogue, which served as a social center offering a familiar environment.[78]

The newcomers had quite a visible impact in the world of arts, theater, music, and publishing, where they introduced styles developed in Weimar Berlin and interwar Vienna.[79] There are also a few studies showing the instrumental role of German Jewish industrialists in sparking new activity in underdeveloped regions, especially in northern England, and in introducing innovative products and marketing methods, especially in the textile, fur, and leather industries.[80]

In the Jewish sphere, German Jewish immigrant teachers contributed to the resettlement of young refugees by establishing their own schools, as was the case in London, albeit for a brief, transitional period.[81] In at least some instances, noted rabbis—such as Rabbi Eli Munk, the son of Rabbi Esriel Munk of Berlin, who established the Golders Green Beth Hamidrash—reconstituted their congregations in Britain.[82]

Britain, as already mentioned, was scarcely prepared for the new task of absorbing immigrants on a large scale, and it was also dominated by an anti-alien tradition that made it unreceptive to newcomers.[83] The new, post-1938 immigrants were seen (and also viewed themselves) as refugees, dependent on the goodwill of the British and Jewish authorities. Given their awkward position as German aliens—after the outbreak of the war, they were "enemy aliens"—the newcomers tried hard to disguise their identity and to refrain from attracting attention. Consequently, British Jews had to organize their support services in an unwelcoming atmosphere of governmental pressure (stemming from the government's policy of permitting only temporary asylum), suspicion, and hostility.

The first organizational aid initiative was undertaken by a German Jew, Otto Schiff (a nephew of Jacob Schiff, the foremost American Jewish leader in his day), who founded the Jewish Refugees Aid Committee. In 1938, the term "refugees" was dropped and the group was renamed the German-Jewish Aid Committee. Then again, in 1939, to avoid the word "German," the initial name was reinstalled. This flip-flop was one of many instances demonstrating a certain insecurity on the part of British Jews over the German Jewish influx.

Another organization, the Council for German Jewry, was founded in 1936 with the aim of collaborating with American Jews, but in 1939 the cooperation ended and the group was renamed the Council for Jewish Refugees. The Central British Fund, founded in 1933, was not meant specifically for immigrants to Britain. On the contrary, as already mentioned, its chief goal was to solve the German Jewish problem through immigration and settlement in Palestine. These institutions made huge efforts to enable the refugees, after their arrival, to continue on their way to other destinations—keeping records of how many people actually left as a measure of their success.[84]

The refugees themselves were constantly reminded that they were neither British nor particularly wanted. Most of the men experienced a period of detention after the war broke out, and some were deported as enemy aliens to the Isle of Man, to Canada, or to Australia.[85] To some extent, they internalized their refugee identity, sometimes for decades, sometimes permanently.[86] As a result of the refugees' insecurity, the Association of Jewish Refugees (AJR) was founded only in 1941—its name, of course, omitting any reference to their national origin. Its publication, which began to appear only in 1946, was naturally in English only, and its main objective was to report on the progress of the refugees' integration into English and the Anglo-Jewish society.[87]

Three Different Destinies

As we have seen, the three groups under discussion varied in terms of demographic, occupational, and economic composition as well as in the timing and dynamics of their migration. All of these factors were closely linked. During the 1920s, both Palestine and the United States served as destinations for migrating German Jews, while Britain experienced hardly any German Jewish immigration. The Jews immigrating to the United States were different from those who chose to go to Palestine. America attracted mainly German Jewish small or middle-class businessmen, while Palestine was the goal of young professionals and academics, mainly in the early stages of building their careers.

During the Nazi era, despite the common grounds for emigration, different groups of German Jews varied in the timing of their decision to emigrate, and accordingly, their options to choose a destination changed. Those who made a quick decision to emigrate were mainly young professionals whose prospects in Germany were dim. For the most part, they chose Palestine as their destination, with the exception of high-ranking academics (both young and old) for whom special arrangements were made in both Britain and the United States. The great majority of German Jews who were driven to emigrate only after the Kristallnacht pogrom reflected more or less the average profile of aging German Jewish refugees who had limited prospects for transferring what was left of their capital. These were accepted mainly in the United States and in Britain, which responded to the events in Germany by loosening their rigid immigration regulations, whereas Palestine became increasingly closed, particularly following the Arab revolt and the Mandate White Paper of 1939, which severely restricted Jewish immigration (Table 12).

Table 12. German Jewish Immigration to Palestine, the United States, and Great Britain, 1933–1941

Period	From Germany Total	To Palestine	% of Total	To the U.S.	% of Total	To Britain	% of Total
1933–1935	81,000	26,000	32.1	9,500	11.7	4,000	4.9
1933–1938	169,000	43,200	25.6	27,000	16.0	10,000	5.9
1938–1941	141,000	14,800	10.5	55,000	39.0	35,000	24.8
1933–1941	270,000	53,200	19.7	82,000	30.4	45,000	16.7

Source: Calculated on the basis of Tables 3, 6, 8, and 10, above.

The outcome of these developments was decisive in shaping the different profile of each of the immigrant groups (Tables 13 and 14). It may be difficult to define with any precision the profile of the immigrants to the United States and Britain. While the estimates for Germany and Palestine apply exclusively to Jews, those for the United States and Britain do not distinguish between Jews and non-Jews. Academics and artists who went to those countries included a significant number of non-Jewish political exiles. Our conclusions will therefore be tentative. However, since many if not most immigrants from Germany were Jews or of Jewish descent, we may apply the estimates in a broad sense to the Jews as a migrant and refugee population. It would appear that the group that went to Palestine was relatively youthful, with considerable means and with skills that helped them to fit into the local economy. German Jews constituted a substantial part of the total Jewish immigration to Palestine at the time and caused the German-speaking element in the country to become much more visible. The group who went to the United States was less homogeneous in terms of age, capital, and skills. It included some stellar personalities and Nobel Prize laureates in the arts and sciences, such as the physicist Albert Einstein, the philosopher-historian Hannah Arendt, the composer Kurt Weill, the conductor Otto Klemperer, the author Alfred Döblin, and the filmmaker Ernst Lubitsch, to name only a few, though as time progressed, this influx was more middle- and lower-middle-class, representing the profile of German Jewry at large. The German Jews who immigrated to Britain came at about the same time as many Austrian and Czech

Table 13. Age Distribution of German Jewish Immigrants to Palestine, the United States and Great Britain (percent)

Age	Palestine 1933–1938	U.S. 1934–1938	U.S. 1938–1941	Britain 1933–1935	Britain 1939
0–20	31.4	30.0	18.0	14.5	12.5
21–50	54.4	55.0	51.0	78.3	62.9
50/51++	13.0	15.0	31.0	7.2	24.6
Total	100.0	100.0	100.0	100.0	100.0

Source: Calculated on the basis of Tables 7, 9, and 11.

Table 14. Occupational Structure of the Jews in Germany and of Nazi Era Immigrants (percent)

Occupation	Germany 1933	Palestine 1933–1938	U.S. 1933–1945	Britain 1933–1934
Business	61.3	26.1	58.5	18.0
Professions / services	13.9	24.4	38.0	68.6
Industry	23.1	18.3	3.5	6.2
Agriculture	1.7	17.4		
Unknown /unskilled		13.8		7.2
Total	100.0	100.0	100.0	100.0

Source: Calculated on the basis of Tables 2, 7, 9, and 11 above.

Jews. Most of the immigrants came in the late 1930s, and with no possessions, though among them (as in the American case) was a small but visible group of artists and academics, many of them of Viennese origin.

In absolute terms, as well as in its proportional share of the total immigration over the entire Nazi period, the United States took in more immigrants than did Britain or Palestine. The latter received similar numbers (Palestine slightly more than Britain; see Table 12), together accounting for about 20 percent more than the number of immigrants to the United States. However, these proportions must be seen against the circumstances of each of the countries. Palestinian Jews had already acquired official status as a national community under the British Mandate, and Jewish immigration was a central and dominant aspect of its life and development. The German Jews immigrating to Palestine comprised more than 20 percent of the Fifth Aliyah, which doubled the size of the Yishuv. They differed socially and culturally in the context of their new home, but it may be said that Central European immigrants of the 1920s and 1930s provided Jewish Palestine with a much-needed, modernizing cohort.

The immigrants to the United States and Britain must likewise be viewed against the general background in these countries, and in particular against the background of their Jewish communities. We may assume that Central European Jews (including Germans, Austrians, and Czechs) constituted the majority of the European immigration to the United States at the time. What bears remembering, as well, was that unlike in the case of Palestine, there was a significant Central European descent group among American Jewry, established over the course of the previous century. Representative figures of German American Jewry still maintained their hegemonic position after the First World War, and through much of the 1930s. Given this background we may conjecture that the latter-day immigration from Nazi Germany had very little qualitative or differentiating impact on the established Jewish community.

In some ways, the Central European Jewish immigration of the 1930s was as significant for British Jewry as it was for Palestine. In both countries, we saw that this influx brought a new cultural element into the existing mix of East European and Sephardic Jewry. In Britain, though, it is hard to distinguish the Germans from the Austrians and the Czechs, who made up about one third of the refugee migration. Thus, whereas for Palestine we can estimate the German Jewish component as 22 percent (and together with other Central Europeans, 25 percent) of the total Jewish immigration of that time, the 83,000 German-speaking Jews who reached British shores after 1933 actually comprised the entire Jewish immigration to Britain in this period, and accounted for an increase of 28 percent in the Anglo-Jewish population (this figure drops to 17 percent, if we consider only net immigration). In the United States, it may be recalled, the influx of German-speaking immigrants during the Nazi era added only slightly more than 3 percent to the total Jewish population. Britain, like Palestine, experienced the presence of many German Jews as unprecedented. But as against Palestine, Britain and its Jewish community were far less prepared for absorbing the newcomers, and the fortunes of the refugees were dominated by an anti-alien tradition.

In Palestine, the immigrants were assisted by their predecessors and by the machinery created by the Zionist Organization and Jewish welfare institutions. They quickly formed a landsmanschaft, and also a political party that got involved in the politics of the Jewish national home—not in order to advance narrow sectoral interests, but rather those values deemed of particular importance to the national Zionist project. Political activism of that sort was not possible in the United States or in Britain, where even the most effectively integrated could not exert any palpable public influence. Even if we ignore the political dimension, the Palestinian case was unique in terms of the immigrants' high level of self-confidence. The British case displays the extreme opposite situation, where the mistrust of the general public and the lack of confidence among the established Jewish community prompted a low-profile policy. It might also be noted that the extent to which German Jewish immigrants tended to live separated from other Jews was highest in the British case.

Common sense, or intuition, leads us to believe that the encounter of the immigrants with their new host societies had much in common, given their common German heritage, social and economic fabric, and education. In all three countries, the immigrants suffered from losing their former social and economic status. In all three cases, they tenaciously worked their way up the economic and social ladder. Despite initial difficulties, they did not give up their aspirations for cultural consumption at a high level. As for the encounter with the local Jewish community, in all three cases it was marked by mutual frictions that hampered complete social integration. However, it seems that the differences between the receiving countries were much more decisive than the common features, with Palestine and Britain representing two extremes along a continuum and the United States positioned somewhere in between.

Although the immigrants to Palestine experienced a drop in their standard of living, it is likely to have been less difficult for them compared with the loss of social status experienced by those immigrating to the United States or Britain. This assumption is based on four factors. First, immigrants to Palestine usually did not come from among the most prosperous echelons of German Jewish society, whereas many of those who went to Britain and the United States came precisely from among the most integrated and the most affluent German Jewish circles. Second, many of those who immigrated to the United States and Britain did so quite late, when they were prohibited from taking much or any of their possessions. Immigrants to Palestine, in contrast, came early enough, and under a more permissive emigration regime, to enable them to bring along a considerable part of their capital. Third, many of the newcomers to Palestine could apply their skills and professions, for which there was a demand, almost immediately, so that they experienced a relatively minor amount of status dislocation. And fourth, the Palestinian Jewish middle class was much less prosperous, on average, than its counterparts in the United States and Britain. Therefore, the new immigrants did not suffer from relative deprivation as measured by local criteria.

It seems that the effort to rebuild a solid existence, not to speak of moving up economically, academically, or occupationally, was much harder in the United States and Britain than in Palestine, where the economic integration of the olim was rapid, and where their impact on various economic and cultural sectors was recognized and appreciated.

At the same time, those who came to Palestine experienced significant culture shock, encountering a society whose Middle Eastern and East European components alike appeared to be "inferior" to their own culture. In comparison, immigrants to the United States and Britain were ostensibly "cushioned" by a more familiar, western social and cultural environment. The cultural issue in Palestine may have offset somewhat the comparative economic advantage of the immigrants but may also have added a special impetus to their unique organizational behavior.

The German immigrants revolutionized the Palestinian economy. The high proportion of industrialists and the diversity of new branches they established helped to modernize the infant Palestinian Jewish industry. In Britain, the impact was limited to less developed parts of the country. The proportion of agricultural workers in Jewish Palestine was the largest of any Jewish community, and the German Jewish impact in this field was also unparalleled among the receiving countries. The transfer of German Jewish medical and social services had a profound impact in Palestine, whereas many of the physicians who immigrated to the United States or Britain were confronted with restrictions that delayed or blocked their professional reintegration.

The top German Jewish scientists went to the United States or Britain, which offered not only attractive academic environments but also created special mechanisms to facilitate the migration and absorption process. Palestine's academic infrastructure, in contrast, was still in its infancy, and no special incentives were available to the new immigrants. However, though both the United States and Britain gained substantially from German refugee scientists, this input was only an addition, albeit qualitatively significant, to an existing and well-developed infrastructure. In Palestine, the immigrants who came with academic credentials quite literally changed their new land. Moreover, this had a Jewish-cultural aspect. The intellectual transfer to the United States and Britain was universal in character, possessing little, if any, specific Jewish dimension. In contrast, the transfer to Palestine was evident, first of all, in the field of Jewish studies, which developed as a modern academic endeavor in the German context. Among the olim was a high percentage of teachers who had a distinctive and lasting impact on Jewish education at large, both secular and religious.

In the realm of the arts, the picture is different—here, the United States and Britain derived more benefit from immigrant artists and performers. In certain fields, such as the film industry, the German-Austrian immigration to the United States was of crucial importance. In other fields, such as music and publishing, Britain experienced a revolution as a result of the immigration. Palestine, in contrast, was influenced less by immigrating artistic creators and products and more by the implementation of new standards and concepts of cultural demand and consumption.

If we were to ponder which German Jewish diaspora largely preserved its self-awareness as a cultural community, we might well choose the German Jews who settled in Britain.[88] But were we to pose the question of which branch succeeded best in implementing its German Jewish legacy, the answer would be Palestine/Israel. This is manifested by the ways in which each of these two groups remembers and memorializes its immigration experience, whereas the American group is undoubtedly the most successfully integrated and socially dispersed.

Notes

This essay is the outcome of a research project on interwar Jewish migration conducted by Jacob Metzer and myself at the Hebrew University, which has been supported by the Hebrew

University President's Fund, by the Israel Scientific Foundation, and by the Israel Foundation Trustees. Jacob Metzer provided advice throughout the course of research; Nahum T. Gross commented on various drafts; Gur Alroey collected and analyzed data and made useful comments; Yael Jonas-Dinowich, Liraz Davidowich, and Rona Israel-Kolatt collected some of the source materials. My students in the seminar on interwar Jewish migration (2003) and the participants in the departmental seminar of the Institute of Contemporary Jewry at the Hebrew University (2007) provided stimulating discussions and productive comments. The Center for Advanced Holocaust Studies at the United States Holocaust Memorial Museum supported this study in a generous manner by granting Visiting Scholarship Fellowships during 2005 and 2007.

1. See, for instance, Lloyd P. Gartner, *The Jewish Immigrant in England 1870–1914* (London: 1960); Uri D. Herscher (ed.), *The East-European Jewish Experience in America: A Century of Memories 1882–1982* (Cincinnati: 1983).

2. See, for instance, Michael Marrus, *The Unwanted: European Refugees in the 20th Century* (New York: 1985). Historical research has only recently begun to challenge this assumption; for several recent examples, see Lloyd P. Gartner, "The Great Jewish Immigration—Its East-European Background," *Tel Aviver Jahrbuch für Geschichte* 24 (1998), 107–136; Aubrey Newman and Stephen E. Massil (eds.), *Patterns of Migration, 1850–1914* (Proceedings of the international academic conference of the Jewish Historical Society of England and the Institute of Jewish Studies, University College London) (London: 1996); Gerald Sorin, *A Time for Building: The Third Immigration, 1880–1920* (Baltimore: 1992); Gur Alroey, *Imigrantim: hahagirah hayehudit leerez yisrael bereshit hameah ha'esrim* (Jerusalem: 2004).

3. The discussion of Jewish migration in Jacob Metzer's *The Divided Economy of Mandatory Palestine* (Cambridge: 1998), 59–83, which uses a social science framework as an organizing theme, is a recent exception to this pattern.

4. Doron Niederland, *Yehudei germanyah: mehagrim o pelitim? 'Iyun bidfusei hahagirah bein shetei milhamot ha'olam* (Jerusalem: 1996).

5. Colin Holmes, *A Tolerant Country? Immigrants, Refugees and Minorities in Britain* (London: 1991).

6. Aviva Halamish, *Bemeruz kaful neged hazeman: mediniyut ha'aliyah haziyonit bishnot hasheloshim* (Jerusalem: 2006), 99–125.

7. Avraham Barkai, "Bevölkerungsrückgang und wirtschaftliche Stagnation," in *Deutsch-jüdische Geschichte in der Neuzeit*, vol. 4, ed. Avraham Barkai and Paul Mendes-Flohr (Munich: 1997), 39.

8. Niederland, *Yehudei germanyah*, 21–23 (estimation of the negative balance of migration for the years 1925–1933, including East European Jews leaving Germany).

9. This is the estimate given by Michael Traub, *Die jüdische Auswanderung aus Deutschland: Westeuropa, Übersee, Palästina* (Berlin: 1936), 10–11. Herbert A. Strauss gives a somewhat higher figure of 525,000; see his "Jewish Emigration from Germany: Nazi Policies and Jewish Responses (I)," *Leo Baeck Institute Year Book* 25 (1980), 313–336, esp. 317 (Table 1).

10. Strauss, "Jewish Emigration from Germany (I)," 318 (Table 3a); Barkai, "Bevölkerungsrückgang und wirtschaftliche Stagnation," 37–49.

11. Barkai, "Bevölkerungsrückgang und wirtschaftliche Stagnation"; Traub, *Die jüdische Auswanderung aus Deutschland*.

12. Council for German Jewry, *First Annual Report for 1936* (London).

13. American Jewish Joint Distribution Committee, Aid to Jews Overseas, "Report of the Activities of the American Jewish Joint Distribution Committee for the Year 1938," YIVO.

14. Bat-Ami Zucker, *In Search of Refuge: Jews and US Consuls in Nazi Germany, 1933–1941* (London: 2001).

15. Niederland, *Yehudei germanyah*, 25–26; Walter F. Willcox and Imre Ferenczi (eds.), *International Migrations* (New York: 1929–1931), 1:897.

16. Hagit Lavsky, "Hainflaziyah begermanyah vehamashberim shebe'ikvoteha (1922–1926) minekudat reut ziyonit," *Haziyonut* 12 (1987), 165–181; Traub, *Die jüdische Auswanderung aus Deutschland*.

17. Hagit Lavsky, *Before Catastrophe: The Distinctive Path of German Zionism* (Detroit: 1996), 88–105.
18. Ibid., 246–249.
19. Ibid., 249–251; Council for German Jewry, *First Annual Report for 1936*.
20. Halamish, *Bemeruz kaful neged hazeman*, 49–98.
21. There were some exceptions, however, as demonstrated in a recent study by Adi Gordon: *"Bepalestinah banekhar": hashavu'on "Oriyent" bein "galut germanit" le"'aliyah yekit"* (Jerusalem: 2004), which deals with a group of Left-oriented Jews who identified themselves as German exiles in Palestine.
22. Calculation based on Yoav Gelber, *Moledet hadashah: 'aliyat yehudei merkaz eiropah uklitatam, 1933–1948* (Jerusalem: 1990), 55–62; and "Report of the Executive of the Zionist Organisation and of the Jewish Agency for Palestine, submitted to the 21st Zionist Congress and to the 6th session of the Council of the Jewish Agency at Geneva," August 1939 (Jerusalem: 1939), 292–331.
23. Gelber, *Moledet hadashah*, 344.
24. Israel Central Bureau of Statistics, "Hatekhunot hademografiyot shel haukhlusiyah," part 2, "Mifkad haukhlusin vehadiyur 1961" (Jerusalem: 1962), Tables 24–27; Roberto Bachi, *The Population of Israel* (Jerusalem: 1976), Table 1.2.
25. According to Gelber, *Moledet hadashah*, 57 (in table based on Jewish Agency data), professionals alone accounted for 20 percent of the German Jewish olim.
26. This fact is reflected throughout the volumes devoted to the history of the Hebrew University—see Shaul Katz and Michael Heyd (eds.), *Toledot hauniversitah ha'ivrit birushalayim*, vol. 1, *shorashim vehathalot* (Jerusalem: 1997); Hagit Lavsky (ed.), *Toledot hauniversitah ha'ivrit birushalayim*, vol. 2, *Hitbasesut uzemihah* (Jerusalem: 2005).
27. Anat Helman, *Or veyam hikifuha: tarbut tel avivit bitkufat hamandat* (Haifa: 2007), 24–25, 163–164, 176–178; Gelber, *Moledet hadashah*, 466–472; Joachim Schloer, "Berlin in Tel Aviv," *Exilforschung—Ein internationale Jahrbuch* 13 (1995); Gideon Ofrat, *Bezalel hehadash 1935–1955* (Jerusalem: 1987).
28. Hagit Lavsky, "Leumiyut, hagirah vehityashvut: ha'im hayta mediniyut kelitah ziyonit?" in *Kalkalah vehevrah bimei hamandat 1918–1948*, ed. Avi Bareli and Nahum Kalinsky (Sdeh Boker: 2003), 153–178, esp. 172.
29. Doron Niederland, "Hashpa'at harofim ha'olim migermanyah 'al hitpathut harefuah beerez yisrael, 1933–1948," *Cathedra* 30 (1983), 111–160. At a certain point, though, the government restricted the entrance of physicians because of a growing surplus that was leading to unemployment among the doctors. On the introduction of psychotherapy in Palestine, see Eran J. Rolnik, *'Osei hanefashot: 'im Freud leerez yisrael 1918–1948* (Tel Aviv: 2008); Rakefet Zalashik, *'Ad nafesh: mehagrim, 'olim, pelitim, vehamimsad hapesikhiyatri beyisrael* (Tel Aviv: 2008). On social services, see Lavsky, "Leumiyut, hagirah vehityashvut," 153–177; Nissim Levi and Yael Levi, *Rofeha shel erez yisrael 1799–1948* (Zikhron Ya'akov: 2008).
30. Gelber, *Moledet hadashah*, 385–475.
31. See, for example, Amiram Oren, "The 'Kfar Shitufi': A New Settlement Type Founded by German Middle-Class Immigrants," in *The Land that Became Israel*, ed. Ruth Kark (New Haven: 1990), 233–249.
32. Lavsky, "Leumiyut, hagirah vehityashvut"; Mathias Marburg, "HOG und Landsmanschaften" (unpublished seminar paper).
33. Gelber, *Moledet hadashah*; Guy Miron, *Mi"sham" le"kan" beguf rishon: zikhronoteihem shel yozei germanyah beyisrael* (Jerusalem: 1998); Miriam Getter, "Ha'aliyah migermanyah bashanim 1933–1939," *Cathedra* 12 (1979), 125–147.
34. Getter, "Ha'aliyah migermanyah bashanim 1933–1939"; Miron, *Mi"sham" le"kan" beguf rishon*.
35. Hagit Lavsky, "The Riddle of Absence': Why Did German Jewish Leaders Not Integrate into the Yishuv Leadership?" lecture given at the 15th World Congress of Jewish Studies (Jerusalem), August 2009; Anne Betten and Miryam Du-nour, *Sprachbewahrung nach der Emigration—Das Deutsch der 20er Jahre in Israel* (Tübingen: 2000).
36. Lavsky, *Before Catastrophe;* idem, "German Zionists and the Emergence of Brith Shalom," in *Essential Papers in Zionism*, ed. Jehuda Reinharz and Anita Shapira (New York:

1995); idem, "'Realpolitik' and Moderate Nationalism: German Zionism and the Arab-Jewish Conflict in Palestine," in *Zionism and the Return to History: A Reappraisal*, ed. S.N. Eisenstadt and Moshe Lissak (Jerusalem: 1999), 325–332.

37. Yoav Gelber, "Deutsche Juden in politischen Leben des jüdischen Palästina, 1933–1948," *Leo Baeck Institut Bulletin* 76 (1987), 51–72; Yael Yishai, "'Aliyah hadashah uve'ayat hahaverut hakefulah beMapai," *Haziyonut* 6 (1981), 241–273; Ruth Bondy, *Felix: Pinhas Rosen uzemano* (Tel Aviv: 1990).

38. Hartmut Bickelman, *Deutsche Überseeauswanderung in der Weimarer Zeit* (Wiesbaden: 1980), 146 (Table 6). Harry S. Linfield, the director of the Jewish Statistical Bureau in New York, cites a figure of 6,670 Jewish immigrants from Germany between 1920 and 1930—see his *Jewish Migration: Jewish Migration as a Part of World Migration Movements, 1920–1930* (New York: 1933), 41–42 (Table 3).

39. Barkai, *Branching Out*; Hasia R. Diner, *A Time for Gathering: The Second Migration, 1820–1880* (Baltimore: 1992).

40. Max Malina, *Deutsche Juden in New York nach dem Weltkriege* (New York: 1931), 23–26.

41. Ibid. Malina devotes most of his account to the various organizations; he was the founder of the German-Jewish Center in New York.

42. Maurice R. Davie and Samuel Koenig, *The Refugees Are Now Americans* (New York: 1945), 3–11.

43. Claus-Dieter Krohn, Patrick von zur Mühlen, Gerhard Paul, and Lutz Winckler (eds.), *Handbuch der deutschsprachigen Emigration 1933–1945* (Darmstadt: 1998), 446.

44. Davie and Koenig, *The Refugees Are Now Americans*. In his book *Refugees in America: Report of the Committee for the Study of Recent Immigration from Europe* (New York: 1947), Davie wrote that the number of Jews arriving in the United States between 1933 and 1944 who were born in Germany was 97,374 (HIAS figure of 81,500 in YIVO Archives [henceforth: HIAS/YIVO], RG 245.4.5, MF 15.12 V-I, II: table titled "Jewish Immigrant Aliens Admitted from July 1st 1933 to June 30, 1943 by Last Permanent Residence, Including Austria from 1937/8"). Another estimation of the total (Jewish and non-Jewish) German immigration, excluding Austria, during the years 1933–1941 quotes a figure of 104,000: see Donald Peterson Kent, *The Refugee Intellectual: The Americanization of the Immigrants of 1933–1941* (New York: 1953); Martin Jay, "The German Migration: Is There a Figure in the Carpet?" in *Exiles and Emigrés: The Flight of European Artists from Hitler*, ed. Stephanie Barron with Sabine Eckmann, contributions by Matthew Affron et al. (Los Angeles: 1997), 320–326.

45. Traub, *Die jüdische Auswanderung aus Deutschland*, 10–11, 14–17.

46. Based on Joseph Perkins Chamberlain's tables in the Chamberlain Collection, YIVO Archives (YIVO), RG 278, Box 4; American Friends Service Committee (henceforth: AFSC), *Refugee Facts* (Philadelphia: 1939). The tabulation of immigrant entries according to the U.S. fiscal year at that time (July-June) effectively extends the estimate of a given calendar year into the first six months of the next calendar year, and this affects the estimate.

47. Werner Rosenstock, "Exodus 1933–1939, A Survey of Jewish Emigration from Germany," *Leo Baeck Institute Year Book* 1 (1956), 376; Herbert A. Strauss, "The Migration of Jews from Nazi Germany," in *Jewish Immigrants of the Nazi Period in the USA*, vol. 1, *Archival Resources*, ed. Steven W. Siegel (New York: 1978), xx.

48. Zucker, *In Search of Refuge*, 36–48.

49. HIAS/YIVO, "Jewish Immigrant Aliens Admitted from July 1st 1933 to June 30, 1943." Because data were calculated on a fiscal-year basis, the dramatic rise in numbers (from Germany and Austria) is visible: 30,096 in fiscal year 1938/1939 and 19,880 in 1939/1940.

50. Norman Bentwich, *The Refugees from Germany, April 1933 to December 1935* (London: 1936); *The Academic Assistance Council Annual Reports* (1934 and 1935) (London); "Report on the Work of the Jewish Refugee Committee from March, 1933 to January, 1935," Wiener Library London (henceforth: WLL), Central British Fund (CBF), MF 318/5, 123; also see various tables in YIVO, RG 278, box 2, files 27, 31.

51. Krohn et al. (eds.), *Handbuch der deutschsprachigen Emigration 1933–1945*, 446–466.

52. YIVO, RG 278, box 4; Harold Fields, *The Refugees in the United States* (New York: 1938); Leo Grebler, "German-Jewish Immigrants to the United States during the Hitler Period"

(unpublished ms.: 1976), Leo Baeck Institute, New York (henceforth: LBINY), ME 716, MM 29.

53. Davie and Koenig, *The Refugees Are Now Americans*, 3–11.

54. Yonathan Shapiro, *Leadership in the American Zionist Organization* (Urbana: 1971); Henry L. Feingold, *A Time for Searching: Entering the Mainstream, 1920–1945* (Baltimore: 1992).

55. Davie and Koenig, *The Refugees Are Now Americans*; Jay, "The German Migration." Cf. Krohn et al. (eds.), *Handbuch der deutschsprachigen Emigration 1933–1945*, who note that two thirds of the immigrants settled in New York City and that Los Angeles accounted for the second-largest concentration (p. 460). See also Ehrhard Bahr, *Weimar on the Pacific: German Exile Culture in Los Angeles and the Crisis of Modernism* (Berkeley: 2007).

56. Davie, *Refugees in America*; Steven M. Lowenstein, *Frankfurt on the Hudson: The German-Jewish Community of Washington Heights, 1933–82, Its Structure and Culture* (Detroit: 1989); Deborah R. Weiner, "The Third Wave: German Jewish Refugees Come to Baltimore," in *Lives Lost, Lives Found: Baltimore German Jewish Refugees, 1933–1945* (Exhibition catalogue of the Jewish Museum of Baltimore, 2004), 18; Bahr, *Weimar on the Pacific*.

57. Bentwich, *The Refugees from Germany, April 1933 to December 1935*, 183.

58. Avi Y. Deter, "Introduction," *Lives Lost, Lives Found: Baltimore German Jewish Refugees, 1933–1945* (Exhibition catalogue of the Jewish Museum of Baltimore, 2004), 11; Weiner, "The Third Wave," 18.

59. Fields, *The Refugees in the United States*; Grebler, "German-Jewish Immigrants to the United States."

60. Walter Laqueur, *Generation Exodus: The Fate of Young Jewish Refugees from Nazi Germany* (Hanover, N.H: 2001), 129–134.

61. Guide to the papers of Joseph Perkins Chamberlain (1873–1951), 1933–1951, YIVO, RG 278; Richard Breitman, Barbara McDonald, and Severing Hochberg (eds.), *Refugees and Rescue: The Diaries and Papers of James G. McDonald, 1935–1945* (Bloomington: 2009), 2–3.

62. German-Jewish Club, LBINY, AR 6466.

63. American Federation of Jews from Central Europe, Inc., *Ten Years, 1941–1951* (New York), LBINY.

64. Davie and Koenig, *The Refugees Are Now Americans*, 15. The extent to which these patterns influenced relationships between East European Jews and the German Jewish newcomers has yet to be carefully explored.

65. Austin Stevens, *The Dispossessed* (London: 1975); Anthony S. Travis, "From Color Makers to Chemists—A Jewish Profession Elevated," *Jahrbuch des Simon-Dubnow-Instituts* 3 (2004), 199–219.

66. Pamela Shatzkes, *Holocaust and Rescue: Impotent or Indifferent? Anglo-Jewry 1938–1945* (Basingstoke: 2004), 47.

67. Traub, *Jüdische Auswanderung*, 14–17.

68. Refugee Aid Committee Report (April 1939), WLL, MF CBF, reel 2, file 190.

69. Rosenstock, "Exodus 1933–1939, A Survey of Jewish Emigration from Germany"; Salomon Adler Rudel, "Die jüdischen Refugees in England" (1943), Salomon Adler-Rudel Collection, LBINY, AR 4473; Waltraud Strickhausen, "Grossbritannien," in Krohn, et al. (eds.), *Handbuch der deutschsprachigen Emigration 1933–1945*, 251–269.

70. Based on a calculation of Home Office statistics and cited by A.J. Sherman, *Island Refuge: Britain and Refugees from the Third Reich, 1933–1939* (London: 1973), statistical appendix.

71. Anthony Grenville, *Continental Britons: Jewish Refugees from Nazi Europe* (London: 2002), 21–29.

72. Werner Rosenstock, "The Jewish Refugees, Some Facts," in *Britain's New Citizens: The Story of the Refugees from Germany and Austria 1941–1951* (tenth anniversary publication of the Association of Jewish Refugees [AJR]) (London: 1951), 15–19.

73. Calculation based on Home Office data, cited by Sherman, *Island Refuge*, statistical appendix; Granville, *Continental Britons*, 21–29.

74. *AJR Information* 6 (June 1946).

75. Marion Berghahn, *German-Jewish Refugees in England: The Ambiguities of Assimilation* (London: 1984), 75.

76. Jewish Refugee Committee Report (1933–1935), WLL, CBF, MF 318/5, 123.

77. Ibid.

78. Anthony Grenville, "The Integration of Aliens: The Early Years of the Association of Jewish Refugees Information, 1946–1950," in *Yearbook of the Research Centre for German and Austrian Exiles Studies*, vol. 1, *German-Speaking Exiles in Great Britain*, ed. Ian Wallace (Amsterdam: 1999), 1–23; idem, *Continental Britons*; Bea Lewkowicz, "Belsize Square Synagogue: Community, Belonging, and Religion among German-Jewish Refugees," in *Yearbook of the Research Centre for German and Austrian Exile Studies*, vol. 10, *"I Didn't Want to Float; I Wanted to Belong to Something": Refugee Organizations in Britain 1933–1945*, ed. Anthony Grenville and Andrea Reiter (Amsterdam: 2008), 113–136.

79. Günter Berghaus, *Theatre and Film in Exile: German Artists in Britain, 1933–1945* (Oxford: 1989); Daniel Snowman, *The Hitler Emigres: The Cultural Impact on Britain of Refugees from Nazism* (London: 2002).

80. *AJR Information* 5 (May 1946); Berghahn, *German-Jewish Refugees in England*, 106; Werner E. Mosse, Julius Carlebach et al. (eds.), *Second Chance: Two Centuries of German-Speaking Jews in the United Kingdom* (Tübingen: 1991), esp. the following articles: Harold Pollins, "German Jews in British Industries," 361–377; Herbert Loebl, "Refugees from the Third Reich and Industry in the Depressed Areas of Britain," 379–403.

81. Interviews with Charles Hofner and Elly Miller (London), June 2007.

82. Bernard Homa, *Orthodoxy in Anglo-Jewry, 1880–1940* (London: 1969); Anne J. Kershen and Jonathan A. Romain, *Tradition and Change—A History of Reform Judaism in Britian 1840–1995* (London: 1995); Ignaz Maybaum, "German Jews and Anglo-Jewry," in AJR's 10th anniversary publication (*Britain's New Citizens*), 20–23; *AJR Information* 5 (May 1946).

83. Laqueur, *Generation Exodus*, 189–214.

84. For the facts (without interpretation), see Ami Zahl Gottlieb, *Men of Vision: Anglo-Jewry's Aid to Victims of the Nazi Regime, 1933–1945* (London: 1998). Central British Fund sources (addresses and budgets), Council for German Jewry sources, and Jewish Refugee Committee sources are all found in WLL. For an alternative interpretation of England as a focus for helping the refugees, see Grenville, "The Integration of Aliens."

85. The saga of detention in the Isle of Man and deportation to Australia and Canada has been dealt with extensively. See, for example, Ronald Stent, *A Bespattered Page? The Internment of "His Majesty's Most Loyal Enemy Aliens"* (London: 1980).

86. Grenville, *Continental Britons*, 29–65; idem, "The Integration of Aliens"; Laqueur, *Generation Exodus*, 189–214. This feeling of forever being "refugees" was clearly expressed in a series of interviews screened at the exhibition titled "Continental Britons," at the Jewish Museum in London, Summer 2002.

87. *AJR Information* 5 (May 1946).

88. Grenville, "The Integration of Aliens."

Book Reviews
(arranged by subject)

Antisemitism, Holocaust, and Genocide

Susannah Heschel, *The Aryan Jesus: Christian Theologians and the Bible in Nazi Germany*. Princeton: Princeton University Press, 2008. xvii + 339 pp.

Building on the historiography that has taken a much more critical look at the complicity of the German Protestant church with National Socialism, Susannah Heschel begins the book under review by explicitly acknowledging the pioneering work of Robert Ericksen and Doris Bergen. *The Aryan Jesus* is a worthy, indeed essential, addition to that body of scholarship. Heschel has written a dense and multifaceted study of the Deutsche Christen, the most notable strand of nazified Protestantism, which vainly attempted to create Christianized Nazism during the Third Reich. It is a theological and church history, an institutional study, and a collective biography combined. Most disturbing are Heschel's three conclusions: first, there was considerable continuity between the theological and racist thought of the pre-Nazi period and the "dejudaization" and nazification campaigns of a cohort of German Protestants in the Third Reich; second, this cohort was not a small group of marginalized or fringe players but a significant strand of Protestant response; and third, the degree of their complicity and impact was never seriously confronted and admitted in the postwar period.

Heschel begins with a study of the theological pedigree of Christian "dejudaization" going back to the 19th century. On the one hand, she traces the emergence of arguments for a non-Jewish Jesus who was allegedly born in a racially non-Jewish Galilee and shaped by any number of suggested non-Jewish contextual factors; as his teachings constituted a challenge to the Pharisaic-dominated Judaism of the Jews of Jerusalem, he was killed by them. Such claims were supported at least in part by advocates of a liberal, contextualizing "history of religions" approach against advocates of the more traditional, doctrinal approach. On the other hand, Heschel argues against a sharp division between religious-cultural and racial-biological antisemitism. From the perspective of post-1945, such a division has become a standard and all too convenient church apologia; during the 19th century, the lines between the physical and the spiritual, the body and the soul, the cultural-linguistic and the biological were not clearly drawn. For many Europeans, secular as well as religious, the soul or mind, not the body, was the ultimate carrier of immorality and degeneracy—a reality merely reflected in the ugliness and deformity of the body. Indeed, in this regard Heschel could have gone back to the Middle Ages, noting Gavin Langmuir's argument that the "essentializing" of Jewish inferiority in a broad negative stereotype can be traced back to the 11th and 12th centuries.

Thus the "Deutsche Christen" who were trying to bring the German Protestant Church into partnership with the new Nazi regime by means of racializing and "dejudaizing" its theology and liturgy were not aliens speaking a totally incomprehensible language. They represented a plurality of German Protestants, the product of nationalist, illiberal, and antisemitic political traditions combined with "supercessionist" theological views (Heschel terms supercessionism a "colonization of Judaism"). At the forefront of the campaign for a Nazi-Protestant partnership among Deutsche Christen was a cohort of theologians centered around Walter Grundmann, the founding director of the Institute for the Study and Eradication of Jewish Influence on German Church Life. This institute was parallel to myriad other institutions and agencies that sprang up in Nazi Germany to provide expertise on and to lobby for anti-Jewish measures. In this regard, the various "Jewish desks" of the German bureaucracy and the Reich Institute for the History of the New Germany come to mind immediately. Grundmann's Institute was no isolated affair, but in fact was tightly connected to the highly nazified University of Jena (on which Heschel writes an especially fascinating chapter), the Thuringian church, and also—by virtue of its numerous publications, conferences, and workshops, the support it received from prestigious scholars such as Gerhard Kittel, and other forms of networking—the wider Deutsche Christen movement throughout Germany. In short, the Institute reflected a widespread and flourishing institutional development in Nazi Germany, and the ideology it promoted was shared by far too many German Protestants.

Ultimately, Grundmann and his colleagues (whose collective biography is yet another fascinating aspect of this book) articulated a version of Christianity based on a manly, Aryan Jesus who struggled against the Jews and was killed by them, but who triumphed in spirit. They excised the Jewish Old Testament in its entirety as irrelevant to Christianity and purged Protestant hymns of any Jewish "taint." They proclaimed Germanic affinity and sought alliance with Nordic neo-paganism. But they could not reach consensus on the problematic issue of Paul (the Jew) and his central role in both Christian theology and the New Testament. Nor, ultimately, no matter how great the self-amputation they carried out, could they prove their worthiness as full partners of the Nazis. Theirs was an unrequited love for Nazism. For hardliners such as Martin Bormann and Alfred Rosenberg, Christianity—like liberalism and Bolshevism—remained a manifestation of Jewish conspiracy which—by definition—could not be "dejudaized" and still exist. And though Hitler had no reticence in appropriating politically useful Christian language and metaphors (such as "savior" and "resurrection"), his private tirades (admittedly recorded in the "table talk" by Bormann, who had an interest in emphasizing these statements) indicated a deep antipathy to Christianity as well.

After the war the most notorious Deutsche Christen lost their university positions, but virtually all remained employed within the church in one capacity or another. And German Protestant leaders for the most part expended much more energy on indignantly protesting both denazification ("Persilscheine," or "soap certificates"— documents provided by pastors as a means of cleansing one's Nazi past—were an essential component of any suspect's defense) and "vindictive" Allied war crimes trials than they did on coming to grips with their own role in the Third Reich. They portrayed themselves as victims of Nazi anti-Christian persecution and the Deutsche Christen as a tiny minority who erroneously, though sincerely and honestly, went just a little too far in trying to compromise with the Nazis in order to save the church, and whose antisemitism (like their own) was religious and theological, not racial and political. Grundmann, living in the German Democratic Republic, remained not only a prolific writer on religious matters but also, in accordance with his unquenchable thirst to be connected with power, became a Stasi informer on his fellow Protestants.

Heschel cuts through this litany of apologetics with devastating effect. Indeed, finding Grundmann's Stasi file must have been one of those "eureka" moments all scholars yearn for. Ultimately, she concludes, the Protestant racial theologians and "dejudaizers"—like the desk murderers and academic fellow-travelers of other disciplines—did not directly kill Jews in the Holocaust, but they never ceased to provide the legitimacy and moral authority for denigrating and despising Jews even as they were being murdered. Their moral responsibility is great.

CHRISTOPHER R. BROWNING
University of North Carolina at Chapel Hill

Steven T. Katz, Shlomo Biderman, and Gershon Greenberg (eds.), *Wrestling with God: Jewish Theological Responses during and after the Holocaust*. New York: Oxford University Press, 2007. 689 pp.

In this voluminous edited work, Steven T. Katz, Shlomo Biderman, and Gershon Greenberg bring together a host of theological responses to the Holocaust on the part of philosophers, rabbis, and historians of the most diverse Jewish backgrounds and orientations. Judiciously culling from a vast array of materials, they usefully balance classical with lesser-known texts that have never before been anthologized.

Wrestling with God is primarily arranged according to the authors' places of residence—for instance, the United States, Europe, or Israel. The main exception is a section titled "Ultra-Orthodox Voices during and after the Holocaust," which is placed at the start of the volume. The same temporal preposition "during" is repeated for the other sections that are arranged according to place, although almost all of the texts in these sections were written decades after the Shoah. The only ultra-Orthodox voice from the end of the 20th century, Yoel Schwartz, appears in the Israeli section.

While most of the ultra-Orthodox texts have not been published in English before, many of the American contributors are known among the international public as "Holocaust theologians." Among the Europeans we find a number of prominent Jewish philosophers, most of whose works do not, however, primarily focus on Holocaust themes. With the exceptions of Eliezer Schweid, Yehuda Bauer, and more recently Yehoyada Amir, the Israeli contributors likewise have not extensively written on the Shoah.

Both the timing and the placing of Jewish theological responses to the Shoah are problematic. Reactions written in 1942 are very early responses to the Shoah that were produced in the midst of the catastrophe. And with regard to place, Jewish intellectuals are difficult to pin down geographically not only during but also after the Shoah. Emil Fackenheim, for example, was born and educated in Germany, found refuge in Canada, and later decided to immigrate to Israel. National identities cannot easily comprise his biography: a knowledge of his German origins is vitally relevant for comprehending his philosophy, whereas his aliyah was central to his Zionist self-understanding. Nevertheless, Fackenheim wrote his post-Shoah philosophy mostly while residing and teaching in Toronto.

A useful feature of *Wrestling with God* is its juxtaposition of well-known texts by Fackenheim, Richard Rubenstein, Eliezer Berkovits, and Ignaz Maybaum with valuable commentaries. This excellent editorial decision has resulted in the classical texts being seen in a new light. For example, the frequently quoted works of Fackenheim find a sharp theological response in Michael Wyschogrod's much-overlooked 1971 critique. Also included are a number of writings by Irving Greenberg, most of which have not received adequate attention. Greenberg's notion of the modern state of Israel as a framework for a "third phase of the covenant" under human rather than divine leadership is unusual in that it combines traditional Jewish religious thought with Zionist thought, and in this way bridges the gap between the American and (secular) Israeli mindsets. Steven Katz's open-ended commentary on Greenberg's text functions as an invitation to further dialogue. In contrast, his critique of Maybaum has the hallmarks of a concluding argument: he takes Maybaum to task for an excessive reliance on Christian metaphors when Jewish argumentation is what is really called for. In Maybaum's defense, it should be noted that his deployment of such metaphors is far from unself-conscious or naive, nor can he be accused of "assimilative thought." On the one hand, Maybaum is well-informed about Christian thought, including the earliest stages of the process of Christian theological reevaluation after the Shoah; as early as 1965, the last year of the Second Vatican Council, he was already quite aware of this phenomenon, which at the time was still rather inchoate. On the other hand, it must be emphasized that Maybaum employs Christian metaphors in an unusual or even a "Jewish" way—that is, in a manner that effectively subverts Christianity as, similarly, Marc Chagall painted a crucified Jesus wearing a *tallit*.

Well-known Jewish philosophers such as Martin Buber, Abraham Joshua Heschel, Joseph B. Soloveitchik, and Emmanuel Levinas are represented through short but intense texts, such as Soloveitchik's beautifully sad reading of the Song of Songs and an exceptional text of Levinas in which, in contrast to his later great works, he directly addresses the Shoah. This short text formed part of a 1988 collection of essays that had a wide impact in Israeli philosophical circles, although this is not indicated in the present collection.

The editors' greatest innovation is their aforementioned inclusion of manifold ultra-Orthodox writings, many of which have been translated for this volume. The decision to include these texts amid Reform, Conservative, Modern Orthodox, secular, and unaffiliated Jewish responses casts a spirit of Jewish solidarity over an anguished discussion. In this section, the editors' brief introductions take on added poignancy in relating the authors' tragic biographies: many of them were murdered within a short time after having written their testimonies. Indeed, the genre of these texts—most of which are exegetical in form, presenting interpretations of biblical texts and homilies—might better be described as "contemporaneous witness" rather than as "post-Shoah thought."

One question often posed in these ultra-Orthodox texts later became typical of many post-Shoah writings; namely, are inherited theological formulae adequate to address the profundity of current suffering? The prevailing assumption is that ultra-Orthodox witnesses strived to bring the mounting catastrophe into continuity with the earlier history of Jewish suffering, a stance rooted in piety and theological rigidity. Examination of these writings reveals something quite different, however. First, the authors display a clear awareness that the option exists to perceive this catastrophe as qualitatively different from previous historical destructions. This is explicitly the case even in texts from 1941-1942, when the dimensions of industrialized mass murder were impossible to fully discern. The question is dealt with squarely by various rabbis, such as Kalonymous Kalman Shapira, who himself was shot by soldiers of the SS in 1943. His main argument, that we should not speak of a fundamentally new dimension of Jewish loss, is based on a strong sense of historical solidarity with former generations: "What excuse does a person have to question God and have his faith damaged by this prevailing suffering more than all the Jews who went through suffering in bygone times?" (p. 45). His words express the sense that the claim of a new dimension of catastrophe and suffering would undermine this historical chain. Yet the explicitness of both the question and its deliberate answer shows that the idea of entering a new epoch is not remote or proscribed by religious taboo. It is precisely the commitment to Jewish continuity that precludes viewing the Holocaust as unparalleled. Jewish belonging is expressed by not exempting oneself and by not claiming essential difference in suffering.

The selection of Israeli authors was undoubtedly an editorial challenge. On the one hand, almost any Israeli intellectual might have something to contribute; on the other, few Israeli academics would feel comfortable with labeling their response to the Shoah as "theological." Some voices are strikingly missing here, such as Asa Kasher, Avishai Margalit, and, of course, Yeshayahu Leibowitz. Nevertheless, the selected authors contribute to the discourse in various interesting ways. Zeev Harvey, for instance, contrasts Gershom Scholem's representation of evil in the Kabbalah with Maimonides' concept of evil as privation. Harvey argues against the kabbalistic personification that accepts evil as a given reality instead of encouraging its diminution. This internal Jewish divergence is particularly interesting since the discussion concerning evil as an irreducible quality versus its being a reducible *quantity* has its secular counterpart: presenting the evil in the Holocaust as inexplicable and even mysterious is criticized by those who are committed to preventing and opposing it and who thereby wish to subject evil to a rational analysis. One of the many interesting interjections in the Israeli debate is the essay of Yehoyada Amir, whose Zionist approach to the Shoah emphatically insists upon the necessity of acting against evil committed against others, explicitly including the case of evil carried out by Jews.

Among the Israeli authors, Yoel Schwartz stands out. A contemporary ultra-Orthodox rabbi, Schwartz offers a critique of the phrase "like sheep to the slaughter," which was commonly used during the early postwar years in Israel and elsewhere to criticize what was perceived to be the victims' passivity in the face of the Nazi murderers. His is a cutting analysis of the Zionist contempt for weakness, all the more surprising in its resemblance to secular antimilitaristic indictments of Israeli society.

Wrestling with God concludes with a short text of Elie Wiesel, but the last extensive essay is by Jonathan Sacks, the chief rabbi of Britain and the author of many books on the topic. Sacks offers a beautiful interpretation of the ultra-Orthodox response to the destruction of East European Jewry: rebuilding is in children more than in theology. The book is thus framed by its efforts to acknowledge the ultra-Orthodox response and sense of obligation after the Shoah.

The question of how to relate to God in a state of despair marks the center of Jewish post-Shoah discourse, though, as indicated by the variety of themes, theodicy is not the leading question and "because of our sins" is not the overriding answer. In this collection, the editors have done far more than simply bring together diverse and seemingly irreconcilable views. They have produced a comprehensive work that invites discussion, dialogue, and debate as a common endeavor in the post-Shoah world.

BARBARA U. MEYER
The Hebrew University

History and the Social Sciences

Gur Alroey, *Hamahpekhah hasheketah: hahagirah hayehudit mihaemperiyah harusit 1875–1924* (The quiet revolution: Jewish emigration from the Russian empire 1875–1924). Jerusalem: Zalman Shazar Center, 2008. 281 pp.

The vastness of the Jewish emigration from Eastern Europe is well known, and its significance is generally realized. We may ask, then, why Gur Alroey has titled his original and valuable work *The Quiet Revolution*. Its subject is huge—more than two million Jews who crossed international borders and voyaged to new lands, teeming emigration ports, and packed ships—all of which appears to sharpen our question. An answer seems to lie in the habits of Jewish public discourse during the years of maximum migration. During those 15 peak years before the First World War, Jewish ideologies dominated public discussion, while migration, omnipresent though it was, usually was mentioned only incidentally or superficially. Alroey emphasizes as well that Jewish emigration has been examined in terms of statistics and sociology, but rarely as history. Moreover, the study of Jewish migration most often begins with the migrants' arrival and settlement in some new country, whereas the discussion of its causes in the countries of origin has generally amounted to little more than routine clichés.

Alroey, who teaches at Haifa University, reverses all that. His account commences with where and why Russian Jews decided to emigrate and then documents the various arduous emigration procedures they had to undergo before finally arriving at Ellis Island in New York and at lesser ports of arrival. No study of Jewish migration such as Alroey's has yet been written; it reminds the informed reader of Marcus L. Hansen's classic *The Atlantic Migration, 1607–1860,* which was published back in 1940. Alroey's basic sources are the records of the Jewish Colonization Association (JCA), stored and accessible in Jerusalem, out of which he has constructed a database to provide answers to questions most other scholars have never thought to ask. Now we know, or so it seems, the regional sources of emigration. Even more so, we are told which geographic areas tended to send their emigrants to which countries. It is surprising to learn, for example, that Eretz Israel drew its immigrants particularly from the areas near Odessa, the premier port of embarkation, more than from areas of greater Zionist activity to the north. Another important source used by Alroey is the widely used Russian census of 1897. Finally, he makes effective use of a mass of emigrant memoirs, many of them still unpublished.

The JCA operated information bureaus in hundreds of towns throughout the Pale of Settlement, to which prospective emigrants could address their questions about routes of travel and conditions of life and work in their destined country. Naturally enough, the questioners often included information about their personal situation. Thousands of such letters of inquiry have been preserved, constituting a source of utmost value. Alroey also devotes considerable attention to the emigrants' journey. This has been a subject of study, but his work is perhaps the most detailed to date on the subject. Emigrants, as he shows, had to decide between obtaining a passport—a tedious bureaucratic procedure that invariably required a bribe—or else crossing the border illegally, usually as part of a group whose guide was often slippery or crooked. The other side of the border was Germany. (Alroey does not mention that the German government had no objection to illegal arrivals.)

Before emigrants could sail, they often had to wait some days for their ship to be ready. The entire process was not only physically wearing but was also exploited by dishonest operators. However, Hamburg, the greatest emigration port, had a decently kept emigrant village where travelers were kept safely in isolation. A brass band accompanied emigrants from their quarters to their ship (is it an omission that Alroey does not tell us what music they played?). So much is said about thieves and the exploitation of emigrants that the reader may be surprised to learn that the great majority of emigrants, even those who were smuggled over the border, arrived intact in person and possessions. Nonetheless, their trials were not yet at an end. Emigrants whose destination was the United States feared the eye examination that detected and turned back bearers of contagious eye diseases. Alroey gives only scant mention to the two hospitals in Russia where prospective emigrants' eyes could be examined before they set forth and, where necessary and possible, cured.

Much was written at the time about the need to organize or direct Jewish migration, but it is clear that emigrants, millions of whom disregarded warnings and appeals not to leave, did not readily let themselves be directed. Although international Jewish conferences were held about migration, those which met in the peak migration years did not attempt to limit or prevent the vast flow, but rather to aid and inform the emigrants. Alroey discusses the doctrines of Jewish social, religious, and political movements concerning migration, though his contribution to this interesting subject tends to be rather thin. He devotes considerable space to the story of the Galveston movement, an organized emigration project involving about 7,000 Russian Jews who sailed from Europe to the port of Galveston, whence they were distributed throughout the western United States. The two persons who were central to this movement, Israel Zangwill and Jacob H. Schiff, entertained conflicting purposes. Zangwill, the author and territorialist, wanted a sort of Jewish territory to arise in the western United States, whereas the banker-philanthropist Schiff, whose ample means financed much of the movement, saw it as a project to divert immigration from heavily crowded New York City, Boston, and Philadelphia. Immigrants coming through Galveston did much to enlarge small Jewish communities in the trans-Mississippi west, but nothing came of both men's unrealizable hopes, as masses of immigrants continued to crowd into the eastern cities. Here, Alroey puts to good use the standard work of Bernard Marinbach, *Galveston: Ellis Island of the West* (1983).

Despite a few weaknesses that have been noted, Alroey's book ranks as one of the most important studies of Jewish migration yet published. His theme is original, and his research digs deeply and thoroughly. One hopes to see this volume translated into some western language, as it is an invaluable guide to those wishing to further their research.

LLOYD P. GARTNER
Tel Aviv University

Edith Bruder, *The Black Jews of Africa: History, Religion, Identity*. New York: Oxford University Press, 2008. 283 pp.

Edith Bruder's fascinating book on the "black Jews" of Africa is a work of the future. While Bruder herself elucidates the past, one is left wondering what is to come. Surely the term "black Jews" will become politically incorrect sooner rather than later? In addition, almost all the groups mentioned in *The Black Jews of Africa* started identifying themselves as Jews from the 1980s on. Intertwined with their fate is the destiny of the Jewish people and multiculturalism in the state of Israel; it appears that their story is just beginning to unfold.

Perhaps the most famous of Africa's Jews are the Beta Israel, once known as the Falashas. This group has been well studied both in its historical context and in its new sociological landscape in Israel.[1] While many of the themes that the Beta Israel conjure up are relevant for other African Judaizing groups, Bruder's book goes far beyond the particulars of Ethiopia's well-known minority. It presents the narratives of a far-ranging collection of groups in West, East, Central, and South Africa, including some of the Timbuktu in Mali, the Igbo of Nigeria, the House of Israel in Ghana, the Tutsi of Rwanda, and two other groups that have been gaining a reputation in the West in the past few years: the Abayudaya of Uganda and the Lembas of Zimbabwe and South Africa. In true African style, most of these groups trace lineages to putative or real ancestors, who may have been of Jewish origin.

The book is divided into three parts: the prehistory of African Judaism, the genesis of black Judaism, and a discourse on Africa, Judaism, and African "Jews." In the first part, the myth of the Ten Lost Tribes is examined (this myth, of course, is not restricted to Africa).[2] Alongside this pervasive myth, Bruder deals with other ancient legends such as the encounter between King Solomon and the Queen of Sheba, so prominent in Ethiopic tradition, which lives on.

In the second part, Bruder attributes the development of the invention of Judaism in Africa to the western colonizers, including European missionaries who found similarities between African religion and ancient Judaism. Particularly interesting here are the 19th- and early 20th-century western representations of blacks as well as Jews (and Moors) as "promiscuous," based on earlier accounts of primitive black and foreign tribes. Historically, Jews were often portrayed as blacks. In brief, as Bruder demonstrates: "Blackness as a common denominator of the inferiority of Africans as well as Jews has a long history in Western culture" (p. 49). This idea became commonplace by the 19th century and was even adopted by some early 20th-century anthropologists.

Today, of course, such a representation is totally eschewed. In the 21st century, President Barack Obama's Jewish half-brother, Mark Ndesandjo, points to a new narrative distant from the early colonialists. In the United States, there are communities of black Jews who have been practicing Judaism for more than 150 years, a fact that simultaneously highlights the tensions between race and religion and expands the margins of Judaism. Both in Africa and among certain black Jewish groups in America, an Afrocentrist ideology has arisen—one that claims not only that blacks and Jews are linked but that Africans are the "true" Jews. A case in point is the Rastafarians of Jamaica, who originated in Ethiopia. In November 2009, I attended a Rastafarian event in one of Addis Abeba's older neighborhoods, where participants from different countries reiterated their belief in God as black, and in the former Emperor Haile Selassie as Messiah. I had previously visited the Rastafarians in Shashemene, south of Addis Abeba, in 2004, as well as in the 1990s and the 1980s. While their narrative changes from time to time, the essential idea continues to be that Rastafarians represent the authentic Jews, whereas other "Jews" cannot be Jewish since they are not "black."

The third part of *The Black Jews of Africa* moves to an examination of Jewish presences in black Africa, including early mythical figures such as Eldad the Danite, a 9th-century Jewish traveler, and medieval Jewish traders. According to Bruder, in Timbuktu today, there are traces of crypto-Judaic practices, albeit no real religious observance. Bruder also points to the growing number of self-proclaimed Jewish communities in Nigeria, where in 2008 some 30,000 Igbos were practicing some Judaic rites. By now, the numbers have probably swelled, urged on by American Jewish groups such as Kulanu, an organization that encourages the propagation of Judaism globally.

The Black Jews of Africa raises disturbing questions for Jews with regard to the meaning of Jewish identity and to membership in a global Jewish diaspora. The essence of Judaism, coupled with the tension between race and religion, are brought into question as readers begin to ask themselves about the meaning of the Jewish national homeland or about the implications of recent trends among black Jews in Africa for the Jewish people. Bruder skillfully avoids these issues of the future.

SHALVA WEIL
The Hebrew University

Notes

1. See, for instance, the reviews by Shalva Weil of works authored by Emanuela Trevisan Semi and by Stephen Spector, in vols. 22 and 24 of this journal.
2. Shalva Weil, *Beyond the Sambatyon: The Myth of the Ten Lost Tribes* (Tel Aviv: 1991).

Beth B. Cohen, *Case Closed: Holocaust Survivors in Postwar America*. New Brunswick: Rutgers University Press, 2007. 223 pp.

Beth Cohen's book *Case Closed: Holocaust Survivors in Postwar America* is a well-researched, eloquent, and extremely readable work. This book makes an important contribution to the field relating to the postwar experiences of survivors as well as to more specific issues concerning their postwar immigration and integration into American society. Her research is based on a rich blend of sources, including oral histories, the case files of Jewish social workers, and minutes from social service agency meetings, all of which describe the survivors' integration process. Cohen's main thesis is that the public image of the survivor story, both in the early postwar years and today, "effaces Holocaust survivors' struggles and impedes our understanding of the impact of genocide on the individual and on society, as a whole" (p. 2). Her work attempts to reinscribe individuals' experiences, difficulties, and struggles into a more complex portrayal of postwar immigration, absorption, and adaptation. This approach results in a welcome addition to the scholarly research on the postwar experiences of Holocaust survivors in their absorbing communities.

Case Closed describes the legal and financial responsibility assumed by the American Jewish community in helping survivors immigrate to the United States, detailing the remarkable infrastructure established by the community both to sponsor new immigrants and to help them establish themselves. At the same time, Cohen argues, the goals of various local communities and the relevant social service agencies were not always congruent with the survivors' needs—especially their emotional needs. Generally, the American Jewish community saw financial independence and entry into the job market as the key indicators of successful immigrant absorption, and it often did not take into account the emotional needs and wishes of the survivors. Cohen argues that the notion of "work" as the "best medicine" defined the communities' strategy toward the survivors. Interestingly, my own examination of Australian Holocaust survivor narratives indicates that this notion was internalized and shaped the way survivors evaluated their own success decades later.

Beyond the gaping divide between the strategic goals of the various institutions and the emotional and physical needs of the survivors, Cohen also demonstrates the unsympathetic and sometimes harsh attitudes expressed by various Jewish agency workers toward the survivors, as well as the often difficult relationships between survivors and relatives in the United States who sponsored their immigration. Especially painful to read is the chapter on young orphan survivors who found it difficult to cope with the readjustment in their new country and the absorbing society's lack of willingness to connect emotionally with their plight.

Although Cohen describes psychological barriers that account for such unwillingness or insensitivity on the part of the absorbing community, she fails to give enough weight to what was articulated as the "incomprehensible" nature of the Shoah and the "inconceivable" horror that the victims experienced. Extensive literature has described how, during the early postwar years, it was difficult for the western imagination to grasp the reality of the Final Solution and the Jews' treatment at the hands of the Nazis. The extent of the Shoah and the victims' plight during the war was not fully known or grasped, and this hindered a deep understanding of the survivors' ordeals. Cohen argues that various agencies were operating in accordance with their previous experience with "ordinary" refugees and immigrants, failing to make the transition to managing these severely traumatized people. However, I would argue that it would have taken some time for mental health professionals to grasp the extent of the problem or to know how to help the survivors. Cohen outlines the developments in the field of social work and psychology in dealing with survivors of war and trauma, but fails to note that this research and teaching may have taken time to filter down to practitioners. Another important factor often complicating the relationship between social workers and survivors was the language barrier, an essential issue that Cohen does not address. While Cohen argues for a more complete picture of the experiences of survivors, I would be keen to know the extent to which the cases she presents are representative.

I concur with Cohen's argument that a more emotionally generous, flexible, and sensitive absorption program would have benefited survivors greatly. However, beyond its own feelings of guilt as identified by Cohen, the absorbing community did not have the psychological and emotional resources to provide what Dori Laub and Marjorie Allard have identified as an "empathic other," someone able to listen and contain the survivors' stories of victimization and suffering.[1] This phenomenon was not unique to the United States, but rather seems to have been universal. Sadly, the pain and misery that survivors felt during those early years was unavoidable, and the difficulties they faced in reestablishing themselves in the United States were probably inevitable. Jewish Americans were not able to console these grief-stricken people. Notwithstanding, such impediments do not excuse what Cohen describes as "hostile or indifferent" responses to the survivors (p. 176). Cohen shows how it was among themselves that survivors felt understood; in the framework of social or communal groups, they were able to derive some comfort and the means to mourn and commemorate their loved ones, homes, and communities. In the end, however, no one could give survivors what they really needed—the restoration of their families, prewar lives, and communities.

SHARON KANGISSER COHEN
The Hebrew University

Note

1. Dori Laub and Marjorie Allard, "History, Memory and Truth: Defining the Place of the Survivor," in *The Holocaust and History: The Known, the Unknown, the Disputed and the Reexamined*, ed. Michael Berenbaum and Abraham J. Peck (Bloomington: 1998), 809.

Henry L. Feingold, *Jewish Power in America: Myth and Reality*. New Brunswick: Transaction Publishers, 2008. 164 pp.

In the course of a recent class I taught on the Holocaust, an Iranian student came to my office one day and demanded, nervously but politely, that I disprove the existence of the Elders of Zion. After some stumbling, I replied that she was essentially asking me to disprove the existence of unicorns. No amount of evidence could prove the absence of a nonexistent thing, I informed her. I could only provide overwhelming evidence for a simpler explanation of reality; I could only demonstrate that the events of the world are more easily and persuasively comprehended without the existence of a secret Jewish conspiracy. I told her that, over the course of the semester, I would provide considerable evidence for a reasonable portrait of a political world that did not rely on the amazing conspiracy theory, and that at the end of my presentation she would be free to decide for herself how the world best made sense.

I could spend most of this review describing how Henry L. Feingold's book combats the increasing amount of academic and popular literature committed to proving the Jewish conspiracy, but as Feingold does not deign to make this his purpose, neither will I. Instead, I will merely note that I wish I had already read his magisterial study of Jewish power in America at the time I was confronted by my Iranian student, because Feingold has succeeded in presenting a coherent and persuasive picture of actual Jewish power in America. He shows that Jewish power, to the extent that it does exist, is right out there in the open, and that it has been unfocused and ineffectual about as often as it has been successful. For those unaware of its basic contours, Feingold's book is by far the best avenue to knowledge.

Feingold's most succinct insight is that, as an ethno-political group in America, Jews have been uniquely successful only in the realm of political public relations. In the international arena, Jewish organizations traditionally direct their resources toward the physical protection of Jews and their public perception. In the United States, where Jews as a group are not violently threatened, the latter purpose of protecting a positive perception has become the most substantial and successful avenue of Jewish politics. That is to say, American Jewish political power is directed at bringing attention to the physical threats facing Jewry elsewhere. Feingold calls this "soft" power, and he is right to distinguish it from direct policing, defensive, and proactive military action (as is undertaken daily by Israelis).

Feingold presents two strong cases of self-identified Jewish political behavior, namely activities during Franklin D. Roosevelt's administration related to European refugee aid and rescue, and matters related to Soviet Jewry both during and subsequent to the administration of Richard M. Nixon. He also considers less peculiarly Jewish political trends such as Jewish American leftism and neo-conservatism in order to determine which portion of these activities, if at all, can be related to Jewish political behavior. In the case of the Holocaust era (on which he has published extensively) and Soviet Jewry (on which he has previously published a volume), Feingold analyzes the multifaceted (and often uncoordinated) political activities of various Jewish groups in the context of the political pulses of the larger world, and also assesses their political successes and failures.

Feingold's basic conclusion is that American Jews have leaned heavily on a simple moral argument in their public relations political work: Jews, goes the argument, constitute an embattled and vulnerable group that is also committed to liberal western ideals: therefore, they merit the continuing protection of the West. This moral argument, Feingold notes, does not gain practical traction unless there is a confluence of larger western national interests—it failed, for instance, during the Holocaust, when such larger national interests were lacking. However, when the two are complementary, as in the late Cold War-era battle to free Soviet Jewry, success is more likely to be ensured.

In his last chapter, Feingold offers a brilliant yet dark critique of the efficacy of soft, moral, and persuasive power as American Jews have chosen to wield it. He argues that the more Jews attain leading economic and political positions, the more their particular moral argument of vulnerability diminishes, leading inevitably to attenuation of their "soft" power. Indeed, coming to terms with the decreasing efficacy of the rhetoric of victimhood will be among the most significant tasks of American Jewish power in the 21st century.

Feingold's essay reads like an uncut diamond. It deals with a gritty reality encompassing both 20th-century industrial genocide and the possibility of a 21st-century thermonuclear version of the same. Perhaps for this reason, Feingold shuns the use of sparkling prose; yet what he mediates in this book feels starkly true. At the very least, he has proven himself to be the finest theorist of American Jewish power of his generation, while those who would follow in his wake have yet to come close to the subtlety of his vision. Indeed, we who study the American Jewish experience seem to be moving away from the harsh truths concerning American Jewish power. Merely to note that this book is a great contribution to the larger fields of both political science and Jewish studies does a considerable disservice to Feingold's real contribution, which is the immense gift of his scholarly life and mind to the well-being of the Jewish people.

MICHAEL SCOTT ALEXANDER
University of California, Riverside

Jonathan Frankel, *Crisis, Revolution, and Russian Jews*. Cambridge: Cambridge University Press, 2009. x + 324 pp.

Jonathan Frankel, one of the leading scholars of modern European Jewish history, passed away in May 2008. Before his death, he finished collating *Crisis, Revolution, and Russian Jews*, which represents a rich and varied illustration of his convictions on how to write history. Taken together, these 11 articles and contributions, published over a period of more than 20 years, constitute a carefully crafted argument.

In his introduction, Frankel emphasizes the crucial impact of individual and collective agency on the course of history. Although this agency is shaped by prior political contexts and traditions, historical and political contingencies play a crucial role in the unfolding of the historical dynamic. This holds especially true for periods of crisis, the "extraordinary moment in the onward flow of time" (p. 16), which often lead to significant transformations of political culture. Thus, the historian needs to find the right balance between long-term trends and structure, on the one hand, and contingent developments, on the other. Frankel considers the collected articles as a demonstration of this basic argument, which obviously echoes Fernand Braudel's call to write history by interweaving the threads of *longue durée* and *histoire événementielle* into one historical narrative. As Frankel lays out in his concise and elegant introduction, his argument focuses on four themes: the development of modern Jewish politics, the role of the radical Jewish intelligentsia in this development, the connectivity of Jewish history in Eastern and Western Europe (as well as in the United States and in Palestine), and finally the impact of periods of crisis. These themes offer ample opportunity to reflect on the relationship between traditional, liberal, and radical political cultures, which the author regards as central for the understanding of Jewish history in the 19th and early 20th centuries. How is traditional messianic faith translated into radical politics? What are the objectives of those individuals engaging in Jewish politics? Who takes political responsibility when there is no continuous institutional framework of a state with a traditional political class? How did Jews from diverse communities and differing linguistic and religious backgrounds interact when a specific situation required international cooperation? What motivated individual Jews to opt for "Jewish" politics, and who chose to function in interethnic contexts?

The first contribution, "Crisis as a Factor in Modern Jewish Politics," originally published in 1987, offers a combined interpretation of the Damascus blood libel in 1840 and the impact of anti-Jewish violence in the tsarist empire in 1881-1882. Both events illustrate Frankel's argument regarding how unexpected and unprecedented crises engendered new movements and formed new leaderships. In both cases, as well as in the context of the Mortara affair (1858), the struggle of Romanian Jewry in the 1870s, the expulsion of Moscow Jews in 1891, the Dreyfus affair, the revolution of 1905, and the First World War, individual Jews as well as communities had to define the most appropriate answers to hardship and duress. A theme developed by Frankel with unparalleled erudition and precision in this and several other contributions is the complex process of negotiating these reactions. Both in the Damascus affair and during the pogrom crisis of 1881-1882, traditional and modern forms of intervention were practiced, and in both cases, the crisis led to a transformation of Jewish politics. The Damascus affair resulted in a substantial growth of the Jewish press, whereas the pogrom crisis was a crucial catalyst in the formation of radical, mass-based political movements.

In "Jewish Politics and the Press," Frankel follows the further evolution of the Jewish press as the major arena in the international debate concerning the advantages and pitfalls attending the Alliance Israélite Universelle, established in 1860. In "Paradoxical Politics of Marginality," Frankel develops the argument of the "crisis impact" in discussing the resourcefulness of Jewish leaders, especially in the United States, in reacting to the extreme hardship of Jews during the First World War. In "Jewish Politics and the Russian Revolution of 1905," "'Youth in Revolt': An-sky's *In Shtrom* and the Instant Fictionalization of 1905," and a more recent contribution on Yosef Haim Brenner, Frankel describes the impact of this upheaval on the Russian and Polish Jewish communities as being both a massive mobilization and a democratization of Jewish political culture. In his essay on Brenner, Frankel also discusses the writer's ideological floating between diverse, even contradicting, political commitments, a topic that reoccurs in his survey on "The Socialist Opposition to Zionism in Historical Perspective" and in a fascinating account of the diverging attitudes among members of the Second Aliyah (Jewish immigration to Palestine between 1904 and 1914) toward eulogizing the guardians of Jewish settlements who were killed by their Arab neighbors. Frankel shows to what degree political background, or encounters with anti-Jewish violence or Jewish self-defense, shaped ideological attitudes in Palestine and "made the emergence of the most extreme forms of nationalism within the labor movement a possibility" (p. 215). Two contributions on Jewish historiography, one about Simon Dubnov as historian and politician, and the other a reflection on the reappraisal of the interdependence of religious tradition and cultural innovation influencing Jewish assimilation, form the last part of the volume.

Crisis, Revolution, and Russian Jews is an impressive demonstration of erudition and scholarship. Any specialist in modern Jewish history will welcome this collection of essays, which are, in part, not easily accessible. Frankel's contribution on the Socialist opposition to Zionism is for the first time published in translation from Hebrew. Although readers need to be aware of the fact that, in most cases, important scholarship has been published in these areas of inquiry since these essays were first published (the bibliographical references have not been updated), the author's mastery of source material in Russian, Hebrew, Yiddish, and a number of other languages remains unequaled. For the many colleagues who miss Jonathan Frankel's exceptional personality, erudite advice, and forceful argument, this volume offers a welcome inspiration and a demonstration of the highest standards in historical writing.

FRANÇOIS GUESNET
University College London

Lloyd P. Gartner, *American and British Jews in the Age of the Great Migration*. London: Vallentine Mitchell, 2009. xiii + 290 pp.

Lloyd P. Gartner has been a creative and prolific scholar of modern Jewry for more than five decades. A devoted disciple of Salo Baron, he has focused his scholarship on England and the United States, but has remained ever conscious of the larger historical forces that shaped modern Jewry. His valuable one-volume survey, *History of the Jews in Modern Times* (2001), reveals the breadth of his scholarly reach.

The present volume brings together 12 of Gartner's previously published articles written over a 50-year period (1955-2005), dealing broadly with "the great theme of Jewish migration and its far-reaching impact" (p. x). Two articles, comprising more than one-third of the volume, focus on Romania, "the principal international Jewish question in the late 1860s and 1870s" (p. 29). The first, "Romania, America and World Jewry: Consul Peixotto in Bucharest, 1870-1876," brilliantly reconstructs the diplomatic mission of the American Jewish consul Benjamin Franklin Peixotto, appointed by Ulysses S. Grant in 1870, without salary, expressly to aid Romania's persecuted community of Jews. Using a wide range of primary sources, Gartner succeeds in explaining why Peixotto set forth on his journey, his aims and accomplishments, and the mission's lasting impact. A second article, "Romania and America, 1873" deals with another angle on this same subject. Together, the two set the stage for understanding both Romanian emigration prior to 1881 and the more significant emigration later on.

Two of Gartner's chapters deal with women immigrants—a welcome addition to a historiography that has not been particularly gender-conscious. "Anglo-Jewry and the Jewish International Traffic in Prostitution, 1885–1914," originally published in 1983, mines previously unknown manuscript sources on this sordid subject and makes an important contribution that subsequent scholarship has built upon. "Women in the Great Migration," originally a 2005 lecture, highlights significant under-researched themes and is a welcome and suggestive, if far from comprehensive, study of the subject.

The majority of Gartner's chapters consist of his important summary statements on the "great migration," written from different vantage points and in different decades of his career. One focuses on the "East European Background of Jewish Emigration," a well-researched study that the recent work of Eli Lederhendler and Gur Alroey, among others, builds upon. Another chapter tackles the role of Germany and Britain in the migration. A third looks broadly at "North Atlantic Jewry"—a concept that at the time broke new ground. A fourth reexamines, 25 years later, Gartner's own landmark work on *The Jewish Immigrant in England, 1870–1914* (1960). Two further articles seek to separate immigrant "realities" from traditions and myths that have clouded too many popular and even scholarly accounts of this subject.

Inevitably, the articles brought together here repeat one another in some significant details. They also reflect the historiography of their day and have not been updated to take account of subsequent scholarship. The articles appear in more or less random order and are not dated, nor are the original places of publication provided. In one case, "From New York to Miedzyrecz: Immigrant Letters of Judah David Eisenstein, 1878-1886," valuable Hebrew-language footnotes have been dropped from this reprint. In other cases, texts are marred by careless proofreading.

Lloyd Gartner has authored well over 40 important articles during his productive career, and it is a pity that only those bearing on immigration are preserved here. The introduction makes clear that the original plan was to produce two volumes of articles, the second containing such fundamentally important articles as Gartner's classic study of "American Jews and Public Schools, 1840-1875" and his survey of "Emancipation, Social Change and Communal Reconstruction in Anglo Jewry, 1789–1881." One hopes that this second collection may appear soon.

In the meanwhile, the present volume highlights the great strengths of Gartner's scholarship on the subject of immigration. He appreciated the virtues of "transnational" scholarship even before that term was invented, recognized the various distinct stages of the migration process, pointed out the economic factors underlying the migration, and uncovered little-known government documents and other unusual primary sources instead of simply relying, as did so many of his peers, on newspaper accounts.

A new generation of historians is today rewriting the history of Jewish immigration, utilizing new sources, new theoretical frameworks, and new historical approaches. Their questions differ in some respects from Gartner's. Thanks to his pioneering scholarship, however, they build upon a firm and well-laid foundation.

JONATHAN D. SARNA
Brandeis University

Zvi Gitelman and Yaacov Ro'i (eds.), *Revolution, Repression, and Revival: The Soviet Jewish Experience*. Lanham: Rowman & Littlefield Publishers, 2007. xi + 406 pp.

This thick volume is based on the proceedings of a conference titled "Soviet and Post-Soviet Jewry" that was held at the Hebrew University of Jerusalem in December 2003 in honor of Mordechai Altshuler, one of the leading scholars of Soviet Jewry. Prominent members of the field took part in the conference and contributed to this impressive collection of up-to-date scholarship dedicated to Soviet and post-Soviet Jews. The division of space in *Revolution, Repression, and Revival* reflects the approaches to the subject that have evolved over the last few years. Only about half of the book is dedicated to the Soviet period, whereas the other half deals with the experience of former Soviet Jews both in the post-Soviet states and in Israel.

The volume opens with an introduction by Yaacov Ro'i that provides an overview of Soviet and post-Soviet Jewish history. This is followed by two essays that serve as a kind of exposition of the meeting between Jews and the Soviets. The first, Oleg Budnitsky's "The 'Jewish Battalions' in the Red Army," deals with the attempts to organize Jewish units in the Red Army during the Civil War. Utilizing lengthy citations from previously unknown archival documents, Budnitsky shows how antisemitism was rampant in the ranks of the Red Army; how the idea of Jewish units was promulgated (mainly by the Poale Zion party) and ultimately accepted by the top Bolshevik leadership; and how it was nonetheless resisted by many lower-level members of the army on the grounds that separate Jewish military units would only increase antisemitic feelings and confirm the perceived equation between the Soviet regime and the Jews. In the second essay, "Zionism in the Early Soviet State: Between Legality and Persecution," Ziva Galili locates the history of Russian Zionism in the liminal space between tolerance and persecution. Departing from the "heroic" narrative of constant and brutal Soviet repression against the Zionists, Galili shows how several important factors allowed for the survival and even the flourishing of Zionism between 1919 and 1925: among them, the change in character of the Zionist movement—that is, its concentration in "some half dozen Zionist youth movements" and especially in Hehalutz, which in general accepted the Soviet regime (p. 51); successful interventions on behalf of the Zionists by the pianist David Shor, a close associate of Bolshevik leader Lev Kamenev, whose supporters in those years included Stalin and formed the most influential group among the Soviet leadership; the tenuous standing of the Evsektsiia (Jewish sections of the Communist party) among the top Bolshevik leaders; and political changes during the transition from the Civil War to the New Economic Plan (NEP). All of these factors, Galili shows, counterbalanced the hostility of the Evsektsiia and the secret police (GPU) toward the Zionist movement and their general suppression of all political groups not belonging to the Communist party.

Three other articles in the first part of the book deal with key venues framing the interwar Jewish Soviet experience: the shtetl, the metropolis, and the agricultural colonies. Arkady Zeltser's "The Belorussian Shtetl in the 1920s and 1930s" shows that, notwithstanding the Soviet policy of social transformation, the traditional East

European shtetl was preserved as a sociocultural phenomenon until the Nazi invasion in 1941. As Zeltser notes:

> The well known axiom of the Haskalah "Be a Jew at home and a human being on the street" acquired a new significance in the Soviet setting. Shtetl Jews continued to adhere to tradition publicly to the degree that this conformed to Soviet ethnic policy (e.g. conversing in Yiddish). They engaged in private craftsmanship to the degree permitted by the government. . . . Religious and national behaviour that conflicted with Soviet norms was concealed from the eyes of outsiders (p. 102).

All this became possible because of the out-migration of the most modern and ambitious strata—the young people and the relatively prosperous sectors of the population. These Jews are discussed in Michael Beizer's "The Jews of a Soviet Metropolis in the Interwar Period: The Case of Leningrad." Beizer divides the Leningrad Jews into three categories. The veterans from the prerevolutionary era tried to revive Jewish public life in the city throughout the 1920s, but lost their prominence in the 1930s. Newcomers who were anxious to integrate into Soviet society, aspiring to upward mobility, were extremely successful, but the price they paid was "the loss of their religion and their ethnic culture and language, as well as of an opportunity to participate in any form of Jewish life" (p. 122). Finally, the traditionalists who moved to the metropolis "sought frantically to preserve their distinct lifestyle and autonomy. . . .They did not want to come into contact with Soviet life at all, anticipating nothing good from such an encounter" (p. 124). (The division between the second and the third group is not always clear-cut.) Beizer's conclusion is that "there were many Jewish Leningraders who were not actually integrated by the Soviet regime, who never internalized its values, but adapted to it outwardly. . . . Many kept the shtetl in their hearts and minds even though they feared transmitting its values to their children" (p. 127). Thus, the conclusions of Beizer fit those of Zeltser, both authors stressing that a majority of the older generation of Jews adapted only externally to the Soviet regime while continuing to adhere, in varying degrees, to traditional norms and practices.

Another option for migration of Jews from the shtetl is discussed in the contribution by Jonathan Dekel-Chen, "Jewish Agricultural Settlement in the Interwar Period: A Balance Sheet," which reassesses Jewish agricultural colonization in Belorussia, Birobidzhan, and the Black Sea region. Dekel-Chen's conclusion is that while Birobidzhan was a cynical project with no chance of succeeding, and whereas the colonization in Belorussia suffered from the shortage of available arable tracts, "the invading Nazi armies, and nothing else, terminated Jewish life in the colonies around the Black Sea" (p. 75). Judging the Jewish colonization in Crimea and South Ukraine a "qualified" success, Dekel-Chen stresses both "a negative correlation . . . between the attractiveness of agricultural resettlement and the general state of the Soviet economy" (p. 83) and the fact that the colonies provided only "short-term relief" (p. 73) for impoverished Jews of the former Pale of Settlement.

The only piece dedicated to the Holocaust period is Kiril Feferman's "Jewish Refugees and Evacuees under Soviet Rule and German Occupation: The North Caucasus." This article discusses the situation of those Jews who found themselves in the area in late 1941 and early 1942, who subsequently came under the German occupation in the second half of 1942.

In "The Genesis of Establishment Anti-Semitism in the USSR: The Black Years, 1948–1953," Gennadi Kostyrchenko elaborates his understanding of the emergence and dynamics of the anti-Jewish persecution in the last decade of Stalin's regime. He traces the beginning of anti-Jewish policies back to 1939–1940, when "officials of Jewish origin were no longer appointed to senior or sensitive positions in the Party Central Committee apparatus and those who had survived the Great Terror were gradually removed from their posts" (p. 180). Stalin's personal antisemitism influenced the new, post 1937–1938 generation of high-ranking bureaucrats. Already during the Second World War, Jewish origin had become an obstacle to advancement, whereas in the Cold War era, Jews were excluded from the state machinery "bit by bit" (p. 187). Kostyrchenko also shows that after the initial outburst of anti-Jewish fury around the time of the alleged "doctors' plot" in January 1953, Stalin began "to phase down the propaganda campaign," realizing "the danger of any further escalation of nationalistic hysteria for the integrity of the multinational communist empire." Likewise, the campaign met with "the latent opposition of the top bureaucracy," which "had no wish to be continually sent to the slaughter, this time for allegedly condoning a Zionist fifth column" (pp. 189–190). All these factors, along with Stalin's declining health, prevented another Great Terror. The events of early 1953, constituting a "hysterical, but nonetheless frightening overture" (p. 190), did not in fact go any further.

The Khrushchev and Brezhnev eras are discussed by Samuel Barnai in "Social Trends among Jews in the Post-Stalin Years." Barnai focuses on the Soviet nationalities policy and on the social transformations that took place among Soviet Jews. His major point is that the authorities' blocking of possibilities for Jews' vertical mobility led to a concentration of Jews in new technological niches such as the nuclear and space industries in the 1950s and 1960s and computer sciences and high-tech in the 1970s. Barnai also outlines the three social alternatives available for Soviet Jews: emigration, opposition to the system or, following the "common pattern of social behaviour," their "paying lip service to the authorities and living out their regular lives in the private domain" (p. 146)—the last option being a clear continuation of the paradigm shown by Zeltser and Beizer in their works.

The remainder of the volume is devoted to the *perestroika* period (under the leadership of Mikhail Gorbachev) and post-Soviet Jewry. Lev Gudkov's "Attitudes toward Jews in Post-Soviet Russia and the Problem of Anti-Semitism" shows the relatively minor place of antisemitism among other ethnophobias and its concentration in "peripheral social groups and milieus" (p. 202). This lengthy article, featuring the results of numerous large-scale surveys, concludes that "Jews have ceased to be the object of any particular aggression, hostility or fear, despite all the significant mass alienation from them" (p. 212) and that "[w]hile anti-Semitism has been preserved as a basic factor in Russian national identification, it has ceased to be a means of political mobilization" (p. 213).

Vladimir Ze'ev Khanin's "The Jewish National Movement and the Struggle for Community in the Late Soviet Period" describes the establishment and development of Jewish organizations in the late 1980s, particularly in Ukraine. In his interesting "The Problematics of Jewish Community Development in Contemporary Russia," Theodore H. Friedgut presents the history of Jewish umbrella organizations, mainly the Russian Jewish Congress and the Federation of Jewish Communities of Russia, and the relationships between themselves and with the government. A third essay, "Putin and the Jewish Oligarchs: Prejudice or Politics?" by Marshall I. Goldman, describes the fates of various Jewish oligarchs (many of whom provided the financial backing to the Jewish organizations) during the presidency of Vladimir Putin. His conclusion is that "you don't have to be Jewish to come under attack by Putin, but if you are Jewish the odds you will be harassed are much higher" (p. 276).

Another two contributions to the post-Soviet half of the volume deal with demography. In "Post-Soviet Jewish Demography," Mark Tolts sketches the demographic portrait of Jews in the former U.S.S.R.: the aging and assimilation processes, the erosion of the "core" Jewish population, migration from the former Soviet republics, and the returning migration from Israel to Russia and Ukraine. In the end, he presents the "demographic fate" of former Soviet Jews in the countries of immigration, pointing out, for example, that "the Jews who emigrated to Israel escaped the dramatic fertility reduction characteristic of the former Soviet Union population as a whole and Jews in particular" (p. 306). All in all, while the share of Soviet Jews among world Jewry was 17 percent in 1970, Tolts estimates the share of the former Soviet Jews in 2004 as 12 percent.

"The Demography of Post-Soviet Jewry: Global and Local Context," by Sergio DellaPergola, shows the interconnection between the general situation in a given country (measured by the Index of Human Development), and the frequency of Jewish emigration to Israel. This global tendency—emigration from less developed countries to more developed countries—is strongly visible both in the emigration from the former Soviet republics and in the emigration from different regions of the Russian Federation. Thus, post-Soviet Jewry does not differ from global patterns affecting Jews, including those in Israel: "The rate of emigration from Israel stands exactly where you would expect to find a rate of immigration to Israel from a country with similar socioeconomic characteristics" (p. 325–326).

The volume's two final essays focus on former Soviet Jews in Israel. Elazar Leshem's "The Russian Aliya in Israel: Community and Identity in the Second Decade" is a sociological study of the Russian aliyah after 1989. Leshem notes that, while the immigrant political parties established in the 1990s eventually dissolved or were co-opted into existing political frameworks, the immigrants continue to form a distinct and separate community. To be sure, there are signs of a slightly growing level of integration on the part of the immigrants and an improvement in their perception of Israeli society (the Israeli perception of the Soviet olim also shows signs of improvement). At the same time, the immigrants have not traded in their Russian identity but rather view themselves as "Russian Israelis." To the question "[w]hether the crystallization of the Russian community will persist" (p. 335), the author indicates the possible prospects of further integration, which is "emerging as the dominant strategy of Soviet immigrants in their relations with the host society" (p. 353). Supplementing this sociological analysis is Moshe Sicron's "Immigrants from the Former Soviet Union in the Israeli Population and Labor Force," which offers a statistical portrait of the immigrant population. Sicron outlines the salient demographic characteristics, including relatively low fertility and aging of the population, as well as geographical distribution, standards of living, and participation in the labor force. Although his analysis indicates that the immigrants' average income is only 60-80 percent of that of the veteran Jewish Israeli population, Sicron's conclusion is that, overall, "the Soviet and post-Soviet migrations have been a success story." The migrants, he notes, have "fuelled the Israeli economy and have made possible the 'high-tech' boom of the 1990s, while making their mark on Israeli music and sports, as well as in other fields of endeavour" (p. 377).

Finally, in a concluding essay, Zvi Gitelman offers his thoughts on two basic topics: the fate of Jews in the post-Soviet realm, and the issue of how to define who is Jewish, both in Israel and in the diaspora.

All in all, *Revolution, Repression, and Revival* offers a broad-based depiction of the Soviet Jewish experience from its early stages during the Civil War to the post-Soviet period both in the former U.S.S.R. and in Israel. It does not, of course, cover the entire range of Jewish history in the Soviet Union, but it does present most of the relevant issues. A number of the case studies are important and path-breaking in and of themselves, and together provide a rich portrayal of Jewish continuity and change during the Soviet era. In the section dedicated to the post-Soviet issues, the material is even more comprehensive, resulting in a strong and valuable basis for further inquiry and research.

VLADIMIR LEVIN
The Hebrew University

Nadia Malinovich, *French and Jewish: Culture and the Politics of Identity in Early Twentieth-Century France*. Oxford: Littman Library of Jewish Civilization, 2008. 280 pp.

Nadia Malinovich's insightful work explores the emergence of an influential group of Jews who started to define themselves in ethnic and cultural terms in the first decades of the 20th century. Rather than constituting a single subculture, this group of thinkers and activists created such diverse institutions as the Reform-oriented Union Libérale Israélite, the Jewish scout movement, and the highly popular Union Universelle de la Jeunesse Juive, which eventually welcomed anyone who identified as a Jew independent of religious affiliation. Malinovich demonstrates how these novel spaces of Jewish sociability and a new literary scene coincided with a turn to a new type of identity politics.

Although the first voices to propose a new ethnic Jewish identity in early 20th-century France emerged before the First World War, Malinovich argues, it was only after the war that a plethora of new associations and journals came to constitute a broader basis for a Jewish cultural and literary renaissance. Malinovich offers three compelling reasons for this renaissance: the continued stream of Jews from Eastern (and, to some extent, southeastern) Europe who were more oriented toward a national Jewish identity than their French Jewish coreligionists; the drop in antisemitism after the outbreak of the First World War; and most importantly, a new acceptance of ethnic identities throughout France, partly made possible by the dominance of a liberal brand of Catholicism between 1905 and the 1930s.

Malinovich portrays the rise of new ethnic Jewish identities in early 20th-century France convincingly, yet she is also careful not to create an overly stark opposition between the self-understanding and self-positioning of the preceding generations of Jewish activists and those of the generations she studies. Following scholars such as Michael Graetz, Pierre Birnbaum and, most recently, Lisa Leff, she notes that even those Jews who enthusiastically embraced the universalistic promises of French republicanism in the 19th century were usually eager to retain some form of Jewish affiliation. Taking this route, *French and Jewish* depicts the Jewish renaissance of the 1920s not as a complete break but rather as a shift from one arrangement of particular interests within a universalistic framework to another, with its own new paradoxes. Whereas the older model of Franco-Judaism envisioned Jews as individuals with no collective interests beyond their continued existence as a religious group, the newer ethnic model of particularism allowed Jews to make broader claims about their particularity as a people. However, unlike the more recent proponents of a Jewish renaissance who began to rediscover an ethnic Jewish identity in France in the 1980s, the authors of the 1920s who form the subject of this book did not engage in a fundamental criticism of republican universalism. Whatever type of particularism they embraced, these French Jews believed that the legacy of the French Revolution and the Third Republic were the best guarantors of their freedom as an ethnic group.

Throughout the book, Malinovich persuasively describes the widespread, if not unlimited, acceptance of ethnic identities in the decade after the First World War, although she sometimes appears overly eager to celebrate the success of these French Jews' coherent vision of an identity that was ethnically Jewish while still nationally French. Her own perceptive close readings of contemporary literature often seem at odds with this assessment. The tensions of this model become clear in her analysis of novels that depict Jewish characters forced to accept their ethnic Jewish identity as a biological fact against their will. In Albert Cohen's novel *Solal* (1930) and Léo Poldès' play *L'Eternel ghetto* (1928), Jewish men try to escape their Jewish environment—even becoming part of the antisemitic movement, in the case of Poldès' main character, Max. Both works depict Judaism as an irrational life force that can be rejected only at the peril of losing one's life or one's humanity. Both certainly phrase the problem of the relationship between Jewish particularism and nationalist universalism in a manner unknown in 19th-century French literature, but they hardly offer a sense of a successful new synthesis of these concepts. Not all readers will agree with Malinovich's depiction of the 1920s as a time without challenges from antisemitism for French Jews; even accepting this premise, it is difficult to see these new identities mostly as an expression of new possibilities and not also of new tensions.

Despite these issues, Malinovich generally maintains a healthy distance from her subjects. She shows that many of the works that depicted Jews as ethnic others, including those written by Jews, were also criticized by the French Jewish press for reproducing antisemitic stereotypes. She also reflects at length on the case of the non-Jewish brothers Jean and Jérôme Tharaud, the most successful non-Jewish writers to depict the "exotic" life of East European Jews. Here Malinovich offers a perceptive analysis of their negative depiction of Jews in the 1920s, which culminated in their public support of Nazism by 1933.

Some of the book's arguments are suggestive even when not fully elaborated. At various instances, Malinovich notes the prominence of people who immigrated as children, or who were the children of recent immigrants, in the institutions that sought to revive Judaism as a culture in interwar France. While its evidential basis is not broad enough to challenge the depictions of a society split between native and immigrant Jewish communities as offered in Paula Hyman's and Nancy Green's classic works,[1] Malinovich's thoughtful book nevertheless offers a welcome corrective to overly stark depictions of this fundamental division.

Engaging as well with the literature on interwar Jewish life in Germany and the United States, *French and Jewish* is suggestive beyond the field of French Jewish history. The comparison of the French case to the Jewish renaissance in Berlin and Frankfurt, which has been traditionally seen as a reaction to rising (not diminishing) antisemitism, raises questions about the relationship between various simultaneous Jewish renaissances. Perhaps future works, building on the literature that Malinovich has significantly enriched, will be in a position to address the Jewish renaissance of the interwar years from a wider transnational perspective.

ARI JOSKOWICZ
Vanderbilt University

Note

1. Paula Hyman, *From Dreyfus to Vichy: The Remaking of French Jewry, 1906-1939* (New York: 1979); Nancy Green, *The Pletzl of Paris: Jewish Immigrant Workers in the "Belle Epoque"* (New York: 1986).

Moshe Rosman, *How Jewish Is Jewish History?* Oxford: Littman Library of Jewish Civilization, 2007. xiv + 224 pp.

Moshe Rosman's incisive introspection of Jewish historiography reviews the theoretical challenges of postmodernism for Jewish history. Postmodernism defies the possibility of grand narratives and opts to see Jewish society as "a 'hybrid' component of the 'hegemonic' society and culture ... within which Jewish identity, culture, and society are 'constructed'—differently in each time and place" (p. 53). Instead of one grand narrative of the Jews, reading the past in this light thus presents the history of the Jews unraveled into myriad experiences shaped by specific historical contexts. Moreover, the belief is that meaning is not discovered but is instead constructed, shaped by interests and power. Clio's followers no longer pursue the noble dream of objectivity as detached scholars, but rather actively create the past, rendering it a product of their imagination.

Without disregarding such challenges, Rosman asserts that an "attempt must be made to multiply sources and perspectives as much as possible, while admitting that the resultant descriptions will always imply interpretation, will always be contingent, and will never be complete" (p. 10). For him, embracing the fragmented nature of historical understanding safeguards against the threats posed by postmodernism and averts viewing historical studies as the production of fiction. He therefore concludes that "postmodern Jewish historiography is possible" but that it "probably must give up on classic metahistories, although it will not be able to avoid replacing them" (p. 186).

Rosman acknowledges the difficulties posed by essentialist notions, yet concludes that the Jews are best defined as a people. His guarded acceptance is contingent upon historicized realization of such concepts, and he remains mindful of the ways that historical context changes the nature of Jewish culture. As he demonstrates in chapter 5, every generation interprets the meaning of "Jew," "Jewish," and "Judaism" against the background of the historical environment. Drawing on his own field of expertise, Rosman illustrates this contention by arguing that halakhic customs in Poland of the early modern period were a product of a confluence of medieval traditions and the Polish context. During this period, Polish Jewry was quite distinct as a separate culture, and yet Jewish and non-Jewish cultures were "at times intertwined, at times embedded, and at times coincident with each other along broad bands" (p. 94).

Confronting those who believe that there is no coherent Jewish history, Rosman detects in current scholarship a contradiction between the proliferation of metanarratives and "multicultural" narratives that emphasize the influence of the local culture on the Jewish community. "Such a view is postmodern enough in its multiperspectivism, but its 'meta-ness' contradicts the spirit of postmodernism" (p. 18). Noting the inherent contradiction between a postmodern posture and a reliance on essentialist concepts, Rosman furthermore charges that there is a resemblance between contemporary multiculturalism and the 19th-century mission theory of Jewish civilization. Books thus extol the extent to which Jews contributed to the making of modernity but also, one might add, struggle with the "blandly generic term secular Jew" as Yosef Yerushalmi put it in his *Freud's Moses* (1991).[1] Indeed, how to interpret the presence of the marginal Jews at the center of modern thought, literature, and science and the convergence of multiple identities in the lives, for example, of Walter Benjamin, Heinrich Heine, Sigmund Freud, Max Liebermann, or Camille Pissarro remains a daunting challenge.

Notwithstanding the apparent paradoxes and the challenges postmodernism poses for the study of Jewish history, the crisis that Rosman perceives emerged not entirely in response to postmodernism. Doubts have vexed scholars of Wissenschaft des Judentums from its inception. In the 19th century, Wissenschaft promised to arrive at a conclusive definition of the essence of Judaism, only to end up with various conflicting versions. By the beginning of the 20th century, the certainty had waned further and research had moved from the realms of "suffering and learning" to painstaking archival research and sociological consideration, which, however, continued to rely to some extent or another on assumptions about the nature of Jews, Judaism, and their tradition. Moreover, as David Myers in his *Resisting History:*

Historicism and Its Discontents in German-Jewish Thought (2003) has demonstrated, the turn toward history also elicited a vocal anti-historicist current in the 19th and 20th centuries. Postmodernism, it could be argued, poses another stage in a crisis that has bedeviled the practitioners of Clio almost from its inception.

At issue here is not solely how postmodern sensibilities have transformed Jewish studies, but the extent to which they pose an obstacle for the production of a usable past. For Rosman, "Jewish history has formed the Jews," and yet, "[o]nly if they believe in it will they continue to exist" (p. 55). Historians, however, are no longer, as in Friedrich Schlegel's saying, "prophets facing backwards." A unified history of the Jews might indeed have only existed within a theological perspective that gave coherence to the scattered records, for example, on the pages of Jacques Basnage's *L'Histoire et la Religion des Juifs* (1707). Even the grand narratives of the 19th century embedded fragments and shreds of conflict, and Zionist critics of Wissenschaft des Judentums, including the historian of Jewish mysticism Gershom Scholem, who wholeheartedly subscribed to ideals of historical objectivity, denied in his *Sabbatai Sevi: The Mystical Messiah* the existence of a "well-defined and unvarying 'essence' of Judaism."[2]

Yet unlike 19th-century scholars of Wissenschaft, professional historians are no longer required to write histories of nations and minorities in order to foster heritages. As scholars of memory have long noticed, the pursuit of scholarship does not always mesh with collective memories. Today, the construction of the Jewish past is shaped and created in multiple disciplinary, national, and international contexts and public arenas. Moreover, as Roger Chartier and others have argued, meaning is no longer perceived as something that is created by the author but as a process in which the reader partakes. What matters therefore is whether students engage the Jewish past in varied ways and make history and tradition meaningful to themselves and their communities. To be sure, historians contribute to this process, but they are no longer the high priests of the past.

Thus, the perceived loss of certainty and increased fragmentation are not identical to relativism or crisis but rather have opened up Jewish history to social history and to feminist and cultural studies in the widest sense. Furthermore, Jewish studies has created a field of communicative action (in the realms of conferences, reviews, and other forms of exchange) that defines a procedural rationality capable of differentiating fact from fiction. The influence of postmodernism on Jewish studies testifies to vibrancy within the field as much as do conflict and dispute, and these are not signs that portend a crisis.

NILS ROEMER
University of Texas at Dallas

Notes

1. Yosef Hayim Yerushalmi, *Freud's Moses: Judaism Terminable and Interminable* (New Haven: 1993), 9.

2. Gershom Scholem, *Sabbatai Sevi: The Mystical Messiah, 1626-1676*, trans. R.J. Zwi Werblowsky (Princeton: 1973), xi.

Charlotte Schoell-Glass, *Aby Warburg and Anti-Semitism: Political Perspectives on Images and Culture*, trans. Samuel Pakucs Willcocks. Detroit: Wayne State University Press, 2008. xii + 250 pp.

The reception of the works of Aby Warburg (1866-1929) can be said to have proceeded in several stages. Three years after his death, the Kulturwissenschaftliche Bibliothek Warburg in Hamburg that he had founded published two large volumes containing writings that had appeared during his lifetime, with a preface by Gertrud Bing, who had been his devoted assistant. These were meant to be followed by three additional volumes containing drafts, unfinished sketches, and other material, though this plan could not be realized. From these years onward, Warburg's ideas achieved a certain diffusion as refracted principally through the work of collaborators and disciples—most notably Fritz Saxl, Edgar Wind, and Erwin Panofsky—though the manner in which these ideas, often formulated in difficult and aphoristic language, were both understood and propagated by his followers is itself a complicated issue. An English translation of the corpus came out somewhat belatedly in 1999 under the sponsorship of the Getty Research Institute, and some of Warburg's most important articles have more recently appeared separately in various European languages.

The publication of E.H. Gombrich's *Aby Warburg: An Intellectual Biography* (1970), however, placed Warburg's ideas and their sources on much firmer footing and contributed substantially to a renewed interest in them. Commanding an impressive erudition, and drawing judiciously on the substantial archive of unpublished material housed in the Warburg Institute in London, Gombrich seems to have found his project no doubt daunting, if not uncongenial. All subsequent writers who have chosen to deal with the subject have had to take this authoritative text as a point of departure in what has evolved into a burgeoning literature, expanding on its insights or finding reasons to dissent from its governing assumptions or conclusions.

The work under review is a translation of Charlotte Schoell-Glass' *Habilitationsschrift*, accepted by the University of Hamburg and published in 1998, to which a new preface has been added. Its thesis, baldly stated, is that antisemitism, on the rise in Germany after the proclamation of the empire in 1871, provided the decisive impetus for the formation of Warburg's ideas, and that even the origins of his work "must be seen as conditioned by his Jewish background to a degree not previously recognized" (p. 2). Warburg's relatively small scholarly production, primarily devoted to such topics as the Florentine Renaissance, the lore of astrology, and more broadly, the *Nachleben* of classical antiquity, does not provide explicit evidence of a concern with Judaism, but these preoccupations are documented in the papers preserved at the Warburg Institute. Warburg, it has been observed, never discarded the smallest bit of paper, and this mass of writings, consisting of letters, diary entries, notes, and newspaper clippings, has been thoroughly mined by Schoell-Glass in support of her argument.

Warburg's attitude toward his Jewish heritage and his pained discovery of the hostility engendered by his religious affiliation are first registered in letters of 1887 and 1889 that were addressed to his mother after he had left the protected environment of his wealthy parents' home to pursue his studies at the university. These letters are printed in an appendix and are also discussed in the second chapter of Schoell-Glass' book. In the first letter, written from Bonn, Warburg announces that he will no longer adhere to Jewish dietary laws, and, while insisting that he is not ashamed to be a Jew, asks for his parents' understanding for his efforts to accommodate himself to the expectations of the cultural milieu. In the second, sent from Strasbourg, he reports on the slights of which he has been a victim: in the streets, he regularly hears himself apostrophized in a vulgar manner as a Jew by people walking behind him; in the tavern, his card-playing fellow students amuse themselves at his expense by mockingly muttering something in Yiddish (*etwas vorzumauscheln* in the German text, here inadequately translated as "murmuring"). We learn further from the author that in the following years, Warburg paid close attention to press reports about atrocities that had antisemitic overtones, such as the Konitz and Stavropol affairs (1901, 1905) and the Beilis ritual murder trial in Kiev (1913), in which he saw a disturbing irruption of primitive, pre-rational violence under the complacent reigning ideology of civilization and progress.

Warburg's self-understanding as a Jew, to be sure, was marked by ambivalence and complexity. Schoell-Glass draws on a memoir first published in 1947 by one of Warburg's early disciples, Carl Georg Heise, for other revelatory incidents of his biography. In Rome, where in 1912 he was about to deliver his famous paper on the frescoes of the Palazzo Schifanoia in Ferrara, Warburg was asked to preside over the International Congress of Art Historians. He refused to accept this honor, fearing that this would be exploited to bring discredit to the cause of art history. According to Heise's testimony, whose reliability cannot be taken altogether for granted, Warburg, in a moment of despair at the onset of his mental collapse in 1919, confessed to his friend that: "Fundamentally, in my soul, I am a Christian," professing shame for this betrayal of his family and people, and swearing his listener to secrecy.

In bringing to light this dimension of Warburg's personality, Schoell-Glass has performed a very useful task, and her book is thus a welcome contribution to its subject. However, whether (and, if so, to what extent) Warburg's sense of his Jewishness, or the animus to which he was exposed as a result of antisemitism in the German culture of his time, were powerful motivating factors for the development of his ideas is another, more contestable issue altogether. Warburg's major antecedents, as is generally recognized, were Jacob Burckhardt's *Civilization of the Renaissance in Italy* and Friedrich Nietzsche's *Birth of Tragedy*. Gombrich's more detailed treatment of the sources makes only a few brief references to Warburg's Judaism, and these concerns, we read, were his subject's struggle to liberate himself "from the confining bonds of Jewish ritualism" of his forebears, and not the hostility that he encountered in the ambient Gentile world. It may be that Schoell-Glass' argument would have benefited from a somewhat wider exploration of the conditions by which Jews sought, gained, or were denied access to high culture in Wilhelmine Germany, involving other Jews among Warburg's contemporaries who became eminent art historians, such as Adolph Goldschmidt (a fellow Hamburger), Max J. Friedländer, or even the expatriate American, Bernard Berenson. Ultimately, we are presented, I believe, with two distinct models for the construction of a cultural biography, whose different implications are well stated in a concluding paragraph of Schoell-Glass' book (p. 164; I have slightly altered the translation):

> Whoever holds that there is an objective process inherent to scholarship that specifically omits all that is conditional and period-specific, will reckon that personal motives for scholarly accomplishment (in this case, the reaction to antisemitism) should be considered less important: the result is what matters. Whoever, on the other hand, believes that the human sciences cannot do otherwise than to construct what they claim to analyze at a distance, will argue that the motives for an inquiry must be given greater weight.

WALTER CAHN
Yale University

Aviva Weingarten, *Jewish Organizations' Response to Communism and to Senator McCarthy*, trans. Ora Cummings. London: Valentine Mitchell in association with the European Jewish Publication Society, 2008. 164 pp.

There are good reasons why most doctoral dissertations never see the light of day as published books. Most don't warrant publication. Unfortunately, *Jewish Organizations' Response to Communism and to Senator McCarthy* falls into that category. Carelessly translated from the Hebrew by Ora Cummings, this slim volume brings little new historical knowledge to its subject. Much of the material found in this book was previously covered by Stuart Svonkin in the early chapters of his book (also a revised dissertation), *Jews against Prejudice: American Jews and the Fight for Civil Liberties* (1997).

Although Aviva Weingarten sought to examine the major American Jewish defense organizations, including the American Jewish Committee, the Anti-Defamation League of B'nai B'rith (ADL), the American Jewish Congress, and the Jewish Labor Committee, she succeeded in gaining access only to the rich archival resources of the American Jewish Committee, as these have been made available to scholars. Her discussion of the other organizations is largely limited to published materials. Even here, Weingarten does not comb the *ADL Bulletin*, for example, for the four and a half years of Senator Joseph McCarthy's anti-Communist crusade, beginning with his February 1950 speech to the Ohio County Women's Republican Club in Wheeling, West Virginia, in order to portray the complexities of the ADL's public positions. Rather she relies heavily on a handful of documents and a few memoirs and oral histories in order to support her contention that these American Jewish organizations were consistently anti-Communist even as they remained committed to the defense of civil rights. The term "civil rights" is itself a misnomer since Weingarten for the most part is concerned with civil liberties relating to the freedom of individuals and organizations to express unpopular opinions.

So what can be learned from this book? Weingarten ably summarizes a number of internal American Jewish Committee memorandums on the subject of Communism and how to oppose it. She details the approaches designed for use within the Jewish community and those aimed for a non-Jewish American audience. Her presentation of these memos does occasionally highlight the complex challenge facing Jewish communal professionals as they tried to balance anti-Communism with some support for the rights of individuals—especially those unfairly penalized in the highly charged witch-hunt atmosphere generated by McCarthy and the House of Representatives' Committee on Un-American Activities. Yet Weingarten seems to have missed the tragedies of careers ruined, lives lost, and dreams shattered by McCarthyism even as she conveys some aspects of the debates within the American Jewish Committee regarding the reasons for fighting Communism and the methods for combating liberal Jews' inclinations to oppose the anti-Communist crusade.

There was considerable potential in such a study, many ways in which it might have elucidated internal differences of the Jewish defense organizations as they struggled to come to terms with McCarthy's anti-Communism and its threat to Jewish security in the United States. Weingarten does not address the power of smears and innuendo that concerned some of the more sensitive men and women working at the Committee, nor does she convey the vehemence of other staff members' bitter anti-Communism. Reading her book, it is hard to tell the difference between the ADL and the American Jewish Committee, though their ideology and methods diverged in important ways. Nor does she discuss the purges of American Jewish Congress members—who they were or how they were ejected from the organization—or struggles within the world of Jewish labor to deal with pro-Communist unions, such as Ben Gold's Furriers Union, in the face of McCarthy's onslaught. Although she mentions Jewish leaders of these organizations, they remain names without biography so there is no real analysis of motivation. The exceptions are those figures, like Roy Cohn, who cluster around McCarthy.

Weingarten devotes a third of the book to McCarthy and the Jews who worked for him, Jews he targeted, and his relationship (or lack of) with some of the Jewish organizations. She does not clarify why McCarthy's entourage mattered to the Jewish organizations or how it might have influenced their responses to McCarthy. Weingarten concludes, as have most scholars, that McCarthy was not specifically antisemitic, though many of his supporters were. She discusses several cases of Jews pursued by McCarthy, including that of Anna Rosenberg, who was smeared as a Communist by antisemitic agitators when she was nominated for an appointment as assistant Secretary of Defense. In a brief six pages, Weingarten suggests the complexity of the case, but she never uses it as a means to explore in depth the difficulty of balancing anti-Communism and cooperation with McCarthy or the differences among Jewish organizations. This is a pity because a close analysis might have yielded real insight into how Jewish organizations made decisions when faced with aggressive antisemitic anti-Communism. Rosenberg's case also offered an opportunity to explore motivations of Jewish antisemitic anti-Communists and their role in the spread of McCarthyism. These internal Jewish struggles over betrayal deserve elucidation.

Had Weingarten honed a section or two of this book into an article, digging deeply into archival material and revealing through an incisive case study the issues she sought to discuss, she would have brought far greater understanding to American Jewish organizations' responses to McCarthy than she did in this flawed volume.

DEBORAH DASH MOORE
University of Michigan

Arkadii Zeltser, *Evrei sovetskoi provintsii: Vitebsk i mestechki 1917–1941* (Jews of the Soviet provinces: Vitebsk and *shtetlekh* 1917–1941). Moscow: Rosspen, 2006. 478 pp.

If there existed any gaps in our knowledge of how Jews of Vitebsk reacted to the Russian Revolution, the New Economic Plan (NEP), civil war, and economic and cultural policies of the Soviet government between 1917 and 1941, they are now completely filled in by Arkadii Zeltser's study. Based on an impressive amount of archival sources, the author recreates the vibrant atmosphere of Jewish life in Vitebsk with astonishing detail.

Most importantly, the book reveals how policies of the central Soviet regime were implemented in specific locales; who was responsible for implementing such policies; and what they meant for Soviet Jewry. Zeltser's nuanced reading renders more complex the established historiography of Soviet Jewry, which tends to present Soviet Jews as a monolithic mass. In contrast, Zeltser demonstrates that those involved in designing and implementing government policies toward the Jews had to negotiate their understanding of the revolution and of Jewish identity in order to be able to conform with the regime. Day by day (the author literally documents almost every day of the period being studied), all of the Jews of Vitebsk and the surrounding provinces had to make choices about their future: some dealt with the prospects of being arrested; others with economic policies that could destroy or create their livelihood; and others with various possibilities for education. Numerous conflicts among leaders of the "Jewish sections" of the Communist party, which are analyzed and described in detail, reveal the fact that many Vitebsk Jews were not aware of the "central plan" designed to "Sovietize" them, preferring to believe that they themselves had a say in Soviet policies vis-à-vis the Jews. Zeltser's detailed account of these conflicts is an important contribution to our knowledge of how the establishment of Soviet institutions worked on the local level.

The chapter on Jewish education provides a detailed periodization of the development and later dissolution of the Soviet Jewish school system. Zeltser's analysis covers six distinct periods—1917, 1918–1920, 1921–1923, 1924–1928, 1929–1934, and 1935–1938—that were marked by changing attitudes toward the Jewish school system on the part of government officials, parents, students, and Jewish cultural activists. The financial support of schools in the early 1930s led to a rise in the number of children attending these schools, creating a shortage of qualified teachers.

Among Yiddish-speaking youth, the teaching profession lacked prestige, a situation that led to the inevitable decline of the popularity of schools and teacher-training *technicums*—even though the Yiddish-speaking intelligentsia believed that the development of Yiddish culture was crucial in order to maintain Jewish identity and culture in the Soviet Union.

Zeltser convincingly argues that the major manifestation of Jewishness moved away from the public to the private sphere, with greater emphasis placed on family relations, celebrations, and practices. He provides invaluable data on how exactly this process took place in Vitebsk. In his conclusion, Zeltser argues that Vitebsk Jews pursued three different strategies with regard to Soviet policies and their own Jewish identity. The first was to fully accept the Communist way of life; the second was to actively oppose it; whereas the third—practiced by a majority of the Jewish population—was based on careful balancing and adjustment. Moreover, people belonging to the second and third categories gradually developed a double standard with regard to Jewish identity and culture outside and inside the home, which determined the nature of Jewish life in the Soviet Union for many decades.

Zeltser's detailed analysis of the local history answers some of the questions raised by the historiography of this period. Most significantly, it provides important sources on how Soviet Jewish residents, be they intellectuals, politicians, or average citizens, dealt with the Soviet economic and social reforms. As Zeltser shows, while Jews as an ethnic group were not officially discriminated against, there existed a de facto discrimination based on their economic and social standing. In fact, such discrimination might even have been more far-reaching than one solely based on ethnicity. Scholars have speculated about this issue for decades—Zeltser, relying on data from the Vitebsk region, supplies the proof.

Indeed, the only real drawback of this study derives from its almost exclusive focus on the local context. While the detailed descriptions and analysis are extremely valuable, they cannot support more far-reaching conclusions that relate to other places in the Soviet Union. I would welcome an introductory or a concluding chapter in which the similarities and differences of developments in other areas of the Soviet Union are discussed in greater detail. As it stands, the reader is required to fish out such conclusions from bits and pieces of comparative information that are offered in each chapter. Notwithstanding this criticism, I cannot stress too strongly the importance and significance of this book for the scholarship of Soviet Jewish history. I also enjoyed its fluid, clear, and captivating writing style. It is my pleasure to strongly recommend Zeltser's book and to encourage its translation into English.

ANNA SHTERNSHIS
University of Toronto

Religion, Literary, and Cultural Studies

Glenda Abramson, *Hebrew Writing of the First World War*. London: Vallentine Mitchell, 2008. 405 pp.

Glenda Abramson's *Hebrew Writing of the First World War* deals with a fascinating topic. Writing about a historical event can be most challenging, especially when the writers are poets and authors of fiction. For what distinguishes literature from history? This question is as old as Aristotle's claim that history tells what has happened whereas poetry tells what may happen.[1] Abramson does not need to go that far, of course. At the beginning of her book she does, however, mention Goethe's literary autobiography, *Dichtung und Wahrheit*, in which the German poet reveals the productive tension between poetry and truth, the fictive and the factual, imagination and documentation. These tensions, which have long been a source of inspiration for writers and scholars, have become crucial in dealing with the Holocaust, and they continue to inspire a contemporary body of work that goes beyond the issues of the Second World War and the catastrophe of European Jewry.[2] Abramson is well aware of these tensions and of the ways they challenge our understanding of the historical event. Furthermore, her book demonstrates the complexity of acknowledging the separation of the realms and the disciplines, on the one hand, and admitting to the way they collapse and merge with each other, on the other. As she claims: "The nature of the texts led to questions about their exact genres since the labels 'historiography,' 'memoir' or 'fiction' do not accurately define them" (p. xi).

In focusing on an impressive scope of Hebrew writing by Jewish authors and poets who responded to the First World War, Abramson offers an insightful perspective on these questions. The authors poetically document and testify to the horrors of the human condition—from the angst and dismay of the war experience to the devastation that is engraved in the "flesh"—as conveyed in the body of modern Hebrew literature.[3] Their writings shape narratives in a way that can also point to their limits and failures. They construct a story while at the same time reflecting on its potential digressions and breakdowns. The work of a poet thus corresponds with moments of pain and suffering, violence and aggression that transcend national boundaries and political identities.

The three sections of *Hebrew Writing of the First World War* demonstrate the dialectics of the place (Europe/Palestine) and of the roles (soldiers/civilians) played by Jewish writers in the Great War. In her introduction, Abramson points to the elements that constitute the core of her proposed readings. First, Zionism as a crucial element in the authors' war experience, which they saw less as a global political conflict than as a catastrophic end to the Enlightenment. Second, modernism and the understanding of the war as a violent transition into modernity, which was imprinted in the literature of wounded bodies, psychic anxiety, and generational instability. Third, the problem of representation and documentation, as reflected in the question of the genre.

In her inquiry into the experience of Jewish soldiers in Europe, Abramson points to the vulnerable state of those Jews who served in the Russian and other Imperial armies and were caught up in a complicated conflict of ethnic and national loyalties. She concludes her analysis of Avigdor Hameiri's war literature with a prisoner's testimony to suffering, not only of the Jewish soldiers, but of "all fighting men caught up in a war that they do not understand" (p. 63). One of these soldiers was Uri Zvi Greenberg, who survived the war as a "terrified man" (p. 83). Abramson devotes attention to his expressionist postwar poetry: its obsession with death, disgust at the condition of humanity, and the use of the human body as a metaphor of the decay of civilization. Another experience was that undergone by Shaul Tchernichovsky, who served as a medical officer in the Russian army. Looking at his war writing, Abramson notes how even a description of the atmosphere of the military hospitals can be an essential source for historical understanding, and concludes that while the activities of Jewish soldiers are not central to the war poetry, the East European Jewish experience is its central motivation.

The second section explores various responses of civilians to the First World War. There is S.Y. Agnon's reflections on Berlin in '*Ad henah*, an expressionist novel that embodies the "deformed nature of war and the shattered body of a society that represents the end of one of the most significant periods in Jewish history" (p. 179). Yehuda Ya'ari's negation of exile—the victimhood and distortions of the exilic Jew, which cannot, however, be redeemed in the new settlement of the pioneers—is conveyed through the novel *Keor yahel*. Written by one of the major voices of the Third Aliyah, this novel responds to the famous pioneering experiment of the Hashomer Haza'ir movement in Bitanyah, a fascinating social project that also demonstrates the limits of the Zionist vision. And in the work of Gershon Shofman and David Vogel, the war uncovers the true face of Vienna and the bareness of the human condition. In her reading of Vogel's diary accounts of his arrest and imprisonment, Abramson convincingly shows how Vogel's writing should be read in the context of European modernity and how it reveals above all a disjunction between the Hebrew language and the national aspirations its use encoded. For Vogel, Hebrew was less a badge of national identity than a marker of difference.

The third section deals with the war in Palestine and its effects on the Yishuv. It opens with Aharon Reuveni's trilogy, '*Ad Yerushalayim*, which represents the dialectics of secularism, as well as Reuveni's view of both the possibilities and the dangers of the Zionist enterprise, which ultimately depended on heroes, not anti-heroes. Abramson then moves to Arieli Orloff's novel *Yeshimon*, which is based on his experience as a musician in a Turkish military band during the war years. In referring to the homoerotic relationship between the Jewish protagonist and the non-Jewish men around him, Abramson points to the breakdown of taboo in war literature. She shows how the novel offers striking insights not only into political discussions but also into private preoccupations and the way in which the Hebrew Renaissance was celebrated in the Yishuv; she reads Orloff's decision to leave Palestine as evidence of his distrust of Zionism's ability to sustain its ideology.

A different perspective is found in the works of Ya'akov Hurgin and Yehuda Burla, two "native-born Palestinians" who served as interpreters in the Turkish army, who represent familiarity with the local languages and the Middle Eastern landscape, without any display of the Orientalism so prominent in other writers. According to Abramson, the question of Jewish nationalism does not feature in their war stories, which therefore avoid the ideological dimension so prominent in other war novels. The book culminates in a reading of Y.H. Brenner's narrative fiction from 1917–1919 in the light of Joseph Zevi Falk's memoir, *Hagerush*. The expulsion of Jews and the final year of the First World War provided the framework for Brenner's seven stories, which draw heavily on documented events and eyewitness reports. Abramson claims, however, that despite Brenner's "truthful" presentation of the effects of the war on the Yishuv, his account indicates the reinforcement of his subjective "obsessions"— his pessimistic view of the unchanged fate of diaspora Jewry. But perhaps this obsession, which resonates with what is repressed in culture, and which creates a disturbing account in retelling and rejecting, constructing and contradicting the narratives offered by memoirs and documents, does bear true witness to the complexities of the historical experience.

Indeed, Abramson is strongly aware of the genre and its blended boundaries, as shown in her discussion of concepts such as "fictionalized memoirs," "autofiction," "documentary novel," or "non-fictional novel." Yet at some point, focusing on the structural categories and their definitions seems to fixate the proposed readings. Her book, however, does encompass an interesting mix and a wide scope of writings inside and outside the canon of modern Hebrew literature, including an informed response to the vast corpus of scholarship in the field, and a historical contextualization for the authors' war experience and their conceptual and creative dilemmas. This provides a remarkable perspective on a most pertinent and challenging set of questions. What is revealed in the writings of the war and what kind of encounter do they promise readers? What is opened throughout these readings? What does the writing recall? Here, for example, is one of Agnon's replies:

> I dreamed that a great war came to the world and I was called to the war. I made an oath to God that if I return fit and well from the war I would offer as an offering anyone coming out of my house to meet me when I returned from the war. I returned to my house fit and well and behold, it is I who came out to meet me.[4]

Agnon's narrator dreams that he returns home from the war. However, the verbal repetition (return) that amplifies the move back (home) transcends the limits of historical time (1912–1924). Thus the house, a repetitive figuration in Agnon's literature, condenses different places and time periods. It is a poetic zone where that which "is" and "is not" a house merge together, encoding security but also anxiety, settling down but also immigration and nomadic movement. It is a site of guarding and preserving, of settlement, reconstruction, and revival, but also of loss, expulsion, and destruction; of exile and homeland; pogroms and wars; Europe and the Yishuv in Eretz Israel; (Jewish) Israel and Palestine. This Hebrew writing offers the readers a medium that testifies not only to collective dreams and ideological visions but also to the limits, failures, and that which dreams and visions deny.

Standing at the gate to his house, Agnon's narrator returns to the "home" in the fullest sense of the word—that is, to the unbearable consciousness of death. This oscillation over worlds of war and peace, soldiers and civilians in hospitals and cafés, reverberates with the mechanical rhythm of the trains, which tends to blur the boundaries and to dismantle and redefine the lines between dream and reality, tradition and innovation, fiction and testimony. This movement opens up a striking view, revealing the horror of an uncompromising moment—a disturbing glimpse into the human condition. Abramson's *Hebrew Writing of the First World War* facilitates a critical reading and a noteworthy exploration of those uncompromising moments, whose relevance today, perhaps more than ever, cannot be ignored.

MICHAL BEN-HORIN
University of Florida

Notes

1. See Aristotle, *Poetics*, ch. 9.
2. See, for example, Theodor Adorno's famous claim regarding poetry after Auschwitz, in *Prisms* (Cambridge: 1981), 34; Shoshana Felman and Dori Laub, *Testimony: Crises of Witnessing in Literature, Psychoanalysis and History* (New York: 1992); Saul Friedlander (ed.), *Probing the Limits of Representation: Nazism and the "Final Solution"* (Cambridge: 1992). For a recent study of fiction that moves beyond the specific complexity of the Second World War and the Holocaust, see Azade Seyhan, *Tales of Crossed Destinies: The Modern Turkish Novel in a Comparative Context* (New York: 2008).
3. Abramson, who acknowledges the comparative potential of her study (German, Austrian, English, French, and Italian), works within the field of modern Hebrew literature and responds to a body of scholarly work by Hillel Barzel, Gershon Shaked, Dan Miron, Robert Alter, Avner Holzman, and Hannan Hever, among others.
4. S. Y. Agnon, *'Ad henah* (Jerusalem: 1966), 86; quoted in Abramson, 170.

Justin Cammy, Dara Horn, Alyssa Quint, and Rachel Rubinstein (eds.), *Arguing the Modern Jewish Canon: Essays on Literature and Culture in Honor of Ruth R. Wisse*. Cambridge, Mass.: Center for Jewish Studies, Harvard University, 2008. ix + 721 pp.

There is an anticipatory thrill in holding in one's hand such a voluminous volume (or, as it is a festschrift, a *Heft* of such heft), filled with so many stimulating ideas, as *Arguing the Modern Jewish Canon*. It is an impressive presentation of some 36 articles and essays in which the festive element of the festschrift is on clear display, as is the emotion engendered in these students and colleagues by the honoree.

This volume's editors have chosen as its organizing theme the subject of one of Wisse's most recent works: *The Modern Jewish Canon: A Journey through*

Language and Culture. It is a clever choice in that both the literary and the political can not only be slotted in under that pithy rubric, but the idea of the canon is also a site of their dramatic interplay. However, despite this potential, it is ultimately somewhat disappointing that not more of the articles confront the issue head on and address that complicated intersection directly. It is quite fair for edited volumes to fall back on their anthological nature to deflect such carping. Nevertheless, it points to one of the larger structural drawbacks of the volume in general. Whether to address literariness or politics, taken individually or in combination (and several of the authors do explicitly link them), may be the choice of the individual authors; but the representation of the very idea of canonicity at the heart of the project is a function of the editors' discretion. The elision of canonicity per se is therefore at least curious, if not a missed opportunity. While laboring under the long canonical shadow of Bloom Agonistes, the engaged and engaging debate about canons—certainly from Robert von Hallberg's collection *Canons* (1984) into the modern Jewish literary milieu with Michael Gluzman's *The Politics of Canonicity* (2003)—is given very little reference in these articles.

This is made all the more problematic by following the lead of Wisse's book and focusing the bulk of attention on the novel, a form that, certainly since Bakhtin's notable work, can be considered far more a frustrater than a bulwark of traditional notions of canonicity. It is true that the articles in the opening section of the book do address canons more generally, and in two notable cases (Alan Mintz's "Knocking on Heaven's Gate: Hebrew Literature and Wisse's Canon" and Ezra Mendelsohn's "A Jewish Artistic Canon") with that careful attention and balance which one has come gratefully to expect from those scholars. Traditional conceptions of canons maintain that they are designed to hedge, to proscribe, to circumscribe. The real work of modern critical scholarship is to follow the lead of this book's title and "argue" the nature and function of canonicity, opening a debate—not ending one. (For example, Mendelsohn's essay makes the "iconic" far more ambiguous than its monumental façade would seem to suggest.) The book's title thus becomes a diversion, or straw man. *The* modern Jewish canon is an imaginary thing whose presupposition makes the "arguments" about it seem of little consequence, in the end.

One of the more important of the problematic terms in the larger debate is that elusive "Jewishness" which haunts any "modern *Jewish* canon." Each author defines for him- or herself the parameters of that concept, which is only to be expected. Nevertheless, Jewishness is more often presumed than parsed, thus avoiding the interesting question of what is so Jewish about a "modern Jewish canon." A modern Jewish artist, let us say, is as much an artist as a Jew; as much an individual (if not more so) as a representative of a community. So many of the works of art dealt with in this volume are so ramified, their authors so confounding, their themes so complex, their implications so imbricated that, though one may be hard pressed to essentialize any identity sufficiently to establish a standard of Jewishness, one wants something more synthetic to organize the book's valuable readings.

This last notwithstanding, there is an underlying attitudinal dimension to many of the pieces, which is only in a few cases made explicit. Viewed schematically, there are two endpoints of opinion: Jewish exceptionalism, on the one hand and Jewishness as *inter plures unum*, on the other. That is to say, on one end of the spectrum there is the idea that Jewish literature may not only present a unique voice, but perhaps one of the guiding voices (literarily and ethically) in Western literature and culture. On the other end, one finds the notion that Jewish writers, belonging as they do to a people among other peoples, reading other literatures and speaking other languages in addition to their own, cannot but be understood as products of those dynamic and fertile contexts; the literature they produce is consequently and necessarily *part of* a larger network of literary systems. By way of caveat, the articles in this volume, consonant with the honoree's work, do tend more toward the former than the latter.

Among the articles there is an unevenness of quality, which may ultimately be inevitable for a work of such size. Instead of attempting an overall critique I will rather describe the primary methodological approaches and point out a few of the volume's highlights. The two primary methodological approaches are the close reading and the broad reading. As for the first, the paragon is Dan Miron's "The Pleasure of Disregarding Red Lights: A Reading of Sholem Aleichem's Monologue '*A Nisref*'," whose extended closer reading of that text offers a strong argument in favor of—not to mention an active participant in the tradition of—applying to a given Yiddish literary work the fine-toothed comb of close reading, focusing on idiomatic material, clever and nuanced reformulations of "canonical" texts and intertexts, interlinguistic puns, and the polyphony of Jewish discourse and its considerable tools. Some other close readers in the volume, however, are not as successful with a similarly pared-down apparatus and discursive style. This last notwithstanding, the technique in general is well represented in this book, concentrating on presenting skilled readers' close readings of an individual text or small set of texts, rather than focusing on a closely reasoned but larger argument. In the great orchard of a Jewish literary canon, such readings are the low-hanging fruit: easily plucked and tastily, enjoyably consumed. While these are potentially useful and often interesting, one runs the risk of losing sight of a larger field of vision and significance, that is, what is at stake in making the reading in the first place.

The second methodological approach consists of the more involved disquisition on an issue or a set of historicized readings. These tend to be more successful overall precisely because of the careful contextualization. So, for example, Ken Frieden's "Innovation by Translation: Yiddish and Hasidic Hebrew in Literary History" underscores the centrality of translation to the development not only of literary styles in Jewish languages, but of Jewish literatures themselves. Marion Aptroot's "Creating Yiddish Dialogue for 'The First Modern Yiddish Comedy'" focuses our attention not only on the importance of West Yiddish texts but also on the innovation of using spoken norms in some of these texts in advance of East Yiddish; or, put another way, on the importance of spokenness and orality to both West and East Yiddish as a major avenue of literary innovation. In his estimable essay "What's So Funny about Yiddish Theater? Comedy and the Origins of Yiddish Drama," Jeremy Dauber's selection of plays presents us with the very important notion of comedy (and, to some extent, satire) as a canonical form. Following quickly on its heels is Alyssa Quint's fine assessment of Avrom Goldfaden ("Avrom Goldfaden's *The Fanatic or the Two Kuni-Lemls*"), where Quint shows how the larger problem of Jewishness is foregrounded in Goldfaden's own emphasis on the multiplicity and partiality of modern Jewish identities, which form the core of the play's anxieties as well as its humor. In so doing, Quint also problematizes the very idea of a "community of readers" at the time, especially as a unified community of Jewish readers.

This idea of readership points to another undercurrent in the book as a whole. The type of canon presupposed is in some sense designed to counter a certain kind of taste associated with popularity. Were one to posit a law of aesthetic supply and demand, then what is demanded is in some sense popular. The above idea of canon in its way dismisses the popular, and organizes itself around works designed to meet the expectations of a highbrow readership; or at least the justification for works to be included in that canon is one that appeals to the "inherent" authority of the highbrow. That is why perhaps one of the more interesting and useful sections of the book is Justin Cammy's introduction to, and translation of, Sholem Aleichem's polemical satire "The Judgment of Shomer" (*Shomers mishpet*) in which precisely this competition is being waged. Shomer, the pen name of Nokhum-Meyer Shaykevitsh, was an immensely popular and prolific writer of stories, novels, and plays. Based inter alia on their romantic plot devices and sensationalism, they were derogated as *shund*, "trash," but their role in the history of Yiddish literature and the creation of a wide and avid readership is both significant and in need of further scholarly exploration. Sholem Aleichem's broadside against Shomer uncovers the fault lines in a literature undergoing seismic shifts.

What "The Judgment of Shomer" brings in through the canon's backdoor is in a curious way Shomer himself; and through that introduction, we begin to see the intersecting visions of canon-making in this volume. The first (consisting, by my rough count, of about three quarters of the articles) involves new readings of accepted works or authors: Joyce, Babel, Salinger, the Roths (Henry and Philip, but interestingly not Joseph), Mendele Moykher-Sforim, Sholem Aleichem, Peretz, I.B. Singer (three articles), Aharon Appelfeld (two articles), to name just some of them. It is also noteworthy if curious that if this book is, at least in part, about the Wissean canon, two of the figures whom Wisse has spent much time, care, and effort in effect to canonize—the Yiddish poets Mani Leyb and Moyshe-Leyb Halpern (in her book *A Little Love in Big Manhattan*)—get almost no attention. That is a missed opportunity.

The next group concerns lesser-studied works by accepted authors. Here Avraham Novershtern's lengthy case for one of Yankev Glatshteyn's novels is notable ("The Open Suitcase: Yankev Glatshteyn's *Ven Yash Iz Gekumen*"), as is Janet Hadda's comparatively brief but pithy alignment of the poets Tsilye Drapkin and Allen Ginsberg on the axis of poetic anger. This article has the great added benefit of treating two kinds of text noticeably and regrettably underrepresented in the book: poetry, and works by women writers.

The third approach introduces what are in effect recovery projects, which make a case for including lesser-known works by lesser-known writers into this canon. Monika Adamczyk-Garbowska's case for investigating Polish literature ("Fiddles on Willow Trees: The Missing Polish Link in the Jewish Canon") is well founded; Beatrice Caplan's work on Shmuel Nadler ("Shmuel Nadler's *Besht-Simfonye*: At the Limits of Orthodox Literature") opens a door to a body of literature beyond the secular worldview of many of the other literary works included in this volume; and Mikhail Krutikov's exposé of the novel *Kolev Ashkenazi* ("Memory as Metaphor:

Meir Wiener's Novel *Kolev Ashkenazi* as Critique of the Jewish Historical Imagination") is a careful study, as well as an illuminating part of a larger project on Meir Wiener.

One of the goals in making these observations has been to elucidate the sometimes competing conceptions of canon that inform the projects presented in this book, beyond the level of organizational expediency. That a good deal of the best critical scholarship today explores the margins of the canon makes the relative paucity of such readings in a tome ostensibly devoted to "arguing" that canon all the more striking. Furthermore, until the final three works of the book, in which novelists, including Cynthia Ozick and Dara Horn, take up ideas about Jewish canonicity (and sometimes ardently so), these essays by and large steer clear of tackling the political issues that have in many ways informed Wisse's thinking about literature and certainly about her Jewish canon. Still, for whatever faults one may encounter in a given article, and for whatever complaints or cavils one may engage in over the book itself—an important one being the absence of an index, especially for 700 pages of articles on a wide variety of subjects—this volume as a whole can be seen as the belated bellwether of a scholarly trend in Jewish canonical thinking, and one that will very likely make good on its promise to rouse an argument.

JORDAN FINKIN
University of Oxford

Ben-Zion Gold, *The Life of Jews in Poland before the Holocaust: A Memoir*. Lincoln: University of Nebraska Press, 2007. 152 pp.

For many years, Ben-Zion Gold has been a unique presence in the world of American Jewry and American Judaism. He combines, as do few Conservative rabbis (or any rabbis, for that matter), a profound knowledge of Orthodox Judaism, the result of his traditional yeshiva education in prewar Poland, with an intimate acquaintance with modern culture, Jewish and general. His loyalty to the Jewish tradition is matched by his humanism, his progressivism, his hatred of injustice, and his willingness to place himself on the line in the struggle for human rights. His support for the state of Israel, where he has many friends, is accompanied both by a severe critique of its policies regarding the territories captured in the war of 1967 and unease with the stranglehold of government-supported Orthodoxy on so many facets of life. It would be difficult to imagine him as a synagogue rabbi in American suburbia, but as Hillel director at Harvard—the ideal position for him—he served as an inspiration to generations of young men and women who wished to remain within the fold of Jewry while partaking of the incomparably rich cultural menu served up to them by that great institution. In the interests of full disclosure, I must reveal that I am proud to call myself his friend, and that I, too, find him to be inspirational. He is an exceptional, if sometimes rather lonely voice within the American rabbinate.

At the very outset of his memoirs, Gold informs us that he has an agenda. As he puts it: "There is an imbalance in the way we remember the Jews of Europe. Thousands of books have been written about the Holocaust, but only a few have been written about the life of Polish Jews before they were murdered" (p. ix). This is not strictly accurate (I can think of scores of books on interwar Polish Jewry—I have written a few myself), but I take his point. There is, no doubt, a moral and political message here: Gold feels that Jews are too prone to enlist the Holocaust in support of unworthy causes—for example, to justify their own bad behavior (as in the case of certain Israeli policies), and to maintain attitudes of hostility toward non-Jews ("they're all antisemites"). Sweet are the uses of adversity, he knows, but he does not want any part of it. As a result there is very little in this memoir about Gold's near-miraculous survival in Nazi-occupied Poland and in German captivity during the years 1939–1945. He is a survivor, but unlike Elie Wiesel, Primo Levi, and so many others, he does not want to write about it.

There is another way in which this book is unusual. Most memoirs of interwar Polish life have been written by more or less secular Jews—political activists (Zionists, Bundists, etc.), cultural figures, and the like. Gold's book is entirely taken up with Orthodox Jewish life. His is the story of a minority within a minority, since by his own reckoning (p. 16) less than one-third of Polish Jewry in this period still conducted their lives according to the commandments of Jewish law (halakhah). His family had hasidic leanings, although his father, a leader of the community of Radom and a member of the city council, knew Polish well and read a Polish newspaper. Still, the young Ben-Zion was given a traditional Orthodox education at heder and yeshiva and hardly studied secular subjects, which were not highly valued in his family. He was aware of the decline of Orthodox Judaism in Poland, a phenomenon that he attributes to the impact of the First World War, the Bolshevik revolution, the Balfour Declaration, and the economic crisis that made it increasingly difficult to devote one's life to the study of Torah. But his family remained more or less immune to the wave of secularization, and Ben-Zion lived in the cocoon of the Orthodox Jewish world until the war.

This world is described with great warmth, and the entire memoir is saturated by a deep and moving nostalgia for a unique civilization destroyed by the war (although it has, of course, been partially reconstructed, above all in Israel and America). We are given detailed descriptions of the celebration of Shabbat and the holidays among the Golds, when family love alongside the meticulous observance of Jewish tradition created a world of great beauty, combining as it did the certain faith in a stern but ultimately benevolent God (who, if obeyed, would look after his own people), inspiring singing, and delicious food. No one can read these pages without gaining an understanding of the tremendous attraction of Orthodox Jewish life, and of the ways in which this world was able to deal, although not all that successfully, with the difficulties of economic decline and considerable hostility emanating from the Gentile majority. One of the ways in which it managed to do so was by giving the children a firm sense of identity and belonging that was rooted in the biblical past and in the glories and heroism of Jewish history. Gold records that "we felt as if the patriarchs were our great-grandparents" and that the story of Ruth "brought to our minds the sunny fields of Bethlehem that we, children in anti-semitic Poland, longed for" (p. 33).

Gold is not so positive with regard to the heder, the much-maligned Jewish elementary school where boys were taught by antiquated methods and where the rod was not spared (the cover of the book reproduces a photograph by Alter Kacyzne of a rather wretched-looking institution of this type, presided over by a disheveled melamed).[1] He notes that his sisters' elementary education, also Orthodox, was more modern and much better than his. But he found his yeshiva studies rewarding, and he lauds his teachers and the atmosphere of learning and piety that prevailed. He includes highly appreciative thumbnail sketches of various religious types whom he encountered during his studies, including adherents of the musar movement, which spread to central Poland during the interwar years. Indeed, much of Gold's book is a paean of praise to Polish Orthodoxy, and a welcome corrective to the usual portrait of interwar Polish Jewry as a community committed to Zionism, or socialism, or some combination of the two. It is a labor of love, and it is extremely moving, all the more so as one reads with the certain knowledge that doom is fast approaching and that this world will soon be crushed.

A brief but interesting chapter deals with the question of relationships between Poles and Jews, about which much ink has been spilled in recent years. Gold is a humanist, but he does not wish to deny the reality of intense Polish antisemitism. For him, growing up in Poland, there was no question that "Jews" were not "Poles" and that "assimilationists," as he calls those Jews who both thought they were Poles and tried to live as Poles, were suffering from a dangerous illusion. Gold attributes much of Polish antisemitism to the venom of the church, and notes that, in general: "Despite having lived in Poland for centuries Jews were viewed as strangers" (p. 78). But he also records that many Jews despised and looked down upon Poles, who were regarded as children of Esau, "with all of the vile characteristics that our tradition ascribed to him: a depraved being, a rapist, and an inveterate enemy of Jacob" (p. 76). Yet his father was on good terms with some Poles, and the Polish nation had, after all, never expelled the Jews, unlike so many other European states. Ben-Zion, fluent in Yiddish and Hebrew, learned to speak Polish as well. The Poles and Jews also shared a common enemy—Nazi Germany—but this did nothing to improve relations between these two peoples, destined by history to share a common land but never to love one another, or even to live together in mutual respect.

Ben-Zion Gold came to America after the war, and the book ends with a discussion of his crisis of faith, engendered by his terrible experiences of the Holocaust, in which his family was murdered. He found himself, at first, "being in exile from God" and no longer able to pray, although he remained fiercely attached to his Jewish identity and to the ways of his fathers (p. 146). He solved this existential problem by pursuing a secular higher education and then studying for the rabbinate at the Jewish Theological Seminary. There he was exposed to the principles of modern Jewish scholarship, and there he gave up "the comfort of a personal deity" and the absolutism of the old Jewish world, while continuing to cherish Jewish tradition and a variety of Judaism that renounces its exclusiveness while holding on to the ethical principles and cultural riches that form the religion's core. This synthesis enabled him to function with great success as spiritual mentor to the remarkable Jewish community of America's greatest university.

We can be happy that Ben-Zion Gold found the courage to write this memoir, although it must be said that the uniqueness of the man does not entirely come through. I think that the author, perhaps because of an innate modesty, was not really prepared to reveal himself to his readers in all his complexity and richness of character. For whatever reason, he will not give himself up to us, as great memoirists must do. His book is interesting, moving, well worth reading, but to know the man in all his subtlety and variety, one must go to Cambridge and spend some time with him. If you are lucky, you might enjoy an erev Shabbat in his company, and hear him sing some old hasidic *zmires* (melodies). At such moments old Polish Jewry, in all its glory, comes back to life.

EZRA MENDELSOHN
The Hebrew University

Note

1. Another, closer friend, Prof. Immanuel Etkes of the Hebrew University, has overseen the translation of this memoir into Hebrew and has written a warm tribute to the author. See Gold, *Yehudim veyahadut bepolin lifnei hashoah: pirkei zikhronot* (Jerusalem: 2009). The title of the Hebrew edition differs slightly from the English (Jews and Judaism in Poland before the Holocaust) and features a different image on the cover—instead of Kacyzne's run-down heder, we see a fine-looking young man studying alone, perhaps in a beit midrash, with no teacher present.

Benjamin Harshav, *The Polyphony of Jewish Culture*. Stanford: Stanford University Press, 2007. 285 pp.

In this work of reasoned critical arguments and cultural manifestos, Benjamin Harshav grants the reader several fascinating glimpses into his autobiography that help to make sense of his distinguished yet unconventional scholarly career. One of these is delivered as an aside to his introduction to his translation (together with his wife, Barbara Harshav) of Herman Kruk's diary of the Vilna ghetto. Harshav (né Hrushovski) is himself a native of Vilna (as was Abraham Sutzkever, the subject of another essay in this collection); his parents were teachers—his mother taught mathematics and his father history—in various Hebrew, Yiddish, and Polish schools. In the summer of 1941, his parents took the family east in advance of the German occupation. Harshav "celebrated" his bar mitzvah traveling on foot through the Belorussian forests before the family eventually arrived in the Urals and were spared the fate of Kruk and Vilna Jewry. A childhood in which Hebrew, Yiddish, and Polish were in active use (extensive reading in Russian, German, and French added to the mix) provided Harshav with a multilingual fluency that made him a rarity among the young students at the Hebrew University who came to study in Jerusalem after their service in the War of Independence. As an aside to another piece, an essay on the beginnings of Israeli poetry, Harshav recalls that he typed the early poems of Yehuda Amichai, Natan Zach, and David Avidan on a precious "Hermes Baby" Hebrew typewriter given to him by an uncle in New York. These poems appeared in the mimeographed issues of *Likrat*, the revolutionary poetry journal that challenged the hegemony of Natan Alterman and his generation. As products of the schools of the Yishuv, Amichai and the others were exposed to little more than Bialik and the odd Shakespeare play when it came to literature, and it was through discussions with their cosmopolitan contemporary, Benjamin Hrushovski, that they were given access not only to the kaleidoscope of European modernist poetry but also to the theory of prosody and verse forms that lay behind the making of poems.

Such has been Harshav's career. To be sure, his scholarly achievements have been significant. His lengthy entry on Hebrew prosody in the *Encyclopaedia Judaica* is perhaps the finest contribution to Jewish historical poetics ever made. His article on the frame of reference in the production of literary meaning is an important addition to the general theory of literature. Yet Harshav's greatest role in Jewish literary studies and Israeli culture has been as a mediator of the multilingual modernism folded into his upbringing in Vilna. As the teacher (and later, colleague at Tel Aviv University) of Menakhem Perry, Meir Sternberg, Ziva Ben-Porat, and other key scholars, and as the editor and impresario of the influential journal *Hasifrut* (and later *Poetics Today*), Harshav worked tirelessly to rescue the study of Jewish literature from the mire of impressionism and the dust of literary history. The alternative model he advocated was a science of literature rooted in the theoretical inheritance of Russian Formalism. Harshav sought to make the study of literature an advancing body of knowledge that investigated how literature works at its most fundamental level rather than a baggy agglomeration of subjective interpretations of individual works of writing.

Harshav's move from Tel Aviv to Yale University in the late 1980s enacted a further stage in the unfolding of his identity. The focus of his work moved from the rarified realms of literary theory to a more applied attention—through prodigious projects of translating, editing, anthologizing, and redacting—to the varieties of modern Jewish literature, especially Yiddish modernism. It is as if, once relocated in the diaspora and freed from the centripetal intensity of Israeli culture, Harshav could turn himself to restoring what he calls the "polyphony of Jewish culture," the title of the present work under review. This is essentially a collection of introductions to the projects of translation and anthology that Harshav has undertaken over the past twenty years; the volume is provided with two introductions to the introductions, one titled "Theses on the Historical Context of the Modern Jewish Revolution," which reprises the positions staked out in his *Language in a Time of Revolution* (1993), and the other, simply, "Multilingualism." The recurrence of the term "revolution" indicates Harshav's polemical stance toward the notion of renaissance, or *teḥiyah*, the name traditionally given to Hebrew literature written in the late 19th and early 20th centuries. The model of renaissance was congenial to Zionist historiography because it imputed to the new culture an essential continuity with the arc of classical Jewish culture and at the same time blunted the utter break with religious authority and tradition. Like Baruch Kurzweil in the 1950s, Harshav insists that the upheaval was undeniably a revolution. Yet whereas for Kurzweil the break was a tragically doomed renunciation, for Harshav it was the highest achievement of the Jewish people in modern times. The first decades of the 20th century are for him a heady consummation of intersecting vectors of Jewishness and modernity. The most richly combustible mix was to be found in Jewish languages—Yiddish and Hebrew in their differential resources—because of the endless opportunities they provided for internal irony and the juxtaposition of old and new. (Defamiliarized by Harshav, even S.Y. Agnon becomes a star witness for this position in Harshav's introduction to his wife's translation of *Only Yesterday*, included here.) But Harshav also extends the reach of the revolution of modern Jewish culture to Jewish writers in European languages who were emerging from the corners of the Russian and Hapsburg empires. This was a revolution in the visual arts as well, and Harshav includes here an essay on the role of language in Chagall's early paintings, an offshoot from his major book on the painter, which reclaims him both for modernism and for Yiddish culture.

The centerpiece of the volume is a substantial essay on Introspectivism (*Insikh*) in American Yiddish poetry, which served as the introduction to the 800-page bilingual anthology of that body of verse edited with Barbara Harshav. The key figures in this literary trend, which emerged after the First World War, are A. Leyles, Jacob Glatshteyn, Moshe-Leyb Halpern, J.L. Teller, Malka Heifetz-Tussman, Barysh Vaynshteyn, and H. Leyvik. Chief among the many reasons for which Harshav admires this group is their Americanness. Rather than being an extension of Yiddish literature in the old country, the Introspectivists were "as American as anything written in English in that period. It was in America that the poets sensed freedom of thought and ideas, that their conscious perceptions of literature were formed and their poetic language crystallized." While their contemporaries in Tel Aviv whipped up the "wild poem" of Expressionist and Symbolist verse in Hebrew, the Introspectivists "developed a rather Anglo-American poetics of irony, dramatized and objectified poetic situations, and intellectual understatement" (pp. 93–94). Harshav further admires the maturity, unsentimentality, and bleak realism of their writing. Although individualism was part of the credo—the Introspectivist perceives the world through the prism of his or her own unconscious—their verse responded to the murder of European Jewry by reorienting itself toward the task of communal mourning and self-reflection.

Harshav admires them, finally, because, although they knew English very well (and Hebrew, too, for that matter) they chose to write their verse in Yiddish despite the fact that there was no mass audience in America for their difficult and refined modernism. They were the very embodiment of the ideal of Jewish multilingualism and modernism in which Harshav was steeped in the Vilna of his youth. Felt keenly throughout *The Polyphony of Jewish Culture* is regret over the monolingual nature of the two great Jewish communities of our time. While this critique of American Jewish culture is familiar and widely shared, more interestingly subversive is the implied critique of the one-dimensionality of Israeli culture, a culture wholly lived in the triumphantly revived ancient language of the Jews. By the evidence of this volume, Harshav's recent intellectual energies have been harnessed to the project of making the achievements of high Yiddish culture present to the contemporary Jewish mind and, by so doing, allowing us to hear something of the polyphonic music that has accompanied his life from his earliest childhood until now.

ALAN MINTZ
The Jewish Theological Seminary of America

Mitchell Bryan Hart, *The Healthy Jew: The Symbiosis of Judaism and Modern Medicine*. New York: Cambridge University Press, 2007. 280 pp.

In recent years, a large body of scholarship associated most prominently with Sander Gilman has focused on different aspects of the history of antisemitism, the Jews' racial difference, and racial concepts of inferiority. Mitchell Bryan Hart's *The Healthy Jew* belongs to this growing body of scholarship; yet, while much of that literature repeatedly demonstrates that difference in this context indicates inferiority, Hart's book attempts to recover a discourse that pointed to Jews as the epitome of health and vigor.

Hart examines theories that were promoted by Jews and non-Jews in Germany, Great Britain, France, Italy, and the United States in the 19th and 20th centuries, which postulated that the Jews were civilized thousands of years ago and had moreover helped to civilize Europe. As bearers of medical and biological knowledge, Jews assisted Christian societies to progress in these domains—for instance, by following the Jewish model of preventive medicine.

The Healthy Jew comprises six chapters, each dealing with a different episode in the history of representations of Jews and Judaism in modern medical or scientific discourse. The first chapter recovers the idea that Jews were important in the transmission of Greek medicine to the Latin West. The following chapter focuses on perceptions that Mosaic laws could serve as the basis for current hygienic and eugenic practices and thus as the foundation (either wholly or in part) of modern European or Anglo-American societies. Chapter 3 discusses how Anglo-American medical literature promoted the Bible as a sanitary code. In chapter 4, Hart concentrates on the claim that biblical decrees preceded contemporary Social Darwinist and eugenic ideas; a case study of tuberculosis is offered in the fifth chapter in order to illustrate this point. The final chapter addresses discussions of Jewish ritual law as a model for Christian health.

Hart presents an interesting, albeit brief, analysis of the two general strategies involved in the affirmative writings on Jews: either viewing Jewish health and survival as a result of adherence to Jewish law and ritual, or else reinterpreting Jewish history, particularly the medieval period and ghettoization, as a Darwinian process of natural selection. Perhaps the greatest merit of this carefully argued book is its raising of larger questions that transcend the specific cases it recounts. One pertains to the general historical context of the underlying themes and assumptions that gave rise to the positive association made in this discourse concerning race and Jews. A second, interconnected, question touches on the relationship between non-Jews and Jews within this history.

The crux of Hart's account lies in the larger context of the affirmative writings on Jews. Although his intention, as noted, is to counter or revise the current historical interpretation of perceptions of Jewish inferiority, he does not tell us how common these interpretations were, or what was their relative weight within the then-current discourse. Moreover, although the cases he presents are illuminating and important, it remains unclear whether they really alter—or are even intended to alter—the overall historical picture of the close link between the biologization, medicalization, and racialization of Jews. Thus, in elucidating hitherto unresearched aspects of this discourse, Hart fails to provide a comprehensive interpretation of his findings within the larger historical picture. What, for instance, is the nature of "compliments" made to Jewish character or difference that verge on being expressions of anti-Jewish themes and images?

With regard to this issue, the second, and perhaps even more interesting and sensitive matter raised by Hart's account surfaces: namely, the complex relationship between Jewish and non-Jewish writers in this history. Hart assembles a group of writers who made affirmative declarations regarding Jews. These individuals came from different social backgrounds, operated in different disciplines, had different scientific or social standing, and pursued different goals. Hart presents their biographical background (in particular, their Jewish or non-Jewish background) while sensitively avoiding pitting Jews and non-Jews against each other. In doing this, he clearly implies that the "healthy Jew" paradigm is a co-product of non-Jewish and Jewish writers. At the same time, this strategy leaves the reader wondering whether these authors, despite their similar perceptions, might have been writing from greatly differing scholarly, social, and political motivations. It seems to me that uncovering their motivations would aid in a more nuanced mapping out of the historical terrain.

Hart avoids any systematic interpretation of patterns of relationship between Jewish and non-Jewish writers (many of whom corresponded with one another), and he does not dwell at length on the Jewish background of many of the writers he discusses. Among them were prominent figures such as Alfred Nossig, Cesare Lombroso, Maurice Fishberg, Louis Wirth, and Arthur Ruppin; their Jewish background raises the possibility that their locutions are at least potentially apologetic. Yet Hart does not reflect on these writers' strengths, weaknesses, or effectiveness as compared with other existing apologetic strategies or the different modalities of Jewish/non-Jewish cooperation. Few contemporary authors have Hart's knowledge or ability to address these questions—a fact which makes this omission all the more noticeable, to the extent that one wonders whether it was part of Hart's objective. Finally, as with Sherlock Holmes' famous observation concerning the hound of the Baskervilles, the almost complete absence of Zionism from Hart's discussion is so evident that it calls for interpretation. Yet overall, his book is a significant contribution to the growing literature on the intersection of modern Jewish history and the history of science.

AMOS MORRIS-REICH
University of Haifa

Tova Hartman, *Feminism Encounters Traditional Judaism: Resistance and Accommodation*. Hanover, N.H.: University Press of New England, 2007. 184 pp.

In many ways, Tova Hartman's recent book, *Feminism Encounters Traditional Judaism*, is the book on Jewish feminism for which I have been waiting rather a long time.

I have personally taken part in the revolution aimed at empowering Jewish women (and thereby also Jewish men), starting with my ordination at the Jewish Theological Seminary in 1989 and followed by my service to the Masorti movement as a woman rabbi who also teaches Jewish feminism at various Israeli higher educational institutions. Yet today, approximately forty years after the beginning of the Jewish feminist revolution, I sense that feminist-inspired demands to uproot much of the tradition in the name of fighting patriarchy risks promoting the kind of emotional male backlash that could undo much of what women sought to attain. Radical purists—one is tempted to call their thinking "idolatrous"—are seemingly oblivious to alienation between Jewish men and Jewish women, between traditionalists and non-traditionalists, and the evident rift between many diaspora liberal Jews and Israeli traditional Jewry.

This purism is encapsulated in demands for complete and absolute, gender-blind equality, which is made to take priority over all other Jewish values. One wonders, indeed, whether such initiatives might not end up as more oppressive to Jewish women than the traditional patriarchy with all its ills. Frequently, that version of Jewish feminism demands non-participation in, or even the boycotting of, non-egalitarian *davening* (prayer) communities. It delegitimizes non-egalitarian family life; insists on re-editing all of Jewish liturgy because of its male God imagery; and crosses many halakhic boundaries. Tova Hartman's brand of Orthodox feminism responds in a very gentle way to many of these challenges by means of a dialectic approach that seeks to balance between equality and Jewish tradition.

As Hartman brilliantly analyzes the mainstream Orthodox obsession with women's modest clothing and modest appearance, she highlights the basis of the problem of collaboration between Jewish men and women in the modern world:

> The heart of what is held in common by the sexual discourses of Orthodoxy and the West is that the discourse itself is shaped almost exclusively by males, and accepted by women as if by divine fiat. This lopsided disconnect itself would appear to be the source of all the various forms of corruption to which the different systems of gender give rise—ultimately as harmful to men as it is to women, and ultimately serving neither. . . . [I]nherent to any true model of modesty is an equality, a "witness," between the partners involved. And if, indeed, we are, as men and as women, given the condition of modesty, fit to walk with God, is it possible to conceive that we are unfit to walk *with* each other? (pp. 60–61).

Hartman is the first Jewish feminist thinker to point out how the western and Orthodox paradigms of sexuality mirror each other in objectifying women and depriving them of their personhood. Both paradigms cultivate alienation between women and their bodies and between men and women, and both severely injure men and women. The alienation, I would add, goes beyond the source of discrimination against women that is identified in feminist literature as the "male gaze" (p. 57). While a "gaze" assumes some kind of (paternalistic) relationship, in today's world of alienation we are losing even that gaze and are left with apathy and blindness to the vulnerabilities of the other sex.

Hartman does not specify all the solutions to the legitimate problems raised by non-Orthodox Jewish feminists. A big question still remains as to how we are to educate Jewish men and women so that they can lead synagogues and families *together*. Yet she successfully responds to many of the theological issues raised by other feminists. Thus, following thinkers such as Carol Gilligan and Sara Ruddick, Hartman suggests that male imagery of God might remain in its liturgical place, while inviting new meanings for such imagery. She offers a personalized perspective on *nidah* and the mikveh ritual. Finally, a very important aspect of the book is Hartman's sharing her experience in helping to establish Shira Hadasha, the most egalitarian Orthodox congregation in Jerusalem. Together with other founders of the congregation, Hartman outlined a formula to bring together people with different ideas concerning gender and halakhah. Let us hope that this fragile but extremely creative theological and communal venture will outlast the "conflicting spirits of our time" and pave a middle-of-the-road way for our gender-perplexed Jewish people.

EINAT RAMON
Schechter Institute of Jewish Studies

Meri-Jane Rochelson, *A Jew in the Public Arena: The Career of Israel Zangwill.* Detroit: Wayne University Press, 2008. xxvi + 317 pp.

One early biographer of Israel Zangwill (1864–1926) referred to his subject's "violent contraries," meaning the complicated twists and turns in the writings and life of this fascinating Anglo-Jewish figure.[1] Zangwill's written words and public acts constitute a sprawling, inconclusive dialectic of roughly formulated theses, comparably blunt antitheses, and uncannily eloquent rebuttals of any workable synthesis. With regard to both political and personal identity issues, formal consistency was not Zangwill's greatest concern.

The problem of Jewish continuity figured prominently in Zangwill's plays, novels, and public activities, but on a wide continuum running between assimilation and nationalism, Zangwill concurrently or successively endorsed specific formulas and options that were regarded by contemporaries and subsequent scholars alike as fundamentally incompatible. He married a non-Jew, Edith Ayrton (herself an articulate writer with firm political orientations), and decided not to circumcise his son; many of his writings tacitly or explicitly recommend such private life decisions to the public at large, envisioning the regeneration of Jews and Christians under the auspices of some higher religion fused from the monotheistic faiths. Yet equally apparent in Zangwill's life and literary work is normative commitment to Jewish well-being. Zangwill's devotion to Jewish life found literary expression in works such as *Children of the Ghetto* (1892), which documented past phases of Jewish life from a fundamentally sympathetic standpoint; the same Jewish idealism animated much of Zangwill's public-political activity, most notably his work on behalf of the Zionist movement and for the "territorialist" offshoot he himself spearheaded, the Jewish Territorial Organization (known by its Yiddish acronym, ITO), which sought a homeland for Jews apart from Eretz Israel.

In her thoughtful, well-researched, and highly readable biography, Meri-Jane Rochelson argues that retrospective efforts to identify some underlying unity in Zangwill's ideological eclecticism have been artificial and unpersuasive. In the penultimate Zangwill biography, *Dreamer of the Ghetto: The Life and Works of Israel Zangwill* (1990), Joseph Udelson observed that Zangwill proposed a division of labor for Jews in the future: assimilation in the West, versus national and religious revitalization in the East. While Rochelson can be somewhat churlish in her dismissal of specific arguments and findings in Udelson's work and in other previous Zangwill biographies, her overall objection to this East-West division of Jewish labor, as well as to other proposed syntheses of Zangwill's writings and actions, is cogent. Assembling an impressive array of data and focusing her study on insightful analysis of Zangwill's literary work, Rochelson shows that Zangwill was too conscious of ethical and practical constraints hampering Jewish integration in western countries, and too ambivalent about issues relating to Zionism in particular (and to religion and nationalism, in general), to commit himself to any neat geo-ethical identity formula.

In other words, it may be that the contradictory boisterousness of Zangwill's life militates against a biographer's ability to say any final word about it. Yet Rochelson's admirably candid statement in the final section of her book, namely, that more "needs to be said on Zangwill and assimilation" (p. 224), raises an issue beyond the hard-to-capture quality of Zangwill's complicated personality. That is to say, the methodological choices made by Rochelson enable her to cover much ground and to relate sympathetically to the rich cornucopia of Zangwill's interests in ways that have been lacking in previous analyses. No other volume on the subject contains so much reliable information on such seemingly disparate activities as Zangwill's work for women's suffrage and his leadership of the ITO. Moreover, Rochelson's explanations of possible links between Zangwill's commitment to specifically Jewish issues and broader public topics, while admittedly conjectural, are illuminating and groundbreaking. However, because this biography is more kaleidoscopic than thematic in nature, Rochelson never quite seems able to explain why Zangwill's life and work remain important.

Rochelson portrays Zangwill as an ambitious personality who craftily sought publicity while at the same time nobly refusing to downplay his own Jewish identity and Jewish concerns. Perhaps her claims about the level of his fame in his own time are overstated—she touts Zangwill as "the first Anglo-Jewish celebrity of the twentieth century" (p. 24), whereas Michael Berkowitz, who has probed how Zionism and other modern Jewish political forces relied on (and accelerated) the fame of particular individuals, has had very little to say about Zangwill.[2] Rochelson herself concedes that Zangwill's celebrity status was ephemeral. In fact, much of her analysis of Zangwill's writings recapitulates the tone and design of his *Children of the Ghetto*. In Zangwill's writing, Rochelson perceptively reveals, levels of neo-traditionalism and nostalgia lurk beneath flamboyant declarations about the ways in which the Jewish religion and "ghetto" communalism are fundamentally unsuited to life in the modern world. Similarly, Rochelson herself appears to be writing about a subject which is dead and virtually forgotten, but which she nonetheless thinks is worth documenting, in the hope that Zangwill's reputation might someday be revived.

This once-upon-a-time tone of archaic retrieval seems misplaced, however. After Zangwill, many Jewish writers achieved comparable fame and notoriety and also enjoyed a much more solid and enduring literary reputation. Yet even the most scandalous texts rendered by these writers (for instance, *Portnoy's Complaint* by Philip Roth, a writer whose pedigree, Rochelson suggestively claims, draws from Zangwill's Jewish gadfly status) have clearly demarcated shelf lives and expiration dates. Within a few generations, students who read them might well wonder what all the shouting was about. In contrast, has any Jewish writer in the past century written anything that relates more pertinently to 21st-century politics of multiculturalism and personal identity than Zangwill's 1908 production, *The Melting Pot*?

In a biography framed around Zangwill's literary accomplishments, *The Melting Pot*, his most significant text, seems homeless, mainly because of its dubious artistic quality. Rochelson discusses the play in a chapter devoted to his thoughts and writings during the First World War period. However, this clearly anachronistic placement has no convincing thematic justification. To be sure, Rochelson suggests that Zangwill conceptualized the utopia of Jewish-Christian harmony in the American "crucible" as the antithesis to the Great War "cockpit" of bellicose nationalism that he described in works published after *The Melting Pot*, but this does not mean that the discussion of the play should be placed out of its proper historical chronology. Moreover, as evidenced by a key passage in *Children of the Ghetto*, Zangwill's fascination with America as a possible solution to Jewish identity dilemmas well preceded the crisis of the First World War years. Finally, this chapter about Zangwill during the First World War is flawed by descriptions that underestimate the strain of Zangwill's position during that time—positioned among the patriotic and even jingoistic elites in the Anglo-Jewish community, he was himself skeptical with regard to the legitimacy of the Allies' war effort.

In a different, more thematic biography centered on Zangwill's grappling with the dilemma of modern identity, *The Melting Pot* (and the debates it generated) would most likely be the centerpiece. In contrast, Rochelson's methodological choices, which focus quite successfully on the interrelationship of literature and Jewish politics in the English-speaking world, have the effect of marginalizing Zangwill's famous play. Thus, Rochelson overlooks important scholarly discussions of *The Melting Pot*'s manifest relevance to contemporary debates about multicultural autonomy versus globalized amalgamation.[3]

Students of modern Jewish politics will find here important, even trail-blazing, clues to Zangwill's significance in the larger historical picture. Nonetheless, the complexity of Zangwill's career leaves many key questions for further research. On the issue of Zionism, Rochelson makes one crucial contribution: she cogently interprets Zangwill's territorialism as a function of his lingering English patriotism, suggesting that he broke away from the Zionist movement after it spurned colonial secretary Joseph Chamberlain's East Africa settlement offer. In a corollary to this interpretation, she observes that Zangwill gazed toward the future of Jewish-Arab relations in Palestine through lenses tinted by concerns and assumptions of British colonial control over nonwhite natives. Beyond this, however, Rochelson leaves it to others to sort out what really happened in the breach between Zangwill and Zionist activists.

Happily, the questions are intriguing, and they should attract many individuals both to Rochelson's biography and to future studies of Zangwill's activity. How was it that this Anglo-Jewish writer came to believe that the creation of a Jewish homeland outside of the land sanctified by Jewish religion and tradition was a necessity? How serious was Zangwill's involvement with the ITO? In Zangwill's corrosive description of Mordechai Noah as a con man who preyed upon the messianic naivety of desperate Jews (in the 1820s, Noah had proposed setting up a Jewish territory in America), was he consciously distancing himself and his own work with the ITO from Noah's flawed image? (In this respect, one wonders about the analogy Rochelson draws at the end of her study between Zangwill and Woody Allen's protean character, Zelig; perhaps a better parallel to Woody Allen is the way in which Zangwill's creative work analyzed and anticipated personal moral challenges that the artist then reenacted in his own life.) What was the relationship between Zangwill and Chaim Weizmann (who receives just one passing mention in this text), given that the two reached diametrically opposite conclusions regarding the marriage between Zionism and English colonial power? Finally, is there some causal dynamic or historical lesson to be found in the contrasting fates of Theodor Herzl, who aspired to write popular plays and ended up making a lasting impression on Jewish nationalism, and Zangwill, the popular playwright whose political activities failed to have lasting outcomes?

MATTHEW SILVER
Max Stern College of Emek Yezreel

Notes

1. Maurice Wohlgelernter, *Israel Zangwill: A Study* (New York: 1964), 20–30, quoted by Rochelson on p. 4.
2. Michael Berkowitz, *The Jewish Self-Image in the West* (New York: 2000), 64–67.
3. See, for instance, Philip Gleason, *Speaking of Diversity: Language and Ethnicity in Twentieth-Century America* (Baltimore: 1992), and David Biale, "The Melting Pot and Beyond: Jews and the Politics of American Identity," in *Insider/Outsider: American Jews and Multiculturalism*, ed. David Biale, Michael Galchinsky, and Susannah Heschel (Berkeley: 1998), 17–33.

Anna Shternshis, *Soviet and Kosher: Jewish Popular Culture in the Soviet Union, 1923–1939*. Bloomington: Indiana University Press, 2006. 248 pp.

Soviet and Kosher is a long overdue historical study of the role of popular culture in the formation of Soviet Jewish identity in the 1920s and 1930s. With clear, appealing prose and a highly original methodology, Anna Shternshis offers a fascinating exploration of the central paradox of the early Soviet Jewish experience: at the same time as the Bolshevik state actively eliminated the basic components of collective Jewish identity (religious, social, and cultural institutions) and emphasized Russification, it also openly promoted Yiddish-language secular Jewish culture. The general outlines of this story are by now quite familiar to historians. The great virtue of

Shternshis' book is that she shifts the focus from the state bureaucrats and the Soviet Jewish artistic intelligentsia to the reception of this new culture in the context of everyday Jewish life. In the process, she illuminates the rich private interiors of the unique Soviet Jewish identity that arose as a result of this contradictory ideological revolution.

In successive chapters, Shternshis surveys official Yiddish popular culture, including popular songs, amateur Yiddish-language writing and theater productions, official counter propaganda against antisemitism, and mock trials of the Jewish religion. Analyzing these new texts and rituals leads her to a larger revisionist thesis about their role in shaping Soviet Jewish identity. She argues that the Soviet Jewish cultural experience reflects not so much the power as the limits of Soviet state control over Jewish identity. Rejecting both the older narrative of Soviet repression and Jewish cultural "resistance and survival" and the newer narrative of "assimilation" and universalism typified by Yuri Slezkine's *The Jewish Century* (2004), Shternshis emphasizes a subtler pattern of ongoing Jewish "compromises and adjustments" that reflects the unintended consequences of Soviet propagandistic efforts. Thus official Soviet Yiddish culture, even when targeting Jewish parochialism and denigrating religious traditions, ironically facilitated the development of "positive Jewish identity" and "national Jewish pride." It did so, Shternshis claims, by providing Jews both a license to identify publicly as a national minority and a set of permissible public spaces for Jews to convene as a community. In spite of their obvious ideological content, the new Yiddish-language cultural activities allowed early Soviet Jews to engage in open discussion of contemporary issues such as intermarriage, "assimilation," Jewish participation in Communist politics, and antisemitism.

What this flourishing Soviet Jewish public culture further reveals, according to Shternshis, is that even the crudest forms of state political propaganda could take on new meanings in the hands of average Jews. Thus she documents how polemical anti-religious literature served as vehicles for some Jews to forge a nostalgic connection to pre-revolutionary traditional Judaism. In the absence of access to actual religious life, anti-clerical parodies provided building blocks for a secular Jewish identity beyond religion but still defined in relation to it. Similarly, Shternshis documents how more acculturated Jews read anti-Zionist texts as a means to learn more about aspects of Jewish religious ritual, folklore, and history with which they were otherwise unfamiliar. Perhaps the most telling and colorful example of this process is found in the anecdote with which Shternshis opens her book. Interviewing an 82-year-old former Soviet Jew in Brooklyn, who speaks Yiddish fluently but has never set foot in a synagogue, she finds her informant lecturing her on how to cook "kosher pork." The obvious oxymoron perfectly captures the total estrangement from religious tradition coupled with a creative reappropriation of it into a strong secular Jewish cultural identity.

These sorts of claims about cultural identity and historical agency hinge on the quality of the sources documenting the popular reception of the texts and tropes in question. And the most impressive aspect of Shternshis' work is her methodology. Avoiding the classic pitfalls of overreliance on émigré or refusenik literature, on the one hand, or relying on official propagandistic texts and active Bolshevik Jewish writers, on the other, she combines in-depth, extensive ethnographic fieldwork with careful study of published popular culture and archival first-person writings. In this way, she manages to connect literary popular culture to a context of reception via interviews with living participants, many of them octogenarians. Such an endeavor is fraught with challenges, not the least of them being the problem of relying on individual memory across vast periods of time. Here, fortunately, Shternshis' anthropological skills generally immunize her against taking such testimony at face value.

As compelling as these contemporary ethnographic excursions are, the most interesting part of Shternshis' work lies in her focus on the linguistic dynamics that divide Soviet Ashkenazic Jewry. As she notes, Soviet Jewry produced two different cultures, one in Yiddish and one in Russian. This necessarily must be taken into consideration when generalizing from any one anecdote. "Kosher pork," for instance, would have meant something very different to a Jew raised in a home that still retained awareness of Jewish ritual law (if not ritual practice itself) as opposed to one with no firsthand exposure to Orthodox Judaism. Or would it? What is therefore striking is not so much the differences, as the similarities between these sub groups. Despite the linguistic gulf and very different social and cultural experiences, what appears to link both groups in Shternshis' narrative is a deep nostalgia for pre-revolutionary Yiddish popular and folk culture, even in its Sovietized, politicized forms. This suggests that music and isolated elements of language, humor, and literary symbols became that much more important as common sources of Soviet Jewish identity across the otherwise considerable geographic, cultural, linguistic, and even religious divides of the population.

This notion of a shared nostalgic sensibility among otherwise markedly different Jewish sub populations points simultaneously to the strength and weakness of Shternshis' generational approach. On the surface, her decision to restrict her focus to those Jews born between 1906 and 1930 is sound. It introduces a neat discipline into a potentially unruly subject otherwise ripe for overgeneralization. However, this generational paradigm implies a historical experience tightly defined by historical periodization, in which the language spoken by these very different Soviet Jews actually mattered less than their shared chronological proximity to the pre-revolutionary past. This is a bold, intriguing claim. Yet it seems antithetical to Shternshis' other nuanced arguments about culture's ability to transcend politics and the role of language in defining modern Jewish identity. Expanding the field of vision from a single generation to a broader temporal model might have clarified her view of the larger relationship between language and identity in the lives of early Soviet Jewry.

In spite of these reservations about the generational paradigm, Shternshis' book presents a solid case for a middle ground in the historiographical debates about early Soviet Jewish identity. Shifting the focus from Bolshevik Jewish elites and deracinated texts to a broader swath of the Soviet Jewish public, she shows how these post-revolutionary Jews synthesized new cultural identities on their own terms. Moreover, her study offers a highly convincing model of how oral history techniques and memory studies can be profitably integrated into Soviet Jewish history. So too it raises the bar for Jewish cultural history by demonstrating how any historical interpretation of popular culture must take into account the actual responses of its contemporary audiences. As more studies of Soviet Jewish music, film, and the arts continue to appear,

Shternshis' mixture of textual analysis, oral history, and archival research offers a fruitful ideal that should be heeded by all.

JAMES LOEFFLER
University of Virginia

Barry Trachtenberg, *The Revolutionary Roots of Modern Yiddish, 1903–1917*. Syracuse: Syracuse University Press, 2008. xv + 222 pp.

"Revolution" is the new buzzword of Jewish cultural studies, replacing the "Other" of yesterday and "emancipation" of long ago. *The Revolution of 1905 and Russia's Jews* (2008), edited by Stefani Hoffman and Ezra Mendelsohn, was followed in 2009 by Kenneth B. Moss' prize-winning book, *Jewish Renaissance in the Russian Revolution*. The life and work of S. An-sky, the revolutionary, playwright, and ethnographer, continues to fascinate scholars in Russia, France, America, and Israel. Where the coin of the realm was once German and French, the Jewish cultural historian of today cannot proceed without learning Yiddish, Hebrew, and Russian. That's the easy part. For no sooner did the Russian empire begin to fall apart than its Jews, God bless them, broke into a plethora of political parties, schisms, and coalitions. On one page alone of Barry Trachtenberg's new book on the revolutionary roots of modern Yiddish the reader is barraged with the SERP, the S.S., and the RSDWP; Bundists, Zionists, Territorialists, and liberals; Ukrainians, Jews, and Poles—all because of a young Russian Jew named Nokhem Shtif, who could not decide where to belong until he turned his mind to Yiddish scholarship. It is no small feat, as Trachtenberg has done, to rescue a single strand from the eye of the revolutionary storm.

The author traces the turn to Yiddish on the part of a tiny but highly influential group of Russian-born intellectuals. With one chapter devoted to each, the main players in his drama are Shmuel Niger (1883–1955), Ber Borochov (1881–1917), and Nokhem Shtif (aka Bal-Dimyen, 1879–1933). Their embrace of Yiddish, he demonstrates, was essentially a turn from radical, utopian politics to some form of cultural nationalism, but such were the centrifugal forces unleashed by the first—and failed— Russian revolution that none of his cast of characters remained in Russia for very long. From Mother Russia they branched out in three directions: to Germany, the home of Wissenschaft; to Palestine, to form or inspire the Second Aliyah; and to the United States, where they launched the aesthetic revolution in Yiddish literature. Borochov, the most protean figure in Trachtenberg's gallery, played a major role in all three arenas. Not only did Borochov lay the foundation of a new discipline that he grandly called Yiddish Philology; not only was he a major theoretician of labor Zionism; but during his brief sojourn in America, he managed to provide the scholarly apparatus for M. Bassin's *500 yor yidishe poezye* (Five hundred years of Yiddish poetry) (1917), the hugely ambitious anthological project of Di Yunge. Some, like Shtif, eventually did return, but by then Russia was no longer Russia and the elitist project of Yiddish scholarship for its own sake ran afoul of the new revolutionary cadres. If Shtif hadn't died at his desk, he would have perished in the gulag.

In Trachtenberg's telling, however, it is sometimes difficult to see the forest for the trees. The telltale signs of a Ph.D. dissertation with its mandatory structure are everywhere apparent. The first 60 pages of *The Revolutionary Roots of Modern Yiddish* read like an annotated bibliography, replete with names, dates, and oh-so-many publications. The storyline doesn't really pick up until the middle of the second synoptic chapter. Here Jacob Lestschinsky (1876-1966), the pioneer of Jewish sociology and demographic research, makes his appearance. As politically promiscuous as the rest of them, he at least stayed focused on one discipline long enough to investigate the anomalous life of the Jewish worker and the statistical breakdown of one shtetl. Similarly short-lived were the path-breaking Yiddish literary journals that Trachtenberg describes: *Di literarishe montasshriftn, Lebn un visnshaft, Der pinkes*. When, at long last, we get to the publication of *Di yidishe velt*, which enjoyed an unprecedented five-year lifespan (January 1912 to December 1916), Trachtenberg mercilessly dispenses with it in two pages.

With such a peripatetic and polyglot cast of characters, it should come as no surprise that the course of Yiddish studies never did run smooth. Whom, after all, did they serve? The Jewish worker, staggering under the double yoke of Tsar and Kapital? The ordinary, God-fearing Jew, who still pored over the *Ein Ya'akov* in the house of study? The millions of Jewish men, women, and children who voted with their feet and booked passage to America? And where, after all, could Yiddish studies thrive? If, at the height of his powers and prestige (supported by Boris Kletskin, the greatest philanthropist in the annals of Yiddish, and in Vilna, the Jerusalem of Lithuania) the 36-year-old Shmuel Niger could not make a go of it, then no place would provide Yiddish studies with a secure home. More tragic still was the fate of Shtif. One year after famously calling the YIVO into being as an independent Yiddish academic institute, he crossed over into the Soviet Union, assumed an academic position in Kiev, and burned his bridges behind him. Borochov, ill with tuberculosis, died soon after his return to Russia in the wake of the 1917 Revolution.

As an intellectual biographer, Trachtenberg does a credible job tracing the careers of his triumvirate. As a cultural historian, he misses the main dialectical drama. This is because, taken alone, the revolutionary trope does little to situate the cultural project to which its protagonists were harnessed. Niger, Borochov, and Shtif, insofar as Yiddish was concerned, were a species of revolutionary traditionalists, a cultural phenomenon with its roots in the fin-de-siècle. While Niger and Borochov were inspired by the Promethean presence of I.L. Peretz, Shtif was drawn to Yiddish—nay, captivated by it—after hearing Sholem Aleichem read at a Zionist gathering in Kiev (p. 139). Alone among the Young Turks of his generation, Shtif championed Sholem Aleichem over Peretz as a "democrat" (p. 147) and as a beacon of *bitokhn*, stubborn faith (pp. 148–149). A Yiddish scholarship for Yiddish-speaking Jews remained torn between the two alternative visions of the folk represented by Peretz and Sholem Aleichem.

To pursue the point further, we might well ask: Which of Niger's, Borochov's, and Shtif's scholarly writings are still read today? During his "revolutionary" heyday, Niger produced a single piece of historical scholarship: the essay on "Yiddish Literature and the Female Reader" (1913). Here Niger opened a new chapter of Jewish self-understanding among the secular intelligentsia by insisting that the roots of modern Yiddish culture should be sought in "the literature of *ivre-taytsh*," that is, the semi-sacred texts produced by learned Jewish men for the sake of pious Jewish women (pp. 101–104). So, too, Borochov's pioneering work on "The Library of the Yiddish Philologist (400 Years of Yiddish Linguistic Scholarship)" (1913), which focused on the uncharted realm of Old Yiddish, not to speak of the whole scholarly apparatus that he appended to the first four centuries of Bassin's 500-year anthology. Niger and Borochov turned *tkhines*, those quaint personal supplications by and for Jewish women, into the lyrical source of modern Yiddish poetry.

Shtif is another story. His mini-biography begins with an Oedipal struggle with the Haskalah (p. 138) and with his father's strong desire to raise a good, Russified Jew, in particular. Decades later, Shtif would turn against another surrogate father-figure, YIVO's guiding spirit, Max Weinreich, and become the fiercest exponent of a Soviet-icized Yiddish (p. 182). Left unexplored is Shtif's stunning rehabililtation of the Haskalah in his landmark anthology of "old Yiddish literature" (*Di eltere yidishe literature*, 1929). It was this anthology that inspired the 37-year-old Itzik Manger to write *Noente geshtaltn* (Intimate figures, 1938), a fanciful, fictional rendering of Shtif's pantheon of Yiddish literary forebears.

When all the political parties were ground to dust; when the flames of the revolution consumed itself, what the first generation of scholars-in-Yiddish were able to salvage from the cultural ruins were some forgotten works in *ivre-taytsh*, a few *tkhines*, a somewhat laughable bunch of maskilim, and the folk genius of Sholem Aleichem.

DAVID G. ROSKIES
The Jewish Theological Seminary of America
Ben-Gurion University

Zionism, Israel, and the Middle East

Avraham Burg, *The Holocaust is Over; We Must Rise from Its Ashes*. New York: Palgrave Macmillan, 2008. 272 pp.
Laurence J. Silberstein (ed.), *Postzionism: A Reader*. New Brunswick: Rutgers University Press, 2008. 406 pp.

It did not come as a surprise to me to be asked to review these two volumes together, since I had good reason to believe that they dealt with the same subject. Avraham Burg's book first came to my attention as a result of the lead article in the June 8, 2007 issue of the *Haaretz* weekend magazine, an extremely confrontational interview of the author that was conducted by the journalist Ari Shavit. Titled (in towering red letters) "Post-Zionist," the interview begins with Shavit saying "I read your book," and goes on from there to the inevitable question: "Are you still a Zionist?"

In the interview, Burg, a former speaker of the Knesset and former chairman of the Jewish Agency, doesn't give an unequivocal answer one way or the other. But he does distance himself from political Zionism by saying that "we have to leave Herzl behind us and move on to Ahad Ha'am." In addition, he goes so far as to reject the definition of Israel as a Jewish state, or even a Jewish-democratic state. The latter phrase, he says, is one that people find too soothing. "It's lovely. It's schmaltzy. It's nostalgic. It's retro. It gives a sense of fullness. But 'Jewish-democratic' is nitroglycerine." There is even one passage in the book (seized upon by Shavit at the outset of his interview) in which Burg explicitly identifies himself, to some degree, as a post-Zionist. After deploring the cynical attitude of many Israelis toward today's diaspora Jews, he observes that this "is catastrophic Zionism at its worst: what is bad for the Jews is better for Zionism. In this sense, I am not just a post-Zionist, but an anti-, anti-catastrophist Zionist" (p. 100).

There is a limit, however, to Burg's radicalism. He stops short of reiterating the post-Zionist call to make Israel simply "a state of all its citizens." What he says, instead, in his book, is that "Israel should become the democratic state of the Jewish people which belongs to all of its citizens. . ." (p. 237). Precisely what he means by this is unclear. *The Holocaust is Over* is devoted to a critical analysis of the contemporary Israeli—indeed, Jewish—mentality, not to a comprehensive redesigning of Israel's political structure. It is only at the end of the book that Burg makes a few sketchy comments about concrete reforms that Israel might undertake. And these are not always easy to decipher. When he indicates, for instance, that Israel should remain the "state of the Jewish people," is he reaffirming Israel's special and frequently assailed relationship with Jews outside of the country? It seems more likely, though not altogether certain, that Burg is merely the victim of his far from infallible translator, who has unaccountably rendered "medinat kol yehudeha vekhol ezraheha" (the state of all its Jews and all its citizens), as "the state of the Jewish people which belongs to all of its citizens."

Regardless of whether he sees Israel as (partially) constituting the state only of the Jews (and others) who live there or whether he continues to regard it as the state of all Jews wherever they live, Burg retains high expectations. If the state of Israel could only rise above its Holocaust-induced sense of perpetual persecution at the hands of others, and thereby deny Hitler a posthumous victory, it could yet perform the task for which he believes it is destined. "I want to believe that the Israeli state is not just the incarnation of the Shoah victims and the other Jewish victims of hate throughout history, but that Israel can be a light unto the nations, a light of universal humanity" (p. 144). Burg, it seems, does not simply want to move on to Ahad Ha'am; he wants to get back to Abraham Geiger, albeit from a territorial base. However, it is not entirely clear how attached he remains to that base; in the interview with Shavit, he advises every Israeli who can do so to obtain a foreign passport, as he himself has done. He also describes the European Union in such glowing terms that one has to wonder how much he really believes the world to be in need of Israel's candlepower.

The Holocaust is Over is an illuminating account of the growing disenchantment of one scion of the Zionist elite with the country in whose service he has spent most of his life. It is not an equally trustworthy account of the evolution of that country. Burg's assertion, for instance, that "the majority of the Jewish people opposed the creation of a Jewish state well into World War II" (p. 37) is a gross oversimplification, one that mistakes indifference or lack of active support for actual opposition. He has a great deal to say about the conduct of the Zionist leadership during the Holocaust, but none of it is backed up by reference to the recent research on that subject, much of which is at odds with his claims. On other occasions as well he tailors his summaries of key events and tendencies in dubious ways to support his overall argument.

Despite Burg's marginal status as a post-Zionist, his book (had it only been published a few years earlier) might well have been excerpted by Laurence Silberstein in *Postzionism: A Reader*, an anthology of previously published articles and book chapters. According to Silberstein, it is not important "whether or not a particular scholar writer 'is' or identifies as 'a postzionist.'" What matters is "how and in what ways do particular writings contribute to the production of a postzionist discourse" (p. 6). Burg's critique of Israelis' misplaced sense of victimhood clearly does that, even if it makes less of a contribution than some of the other essays reprinted in this volume, including some by people who could be more accurately characterized as anti-Zionists than post-Zionists.

Silberstein, to be sure, is anxious to avoid any confusion between anti-Zionism and post-Zionism, even displaying a certain amount of indignation against people who attempt to blur the distinction between the two. Anti-Zionism, by his lights, consists of "opposition to the state of Israel itself," whereas post-Zionists seek merely to show how "facing the problematic aspect of its Zionist past does not weaken the state . . . but strengthens it" (p. 5). This argument is disingenuous. Among the post-Zionists in general, and among the authors included in this volume in particular, there are many who regard Zionism as a misconceived, almost entirely egregious project whose worst effects must be undone by the transformation (or the submersion) of Israel into a state no longer demarcated as Jewish and containing, if it were to include the West Bank and Gaza, a majority (or at least a near majority) of Arabs. How such people differ from anti-Zionists escapes me.

Silberstein's distinction between anti-Zionists and post-Zionists serves the purpose of displaying the post-Zionists in a relatively benign light—in this presentation, they are not so nasty as to be "anti" something to which the prospective readers of this anthology might still be (too) attached. It is perhaps for a similar reason that Silberstein has departed in this volume (albeit inconsistently) from one of his usual habits (with provocative intent), that of spelling Zionism and Zionist entirely in lowercase letters. One wonders, too, about the less than candid language in which his introductory remarks about one of the volume's contributors are couched. Azmi Bishara, Silberstein notes, is "a former member of the Israeli parliament" (p. 15). What he neglects to mention is that Bishara left the Knesset—and, for that matter, Israel—under a cloud of suspicion over felony charges of both political and financial wrongdoing.

Postzionism: A Reader is to some extent a companion volume to Silberstein's *Postzionism Dialogues*, published a decade ago. It includes many of the seminal articles and statements discussed in that analytical study but it also contains important new work that has appeared in recent years. Among the many significant, now already venerable pieces that it reprints are Benny Morris' 1988 *Tikkun* article on "The New Historiography," Gershon Shafir's introduction to his book *Land, Labor, and the Origins of the Israeli-Palestinian Conflict*, and Daniel and Jonathan Boyarin's 1993 article "Diaspora: Generation and the Ground of Jewish Identity." The more recent pieces include Yehouda Shenhav's introduction to his book *The Arab Jews*, Uri Ram's retrospective look at "Post-Zionist Studies of Israel: The First Decade," published in 2005, and Caryn Aviv and David Shneer's introduction to their book *New Jews*.

Unlike his earlier book on post-Zionism, Silberstein's *Reader* makes no pretense of elucidating the views of both the supporters and the opponents of the idea and hence cannot be faulted—as *Postzionism Dialogues* should be—for its one-sidedness. It can rather be commended as a well-organized and ample compendium of sources that elucidate the origins and the trajectory of the tendencies that its compiler has for many years sought both to explain and to foster. It does a particularly good job of documenting the Israeli and the American strands of "writings that contribute to the production of a postzionist discourse." It can thus be welcomed as a useful research tool even by those who are utterly opposed to the movement that it charts.

ALLAN ARKUSH
Binghamton University

Motti Golani, *The British Mandate for Palestine, 1948: War and Evacuation*. Jerusalem: The Zalman Shazar Center for Jewish History, 2009. 280 pp.

Over the past decade, a new approach has emerged in Israeli historiography regarding the 1948 War of Independence that might be termed "post-revisionism." In contrast to the preceding stream of "New Historians," a new generation of researchers and a series of new studies now seek to examine different dimensions of the war period, with an emphasis on social and civil aspects rather than exclusively political and military factors. Through the emphasis on the civilian component of war, this approach reveals the mutual relations between ideology, political policy, and social structure, on the one hand, and the management and course of the war, on the other.

One of the hallmarks of this new stream of research is the examination of the 1948 war under such paradigmatic headings as civil war, intercommunal war, and total war. The new approach is critical yet temperate, avoiding a judgmental attitude toward the subjects of its study and recognizing the restrictions, distress, weaknesses, and difficulties faced by all the parties involved in the Israeli-Arab conflict. The same approach has also been manifested in recent research concerning British policy during the latter part of the Mandate in Palestine and the function of the British civil government during early phases of the 1948 war. This field, which connects the end of colonial rule, civilian and military evacuation, and war, forms the subject of Motti Golani's important book, *The British Mandate for Palestine, 1948: War and Evacuation*.

Golani serves as professor of Israel studies at the University of Haifa. As with his previous works and his study of Alan Cunningham's tenure as the last British high commissioner of Palestine, this book reflects Golani's abiding interest in the British Mandatory government in general, and its functioning during the war in particular. By focusing on the British side, it seeks not only to offer an additional perspective on the war alongside the Arab and Zionist standpoints, but also to help change long-standing perceptions of British policy and actions during the war period. Like other scholars who have examined this field in recent years, Golani seeks to challenge the longstanding assumption that the British adopted a hostile and biased approach toward either the Jews or the Arabs, or that it sought to torpedo the 1947 U.N. partition plan. According to Golani, Britain did not materially assist either side, but rather was concerned mainly with evacuating its forces and ending its period of rule in as secure and dignified a manner as possible, thus ensuring that it would continue to enjoy influence and prestige in the region. Golani argues that British policy during the war and the cardinal impact of the war can be understood only against the background of the weakness that characterized the operations of the Mandatory government of Palestine during its last months. As he shows, the evacuation process was marked by confusion, uncertainty, anxiety, and impotence.

The British Mandate for Palestine, 1948 comprises three parts, in addition to an introduction and epilogue. The final and most substantial portion of the book presents the diary of Sir Henry Gurney, the chief secretary of the Mandatory government of Palestine, accompanied by Golani's comments and an appendix providing biographical details. As Golani explains in the introduction to his book, the issues addressed by the diary do not embrace all the aspects of the civil war that raged between December 1947 and May 1948. However, the diary does offer the reader an opportunity to gain a general impression of matters that were of concern to the Mandatory government during this period of evacuation and war.

Golani progresses from the general context to the local level, examining the often tense relationships between the government in London and the administration in Jerusalem; between the high commissioner and the chief secretary; and between the civil administration and the army. The comprehensive discussion in this section is devoted mainly to the connection between the progressive stages of British policy and evacuation and the development of the war. The inability of the British army and civil administration to cope simultaneously with the war and with the task of evacuation was, Golani believes, one of the principle factors behind the decisive outcome of the civil war.

Golani begins by providing the reader with an understanding of the general context, including the state of the British empire after the end of the Second World War; the management of Mandatory government affairs; and the formulation and implementation of the evacuation plan. In the second section, he examines the character of the author of the diary, Chief Secretary Sir Henry Gurney, who epitomized some of the hallmarks of the Mandatory regime and was the very embodiment of British colonial officialdom. Golani succinctly describes Gurney's political work as well as his identification with the colonial administration, showing how he was responsible for the evacuation of civilians and for the work of Arab, Jewish, and British civil servants. This focus on Gurney's role provides an additional tool for understanding British policy and the collective biography of the British officials. Golani also draws systematically on diverse sources in this part, frequently referring readers to Gurney's diary. Thus the first two parts of the book function to some extent as an introduction that prepares the reader for Gurney's diary and for the tragic and dramatic finale to the story of British rule in Palestine.

As with other diaries written during the war that present Jewish and Arab positions and commentaries on the unfolding events, Gurney's diary provides an important source for understanding the decision-making process and the manner in which the British administration evaluated the capabilities of the Jewish and Arab forces. Above all, however, it offers fascinating insights into the character and functioning of the civil administration and into the prevailing mood among the administration's officials during the period of war and evacuation. Golani's use of the term "golden cage" to describe the daily experiences of the British officials accurately characterizes the difficult reality faced by the Mandatory government at the time, as Gurney himself notes in his diary.

Golani concludes his book with an account of his meeting with Gurney's family in London. Titled "Colonial Orphans," this epilogue summarizes the outcome of the twilight years of British rule in Palestine: a colonial rule that began and ended with war, leaving behind not only conflicting historical memories and narratives, but also the foundation for a stubbornly enduring Arab-Israeli conflict.

MOSHE NAOR
The Hebrew University

Anat Helman, *Or veyam hikifuha: tarbut tel avivit bitkufat hamandat* (Urban culture in 1920s and 1930s Tel Aviv). Haifa: University of Haifa Press, 2007. 343 pp.

Thirty years ago, Itamar Even-Zohar published a seminal article, to which several other discussants responded, in which he posed the question of how a local Hebrew culture developed in Eretz Israel and how that topic ought to be studied.[1] Even-Zohar's essay was pivotal in the reframing of Israeli cultural studies. In challenging the prevailing notions of the time, he argued that texts should no longer be at the center of research, and proposed instead that the study of an entire cultural repertoire should include quotidian elements such as food, clothing, and housing—the physical and cultural construction of "home": its furnishings, interior design, indoor and outdoor spaces. Anat Helman's book, *Urban Culture in 1920s and 1930s Tel Aviv*, examines some of these particular elements and more. As such, it is clearly representative of the recent cultural turn in Israeli historiography.

Helman, a perceptive recorder of everyday life, interweaves accounts of the daily practices of the past with a contemporary theoretical framework. In addition to the close attention she pays to patterns of domestic consumption, she binds together material culture and social behavior to examine such topics as changing styles of architecture, parks, transportation, cleanliness and dirt, pets and their owners, the varied use of multiple languages, the prevalence of urban noise, parades, exhibitions, funerals, and holiday and Shabbat activities.

What emerges is a vibrant portrait of Tel Aviv and the evolution of its culture. Helman uses Tel Aviv as a case study to elaborate a theoretical framework by which to decipher the "physics" of culture in general. In the pursuit of that goal, she identifies cultural agents and cultural structures such as the municipality and voluntary associations, points out the separate cultural repertoires of subgroups such as the middle class, the labor movement, and religious and Mizrahi Jews, and details the transmission of ideas and cultural praxis between these subgroups. Hardly less important, geography and climate are considered as factors in the cultural equation: Tel Aviv's beautiful sandy beaches, blue sky, and bright sunshine had a singular influence over the range of social activities and patterns of behavior.

Helman finds that the conviviality of Tel Avivians, who were wont to put their communal identity as well as their private lives on display, was a crucial feature influencing the style of Tel Aviv life as well as the city's image. While she is attuned to the ways in which Tel Aviv's middle-class founders sought to imbue the city with their values and aspirations, she also indicates that the makeup of the city's society was always heterogeneous. The inhabitants were separated by class, ethnic origin, and religious inclinations, and this diversity, she argues, produced an ambiance of cultural tolerance.

Pivotal to her discussion of both material and cultural development is her consideration of modernism, a construct which, in its Tel Aviv variation (unlike in Western Europe), embraced a valorization of both individualistic and collectivist ideas.

As the book progresses, Helman discusses the commonly held view that the eclectic style of Tel Aviv's first buildings was orientalist, flagrantly borrowing "eastern" motifs and mixing them indiscriminately with a "western" aesthetic. Unlike most observers, however, she finds a unique beauty in the eclectic style of the 1920s. Her intention is not to criticize the odd and diversified style, but rather to elucidate its meanings. Helman sees this style as an attempt to reconcile the then-current European-like identity with a renewed identification with the ancient past.

By the end of the 1920s, the Orient no longer inspired Tel Aviv's architects. Helman assumes that it was the deteriorating relationship between Jews and Jaffa's neighboring Arabs that led architects to search for other sources of inspiration, such as the Bauhaus school of modern architecture. The Bauhaus style was meant to offer a link to modernism and the future, frankly relinquishing the attempts to reconstruct an imagined past. Helman bemoans the introduction of the Bauhaus style, describing its products as "box-like buildings" and deploring its debasement of the cheerful colorful eclectic style (p. 25). Ironically, she asserts, although the eclectic style was directed toward the local vernacular while the modernist style was conceived as international, it was the Bauhaus style that actually bore some resemblance to the local Arab architecture. Following Helman's analysis, I would argue that the eclectic style represented an attempt to create not just a private home, but a collective image of what sort of home might speak the language of place. It reflected the ways in which individuals experienced their physical and social setting in accordance with their cultural suppositions.

The degrees of affinity between the new Jewish urban center and its immediate neighboring Middle Eastern milieu shifted between two opposing poles: positive assimilation and separation. One might conclude from Helman's findings that both the co-habitation of space with Arab neighbors and the real or imagined ancient past influenced the desire to increase the affinities between the European immigrants and the Middle Eastern society around them. However, Tel Avivians mostly felt compelled to distance themselves, that is, their culture and social values, from Arab Jaffa. This trend tended to intensify over time in the course of the Jewish drive toward nation-building, in part because of growing inter-group hostilities, but also as an outgrowth of Tel Aviv's conscious embrace of modernity. Reading this history along with Helman, we become aware that the process of differentiation did not follow a direct route, but was a relatively prolonged and complex process.

On another set of issues, Helman notes that Tel Aviv's builders, residents, and city officials were constantly pointing out and criticizing public displays of inappropriate behavior. Similarly, they complained about the inadequate infrastructure and the great difficulty they faced in substantially refining the material and behavioral repertoires needed in order to make Tel Aviv seem sufficiently European. Inefficiency, dirt, noise, and unsupervised behavior were often marked as "Oriental"—meaning Middle Eastern—or else they could often be labeled as provincially "East European." Open-air markets, for instance, were often described as "Oriental," a backward form of commerce, soon to disappear, as the German-born economist Alfred Boneh predicted in 1938. Not only did the markets not disappear, however, they kept springing up haphazardly at locations that met the needs of both merchants and consumers. Although the city authorities did their best to transfer markets to what they deemed a more suitable location, they only engendered discontent. In one such case, the city was forced to build a market where one had spontaneously developed. That was how the city's famous Carmel market was formed.

The competing concepts of order versus chaos, and planning versus the unplanned, are key themes throughout the book. Helman's discussion, although centered on Tel Aviv, clearly takes account of other examples of urban studies. Like generations of planners and builders of ideal cities before them who were similarly preoccupied with social engineering, Tel Aviv's builders, planners, and policymakers all had an ideal city in mind, although they constantly had to reconcile these aspirations with the prevailing social forces.² The effort to enforce order is a difficult task in any city.

Tel Aviv's planners, builders, and critics belonged to the bourgeoisie, or at least were inspired by Central and West European, urban, middle-class values and social order, argues Helman. This cultural disposition led them to a certain kind of "reading" or interpretation of reality. Taking Helman's work a step further, one wonders why certain behavioral patterns or structures were denigrated as "Oriental," East European, or smacking of the diasporic life (a pejorative term in the Zionist lexicon), while others were not. And what, exactly, reminded critics of Eastern Europe as opposed to the Orient? Why, for instance, were Tel Aviv's markets, which were a common form of commerce in Western Europe, labeled "Oriental"?³ Helman does give a few indications, although she does not describe the mechanisms behind them.

The discussion of dirt and disorder in Tel Aviv is similarly part of a longer historical discourse. For instance, when discussing Paris, Elizabeth Wilson demonstrated how filth (for example, that of sewers) and human behavior such as prostitution are identified as disorder, not to mention the fact that a brothel was also termed "a disorderly house" in the United States.⁴ It is through different measures of supervision and control—for instance, by obtaining information about prostitutes—that city bureaucrats aim at regulating, as a form of subduing certain forms of filth. But subduing filth does not mean that the city is able to be rid of it. Zoning can become a preferred way of regulating prostitution⁵ and sewer systems are built to transfer filth away from the vicinity of people. In Tel Aviv, the sewer took the filth into the sea, although, as Helman notes, a modern sewer system was constructed only in the 1940s. As Mary Douglas argues in *Purity and Danger*, it is through the placement of certain categories of the loathsome aspects of life that order is instilled, and the danger of contamination is avoided. Class distinction or social differentiation is achieved through identifying lowly traits through the deployment of contempt and disgust.⁶

For the most part, the "Oriental" market was related to dirt and noise, as described so vividly in the book: flies, chickens being slaughtered on the spot (without hiding the act behind walls), animal blood and rotting fish on the ground, amid the yelling and commotion of vendors, all marked the place as a blighted and low-caste space. Moreover, in Tel Aviv's muggy climate, the dirt and disorder were also associated with foul smells. Finally, the ubiquitous presence of Arabs and the motley of spoken languages combined to create the impression of non-respectable status or "disorderliness," as Helman indicates.

The complexity of the East/West dyad, however, prompts Helman to point out that although the presence of Arab-owned stalls (sometimes thronged by lice-infected children) was viewed as a threat to public hygiene, attempts to exclude Arab vendors were condemned by their Jewish colleagues, who argued that "Tel Aviv's women are accustomed to buying certain goods from Arab vendors" (p. 111). Apparently, implies Helman, these stalls were good for business.

Although the equation of "dirt" with "Arabs," linking disgust and inferiority, seems to have become a fixture of public life, the definition of dirt as Oriental did not necessarily apply to other parts of Yishuv society. Hirsch showed that members of kibbutzim were not perceived by hygienists as great models of cleanliness, yet they were never identified as "Oriental." On the contrary, a certain lack of proper personal hygiene was sometimes consciously adopted by men, as it was interpreted as "manly" and proletarian or expressed the desire to become as rooted in the soil as the local population.[7] Public health officials, however, were not easily convinced. At any rate, it was probably the willingness of the "pioneers" to live a frugal life that defined their conduct and social enterprise as worthy, and thus enabled undesired characteristics (such as dirt) to be ignored.

In contrast to kibbutz society, Helman reports, Tel Aviv was considered a den of hedonism. By the end of the 1930s, Tel Aviv had more than 3,000 shops, meaning one store to 44 people. By comparison, in Britain the ratio was one shop to every 40 people. In addition, hundreds of kiosks were spread along its main streets, offering soda, snacks, newspapers, and cigarettes. Already in the early 1920s, the growing number of retail businesses was considered a betrayal of Zionist ideals. Since most immigrants to Palestine chose to reside in Tel Aviv, the claim was made that the city had become a mirror image of the Pale of Settlement in Russia.

Most shops were utilitarian, and aesthetic values played little part in their exterior or interior design, notwithstanding the municipality's efforts to Europeanize their look. Critics were no doubt bothered by the relative scarcity of respectable shops for bourgeois, refined tastes. In fact, one could argue that the ample array of consumption culture and its wide distribution throughout many of the city's streets affected Tel Aviv's image. Today, when the marketplace is confined to its limited territory— when there are no children selling shoelaces and newspapers, no children offering shoeshine service on the streets, and very few street vendors—and when Tel Aviv is packed with first-class, name-brand shops, the market is no longer perceived negatively.

Yet another explanation of official sensitivity to the condition of the streets and the shops that lined them is suggested in Helman's chapter on public events: civic life took place on the streets. The benevolent weather as well as meager means led to such a vast and intensive performance of outdoor activities. Since everything was on display, and since public performances were so vital to the culture, the gap between the imagined and the real was stark.

This book is scholarly, rigorous, and reliable, but also written with a heartfelt and broadly humanistic outlook. Helman, through her novel approach to the topic, is able to broach critical observations while at the same time portraying the city planners and its early inhabitants empathetically, offering a close and intimate depiction of their lives.

ORIT ROZIN
Tel Aviv University

Notes

1. Itamar Even-Zohar, "Haẓemihah vehahitgabshut shel tarbut 'ivrit mekomit veyelidit beereẓ yisrael, 1882-1948," *Cathedra* 16 (1980), 165–189.

2. Wolfgang Braunfels, *Urban Design in Western Europe: Regime and Architecture 900-1900* (Chicago: 1988), 151.

3. Thomas Hall, *Planning Europe's Capital Cities: Aspects of Nineteenth-Century Urban Development* (Oxford: 1997), 310.

4. Elizabeth Wilson, "From *The Sphinx in the City*: Urban Life, the Control of Disorder, and Women," in *The Blackwell City Reader*, ed. Gary Bridge and Sophie Watson (Malden, Mass.: 2002), 421; Mary E. Richmond, *Child Marriages* (New York: 1925), 70.

5. Deborah Bernstein, *Nashim bashulayim: migdar veleumiyut beTel Aviv hamandatorit* (Jerusalem: 2008).

6. Mary Douglas, *Purity and Danger: An Analysis of the Concepts of Pollution and Taboo* (London: 1966); See also William Ian Miller, *The Anatomy of Disgust* (Cambridge, Mass.: 1997).

7. Dafna Hirsch, "Banu hena lehavi et hama'arav: hanhalat repertuar 'higiyeni' bekerev haḥevrah bepalestina bitkufat hamandat" (Ph.D. diss., Tel Aviv University, 2006), 167–218.

Arie Morgenstern, *Hastening Redemption: Messianism and the Resettlement of the Land of Israel*, trans. Joel A. Linsider. New York: Oxford University Press, 2006. 304 pp.

Hastening Redemption: Messianism and the Resettlement of the Land of Israel is the English translation of Arie Morgenstern's *Meshiḥiyut veyishuv erez yisrael*, published in Hebrew in 1985. The book is a study of the activities of the *perushim*, the disciples of Elijah ben Shlomo Zalman, the Vilna Gaon (1720–1797), who immigrated to Palestine between 1808 and 1840. Morgenstern makes a convincing case that among the perushim were men whose emigration was motivated by the conviction that God had chosen the year 1840 as the start of the messianic era, and who believed that their appropriate response was to build a permanent and productive Jewish community in the land of Israel. Unfortunately, none of the perushim penned a thoroughly formulated messianic theory with a detailed messianic scenario. Consequently, Morgenstern must state his case tentatively and acknowledge the limited scope of his conclusions. That he did not always do so provoked quite a bit of criticism of the original Hebrew version of this book. This English version, produced nearly 20 years later with no revisions, remains problematic but is nevertheless a welcome addition to the field.

Expressions of hope in an imminent messianic redemption were ubiquitous in medieval and early modern Jewish life. Was there ever a generation that did not produce Jews who could claim with the help of sacred prooftexts that the messianic era was at hand? Morgenstern begins his book by presenting statements made by individuals from a variety of countries (the United States, the Russian empire, France, Palestine) who regarded events of the late 18th and early 19th century as harbingers of the messianic era. In Chapter 2, he turns to the belief that the Jewish year 5600, equivalent to the Gregorian year 1840, would be the start of the redemption. Hillel of Shklov, one of the disciples of the Vilna Gaon, expressed this view. He attributed to his master the importance of this year based on the Zohar's statement: "In the 600th year of the sixth millennium, the gates of wisdom above and the wellsprings of wisdom below will be opened." Claims for the importance of 5600, not always tied to the Zohar, were found as well among the region's hasidim, and among Jews in Western Europe, northern Persia, Jerusalem, and Morocco. There is no reason to doubt this point, or the fact that there was a marked increase in the immigration of Jews to Palestine in the first half of the century, but such correlations do not entitle Morgenstern to assert that the aliyah from various lands of the diaspora was "motivated *primarily* by the expectation that the Messiah would arrive in A.M. 5600 (1840)" (p. 201, emphasis added).

When Morgenstern turns to the express opinions of the Vilna Gaon's disciples, his material becomes richer and more detailed. The perushim claimed their opinions were those of their deceased master—a man of such genius, breadth of learning, and integrity that any opinion attributed to him received tremendous respect. Because the Vilna Gaon did not write in an organized fashion, we are dependent upon his students for recalling his remarks and for interpreting the notes he wrote in the margins of books. Morgenstern does not claim to be an expert in this esoteric literature, but rather focuses on statements and activities of the disciples that are preserved in more prosaic writings. Such sources include the personal correspondence of the perushim and the people around them; the accounts written by British missionaries for their home readership; and the letters and documents in the archives of the funding agency for Ashkenazic Jews in the Yishuv, translated here as the Clerks Organization of Kollel HOD (Holland and Germany), headed by Zvi Hirsch Lehren of Amsterdam. Morgenstern's volume would have been stronger had it included a clearer description of the perushim. It is clear that the size of the group varied, but how many were present during the period in question? What were their names? Were some more authoritative than others? How exactly were "the Nobles of Vilna" (an important source of funds for the perushim) connected to "the disciples of the Vilna Gaon"? In addition, Morgenstern's work suffers from his tendency to assume that explicit statements made by various disciples express opinions held by the group as a whole.

Morgenstern's central thesis is that "the Vilna Gaon's disciples immigrated to and settled in the Land of Israel for the purpose of redeeming it, and they regarded the rebuilding of Jerusalem as the most direct path toward that goal" (p. 95). He maintains that the perushim agreed on the following four principles. First, the appearance of a Torah scholar such as the Vilna Gaon heralded the imminent messianic era, preparing the Jews for their entry into the Holy Land. Second, the difficulties experienced by the Jewish people during the Vilna Gaon's lifetime and thereafter were premonitions of messianic tribulations. Third, the date of redemption was predetermined as the year 5600, and was not contingent upon the repentance (that is, exemplary behavior) of the Jewish people as a whole. Fourth, the redemption would be initiated by "the awakening from below." This kabbalistic phrase ("the awakening above is dependent on the awakening from below") was interpreted by the perushim to mean that God's promise of a full and miraculous deliverance would be triggered by tangible, human deeds; in this case, the activities would be those of a group of unblemished individuals (the perushim) who engaged in intense Torah study, emigrated to the Holy Land, and developed a sizable and thriving Jewish community there. Morgenstern concedes that "not all who saw themselves as students of the Vilna Gaon endorsed his leading disciples' view that the End was a necessary, inevitable event utterly unconnected to human action such as repentance in the generally accepted sense of the term" (p. 92). Those who differed, he argued, insisted that repentance was one of the preconditions of redemption. In short, the perushim believed that God had indicated His readiness to end the Exile, and they were to respond by naturalistic progress toward that end. If not, the "window of opportunity" would close and the routine hardship of unredeemed Jewish life would resume its course.

One would expect that religious Jews who exerted themselves to move from their homes in the diaspora were likely to harbor strong messianic hopes. After all, messianic teachings consistently place the locus of redemption in the land of Israel. Jews who want to be on hand to witness the events, or to serve as the advance guard and participate directly in the process, have for centuries expressed these desires upon undertaking their voyages or arriving at their destination. Biblical writings appeared to sanction the conviction that the Jews' exiled condition would end as a result of their decisive activities and God's approval. Whether through conquest under the command of Joshua, the return from Babylonia in response to Cyrus' decree, or the establishment of political sovereignty at the hands of Davidic, Solomonic, or Hasmonean battles, the biblical authors regarded Jewish efforts to gain or reinstate possession of the land as vital, just as much as human acts were held responsible for exile and expulsion.

Yet at some point after the disastrous revolt of Bar Kokhba and the transference of the center of rabbinic authority to Babylonia, rabbinic leaders routinely taught that the only permissible efforts to "hasten the end" were prayer, repentance, and good deeds—and even then, such efforts should not be excessive. In consequence, hopeful pleas for and expectations of a sudden and miraculous redemption infused Jewish liturgy, midrash, and narrative literature. Messianic figures such as Abu 'Isa and Shabbetai Zevi periodically fanned Jewish anticipations of a supernatural deliverance.

However, the earlier pragmatic and more realistic perspective on how the Jews would return to and gain sovereignty over their land was never entirely discredited. Here and there in rabbinic writings, more gradual and naturalistic descriptions of the redemption can be found: for example, Maimonides described the messianic process in such terms. Similar perspectives would surface at times of political flux in Palestine or when the ruling regime was positively disposed toward the land's Jewish inhabitants. At such times, some Jews suspected that God was signaling His readiness to redeem them and was merely awaiting their response. Both the beginnings of European colonialism in the Ottoman empire and Muhammad Ali's expansion of authority into Palestine triggered Jewish messianic expectations, as did the emancipation of the Jews in France. Some Jews regarded these events as signs of an impending miraculous deliverance, while others—such as the perushim—regarded them as part of a process that began gradually and naturalistically.

Morgenstern's research is a significant addition to the historiography of these ideas. Unfortunately, he pays scant attention to the preexisting or contemporary manifestations of realistic messianism. While Morgenstern is no doubt correct that the perushim helped spread these ideas, they were not operating in a vacuum. According to Morgenstern, the application of the kabbalistic maxim "the awakening below leads to the awakening above" to the messianic process was "so revolutionary that only by reliance on divine revelation, as expressed through the person of the Vilna Gaon, could it be advocated against the traditional view" (p. 88). If so, how do we explain the fact that Rabbi Elijah Guttmacher of Graetz made the same point during the 1850s, without any ostensible contact with the perushim? Moreover, belief in a naturalistic and gradual messianic redemption had already been elucidated by Zvi Hirsch Kalischer in 1836 and was the basis for messianic movements in mid-century in Yemen. Neither Kalischer nor the Yemenites had significant contact with the perushim, nor did they regard the year 5600 as especially significant, or identify Kabbalah as the basis of their ideas.[1] Considering these figures together with the perushim would enhance our understanding of the transformation in religious thought during the 19th century.

Morgenstern's tendency to paraphrase (rather than quote) sources and to extrapolate upon them poses a challenge to the cautious scholar who wants to ascertain how many of the disciples embraced realistic messianic ideas and how, precisely, these ideas were presented. For example, as evidence for the widespread belief in 5600 among the disciples of the Vilna Gaon, Morgenstern quotes a statement by Menasheh of Ilya, a disciple of the Vilna Gaon known for his opposition to messianic speculation, scolding people who foolishly interpret the Zohar in that manner. Morgenstern can only surmise that the said fools were "apparently . . . a group of Lithuanian scholars" (p. 37). In his eagerness to prove that rabbinic leaders had cancelled the prohibition in the "Three Oaths" instructing the Jews not to pray excessively for the end of days, Morgenstern twice cites Rabbi Israel of Shklov's letter (pp. 17 and 104). However, the text of the letter does not, as he claims, identify the generic "Gentile persecution" with the 1827 tsarist decrees instituting military conscription for Russia's Jews (see p. 239, n.5). Nor did Israel of Shklov actually sanction group efforts "to scale the walls of the land of Israel"—that being, once again, a prohibited form of collective redemptive activity. Indeed, he described the group's excessive praying as "His people's sin" that would anger God (p. 104).

Elsewhere, Morgenstern supplies the prooftexts for a messianic process suggested by Israel of Shklov, but it is not clear whether Israel of Shklov or Morgenstern is providing these sources. The perspective of the perushim is quite similar to the realistic messianism later articulated and amply supported by a wide variety of rabbinic writings in Kalischer's *Derishat ziyon*. Religious Zionists adopted these arguments and prooftexts in the 20th century, and one wonders whether Morgenstern's scholarship is unduly shaped by them.

Furthermore, Joel A. Linsider's translation of Morgenstern's original Hebrew volume would be improved by more often including the Hebrew terms appearing in the primary sources upon which so much of Morgenstern's argument rests (or better yet, the entire texts). Truly confounding is the decision that was made "for logistical reasons" not to use the original English of the quoted 19th-century sources, such as excerpts from newspaper articles and missionary journals. Instead, they appear in Linsider's English retranslations of Morgenstern's earlier translations into Hebrew (p. viii, n. 3).

Despite these shortcomings, Morgenstern's research on the perushim is an important contribution. He has integrated archival materials into an engaging narrative history of the Yishuv. The vicissitudes of life in the Yishuv are vividly portrayed, and the community of perushim comes to life as it fluctuates in size and in spirit. People arrived in hope and left in despair, suffered losses from disease and epidemics, competed with other Jews for limited funds, paid the debts left by previous immigrants, and attempted to explain the series of hardships that never seemed to end. By 1847, when the expected divine fruits of their labors did not materialize, most of them regretted their previous activism and resolved to focus primarily on prayer and Torah study. Morgenstern's version of their story will enhance the possibility that the growth of the Yishuv will be understood as a complex process involving real individuals, political bodies, and an array of distinctive institutions.

JODY MYERS
California State University, Northridge

Note

1. See Jody Myers, *Seeking Zion: Modernity and Messianic Activism in the Writings of Tsevi Hirsch Kalischer* (Oxford: 2003); Bat-Zion Eraqi-Klorman, *The Jews of Yemen in the Nineteenth Century: A Portrait of a Messianic Community* (Leiden: 1993).

Avinoam J. Patt, *Finding Home and Homeland: Jewish Youth and Zionism in the Aftermath of the Holocaust.* Detroit: Wayne State University Press, 2009. 373 pp.

During the past two decades, there has been an abundance of research on the Jewish displaced persons (DP) population in Germany. Most historians agree that the public atmosphere in the DP camps in postwar Germany was generally pro-Zionist. The question is why this was the case. Why did so many of the *sheerit hapeletah* (surviving remnant) turn to the Zionist option—given that, before the war, only a small minority of European Jews had been drawn to the Zionist movement? Moreover, to what extent was this "turn to Zionism" an autonomous decision? Might it be the case, as a number of Israeli historians have argued, that the refugees' decision was essentially forced on them by emissaries from the Yishuv (the Jewish community in Palestine) who had been sent to the refugee camps?[1]

In *Finding Home and Homeland*, a work based on his doctoral thesis, Avinoam Patt argues that previous research on this issue has been inadequate for two reasons: first, because scholars drew their conclusions mainly on the basis of what was written and said about DP attitudes and behavior by outsiders, namely institutions and individuals such as the United Nations Relief and Rehabilitation Administration (UNRRA), the Joint Distribution Committee (JDC), the U.S. Army, and the various Zionist *shelihim* (emissaries) active in the DP camps. Second, the historical literature has generally regarded Jewish DPs as an undifferentiated mass, failing to take note of their disproportionately young and middle-aged composition.[2]

Although the *yidishe yugnt* (Jewish youth), as he notes, comprised no more than 10 percent of the total DP population, they were regarded by the Jewish DP leadership as representing the future of the *sheerit hapeletah*. Patt seeks to explore their inner motivations: why did they decide to leave Europe forever, and why did they choose the risky option of Eretz Israel as their destination? Why did they seek to join the "kibbutzim" and *hakhsharot* (agricultural training centers) that were set up in the vicinity of DP camps in the face of numerous bureaucratic obstacles? Why did they attach themselves to illegal immigration efforts that were designed to bypass the British Mandatory restrictions, which often resulted in their being arrested and sent to detention camps in Cyprus? What motivated them to persist in their efforts to reach Palestine, which, in the period after the war, was in the midst of a prolonged armed struggle?[3]

These youths, Patt shows, came from two different sources. One group consisted of concentration camp survivors who were liberated in Germany and who immediately established a number of Zionist initiatives, including "Kibbutz Buchenwald"; the United Zionist Organization and a youth movement known as No'ar Chalutzi Meuchad (Nocham); a Hebrew newpaper, *Nizoz* (the Spark); and the Central Committee of Liberated Jews.[4] By these initiatives, claims Patt, the young survivors "succeeded in monopolizing the question of youth, turning [their] future . . . into a political issue whose resolution would define the future of the *She'erit Hapletah* as a whole" (p. 66).

The second group consisted of young survivors in Eastern Europe, mainly Poland, who belonged to or were recruited by Zionist youth movements. At war's end, there were no more than 3,000 Zionist youth group members in Bavaria, where many of the Jewish DP camps were located, but their numbers soon increased with the arrival of thousands of youths who had survived the camps or else had fled to the Soviet Union, to the forests, or to various hiding places. The postwar activity of the Polish Zionist youth movements, Patt argues, was a continuation of their efforts during the war, which had turned them into a leading force in Polish Jewish society as a whole, and certainly in the ghetto resistance and partisan organizations.[5] By the beginning of 1947, some 33,000 kibbutz members left Poland with the assistance of the clandestine immigration movement sponsored by the Yishuv. Approximately half this number (16,000) were members of kibbutzim set up by pioneering movements such as Dror, Hashomer Hatzair, Gordoniah, Nocham, and Pachach (a group of former partisans and soldiers), while an additional 11,000 youths belonged to the Ihud Hano'ar Haziyoni and to the religious Zionist Mizrachi/Bnei Akiva movement.

Relying on a rich array of archival sources—newspapers, diaries, letters written by the kibbutz members, and correspondence between the local leaders in the camps and the centers of the youth movements in Eretz Israel—Patt describes the organization and daily routine of the communal frameworks, and the relationships among their members. His conclusion is that "the appeal of Zionism for these youths was primarily functional in nature, having little to do with any ideological appeal" (p. 89). In this, he goes against previous research that emphasizes (or perhaps overemphasizes) the ideological diversity among the postwar Zionist pioneering groups;[6] attributes internal tensions between the youth movements to the political struggle among the political centers in the Yishuv;[7] or depicts youth movement activity in the DP camps as a function of mutual dependence between groups in the diaspora and the settlement movements in Eretz Israel.[8]

Patt, in contrast, emphasizes the practical aspects of the Zionist frameworks and claims that it provided two distinct benefits for its members: active assistance in leaving Europe for a new life in Palestine, and a form of replacement family. The kibbutz experience, Patt believes, had psychologically therapeutic value: it "provided work, family and structure while simultaneously empowering members of the kibbutz with educational, social, and leadership skills in the embrace of a new national identity" (p. 103).

Paradoxically, the climax of Zionist activity in the DP camps was the establishment of *hakhsharot* on German farms, in preparation for the encounter with Eretz Israel. The farming project was a combined effort by the Central Committee of Liberated Jews, the Jewish Agency, the youth movements, the JDC and UNRRA. Patt argues that the kibbutz members agreed to move to the farms in order to remain within the kibbutz framework and to promote their chances to reach Eretz Israel, even though doing so meant removing themselves from the educational and cultural opportunities available in the DP camps.

Patt tends to underestimate the great influence of the emissaries and their own educational activities among the kibbutz members. As representatives of various settlement movements in Eretz Israel, the *shelihim* devoted their efforts to strengthening Zionist consciousness, by both direct and indirect means. Among other things, they published newspapers featuring material provided by their movements; organized classes in Hebrew and in Zionist history; sponsored conferences attended by leading political figures in the Yishuv; led holiday and festive events (with an emphasis on Zionist themes); organized support for Keren Kayemet Leyisrael (Jewish National Fund); taught Zionist songs and dances; promoted special uniforms and badges associated with their specific movements; and set up paramilitary training programs in preparation for the coming military struggle in Eretz Israel. All these educational activities helped to transform the vague notion of Eretz Israel into something real and vivid.

Finding Home and Homeland ignores the great contribution of the existing Zionist establishment in molding the young survivors into active players in the Zionist enterprise.[9] Yet the book succeeds in presenting a vivid collective profile of a social group that was too often judged apathetic or passive by outsider observers. Patt's own conclusion is that "Zionism was highly successful in filling a positive function for DP youths in the aftermath of the Holocaust by providing a secure environment for vocational training, education, and rehabilitation and a surrogate family that could ultimately restore their belief in humanity" (p. 268). His comprehensive research—based on hundreds of archival sources found in Israel, Germany, and the United States and many other secondary sources in Hebrew, English, German, and Yiddish—exhibits both love and esteem for those Jewish youngsters who found their home and homeland in the new Jewish state.

ADA SCHEIN
Yad Vashem

Notes

1. See, for instance, Idit Zertal, *From Catastrophe to Power: Holocaust Survivors and the Emergence of Israel* (Berkeley: 1998); Yosef Grodzinski, *Homer enoshi tov: yehudim mul ziyonim, 1945–1951* (Or Yehudah: 1998).
2. According to Patt, some 80-85 percent of the DP population was between 15 and 40 years of age (p. 22).
3. Emanuel Sivan, *Dor tasha"h: mitos, diukan vezikaron* (Tel Aviv: 1991).
4. Zeev W. Mankowitz, *Life between Memory and Hope: The Survivors of the Holocaust in Occupied Germany* (Cambridge: 2002). On Kibbutz Buchenwald, see Judith Tydor Baumel, *Kibbutz Buchenwald: Survivors and Pioneers* (New Brunswick: 1997).
5. Israel Gutman, "The Youth Movements as an Alternative in Eastern Europe," in *Zionist Youth Movements during the Shoah*, ed. Asher Cohen and Yehoyakim Cochavi (New York: 1995), 7–18.
6. Patt does not mention Yehoyakim Cochavi's research on youth movement newspapers in the DP camps in Germany. See Yehoyakim Cochavi, *Shoresh la'akurim: tenu'ot hano'ar bemahanot ha'akurim begermanyah, 1945–1949* (Kibbutz Dalia: 1999).
7. Anita Shapira, "The Yishuv Encounter with the Survivors of the Holocaust," in *She'erit Hapletah 1944–1948: Rehabilitation and Political Struggle*, ed. Israel Gutman and Avital Saf (Jerusalem: 1990), 80–106; Irit Keynan, *Lo nirg'a hara'av: nizolei hashoah ushlihei erez yisrael: germanyah, 1945–1948* (Tel Aviv: 1996).
8. Ada Schein, "Ma'arakhot hahinukh bemahanot ha'akurim hayehudiyim begermanyah uveostriyah, 1945–1951" (Ph.D. diss., Hebrew University, 2000).
9. See, for example, Ada Schein, *Homeless Displaced Persons as Partners in the Zionist Enterprise: Survivors in German and Austrian Displaced Persons Camps and the Jewish National Fund* (Jerusalem: 1997). Also see Shlomo Bar-Gil, *Mehapsim bayit mozim moledet: 'aliyat hano'ar behinukh veshikum sheerit hapeletah 1945–1955* (Jerusalem: 1999) whose translated title (Seeking a home, finding a homeland) is strikingly similar to that of the book under review.

Arieh Bruce Saposnik, *Becoming Hebrew: The Creation of a Jewish National Culture in Ottoman Palestine*. New York: Oxford University Press, 2008. 328 pp.

As Arieh Saposnik's book *Becoming Hebrew* draws toward its conclusion, the author presents his credo, in which he sets out his conceptual framework:

> I have attempted to write a cultural history that is at once the story of interaction among different, and at times competing, cultures that are engaged simultaneously, however, in an effort to forge a unifying and homogeneous life whose shared meanings would be generated through a range of cultural images and practices. Seen in this light, the cultural history of the Yishuv ought to be understood as one in which unity and diversity exist in conjunction and in dialectical tension with one another at virtually any historical moment and in each cultural artifact (p. 259).

Saposnik makes it clear that his main purpose is to describe the cultural *becoming* rather than its *being*, leaning in that sense upon the anthology edited by Geoff Eley and Ronald Suny, *Becoming National* (1996). Therefore, even though he posits a unity of Hebrew culture as it took shape within the Jewish community in Palestine (the Yishuv) between the turn of the 20th century and the outbreak of the First

World War, he focuses on the internal conflicts that accompanied its gestation process over time.

According to Saposnik, the complex of cultural cross-currents can be traced initially to the establishment (in 1899) of the Jewish Colonial Trust: an institutional step intended to displace the erstwhile patronage of Jewish colonies in Palestine exercised by the Rothschild family. This, the author argues, marked the starting point for a range of practical developments in the emergent national culture, including the transformation of Hebrew into the common spoken language, the growth of the Hebrew press, early theatrical performances that fed the development of a popular culture (a key element in the formation of a Hebrew public space), and extending to such developments as the organization of a Hebrew teachers' union.

Reading cultural processes as proceeding via conflicts does not wed Saposnik to a rigid set of binary oppositions. Rather, his account of national Hebrew culture in-the-making is structured by the crucial debates that animated Palestine Jewry at the time, in which the protagonists of the various positions maneuvered through a kind of negotiation with one another.

In selecting conflict as his point of reference, Saposnik avoids the vise-like grip of the Zionist metanarrative. His research perspective is, to be sure, Zionist-inflected in that it seeks to investigate (as he puts it, in teleological-organic fashion) the "seeds of a modern nation" (p. 3). This, he maintains, is the way to delineate the course taken by the historical mainstream, while acknowledging the counternarrative of other players. Thus, he presents a nuanced, comprehensive picture, including the role of such non-Zionist bodies such as the French Jewish Alliance Israélite Universelle and the German Jewish Ezra Verein, alongside such eminently nationalist and Hebrew-oriented groups as the Odessa Committee. In discussing the sharp distinction broached in Zionist thought between the land of Israel and Jewish life in exile (the *golah*), Saposnik brings out the finer points of the dialogue that linked these ostensibly opposing poles—a dialogue that was conditioned by the fact that most residents of the Yishuv were not themselves ideologically committed Zionists (here acknowledging research by Gur Alroey [p. 220]). The internal tension between the attitude taken by the Zionist Organization toward the Yishuv and the Zionist movement's orientation toward Jews abroad was not really resolved until the Uganda controversy (1903–1905) and the Czernowitz conference (1908), which tended to reinforce a close association between Zionism, Palestine, and Hebraism.

Indeed, the book's third chapter devotes close attention to the so-called Uganda affair (Britain's tentative offer to explore the possibility of Jewish colonization in East Africa) and the way the debate over this issue played out in the Yishuv. As Saposnik argues, following the pogroms of 1903, Zionists developed different attitudes over the linkage between national culture and national territory—a dilemma that was only resolved when the Uganda plan was definitively shelved. Saposnik traces the flow of the argument, demonstrating its complexity. Against the backdrop of the crisis in the Yishuv, Eliezer Ben-Yehuda, for example, was supportive of the notion of a temporary solution in Africa for the Jewish plight; yet, as Saposnik points out, Ben-Yehuda also published Palestinocentric articles at the same time. As opposed to others who have studied the issue, Saposnik chooses to show the inner tensions and intertwining terms of debate, as was true not only in the case of Ben-Yehuda, but also with Moshe Smilansky, who had warned that accepting Uganda would split the Jewish people in two.

Saposnik stakes out a middle ground, extracting as much as he can from the "revolutionary" approach, which claims that modern Hebrew culture was a brand-new creation, while also mining the "traditional" view, which ties historical development to the past within a tight, linear sequence. Zionism, as Saposnik maintains, is both the direct heir of the Jewish Enlightenment and at the same time a rebellion against it. This passage into a new mode, as the Palestinian Hebraists saw it, would be wrought by means of the language, serving as a vehicle for the transformation of the Jews.

Thus, in 1910, the socialist Zionist Poale Zion party's ambivalence regarding the relative status of Hebrew and Yiddish was resolved in favor of Hebrew supremacy. But Saposnik does not read this resolution as a definitive ending. Rather, he complicates the discussion, extending and deepening Benjamin Harshav's thesis regarding the dramatic revival of Hebrew by members of the Second Aliyah. According to Saposnik, the linguistic reality was not starkly homogeneous, but rather complex, dynamic, and diverse. Yiddish was used alongside Hebrew, and the "language war" that started in 1913 as a dispute over the language of instruction at the Technion quickly turned into a clash between the Yishuv's cultural elite and the non-Zionist German Jewish philanthropists, and eventually escalated into a popular struggle on behalf of Hebrew.

Likewise, Saposnik's multidimensional analysis permits him to introduce new insight into the achievement of Hebraic hegemony, particularly as regards the role of the Yishuv's women. Alongside the gendered construction of separate social functions for men and women, he observes the role played by gender in the emergent preference for the Sephardic ("masculine") pronunciation of Hebrew as opposed to the common European Ashkenazic pronunciation, so closely associated with the "feminine"-gendered Yiddish vernacular.

Saposnik appropriately relates his discussion of the "language wars" to the link between language and territory, in a multilingual context that included Arabic and Turkish. Yet the entire controversy is discussed solely within the bounds of Jewish society, and the author fails to note that the struggle for Hebrew was also essentially linked to the political struggle between Jews and Arabs. This, to my mind, constitutes one of the book's weak points. Another important lacuna involves the absence of any serious discussion of the Hebrew literature written at that time, although Saposnik is well aware of the centrality of that literature, which was a powerful embodiment of the new culture. Nor can I accept his positing of a theoretical distinction between "myth" in its literary and intellectual uses and the notion of myth in connection with the performance of public rituals.

Bypassing the corpus of Hebrew literature is not mitigated by Saposnik's extensive discussion of Herzl's novel *Altneuland*—which, of course, was not written in Hebrew. Much would have been gained by delving into the dramatic contribution, for example, of Yosef Haim Brenner's writings to the construction of Hebrew culture. Brenner's poetics, in the novel *From Here and There* (1911), did much to craft a national, Hebrew "I," complete with subjective, inner contradictions as the Jewish persona struggles to discover a way to adjust in the territorial context of Palestine. Brenner's strategy of representation might have served as a master key to understanding the mechanisms of linguistic territorialization, for the schisms represented in Brenner's writing were intended as a fitting literary approximation of the fluid reality of the day, calculated to preserve the strong utopian-national impulse behind the literary enterprise. Brenner purposely wrote counter to the generic tendencies associated with writers such as Shlomo Zemach, Moshe Smilansky and Meir Wilkansky, who sought to enshrine the way of life in the Yishuv as having already achieved its fulfillment.

Although he follows Eley and Suny in arguing that cultures formulate their own history, not necessarily by a free process of choosing cultural affinities but rather in terms of their encounters with earlier cultures, Saposnik nevertheless offers a detailed discussion of the impact of the Young Turks' revolution within Hebrew culture. Among the influences that he examines is the Jewish fascination with the Orient and its mystique and the emergence of a Hebraic-Zionist Ottomanism in Sephardic circles, in particular around the newspaper *Haḥerut*. In this connection, he also presents the founding of the journal *Ha'omer*, an early attempt to make the Yishuv a center for Hebrew literary activity, and the establishment of the Herzliya *gymnasium*—a conduit for educating a Hebrew-speaking, Zionist-committed populace in Palestine—as taking shape in the wake of the Young Turks movement.

The Jewish response was therefore complex: on the one hand, it entailed European contra-Oriental conceptions, but on the other hand, it also included a willed affinity with the Orient as a means of returning to older Jewish roots as demi-Asiatics. Saposnik reads this ambivalence as Orientalism, at whose core was a romanticization of the ostensible warmth and healthy balance in the simple life of the Arabs, and whose furthest reaches extended to dubbing the natives as "little Arabs" (p. 157). He dwells here on the music of Abraham Zevi Idelson, who sought to free himself from western musical influence but ended up, like the composer Yoel Engel, by intermingling East with West. Thus, Saposnik demonstrates that in Palestine, the Zionist image of the Arabs was far more diverse than a depiction of the native culture as a primitive threat; indeed, he succeeds in pointing toward a different view entirely: the image of Arabs as a race of long-lost brethren, rooted in a common historical legacy in the time of ancient Judaism and capable of helping to forge a new Arab-Jewish cultural synthesis.

In pursuing these attitudes, Saposnik's book also takes up the subject of those who might be termed "Arab Jews," that is, the Mizrahim, known at the time as Sephardim. He describes the critical perspective toward those Jews maintained by the literary and cultural critic Yaakov Rabinovich and relates to the poor treatment accorded to the Yemenite Jews. Yet, as he also shows, the trends toward finding common ground with the Arabs may be found among Sephardim and Ashkenazim alike. In fact, he finds that the tension between East and West was a constitutive element in every phase of Hebrew culture in Palestine.

While this discussion is indeed rich and complex, in practice Saposnik accepts the denial of Zionism's colonial character and generally overlooks the questions of relative power and the sense of cultural and political ascendancy that Jews brought with them when coming to the East. He himself regards the cultural and political realms as two complementary strands in the nationalist framing of modern life. It would behoove him, therefore, to extend the discussion of relative power beyond the bounds of the Jewish community.

The developing Jewish attitude toward the spatial (including the presence of Arabs) was not unconnected to the matter of asserting control over place and space. But when discussing the phenomenon of "touring the terrain" (*tiyul*), so popular in the Yishuv in the period of the Second Aliyah, the author interprets it as a medium that both reflected and enacted the people's connection to the land, without entertaining the notion that *tiyul* also functioned as a medium of Jewish assertion of political ownership of the landscape, vis-à-vis the Arab inhabitants. There can be no doubt, in any event, that symbolic rhetoric such as the "fire and blood" invoked by the volunteer Hashomer (guardsmen) unit expressed the element of force that entered the political culture of the time and had a profound impact on Hebrew national culture. I would argue, indeed, that the self-styled romantic "beduinization" adopted as a style by Hashomer's members not only did not mitigate the political gap that grew apace between Jews and Arabs, but rather represented a Jewish attempt to assert a form of possession over Arab symbols. It becomes apparent that Saposnik does not sufficiently appreciate the link between the growing strength of Arab nationalism, which he describes, and the growth of Jewish militancy.

The book identifies the year 1908 as a major watershed in relation to the colliding forces that were building up in the Yishuv in the wake of a renewed wave of immigration (the Second Aliyah), which drew upon influences of the radical Left in Eastern Europe and spawned an avant-garde in the Yishuv in Palestine. This avant-garde group staged a sharp debate with the veterans of the Jewish colonies, while in the process contributing to the establishment of schools, museums, a music academy, health care institutions, periodicals, publishing houses, and labor unions. Saposnik argues that, regarding that year (1908), we may observe the marked impact of the Young Turks' revolution on the crystallization of Jewish society in Palestine as a national element in its own right, and with its own national culture. Turning to the incipient "mythicization" of Herzl after his death, Saposnik examines, among other things, the institution of national days of observance, showing how these reflected the dual influences of European culture and the Jewish heritage. Here, once again, he draws attention to the contested nature of the process, such as, for example, around the nationalization of the Hanukkah festival.

Saposnik is particularly impressive in his treatment of the secular, national trends within the culture of the Yishuv. He describes secularism as an ambivalent ideology that defined itself via its attitude toward religion, in the process creating a new articulation of that which it ostensibly set out to demolish. "Secularism," in fact, proposed a new reading of Jewish texts and the perception of Jewish nationalism as a natural continuation of Judaism. Saposnik is undoubtedly correct in his understanding that deconstruction was necessarily intertwined with reconstruction, and he thus liberates his discussion from the burden of binary categories, promoting instead a discursive approach that embraces multi-vocal complexity and dialectic expression.

For example, Zionist culture as framed by *Hashiloaḥ* (the preeminent literary journal of the time) is described as a break from Jewish traditionalism, but one that took shape within, and drew upon, a painful dialogue with tradition. Although writers such as Yitzhak Leib Peretz, Micha Yosef Berdyczewski, and Hayim Nahman Bialik, as representatives of the new culture, waged what they saw as a struggle against religious obscurantism, they also displayed their affection for the light generated by faith. Berdyczewski, who exemplified the rupture within the hearts of modern Jews, was after all seeking a way to discover a way for a holistic Jewish life to exist. This duality is what made these writers so popular, because their readership was caught somewhere between the two extremes of religion and secularity. That was also the view of Yosef Klausner, who took principled views regarding the need for secularism in the educational system but also displayed sensitivity toward the religious dimension within secular nationalism. According to that view, the nationalization of Jewish society at large had to be accomplished via the astute use of the customs and heritage of the past.

This approach earned the ire of those who opposed the instrumentalization of religion, who feared that in waging a struggle for hegemony in the Yishuv at the expense of efforts to win support for Zionism in the diaspora, the national culture of the Yishuv ran the risk of abandoning Judaism to the exclusive province of diaspora Jews. Hence, too, the concern over missionary activity in the Yishuv and anxieties manifested over the creation of a planting and floral festival on Lag Ba'omer—a very minor day in the Jewish calendar which, in the Yishuv, was revived and refocused on Bar Kokhba's revolt against ancient Roman rule.

The culture wars in the Yishuv took extreme form in the famous "Brenner incident," in the course of which Brenner—reacting to a spate of conversions by young Jews—took the position that the choice of faith was not really the main issue, but rather that in a healthy and free national culture one might choose if or how or in what to believe, while still remaining members in good standing of the Jewish collective. The publication of Brenner's article soon snowballed into a major argument over freedom of expression and served to mark the outer boundary of Zionist discourse about religion.

Yet another source of conflict examined in the book is the argument between proponents of "productivization" and the extant system of the ḥalukah (the dividing up of monies collected from Jewish communities abroad), which pitted different segments of the Yishuv against each other, contributing to its ethnic fragmentation. Menahem Ussishkin, speaking for the "practical Zionists," bitterly condemned the ḥalukah system, and the institutional expression of this opposition was the Committee of United Zionist Federations in Palestine, whose establishment was both a cornerstone event in the shaping of a Hebraic public sphere in the country and a step toward the nationalization process in the Yishuv. In this context, Saposnik also draws attention to the significance of the founding of the Hebrew Teachers' Association as a move toward formalizing Hebrew culture in the Yishuv.

The emphasis on "productivization" is also carefully delineated in the discussion of the establishment of the Bezalel school for the arts, epitomizing the quest for a new Hebrew culture in Palestine. The emergence of Bezalel was at once an effort to give rise to a new Hebrew aesthetic and a blow for productive professions as against the culture of the dole. Moreover, Bezalel represented a new way of construing Palestine as a national center in relation to a diaspora that might be depicted as its periphery. Saposnik characterizes the products of the Bezalel workshop as capturing the dualism binding the new Zionism and the old Judaism, the religious and the secular, within an aestheticized "sacrality" of a new, Zionist Judaism capable of projecting a deep, spiritual affinity.

The "native-born" motive—such as in the case of Eliezer Ben-Yehuda's son Itamar Ben-Avi—is similarly described in terms of its inherent paradox: local rootedness alongside a never-ending engagement with the diaspora, which stood at the very foundation of Hebraic identity. This paradox was characteristic of an immigrant society in which, for example, immigrant educators founded kindergartens in which to rear Hebrew children in such a way as to connect them with their native roots.

Saposnik's broad-canvas approach and historical integrity serve him well in forging an impressive and profound answer to the challenge he has set himself in seeking to address the unfinished business of constructing a wide-ranging, synthetic cultural history of the Jewish national movement in Palestine. Toward the end of his book, Saposnik quotes Anthony Smith, who claims that nation-building is a prolonged effort that proceeds by repeating cycles, always-renewed reinterpretations, new discoveries, and reconstructions. This book undoubtedly does render a great service in its attempt to achieve just such a perspective. I would only restate my view, that the status of power relations in the Yishuv might have been treated with more complexity, and observe that the systematic, open-minded, and solid scholarship evidenced in this book results in findings that make it far more possible to arrive at that kind of nuanced and critical reading.

HANNAN HEVER
The Hebrew University

Matthew Silver, *First Contact: Origins of the American-Israeli Connection; Halutzim from America during the Palestine Mandate*. West Hartford: The Graduate Group, 2006. 386 pp.

Americans, it seems, especially American Jews, engendered neither respect nor admiration among nascent Israelis—especially Jews living in Palestine during the British Mandate. Matthew Silver argues that the clash of Jewish cultures increasingly visible after the establishment of the state of Israel derives from earlier experiences of the pre-state years. He specifically locates the conflict around the image and reality of the halutz, the Jewish pioneer whose attributes and ethics appeared to be "diametrically opposed to the main traits of American Jewish life" (p. 4). Despite evidence of the appeal of pioneering to American Zionists and their willingness to promote such "new Jews" as idealistic exemplars of Zionism, the reality grated against other deeply held American Jewish values. These included individualism, pluralism, and democracy—standards of behavior cherished by American Jews and often rejected by Jews in the pre-state Yishuv in favor of collectivism, nationalism, and ideology. Although both groups of Jews drew upon European Jewish traditions, their migration choices shaped their cultural development. By the time American Jews headed for Palestine, they had absorbed ways of looking at the world that accentuated their differences from fellow Jews who had chosen aliyah directly from Europe.

In choosing to focus on the interaction of American Jewish halutzim (as he deliberately terms them) in Palestine during the Mandate era, Silver seeks to expand our understanding of pioneering even as he locates the roots of disagreements in these early pre-state contacts. He argues that histories of Zionism almost consistently ignore American Jews' significant presence in Palestine, in effect perpetuating aspects of the original conflict. As a result, both the Yishuv's cultural diversity and the complexity of pioneering disappear from view, resulting in slanted interpretations of the subsequent interactions of American and Israeli Jews.

Silver admits that he has a personal stake in this story. As an American Jew who made aliyah, he is in a sense retrieving his own history, discovering ancestors erased from Israel's past and claiming them as his own. The book bears some of the marks of such a reclamation project: it sprawls and meanders. Silver mixes the institutional history of Hadassah's American Zionist Medical Unit and the Jewish Legion's "American" 39th Royal Fusiliers Battalion that served during the First World War with biographies of Judah Magnes, Henrietta Szold, and Gershon Agron. He covers familiar territory even as he uncovers more obscure histories. Although he tries to stay focused on cultural questions and their political implications, he often gets mired in details that might have served to illuminate an argument were they not swamped by other, potentially equally illuminating details. This is a pity because, while the book has much to offer, the reader is forced to do the legwork of extracting what is valuable from what is tedious. Silver, it seems, was ill-served by his publisher, who did not press him to trim and sharpen his argument.

Nonetheless, that argument is provocative and bracing. Silver begins his book with the First World War not only because of the Balfour Declaration, which set the stage for the postwar British Mandate, but also because of the Russian Revolution, which dramatically presented Jews with three very different migration choices—each one associated with political idealism and the promise of creating a new society. Pioneering in Palestine needs to be understood as one of several options available to Jews in the heady days after the war ended, Silver argues. Creating a workers' utopia in the Soviet Union also enticed Jews, as did the democratic vistas of the United States. Such a tripartite conceptual framework, which draws upon the critically important comparative work of historian Jonathan Frankel, frames Silver's focus on those who chose Palestine and the Zionist project.

In his discussion of Hadassah's medical unit in Palestine, Silver emphasizes a blend of messianic romanticism and political pragmatism guiding the women. He disagrees with much of the previous scholarship on Hadassah, arguing that the facade of organizational efficiency and rationalism obscures religious dimensions animating the women as well as their Jewish idealism. He explores Hadassah's activities under the rubric of "the cultural politics of healing" and characterizes their efforts as a form of *ḥaluẓiyut*. In exploring the inner life of Hadassah women, he wisely draws attention to the neglected writings of Jesse Sampter as well as to Irma Lindheim's more popular memoir. But it is in his thorough discussion of the vehement opposition to Hadassah projects, from anti-malaria efforts to a nurses' training school, that Silver gets at the heart of the encounter that bedeviled American Zionist pioneers: ultimately, the Americans could do nothing right because they were Americans, that is, outsiders. Zionist pioneers wanted to control their own fate, an idea central to *ḥaluẓiyut*, and any outside assistance undermined their vision of self-determination.

American-style pioneering, irrespective of its philanthropic patron-client model, threatened what had been achieved in the Yishuv.

After a thorough and compelling analysis of Hadassah's early years in Palestine and the cultural politics surrounding its pioneering efforts on behalf of health care, Silver shifts to biographical studies. He first discusses Gershon Agron, an American who succeeded in becoming mayor of Jerusalem (his tenure was cut short by his early death in 1959). Silver calls Agron an "immigrant achiever" (p. 135) who strove mightily from the time of his childhood in an immigrant household in the United States, joining the Jewish Legion at age 21 and then becoming a journalist in Palestine in 1924. Agron, Silver writes, pioneered in developing Zionist public relations rather than propaganda through innovative ways of informing the world about the Yishuv enterprise. Silver seeks to expand the notion of pioneering to include Agron's public relations work, despite the fact that Agron himself considered farming to be true *ḥaluẓiyut* (and regarded himself as being inadequate in that regard). While offering an innovative interpretation of Agron, Silver ends his chapter in 1930, leaving the reader wondering where the new political configuration after the 1929 riots would lead.

Silver's subsequent two chapters, titled "American Democracy and Halutz Zionism" and "The Paradoxes of Jewish Solidarity," discuss, respectively, Judah Magnes and Henrietta Szold. Accounting for almost half the book, these two chapters really should have been a separate project. They carry Silver into the 1930s and 1940s, part of his time period, but they do not succeed in further developing his argument. However, Silver's concluding reflections on the limits and tensions inherent in Jewish solidarity are stimulating. It is to be hoped that others will be encouraged by his example to turn to this form of Jewish cultural history in order to enlarge our understanding of the divergent paths Jews took in the 20th century.

DEBORAH DASH MOORE
University of Michigan

Studies In Contemporary Jewry XXVI

Edited by Richard I. Cohen

Symposium—Jewish Museums as Contemporary Interpreters/Narrators of the Past and Present

Natalia Berger, *Coping with Nationalism and Antisemitism: Jewish Museums in Central European Cities in the Early 20th Century*

Inka Bertz, *Jewish Museums in Germany after the Holocaust*

Richard I. Cohen, *Yad Vashem's Museum of the Holocaust and Its Place in the Changing Attitude of Israeli Society toward the Holocaust*

Ruti Direktor, *Six Exhibitions, Six Decades; Toward a (New) Canonization of Contemporary Israeli Art*

Abigail Glogower and Margaret Olin, *Between Two Worlds: Ghost Stories under Glass in Vienna and Chicago*

Ruth Ellen Gruber, *Post-Trauma Precious Legacies: Jewish Museums in Eastern Europe after the Holocaust and before the Fall of Communism*

Felicitas Heimann-Jelinek, *The Role of a Jewish Museum in the 21st Century*

Tobias Metzler, *Collecting Community: The Berlin Jewish Museum as Narrator between Past and Present*

Robin Ostow, *From Wandering Jew to Immigrant Ethnic: Musealizing Jewish Immigration*

Osnat Zukerman Rechter, *In Between Past and Future: Time and Relatedness in the Exhibitions of Six Decades of Israeli Art*

Lisa Saltzman, *A Matrix of Matrilineal Memory in the Museum: Charlotte Salomon and Chantal Akerman in Berlin*

... plus essays, review essays, and book reviews

Note on Editorial Policy

Studies in Contemporary Jewry is pleased to accept manuscripts for possible publication. Authors of essays on subjects generally within the contemporary Jewish sphere (from the turn of the 20th century to the present) should send two copies to:

> *Studies in Contemporary Jewry*
> The Avraham Harman Institute of Contemporary Jewry
> The Hebrew University of Jerusalem
> Mt. Scopus, Jerusalem, Israel 91905

Essays should not exceed 40 pages in length and must be double-spaced throughout (including indented quotations and endnotes).

Alternatively, email inquires may be sent to the following address:

studiescj@savion.huji.ac.il